1899 - 1927

1927 - 1942

1963 -

1942 - 1955

1955 - 1963

A Sense of Time

The Encyclopedia of Northern Michigan University

Compiled by

Russell M. Magnaghi

A publication of
Northern Michigan University Press
in conjunction with
The Center for Upper Peninsula Studies

Marquette
1999

*A Sense of Time: The Encyclopedia of Northern Michigan University
Compiled by Russell M. Magnaghi*

*©Northern Michigan University Press
1401 Presque Isle Avenue
Marquette, MI 49855
1999*

*Library of Congress Cataloguing
Published 1999
Compiler: Russell M. Magnaghi*

Cloth Cover: ISBN 0-918616-25-5

This work is dedicated to the University community,

then and now.

PREFACE

In the observance of our Centennial, Northern Michigan University is pleased to publish an encyclopedia dedicated solely to NMU's history. Dr. Russell M. Magnaghi, professor of history and University Historian, a revolving staff of student interns, and class students completed the immense task of compiling 100 years of facts that describe who and what Northern is today. We are grateful for their dedication.

The Encyclopedia gives us, the Northern community, a better "sense of time" and documents our rich heritage. A handy reference that creates access to people, places and events significant to NMU's development, the Encyclopedia chronicles NMU's first century. It provides information about the origin of Academic Affairs, as well as containing information about Northern's fascinating faces, like Rico Zenti—complete from A to Z.

The Encyclopedia establishes a record of past traditions as an institution—Rush Day, Color Day, assembly, Ivy Day, the Rose Ceremony, and others—now all memories. For students, faculty, staff, and alumni, the Encyclopedia is an exciting way to experience the richness of Northern Normal School and its transition to a state university.

Professor Magnaghi and his cadre of student historians have brought Northern's first century to a close. The Encyclopedia will be updated on a regular basis, making the transition from one century through the next.

Professor Magnaghi and students, thank you for dedicating your time and talent to this special project.

Judith I. Bailey
President

INTRODUCTION

As University Historian, I began studying Northern's century of growth and development using materials in the University Archives and published works on the subject. I soon found myself keeping statistics, biographies and other vital data because they did not exist in accessible form. By June 29, 1994, I realized that what Northern needed was an encyclopedia with information that was readily available to myself and others interested in the development and history of Northern Michigan University.

I have attempted to include all aspects of the University's history, which has been a long and tedious process. Tedious because the material is scattered and many of the stories had to be reconstructed through newspaper articles, oral interviews and traditional research. Although the encyclopedia format is popular with writers in the 1990s, few university-related encyclopedias have been published. The four-volume, *The University of Michigan, An Encyclopedic Survey* (1942-1953) was available but could not be used as a model given each university's comparative size and different histories. So I developed my own model for this encyclopedia.

The scope of the project required that I obtain a lot of additional assistance. Students in three classes of HS 200: Historical Thinking and Writing devoted their studies and research papers to the history of Northern. Their names appear next to the appropriate articles. These students were also helpful in indexing the University newspapers (1919–1980) and bringing important citations to my attention.

Besides the students who assisted with the project, I have conducted interviews with over one hundred individuals ranging from presidents (Harden, Jamrich, Appleberry, Vandament and Bailey) to faculty, staff, students and alumni. These interviews have been deposited in the University Archives and provide a wealth of personal information and insights into the history of the last eighty years. Over the years, history department work study students, Leanne Dowdy, Dawn Guilbault, Bobbie Makela, Kathy Maki and Soumya Singh, under the direction of Alice M. McKinney, have spent hours transcribing the interview tapes.

Furthermore, there are individuals such as Julane Cappo in Human Resources, Yvonne Niemi in the Registrar's Office, Bernadette Norden in Student Activities, Jean Paquette in Engineering and Planning, Jim Pinar and Steve Easton in Sports Information, Sue Ann Salo in the

College of Arts and Sciences and Connie Williams and Diana Bennett in University Relations who provided me with invaluable assistance. University Archivist, Marcus Robyns, and his able staff, Michael Cross, Clarily Hensley, Rebekah Hoekstra, Robin Kennedy and Andrew Robinson were a constant source of help throughout this project.

Over the years I was also assisted by a number of students who researched and wrote a number of articles. They include: Donovan Cater (History), Michael Fitzgibbon-Rhea (English), Stacey Gibson (History), Larry Harness (History), Kambiz Jamshidi (Communication and Performance Studies), Michelle Kangas (English), Alisa Koski (History and English), Lori Seppanen (History) and Emily Magnaghi (University of Michigan, Biology). My colleagues, Gildo Canale, Jean Choate, Kristi Evans, Miriam Hilton and Suzan Travis-Robyns allowed their material to be used and cited. The campus maps were developed by James S. Thams and Dennis Mors of Engineering and Facilities.

Human memory of Northern is an important ingredient. Robert Bordeau, Gildo Canale, Jim Carter, Lauriann Coffey, Martin Dolan, Miriam Hilton, Michelle Kangas, Thomas Knauss, Diane Kordich, Marilyn Robbert, Karen Wallingford and Gene Whitehouse have all provided me with their time to read and make invaluable comments. The final revisions were made by Madonna Marsden.

Two external agencies have also helped this project: the staff at the Archives of the State of Michigan and Linda Panian, Librarian at the John M. Longyear Research Library of the Marquette County Historical Society, who answered my every request for data.

Finally, I want to acknowledge former President John X. Jamrich for his suggestion of a title, President William Vandament and the President's Council who initially supported this project, and President Judith Bailey who gave this project direction and encouragement.

Every effort was made to make the encyclopedia as accurate and complete as possible. If the reader finds material missing or inaccurate, please contact me in writing with the addition or correction. Since the University is constantly evolving, future editions of the encyclopedia will reflect these changes and developments.

To everyone who assisted in creating this work, it could not have happened without your help. A hearty thank you to everyone.

~Russell M. Magnaghi

The Encyclopedia of Northern Michigan University

The following abbreviations are found at the end of many citations: ASNMU: Associated Students of NMU; CR: Campus Review; GLIAC: Great Lakes Intercollegiate Athletics; MJ: Mining Journal; NCAA: National Collegiate Athletic Association; NCN: Northern College News; NN: Northern News; NNN: Northern Normal News; NW: North Wind; UA: Central Upper Peninsula and Northern Michigan University Archives.

Academic Affairs, Vice President for: During the administration of President Edgar L. Harden (1956–1967), the first Vice President appeared on the administrative roster. Harold E. Sponberg came to Northern with the Harden administration in 1956 as the university's first Vice President. His new position reflected the growth of administrative responsibilities associated with the academic affairs of an expanding college. In 1958, enrollment was 888 students, and it rapidly rose to 4,200 in 1964 and 7,085 in 1967, the last year of the Harden administration.

Sponberg resigned in July 1962. Milton Byrd became the first Academic Vice President on June 1, 1962. Byrd became an advocate for the introduction of the Common Learning Program (*See separate entry*) that made up the Four-Course Plan (*See separate entry*).

As a result of recommendations from a consulting firm, the title of Provost (*See separate entry*) was added to the position of Academic Vice President in 1974. This meant that in addition to normal duties, the Vice President would also fill in for the President in his absence. In 1984, the Provost designation was dropped from the Academic Vice President's title.

At the present time the Office of Vice President for Academic Affairs oversees the work of the following six academic colleges: Arts and Sciences; Behavioral Sciences, Human Services and Education; Walker L. Cisler College of Business, Nursing and Allied Health Sciences; Technology and Applied Sciences; and Graduate Studies and Continuing Education. The office also oversees Academic Information Services; Faculty Research Development; Community College Programs; Registrar's Office; Recreational Facilities and Services; and International Affairs (*See separate entries*).

The Division provides academic programming for an enrollment total of 200,000 credit hours annually and monitors and coordinates course programming in all divisions. It also has responsibility for the overall administration of faculty and other academic staff, which includes efforts in recruitment, affirmative action and professional development for about 500 people. The division administers a budget that totals more than $30 million and a supplemental budget for academic and learning technology equipment. The Learning Technology Fee budget totals more than $350,000 annually.

The Vice President works with the Academic Senate and its committees, the Educational Policy Committee, the University Priorities Committee and the faculty unions: American Association of University Professors and NMU Faculty Association. There are periodic reviews of all academic departments and a periodic Northern Central Accreditation review. Furthermore, the Division reviews and submits program proposals to the Board of Control and the President's Council of State Colleges and Universities.

The other duties of the Academic Vice President include: a) promotion and coordination of study abroad programs and other efforts that encourage international study; b) coordination of efforts to improve basic skills through special advising and instruction; c) biennial production of the *Undergraduate Bulletin*; d) proposals for major and minor facilities renovations affecting the instructional mission; e) Honors Banquet and recognition of the outstanding graduating seniors; f) responsibility for faculty labor relations and contract management of the collective bargaining agreements for the American Association of University Professors and NMU Faculty Association; g) coordination of the NMU Retirees Association (375 retirees); and h) coordination of faculty recognition programs.

Vice President: Harold E. Sponberg, 1956–1960; *Academic Vice Presidents*: Milton Byrd, 1962–1966; Clarence Bjork, (acting) 1966–1967; David W. D. Dickson, 1967; Jacob Vinocur, 1967–1974; Robert B. Glenn, (and provost) 1974–1984; Alan Donovan, 1984–1988; John Kuhn, (acting) 1988–1989; Phillip L. Beukema, 1989–present. (Hilton, p. 141, 166–67; *The 1996–97 University Profile*, 1:8–11)

Academic Apparel: Prior to 1907, female graduates of Northern wore white dresses while the men wore suits as evidenced in old photographs. In 1907 graduates wore black caps and gowns for the first time. The faculty wore academic robes for the first time at spring commencement in 1940. The first book published by the Northern Michigan University Press deals with academic heraldry and apparel. It is one of the few books written on the subject. (MJ 06/19/1909)

Academic Computing: *See*: *Academic Information Services; Computers; Library*.

Academic Information Services (AIS): In the early 1990s, plans were made to unite Lydia Olson Library, Academic Computing, the University and Area Archives and Instructional Media Services. Computing and Media Services had not been part of the library operation in the past. In 1992 Academic Computing and Audio Visual Services were removed from Human Resources and University Relations respectively, and transferred into the library.

Academic Information Services (AIS) was in operation by 1993–1994. It is the primary unit within the University to provide support for instruction. In 1994, Dr. Thomas Peischl became the first dean of the newly created unit.

Deans: Thomas Peischl 1994–1998; Darlene Pierce and John Limback, (interim) 1998–present. (*The 1996–1997 University Profile* 1:12–17) *See*: *Library*

Academic Mall: The academic mall stretches from the Harden Learning Resources Center on the north to Forest Roberts Theatre on the south. It was developed after construction of Jamrich Hall, which completed the complex. In the summer of 1971, parking lots were repaved and general improvements were made. The mall was dedicated on October 16, 1971, accompanied by an open house. In 1995, the parking lots were expanded, changing the contour of the mall a bit. The mall was disrupted during the spring and summer of 1996 when steam pipes were relocated. In July 1997 the "Heart of Northern" was added to the area. (NN 10/15/1971)

Academic Senate: The predecessor of the Academic Senate was the Faculty Council (*See separate entry*), which was created in 1947 by the Faculty Organization. By faculty vote in December 1962, a Constitution Committee was created. In May, 1963, the Faculty Organization of Northern Michigan University created a Faculty Senate, approved a new constitution for it and elected members to it. The Senate consisted of nine members who "met regularly with the

Academic Vice President, selected members for committees, and made proposals in areas of faculty concern such as curriculum, teaching load, library, faculty promotion and tenure, and student life." The Vice President for Academic Affairs was an ex-officio member without a vote.

In October 1969, under the administration of President John X. Jamrich, a new constitution for the Senate was drafted. Thereafter, the Faculty Senate became known as the Academic Senate and was enlarged to 35 members.

Chairs: Earl Hilton, 1962–1964; H. Jean Hedlund, 1964; Vito Perrone, 1965–1967; John P. Farrell, 1967 (5–10); Donald Baker, 1967–1969; Richard O'Dell, 1969; Donald Baker, 1970; James Mansfield, 1971; David Goldsmith, 1972; Donald Heikkinen, 1973; David Cooper, 1974; John Watanen, 1975–1977; Richard Swain, 1977–1979; Russell Magnaghi, 1979; James Livingston, 1979–1981; William Babcock, 1981; Roger Barry, 1982–1984; Richard Gorski, 1984; Kathleen Thompson, 1985; Donald Rybacki, 1988; Donald Dreisbach, 1989; John Berens, 1990–1992; Sara Doubledee, 1992–1994; Jean Kinnear, 1994; William Babcock, 1995; Gloria Urban, 1996–1998; Charles Rayhorn, 1998-present.

Academic Senate, Committee on Undergraduate Programs: Popularly referred to as "CUP," the Committee on Undergraduate Programs was established as one of the major standing committees of the Academic Senate in its charter constitution of 1969 and replaced Committee A (*See separate entry*). The committee was established to create guidelines for the introduction of new courses, to evaluate the merits of new course proposals and to participate in keeping descriptions in course bulletins current.

Because of the demanding nature of the work of this committee and the need for a greater amount of continuity in leadership than was normally required of the committees of the Academic Senate, the Senate departed repeatedly from standard practice and reappointed the committee's charter chairman, Eugene A. Whitehouse as the committee's chairperson each year since the committee was established for consecutive three year terms. This ended in 1998.

Chairs: Eugene Whitehouse, 1966–1998; Marge Sklar, 1998–present. (NMU Archives: Academic Senate: Committee on Undergraduate Programs, Records, UA 95.1.2.5)

Academic Senate, Executive Committee: The Executive Committee is a key committee of the Academic Senate. Its responsibilities include establishing the business agenda that is brought before the Academic Senate and deciding the discussion order for each item. The Committee also investigates matters and formulates policies from time to time for later discussion and approval or rejection by the Senate as a whole. Occasionally the Executive Committee formulates charges for the various Senate committees, which are later discussed, occasionally modified and then approved or rejected by the Senate.

The Executive Committee was created in 1969 as one of the major committees of the reorganized Academic Senate. During the first years of its existence, the Executive Committee consisted of the President of the Academic Senate and of eight of his Senate colleagues who were elected to the committee by the Senate to serve for staggered periods of time. (NMU Archives: Academic Senate: Executive Committee Records, UA 95.1.2.4)

Academic Senate, Faculty Adjudication Committee (FAC): This committee was created in 1971 by the Academic Senate to provide individual faculty members or groups of faculty members with a duly constituted body of colleagues to whom they might air grievances or have them adjudicated. George F. Helfinstine acted as its first chair. With the establishment of the American Association of University Professors in 1975, this body was no longer viable. (Academic Senate: Faculty Adjudication Committee (FAC) Records, UA 95.1.3.1)

Academic Senate, Faculty Grants Committee: The Faculty Grants Committee is responsible for evaluating faculty applications for University grant monies, forwarding its recommendations to the Academic Senate, creating guidelines that applicants must meet and modifying them when appropriate. The Faculty Grants Committee is also responsible for publicizing funds that are available during any particular year for faculty grant purposes.

Prior to the creation of the Academic Senate, faculty entities that performed similar functions existed. These entities have been known by different names such as the Faculty Service Committee. (Academic Senate: Faculty Grants Committee Records, UA 95.1.2.6)

Academic Senate, Faculty Hearing Panel and Work Committee:
In 1971, the Academic Senate and the Administration of Northern Michigan University created a Work Committee to draft a document to

establish a hearing panel and to establish University policies and procedures for processing faculty grievances. Donald D. Heikkinen was appointed chair of the Work Committee. By 1972, a policy was approved and published. Subsequently, additional committee efforts "fine-tuned" certain aspects of the policy. The result was the Faculty Hearing Panel of 1972. The panel was a joint faculty-administration creation. Neil W. Carlson served as its only chairman until 1975, when the American Association of University Professors (*See*: *Union*) created a new mechanism for handling grievances. (Academic Senate: Faculty Hearing Panel and Work Committee, 1972–1975 Records, UA 107.1-.6.)

Academic Senate, Graduate Programs Committee: The Graduate Programs Committee was established as one of the major standing committees in the 1969 charter of the Academic Senate. Its predecessor was the Graduate Council, which worked with the Faculty Senate, the predecessor of the Academic Senate.

Originally, a function of the Graduate Council was to work with the various accrediting associations to get Northern's original graduate program accredited, which occurred in 1964. Over the years, the committee has developed criteria and procedures for the acceptance of additional graduate curricula, the evaluation of graduate course proposals, graduate student admissions policies and graduate student grade standards. (Academic Senate, Graduate Programs Committee Records, UA 95.1.2.7.)

Academic Senate, Library and Learning Resources Committee: The 1969 constitution of the Academic Senate established the Library and Learning Resources Committee (LLRC) as one of the major committees of the Academic Senate. The LLRC continued to function until December 1979, when the Senate abolished it. Later, the Senate reestablished the Committee as the Library Advisory Committee without its former concern for audio-visual matters. During the 1970s, audio-visual matters were the responsibility of the Learning Resources division of the University, not the library, and it remained so well into the second half of the 1980s.

The LLRC concerned itself with many issues that were vital to the development and expansion of the library and to shaping the kind of library that the faculty wished to see. Additionally, the LLRC's support of the library was crucial for obtaining funding the library required to update or modernize library procedures such as switching the library over to the Library of Congress classification system and laying the groundwork for automating some of the library's reference and cataloging work. LLRC also improved the audio-visual equipment and materials available for Academic purposes. (Academic Senate: Library and Learning Resources Committee Records, 1969–1979, UA 95.1.2.8.)

Accidents: Over the century of Northern's existence, numerous members of the academic community have succumbed to a variety of accidents or diseases. Some have died from drowning in Lake Superior due to the violence of lake storms or fatigue. Automobile accidents have taken lives. Airplane accidents, training flights and U.S. Air Force flights have taken lives. One was a victim of spouse abuse and met her death close to campus. (NW 08/28/1997)

Accounting and Finance: The Walker L. Cisler College of Business is home to the Accounting and Finance unit. The curriculum provides students with a strong foundation in the technical and conceptual dimension of the accounting/finance discipline. In addition, students are provided background knowledge in related functional areas of business necessary to understand its dynamic and integral nature. *See: Business, Walker L. Cisler College of*

Accreditation: Northern was first accredited by the Commission on Institutions of Higher Education of the North Central Association of Colleges and Schools in 1916 as a teacher-training institution. It was transferred to the list of colleges and universities in 1929.

Today Northern continues to be accredited by the North Central Association of Colleges and Secondary Schools. All education programs are accredited by the National Council for the Accreditation of Teacher Education (NCATE).

Other accreditations are conducted by agencies such as: the American Chemical Society; the National Accrediting Agency for Clinical Laboratory Sciences; the American Speech-Language-Hearing Association (Speech Pathology); American Medical Association's Committee on Allied Health Education and Accreditation (Medical Laboratory Technician and Clinical Laboratory Science); National Association of Industrial Technology; National Association of Schools of Music; the American Alliance for Health, Physical Education,

Recreation and Dance; the Council on Social Work Education; the Department of Transportation; the Federal Aviation Administration for Aviation Maintenance Technology; the Michigan Department of Natural Resources Water Quality Examining Board Certification; and the American Dietetics Association.

The Nursing Programs (Practical Nursing, Associate Degree, Baccalaureate Degree and Master's Degree) hold accreditation by the Michigan Department of Licensing and Regulation, State Board of Nursing, and National League for Nursing. The College of Business is an Assembly Member of the American Assembly of Collegiate Schools of Business.

Administrative Effectiveness and Information Technology: This office is under the division of Finance and Administration, and includes the Computer Center, Printing and Mail Services, Telephone Systems, and Microcomputer Repair. It was created on July 1, 1996. *(The 1996–97 University Profile* 2:46–51)

The Administrative-Professional Staff Association (APSA): The APSA was established in 1971 to provide advice and counsel to Northern Michigan University's President and to make recommendations on matters of university-wide concern brought to it by the President or by the representatives of the APSA.

In January 1978, a decision was made to discontinue regular meetings unless an issue arose because the APSA no longer served its purpose and other organizations had been formed that dealt with the same subjects as the APSA. The AP Union and NMUFA *(See separate entry)* were formed out of this group. Unionization was the reason it ceased to exist. Michael Fitzgibbon-Rhea

Admissions Office: In the beginning, students could enroll at Northern at the start of any term. The conditions of admission were that the student must bring in certificates of credits taken or proof they had graduated from the schools that they attended. An entrance exam was given for preparatory courses and four-year courses. For the two-year course program, an exam was not necessary if students were applying within three years after high school.

Originally, Northern was a teacher's training institution, and there was a great demand for teachers. Consequently, there was little need to advertise. Various presidents did, however, visit high schools around the

Upper Peninsula and promoted Northern. Large advertisements in the student newspaper and at sports programs promoted summer school and the fact that most graduates easily obtained teaching positions.

The first official Director of Admissions was Luther O. Gant in 1957. Before this time, there were Enrollment Committees who oversaw admissions. In September 1961, Clarence M. Bjork became the Dean of Admissions and Graduate Studies. Over the years the Office of Admissions has been placed variously under Academic Affairs or Student Affairs. The admissions policy has varied from open admissions and "the right to try," to a liberal admissions policy characteristic of regional public universities. In 1985 James Masuga was appointed Dean of Admissions and Enrollment Management. The position was eliminated in 1994. Thereafter the Vice President for Student Affairs, Karen Reese, assumed the responsibilities as Chair of the Enrollment Management Network.

Today the Office of Admissions, which is under the Vice President for Student Affairs, is responsible for undergraduate student recruitment, processing applications for admission to undergraduate programs, hosting potential students and orienting new students. The office personnel work with parents, secondary and community college personnel, community based agencies and organizations and the general public. Recruitment entails identifying potential student markets and obstacles to enrollment, defining enrollment objectives, devising and implementing recruitment strategies, and evaluating the outcomes for their effectiveness and benefit to Northern.

Directors: Luther O. Gant, 1956–1959; Clarence M. Bjork, 1959–1964; Robert L. Bliss, 1964–1969; James W. Hoffman, 1969–1973; John Dudd, 1973–1975; Lowell Kafer, (acting) 1975–1976; John M. Kunkel 1976–1984; Karen Reese, (acting) 1984–1985; Nancy Rehling, 1985–1995; James Gadzinski and Gerri Daniels (associate co-directors) 1995–1997, Gerri Daniels, 1997–present. (*The 1996–97 University Profile* 2:107–112)

Advantages of Northern: From the start of Northern, the advantages of its location were stressed in literature promoting the institution. The points stressed in 1902 were: 1) environment: climate, potable water, infrastructure; 2) laboratory nature of the local mining, timber and transportation industries, and governmental offices and records; and 3) facilities of the institution. During the 1920s, large summer school attendance was encouraged by promoting the advantages. This has been continued over the years. In the 1990s, the concept continues to be stressed as a focus is placed on increasing enrollment. Some of the advantages that are stressed include: 1) safe environment; 2) natural beauty of the region; 3) relatively small classes; 4) faculty willing to work with students. (*Northern Normal Bulletin,* 1901–1902; NCN 07/12/1939)

Affirmative Action: This office is under the President's Division and was organized in 1993. Its mission is to advise and assist the President and other Executive Officers in all matters relating to civil rights. The Affirmative Action Office serves as an advocate for equity and support-enhanced opportunities for the campus community. The office also gives advice and assistance regarding prohibited discrimination and coordinates and conducts the activities of the University's affirmative action programs.

Directors: Doreen Rauch, 1993–1997; Susan Menhennick, (interim) 1997–present. (*The 1996–97 University Profile*, 2:15–20)

African American Students: The first African American students were Bessie and Charlotte Preston (*See separate entry*) of Marquette. Prior to the 1950s, there were few African Americans attending Northern. So few, as a matter of fact that a fraternity on campus put on annual minstrel shows, which were well attended. This ended in 1958.

With the coming of President Harden in 1956, ethnic enrollment patterns changed. Northern's Right-to-Try Program attracted African-American students; K. I. Sawyer Air Force Base had a Black population that was drawn to the University; African American athletes came to Northern due to expanded football and basketball programs; and finally, the Job Corps (which opened on campus in 1966) attracted Black students. Although exact figures are not available, there were around 100 Black students on campus in 1961. This figure grew to around 300 in 1969–1970.

At that time there were a number of incidents involving Black students that many people especially Blacks, saw as racist on the part of the University administration. In the fall of 1969, Charles Griffis was suspended for violating a housing rule. This was followed by protests, a sit-in, acquittal, acquisitions and a general erosion of race relations. As a result, many Black students left campus in the spring of 1970 and the general Black population never returned to its highwater mark. By 1978, when records had to be kept due to a federal mandate, there were 216 Black students on campus. Between 1981 and 1990 there was an average of 211 Black students on campus.

During this period, Black students had their own fraternities and sororities. In April 1971, Ozel Brazil ran for president of NMU's student body as an Independent. He received 578 of the 1,350 votes cast, outdistancing his nearest rival by more than 150 votes. He was the first African American elected as president of ASNMU.

Black Student Services was an African-American organization started around 1970 and developed many branches. One of the most active branches was the Black Student Union as was the Social Cultural Committee. Together they started several celebrations and programs that are continued today:

Black History Month--Starting around 1980 Black History Month was brought to Northern's campus by the Black Student Union, the Social/Cultural Committee and Alpha Delta. This celebrates African American culture, accomplishments and history by bringing speakers, music, meals and cultural events to Northern's campus.

Martin Luther King, Jr. Day—Begun in January 1986 as a one day event in 1993, Martin Luther King Jr. Day began to be celebrated as a week long celebration. This federal holiday is celebrated on campus with varied programs running for several days.

Dr. Arthur Walker Memorial Scholarship Fund Fashion Show—Since 1974, this annual fashion show has been held in cooperation with businesses around Marquette to raise funds for the scholarship created in Dr. Walker's name. Dr. Walker was the first director of Black Student Services on Northern's campus. The memorial scholarship has been in place since his death in 1974.

Around 1990 Black Student Services was combined with the Native American Student Services office under the Dean of Students to form the Multicultural Affairs Office. This office has undergone changes and is now called Diversity Student Services. The role of the Black Student Union has now fallen to organizations such as Ebony Excellence, Sisters of X and Essence.

Other Black student organizations on campus and surrounding communities of Marquette and the former K. I. Sawyer Air Force Base including Orientation/Big Sisters-Big Brothers Program, Aides, Black Unlimited Collegiate Association, Black Collegian Annual Awards Dinner, & the Harambee Gospel Choir, were all overseen by the Black Student Services Office. The Black Students Financial Aid Committee was formed during the 1978 fall semester. There were also Board of Control Black Scholarships. Programs and watchdog groups like the NMU Human Rights Commission and Student Support Service brought a new climate to campus. Since December 1993, the celebration of Kwanzaa has been held on campus every year except 1997.

Over the years ten prominent African Americans have received honorary degrees from Northern: Richard H. Austin (12/1989); John Hope Franklin (8–1978); Patricia Harris (8/1973); Clara Stanton Jones (5/1978); Wade H. McCree, Jr. (5/1985); Gordon Parks (5/1997); Judge Myron H. Wahls (4/1996); Willis Franklin Ward (1/1970); Roger W. Wilkins (12/1994); Clifton R. Wharton, Jr. (12/1975). Stacey K. Gibson

Agriculture, Department of: *See: Conservation & Agriculture, Department of*

Alcohol-Free Weekend: A January weekend set aside for students to make a pledge to remain alcohol free for Friday, Saturday and Sunday. Students purchase a button for $1 and sign a pledge card, which is kept in the Student Activities office and states that the student will remain alcohol free for the entire weekend. Students can use the buttons for discount purchases at select city businesses. On Saturday, a student carnival called the Superior Dome Spectacular is held and has live entertainment, games and other activities. (NW 01/23/1997)

Alibi Rock Theater: Located on Wright Street across from campus and nearby dorms, this was a popular hangout for students. The club opened on December 13, 1974. Previously a bar called the Brat House, it had a notorious reputation. When the new business opened, it had to live down its former reputation.

The Alibi boasted the vibrations of 920 watts (RMS), projectors, and a lighted dance floor. A DJ controlled the music, which was described as "good dance music." Over the years, the Alibi ran into trouble with fights between NMU students and K. I. Sawyer airmen. In the early 1980s, wet tee shirt contests were popular. The Alibi closed and was replaced in the early 1990s by the Power Station, a health club. (NW 12/12/1974)

All Student Judiciary: Referred to as ASJ, this organization dates back to March 3, 1981. The function of ASJ is hearing cases dealing with violation of university regulations in residence halls and food service facilities. It recommends penalties below suspension and expulsion.

Alma Mater: The modern alma mater was written in 1949 by Luther S. West, a noted biologist, dean of the College of Arts and Sciences and a poet, as a contribution to Northern's Semi-Centennial Celebration. The words, melody and harmonization for male voices were the work of Dr. West. Certain transpositions, as needed for band use, were prepared by Gordon D. Gill. Somewhat later Dr. Harold Wright, who subsequently became head of the University's Music Department, provided the piano arrangement.

Each stanza carried a separate message. The first calls attention to the institution's fifty years of service in Michigan's Upper Peninsula; the second reflects more serious thoughts and ambitions of the undergraduate. Stanza three reminds one that the majority of Northern's graduates have traditionally entered the teaching profession. The last four lines belong distinctly to alumni. Reference to "thine ivy'd walls" refers to Longyear and Kaye Halls, which were covered with a generous growth of English ivy when the alma mater was written.

The following are the lyrics to *Hail Northern:*

>Hail Northern, we thy sons and daughters
>Now bring thee tribute long deserved,
>Thou beacon light mid nature's grandeur
>Through passing decades well preserved.
>O may we labor with untiring zeal
>That when these golden days have flown
>We may with honor face the future
>And match thy courage with our own!
>We shall go forth inspired, devoted,
>The light of wisdom to extend
>That liberty of thought and worship
>Within our land may never end.
>And when in years to come, we ponder well
>Our sojourn 'neath thine ivy's walls.
>Our hearts will pledge renewed devotion.
>In hallowed memory of thy halls.
>(NN 10/08/1958)

Alumni Citizenship Award: The award was created in 1994 and is given to alumni who provided exemplary community service. *Past recipients*: Joseph R. Konwinski (3–97); Larry Hassel (3–97); Joseph E. Schmidt (2–95).

Alumni Relations: The history of this office goes back to the opening years of the institution. The first alumnae—Ellan Harshman, Sarah MacLeod, and Ida Mitchell—received limited teaching certificates on July 3, 1900. Within a few years there were enough graduates for the alumni to meet. This occurred on June 18, 1902. The first alumni banquet was held, and it became a Northern tradition. The banquet was held following commencement and was a time to introduce the graduates to their roles as alumni and encourage their commitment to their alma mater. These banquets led to the first reunion dinner held in Escanaba in October 1907. With the completion of Kaye Hall in 1915, the alumni dinner included nearly 600 alumni and former President Waldo. By 1926 the librarian, Lydia Olson was keeping a "Who's Who Cabinet" of alumni in the library.

An alumni publication developed slowly. In 1916 the editor of "Alumni News", librarian Lydia Olson, had several pages in *The Quill*, Northern first literary magazine devoted to alumni activities. After 1919 with the coming of *The Northern Normal News*, several columns were devoted to alumni affairs. At that time the annual alumni fee was one dollar.

As the number of alumni increased and spread across the nation, it became increasingly difficult to keep track of them. In 1920–1921 a group of alumni in the Detroit area called for and then established a local club. As a result, the Northern Alumni Association was formed in 1924. By 1939, about eight alum groups were organized around the Upper Peninsula. To celebrate Northern's 40th anniversary, the alumni united for a special 4th homecoming (*See separate entry*), which has become a campus tradition. This began a new era on campus in which the alumni were considered important to the institution.

In the 1940s, *Alumni News* was published at regular intervals and sent to alumni. Prior to this publication, only a short bulletin was sent out just prior to homecoming. The Copper Country Alumni Club was formed in 1944. John Hogan, who was alumni president in February 1945, had plans to keep a record on over 900 alumni and maintain contact with those in the armed forces.

With the coming of President Harden, Northern's commitment to alumni expanded. In the summer of 1957, the Alumni Relations office was created within the Placement Office. R. Tom Peters (BS 1955) was the first director. Its goals were to identify, locate, and organize alumni. Other goals included organization of chapters, fund raising and the use of alumni to recruit students. Under Peters, an alumni office was established in the Don H. Bottum University Center after previously sharing space with other administrative offices in Kaye Hall.

By 1961, there were over 20,000 alumni whose names were kept on a mailing list. Alumni groups met downstate for regional basketball games, and the Marquette-Alger County Alumni Club began holding dinners prior to football games in Marquette. At homecoming in 1960, four members of the 1910 class were given "Golden N" certificates, while those back for their 25th reunion received "Silver Ns". In 1962, Catholic alumni held a dinner to raise money for the Newman Center and honor their members. The Alumni "N" Club was formed at this time, and the varsity-alumni basketball game became a tradition for many years. In addition to athletic-related receptions, charter jet trips to various destinations became an annual event as well.

As the role of Alumni Relations grew, the director's position became full-time. Under Paul Suomi, who was named director of Alumni Relations in 1984 after serving as the University's Director of Communications, the university's external thrust intensified. In addition to maintaining receptions held in conjunction with key athletic events, particularly basketball, football, and ice hockey, alumni groups took hold in 28 different geographical locations, where dinners or receptions were held on an annual or biannual basis. One of the highlights of these events was the showing of an annual "NMU in the News" videotape, which was produced by alumni.

Awards were established to recognize the achievements of young alumni (*See: Outstanding Young Alumni Award*); citizenship (*See: Alumni Citizenship Award*); service to alma mater (*See: Alumni Service Award*); in addition to expanding the search for candidates for the Distinguished Alumni Award (*See separate entry*). With the approval of NMU Alumni Association Board of Directors, new committees were created to help the University and Alumni Relations; an alumni dues program was instituted to finance *Horizons* and other external operations. *Horizons* was created to help strengthen ties between NMU and its alumni, establish and nurture a supportive relationship with external audiences, and inspire teamwork required between alumni, friends, and current residents of the university community to maintain and advance the institution.

A supplement to *Horizons*, *Horizons Extra*, began publication in November, 1997 to encourage alumni and friends to become active, dues-paying alumni association members. The first issue was printed in a tabloid format, but a more reader friendly, newsletter format was adopted for the next and all subsequent issues. *Horizons* is published six times a year--twice in magazine format as *Horizons* and four times in newsletter format as *Horizons Extra*. .

Alumni Relations also worked with the Admissions Office for several years. Working with Suomi, Carol Sarvello ('64) was liaison with the Admissions Office. At its peak, more than 300 alumni were designated as "Ambassadors" and worked with Admissions to identify and recruit potential students. Sarvello was also co-advisor with Suomi of the NMU Student Alumni Association, which was named the best group of its kind in the nation in 1984 by the Council for the Advancement and Support of Education. Today many of the group's former responsibilities are performed by First Impressions *(See separate entry)*.

Alumni Relations operates around the principle that the alumni represent a primary constituency that significantly affects the University's present vitality and future strength. Successful alumni relations leads to financial contributions to the University, job leads for graduates, on-campus lectures by alumni who are experts in their professional fields, identification of potential students, enhancement of the University's image and opportunities for alumni to strengthen ties with the University.

The Director serves on University and non-University committees such as: Golden Wildcat Club Executive Committee, Homecoming, Golden Z Club, Campus Master Planning Committee, K. I. Sawyer Air Force Association, Economic Club of Marquette County, and Finn Fest '96, to name a few.

Alumni directors: R. Tom Peters; Louis Myefski; Harry Culver; Terry Nyquist; R. Tom Peters; Paul Suomi. (Erin C. Brady. "Alumni Relations," (1996), UA; *The 1996–97 University Profile*, 2:204–209; NNN 12/15/1920, 08/03/1926; NCN 04/22/1930; NN 10/09/1957)

Alumni Service Award: The Award was first given in October 1984. It is given to NMU alumni whose volunteerism, contributions and/or recruitment efforts on behalf of NMU are above the norm, evidenced by loyal and outstanding service in areas such as the NMU Alumni Association; the NMU Development Fund; service to school, departmental, or other University committees; establishment of a scholarship; serving as an Alumni Ambassador; and/or serving as a mentor in the Externship Program.

Recipients have included: Art Allen '53 (10–84); Richard H. Allen '60 (9–92); John Arger '70 (10–94); Barry Axelrod '69 (10–94); Creta Bayee '31 (10–85); Connie (Schwemin) Barto '61 (10–98); Thomas Berutti '63 (10–94); Philip G. Blake '81 (10–96); David Blomquist '62 (9–92); Charles Blossfield '63 (10–85); Robert M. Bordeau '59 (10–87); William D. Brodeur '60 (10–90); W. David Cade '64 (10–91); Gildo Canale '56 (10–95); Connie (Lutz) DelBello '75 (10–98); Thomas H. Finnerty '68 (10–88); Gerald Goerlitz '62 (10–87); Barbara Velin Gusick '60 (10–85); Larry Hassel '67 (10–85); Gloria Jussila Jackson '68 (10–86); Byron J. Johnson '68 (10–90); Jay W. Johnson '65 (10–88); Tyne Kangas '58 (10–85); John Kukuk '76 (10–95); Denise A. Lafferty '82 (10–96); Denham Lord '59 (10–86); Angeline Major '23 (10–84); Dennis Malaney '76 (10–93); Walter McClintock '39 (10–98); Robert A. Mercier '62 (9–92); Bronwen L. Millet (10–97); Norbert C. Murphy '58 (10–89); Michael H. Nelsen '63 (10–97); D. Neil Nystrom '57 (10–88); Jerry Pangrazzi (10–93); Robert L. Pecotte '64 (10–89); Paul J. Roberts '56 (10–91); Ivan Ryan '54 (10–90); Carol Levine Sarvello '64 (10–89); Dominic Sarvello '64 (10–87); Jerold L. Saundri '61 (10–86); Robert Sibilsky (10–95); Gary F. Silc '63 (10–86); Daniel J. Stencil '76 (10–96); Daniel J. Trotochaud '68 (10–97); Frank Wareham '63 (10–9-8); Daune L. Weiss '69 (10–97); Fritz Wilson '58 (10–94). (University Relations Office)

American Indian Movement (AIM): The national actions conducted by AIM during the 1970s were shunned by some local Native Americans. However, AIM turned campus attention to Native American issues. (*See*: *Organization of North American Indian Students*) AIM's first Michigan chapter, which had several NMU students and alumni members, was not started until February 1997 in Norway, Michigan. An AIM tribunal investigating allegations of corruption at the Keweenaw Bay Indian Community in Baraga made a presentation at NMU in October 1995.

Americans with Disabilities Act: Using $380,000 from the State of Michigan Special Maintenance this Federal law (07/26/1990) encouraged the University to make renovations in West Science, Jamrich Hall, Thomas Fine Arts and Cohodas Administrative Center. Renovations included restrooms, ramps, elevator modifications and other accessibility concerns. Improvements continue to be made across the campus, which greatly improves the lives of disabled students.

Anatomy of a Murder: This is considered by many to be the best courtroom drama ever made. It was filmed in Marquette in 1958. At the time, Robert Bordeau was student body president and he was asked by the administration to organize a dance at Lee Hall Ballroom so that the film's Director, Otto Preminger, could pick the couples to be included in the filming of the bar scenes at Mount Shasta Lodge in Michigamme. Numerous Northern students had the luxury of dancing and sitting in Mount Shasta for a whole afternoon doing takes while Duke Ellington played the piano.

Andy's Bar: A popular student bar from 1965 to 1981, Andy's was located on the southeast corner of South Front and Spring Streets. It was a place where students could "get loose." Its famous Tuesday "Peanut Night" was introduced in 1972, and four years later other innovations followed. Students filled the premises. In October 1981, unable to take care of $23,000 in repairs and upgrades, the bar was closed. The brothers of Phi Kappa Tau fraternity were "terribly upset" at the demise of the bar and planned a mock funeral. The building was demolished, and a vacant lot now marks the site.

Annual: The earliest annual is the *Olive and Gold,* published in 1910. It was a paper-bound book containing essays and poems written by students. Sections such as faculty and sports were given long write-ups with a few pictures.

In 1920, the yearbook was called *Echoes of 1920*. In this issue there were more pictures and less reading material, even though the articles were still quite extensive.

The name of the annual was changed in February 1924 when the students elected to called it the *Kawbawgam*. It was named after Charles Kawbawgam, an Ojibwe leader who met the Amos Harlow party when they arrived on the Carp River in 1849. The cover was changed from paper-bound to hard-bound. The contents of the book included a wider range of sports, extra-curricular activities and organizations. The annual was published yearly until 1933 when budget cuts caused by the Depression curtailed most extra-curricular activities.

The *Campuseer*, published in 1941, further developed the organizations section, including the Greek groups. In 1942, *Polaris* was published, dedicated to former students in military service. During the war years, the publication of an annual was suspended. In 1947, when publication was revived, the name was changed to the *Northerner*.

The idea of a yearbook was revived in 1948 with the idea of preserving the 50th anniversary celebration and record of student life on campus. The modern annual, called the *Peninsulan* dated from 1949. The annual emphasized casual pictures with a minimum of writing. It gave more attention to class activities than previous issues had, as well as continuing to portray social life on campus. The editor of the yearbook was a paid position in par with the editor of the campus newspaper.

The *Peninsulan* was published annually until 1980. It was discontinued due to changing student interest in yearbooks. In 1990, a Yearbook Club was formed under the leadership of Keith Cielinski. The members worked with the Dean of Students office only to discover that the production and sale of a year book was financially risky and the idea was tabled. These annuals provide an excellent historical review of university life and times. (NNN 02/14/1924; NCN 12/01/1948; NN 12/05/1962; NW 11/18/1990)

Apartments: With the increase in student enrollment beginning in 1946, apartments were constructed to meet the demand for married students. The first two sets of apartments were known as "GIville" and "Vetville" (*See: Veterans Housing*). They were located in the vicinity of Waldo and Presque Isle and in front of Lee Hall. They were removed in 1951 and 1957 respectively and replaced by modern apartments.

The first apartments on campus were constructed in the College Woods, an area bound by Wilkinson and Summit Streets, Elizabeth Harden Drive, and the Art Annex North. Development of the housing area began in 1956 and the first two buildings designated as "A" and "B", located at 600 and 601 Summit Street, were completed in June 1957.

Within this complex, the first two-story apartments for married students, located at the intersection of Summit Street and Wilkinson Avenue, were built by Proksch Construction Company of Iron River. The apartments were opened on June 15, 1957. Within a month, twenty-four college students and their families occupied the buildings.

In the buildings designated as "A" and "B", there were four, two-bedroom apartments and twenty one-bedroom apartments. In each kitchen, there was a Roper gas range, a Kenmore Automatic washer and dryer, a Frigidaire refrigerator, and a Formica top dinette. The rest of the kitchen was made up of Youngstown steel cabinets.

In each living room, there was an easy chair, davenport, and matching coffee table and end table that were topped with Formica. Located between the kitchen and living room was a wooden room separator, which had a light tan mahogany grain.

Bedrooms were equipped with a bed and bookcase-headboard and a large dresser with a matching mirror. Walk-in closets with sliding doors were in each bedroom, with a separate closet for linens.

All windows, with the exception of the bathroom window, were equipped with venetian blinds. The bathroom window was made of smoked glass.

Each apartment had individual thermostats, so tenants could adjust the temperature to their own liking. Floors and hallways had multi-color tiling to match the walls and ceilings.

Six more units were constructed in the summer of 1958. The first twenty-four families moved into the first completed units at 700, 800, 801 and 821 Summit by mid-December 1958 and another twelve families were in by Christmas. The last units were filled by February 1959.

Each of the new buildings contained ten one-bedroom units and two, two-bedroom units. As the *Northern News* stated, "The apartments, tastefully furnished and decorated, exemplify the comfortable and economical accommodations provided for today's married college student and his family." Each apartment contained a living room, kitchen, one or two bedrooms and ample shelf and storage space. The bedrooms contained large sliding-door wardrobes. Each apartment had its own thermostat-controlled heating unit supplied by the University's central heating plant. Furnishings and appliances in 1959 consisted of a stove, refrigerator, dinette table and chairs, bookcase, room divider between the kitchen and living room, sofa-bed, lounge chair, coffee table, end table, double bed with bookcase headboard and a dresser and mirror. One end of each building contained a mechanical room with a hot water heater and control panels, with a laundry room was located at the opposite end. These apartments have been thoroughly renovated since then.

As the enrollment of Northern grew, so did the demand for housing for the faculty. Many faculty members arrived in Marquette to find limited or no immediate housing. As a result, the first faculty apartments were constructed at 821 Center Street, screened from the street by birch trees. The two-story brick, twelve unit apartment building had two-bedroom units that were painted pastel colors and rented unfurnished with a stove and refrigerator provided. The faculty apartments were ready for occupancy by mid-March 1959. The first faculty resident was Katheryn Marriott of the English Department and supervisor of student publications.

In January 1966, as the demand grew, the first series of 24 apartments were constructed along Center Street to the west of the main campus across Lincoln Avenue. Eventually there would be 72 units in the complex covering 59,292 square feet. These apartments were opened for occupancy beginning in 1967. The street servicing the apartment buildings at Center and Lincoln was named Gilbert L. Brown Court by the Board of Control (09/27/1967), after the former head of the Department of Psychology and Education.

Another series of apartments with one hundred units was completed to the north of the earlier apartments off of Lincoln Avenue in August 1980. They were constructed with Housing and Urban Development funds amounting to $3.6 million and comprise 84,336 square feet. They consisted of 50 one-bedroom units and 50 two-bedroom units. Four of these were made available to handicapped students. Rent from these apartments is used to repay the HUD funding. (NCN 05/29/1957; 07/24/1957; 12/17/1958; 01/28/1959; 02/18/1959; 02/25/1959; 04/22/1959; NN 07/24/1970, 08/28/1980)

Appleberry, James B.: (February 22, 1938–). Dr. Appleberry was born in Waverly, Missouri and began his career as a teacher and principal in a rural Missouri School District. Subsequently, he served education in positions of ever-increasing responsibility. Dr. Appleberry received his bachelor's (1960) and master's (1963) degrees from Central Missouri State University. As the first graduate fellow at the University, he received his education specialist degree in 1967. He joined the faculty of Oklahoma State University following completion of his doctorate at OSU in 1968. He served the University as assistant, associate and full professor, and as chairperson of his academic department. In 1973–74, he was selected by the American Council on Education as a fellow in its Academic Administration Internship Program.

In 1975, Dr. Appleberry joined the University of Kansas as University Director of Planning and Professor of Administration, Foundations, and Higher Education. Nine months later he was designated Assistant to the Chancellor. He was chosen President of Pittsburg State University in Kansas in 1977, where he served seven years.

Dr. Appleberry was appointed President of Northern Michigan University by the Board of Control and began his tenure in office on July 1, 1983. He was inaugurated in a simple ceremony as part of commencement on December 17, 1983.

President Appleberry helped strengthen programs to ensure academic excellence, for example, the Glenn T. Seaborg Center for Teaching and Learning Science and Mathematics, named after the Nobel Laureate was established. With the assistance of the faculty, the University strengthened its promotion, tenure and sabbatical leave policies, revised its procedures for merit salary distribution and established a teaching and learning improvement center on campus. After nearly ten years of declining enrollment, NMU raised its admission standards in 1985. The results were increased enrollments, a jump of nearly two full points in the ACT score of entering freshmen and a dramatic increase in the rate of student retention. In 1987, the University was recognized by the American Association of State Colleges and Universities as one of the top ten institutions in innovation and change in American higher education.

During the period between 1984 and 1989, numerous changes were made on campus. The Glenn T. Seaborg Center for Teaching and Learning Science and Mathematics, the Upper Peninsula Center for

Educational Development, the Olympic Education/Training and Great Lakes Sports Training Centers, the Northern Economic Initiatives Center and the Center for Excellence in Leadership and Personal Development were all established. The Commission on the Future of Northern Michigan University was active between 1986 and 1987. In other areas, a Writing Fellows Program and related courses were created to improve basic student skills. A program was created to improve support services for probationary students. General education requirements were increased from 32 to 40 credits. The University supported new internship opportunities in Washington, D.C. and the Vienna Programs. $250,000 was allocated annually to make the transition to new technology for computers and classroom equipment. At this time, the University Art Museum (formerly Lee Hall Gallery) was renovated and the position of full-time Gallery Director/Cultural Affairs Coordinator was created. A Cultural Affairs Program was also established.

Within academic departments, accreditation was achieved or renewed by agencies such as the American Chemical Society, the American Speech and Hearing Association, the National Association of Schools of Music, the Council of Social Work and the National League of Nursing. Efforts to improve internal communication through the Brown Bag Luncheon Series, Agenda, Campus, and Northern Notes were expanded.

Under President Appleberry's guidance, the University was named an Olympic Education Center by the United States Olympic Committee, becoming the only one in the United States. For the first time, United States Olympic hopefuls trained at an approved center while they completed their education. The Center had a positive economic impact on the region, and provided opportunities for academic programs and research on campus.

During his tenure, President Appleberry added a number of positions to the administration, including a Vice President for Students Affairs, another for Academic Affairs and an Assistant Vice President for Graduate Studies.

In March 1991, Dr. Appleberry resigned the presidency to become president of the American Association of State Colleges and Universities, located in Washington, D.C. This position became effective on July 1, a day after he left NMU. He retired from this position in 1999 and settled in Lawrence, Kansas.

Dr. Appleberry authored and co-authored numerous publications which appeared in national journals. In addition, he lectured and delivered professional papers at meetings throughout the country.

Memberships: Vice Chair of the National Center for Education Statistics Advisory Council, an appointed position by the United States Secretary of Education; served as a member of the National Collegiate Athletic Association Presidents Commission; chair of the Policies and Purposes Committee of the American Association of State Colleges and Universities; American Association of Higher Education; the American Educational Research Association; the National Conference of Professor of Educational Administration; Pi Delta Kappa; Phi Kappa Phi; Kappa Delta Pi; Phi Sigma Phi; and Kappa Mu Epsilon.

He married Patricia Ann Trent, also of Waverly. They are the parents of two sons: John Mark and Timothy David. (MJ 04/05/1983, 12/16/1998; President's Report, 1983–1984 [1989]; Focused Evaluation Report. Marquette: NMU, 1989).

Appleberry, Patricia Ann Trent: Mrs. Appleberry was born in Waverly, Missouri. She and Dr. Appleberry were "high school sweethearts" who attended Central Missouri State University and were married in 1960. They have two sons: John Mark and Timothy David. She received a bachelor's degree in Science and Vocational Home Economics from Central Missouri State University. Mrs. Appleberry supported her husband professionally in the academic environment. She was known for the upscale receptions and parties that she hosted both at Kaye House and on campus. She participated in alumni visits around the country and promoted cultural activities on campus. Mrs. Appleberry was known for her volunteer work in the Marquette community.

Over the years, Mrs. Appleberry suffered from ataxia, a hereditary disorder that affects the nerve cells. As a result of this, she and Dr. Appleberry retired to Lawrence, Kansas in 1999. (MJ 10/18/1983, 02/27/1984, 12/16/1998)

Appropriations: Between 1899 and 1949 Northern received $8,645,746 in state appropriations. This figure does not include monies which came to the institution from other sources on a greater scale. Over the years a high proportion (80%+) has been used for salaries. The appropriations went from $7,500 in 1900–1901 to $27,630 in 1901–1902 and then continued to rise steadily to $288,500 in 1930–1931. The Depression saw a decline to $168,144 in 1933–1934 and 1934–1935 which was followed by a continuous rise. With post-World War II growth, appropriations rose from $311,100 in 1946–1947 to $578,240 two years later.

In a unique development, that only happened once in Northern's history in 1956–1957, the administration requested $896,762 and received a net appropriation of $914,376. Over the years the appropriations have continued to rise. During the Harden years (1956–1967) of great expansion, the amount went from $914,376 to $5,140,342 in 1967–1968. The amounts continued to increased until fiscal years 1992–1994 when the amount of $39,971,586 remained stagnant.

In 1998–1999 Northern received $47,247,801 from the state. However the operating budget was actually a bit over $104 million. The added monies came from tuition, grants, pay for services, auxiliary enterprises, and other designated funds. Over the years, the university has been receiving less from the state.

Archaeology: This field of study on campus dates to the fall of 1971 when Dr. Marla Buckmaster joined the faculty. Her field of specialization is prehistoric archaeology and she has conducted classes in field archaeology, studied important sites in Michigan and published her findings.

Area Training Center: See: *Jacobetti Center*.

Archery: Intramural archery can be traced back to the early days of Northern. The first annual Intramural Archery Tournament was held on May 24, 1957. In 1998 the NMU Archery Organization provides an opportunity for non-archers to learn more about archery. Members are able to compete against other archers. Archery continues to be taught on campus.

Archives: Officially called the Central Upper Peninsula and Northern Michigan University Archives, the Archives are located on the lower level of the Harden Learning Resources Center.

Dr. Ruth Roebke-Berens, chair of the history department, opened talks with Martha Bigelow, director of the State History Division, concerning the development of a state archives branch on the Northern campus. On November 10, 1982 the history department voted to promote the archival program. In June 1983, Dr. Cliff Maier and Dr. Gene DeLon Jones attended a ten-day workshop. The state officials agreed that this workshop would provide the individual with the minimal knowledge to handle the archives.

In 1983, Dr. Maier began to work as Archivist. He worked under difficult conditions with limited funds to develop a physical space for the archives. At this time, the administration saw the archives in a narrow sense; materials related only to the university were to be collected. However due to the foresight of Dr. Maier, non-university materials were collected within the collections of faculty members. Over the years the space expanded and the archives grew.

The archives reached a second phase when Dr. Maier retired in 1992. Through a $72,000 grant from the National Historical Records and Publication Commission, Gayle Martinson was hired as a fully trained Archivist and remained until April 1, 1996. During the period until December 31, 1996 the Archives were under the direction of Krista Clumper and headed by Mary Argeroupolis who retired on that date. During the first four months of 1997, Clumper oversaw the archives. In April 1997, Marcus Robyns began his duties as Archivist.

From the beginning, the Archives were housed in a series of small offices and use of the facilities was extremely difficult and limited. In 1995, the Archives were given renovated quarters, but no sooner had they become partially established than they were moved (February–March 1996) into their present location. The Archives also obtained some 45,000 square feet for remote storage in the Services Building. In the summer of 1997, Robyns began to focus on the collection of the region's labor records and other records housed in the State Archives in Lansing. At this time, Robyns had the rare Moses Coit Tyler Collection removed to the Archives. Guides are available for use of materials in the Archives.

Archivists: Clifford Maier, 1983–1992; Gayle Martinson, 1992–1996; Mary Argeroupolis, (interim) 1996; Marcus Robyns, 1997–present. (NMU Archives, Univ. Series 47, History Department Minutes, 10/21/1982, 11/10/1982; *The Roundtable* 1:5 (March 1992); MJ 10/05/1997)

Arctic House Plunge: Started in the winter of 1987 by a group of hearty students from Hunt Hall, this annual winter plunge into Lake Superior at the mouth of the Dead River has become a tradition at NMU. In February 1995, a group of fourteen noted that it was the coldest day on record for the event, with a reported wind chill of -30°. (MJ 02/11/1995)

Art and Design, Department of: The teaching of Art goes back to the opening of Northern in 1899. At that time it was merely called Drawing, and the instructor also taught Geography. This situation soon changed. Art was an important component in teacher education. During the early days of the Department, Peter White provided special funding for the purchase of art replicas (paintings, lithographs, sculptures) which were found throughout the buildings. The idea was to create a museum-effect. Probably the most famous Art teacher in the department was Grace Spalding (1903–1938).

In 1965, Richard "Mike" Gorski was hired as the new department head. It was his task to restructure the Art Department and bring in curriculum change. There was a shift away from the earlier emphasis on art as a teaching tool to art as a creative and unique experience. The younger faculty Gorski hired were experimental artists, interested in exploring new media of artistic expression with their students.

As evidence of this change in focus, on June 11, 1966 the name was changed from the Department of Art to the Department of Visual Arts. Then effective August 1, 1973 the official name became the Department of Art and Design. In August 1972 the Board of Control approved the Bachelor of Fine Arts degree. The result of Gorski's work was the creation of the multi-faceted department.

Over the years, the department has had scattered quarters around the campus. In the beginning, the department was located in Kaye Hall with adjacent kilns which were demolished in 1970. Classes were then removed to the Russell Thomas Fine Arts Building (*See separate entry*).

In 1969, the department offices were relocated to the Learning Resources Center. Later in the 1970s, offices and work areas were expanded to Lee Hall and the Birdseye Building, which was renovated in 1970. In 1977, a portion of a kitchen area of Lee Hall was developed into dark rooms. This remained the center of Art and Design until late August 1996, when ultra-modern facilities were opened in the old Service Building and Power Plant now called Art and Design Studios North. (*See separate entry*)

The undergraduate objectives of the department are to prepare students of the region and state to participate in the professional fields of art, design and education, broadening the scope of their experience by the intellectual support for art action beyond the limit of studio skills. The department, through the University Art Museum, also performs the regional objective of providing students, faculty and the community with exposure to exhibitions exemplifying the cultural breadth of the visual arts from international, regional and local sources, including the University's permanent art collection.

The graduate objective of the department is to develop art educators who possess advanced knowledge and skills in a specific studio area. The program stresses cognitive and applied aspects of art and design, providing an advanced experience that can be used to create visual art works.

Department chairs or heads: Grace Spalding, 1903–1938; Nadia Thorpe Leonardelli, 1938–1946; Cleobelle Harris, 1946–1965; Richard Gorski, 1965–1975; Thomas Cappuccio, 1975–1978; Michael Cinelli, 1978–present. (*The 1996–97 University Profile*, 1:61–67)

Art & Design Studios North: The name for the former Service Building which was renovated and renamed by the Board of Control on February 16, 1996, opened in the fall of 1996. Earlier in 1995 it was unofficially designated "Art Annex North."

Art & Design Studios South: Originally designated "Art Annex South," it was renamed on February 16, 1996, by the Board of Control. It consists of the work area and University Art Museum while the Lee Hall designation refers to the office area.

Art Museum, University: The original Lee Hall Gallery was established in 1975 by the Department of Art and Design. In 1996, Lee Hall Gallery received art museum status through the action of the Board of Control and the name was changed to Northern Michigan University Art Museum. The American Association of Museums recognized this action soon afterward.

The primary purpose of the Gallery is to exhibit the work of NMU art students and faculty, as well as local, national and international artists. The Gallery serves as both an educational facility for the University, and as a fine arts gallery for the residents of the Upper Peninsula. Various Art and Design faculty members served as interim gallery directors until 1985, when Wayne Francis was hired as director.

In 1988, Lee Hall Gallery underwent an extensive renovation funded by a grant from the Detroit Institute of Art. After the departmental offices were moved to the opposite side of the lobby, a second exhibition room was opened, increasing the Gallery floor space to over 2,000 square feet. The lobby itself was remodeled, the permanent art collection storage improved and the security system upgraded. The newest physical improvements are the installation of an environmental control system and the addition of showcases to show parts of the permanent art collection.

The Museum's permanent art collection consisted mainly of student and faculty work until 1980, when Ralph Slovonko and Norman Pappas donated a collection of silk screen prints. This was followed by a major donation of Japanese prints and objects by Dr. Dorothy Lewis and Captain Arthur and Jo Bennett. Other major donors include Joel Murray (Salvador Dali prints), Ralph and Ann Secord (American illustrations) and Cecilia Kettunen (drawings and paintings). The most recent major donation was a collection of over 250 Native American objects from Everett and Elizabeth Losey. These, along with other donations, have extended the permanent collection which has been recently catalogued.

The Museum's programming has grown steadily. The exhibition schedule includes approximately seventeen exhibitions during the twelve-month season. Funding from various sources, including Northern Michigan University, Friends of the University Art Museum (*See separate entry*), the Jamrich Endowment for the Arts, Michigan Council for the Arts and Humanities, the Detroit Institute for the Arts, the Shiras Institute and the Native American Studies program have provided a variety of distinguished exhibitions.

In 1990, "The Friends of Lee Hall Gallery" was established to raise money to further enhance the Gallery's programming and encourage community involvement in Gallery activities. Each year they fund 4 or 5 high-quality exhibitions which would not be possible without their support. The Friends have also been very active in using the museum to provide educational programs for the community. They have recently begun seeking and purchasing new acquisitions for the Museum's permanent collection and funding a Sculpture Walk (*See separate entry*) on campus.

Director: Wayne Francis, 1985–present. Wayne Francis

Art Works and Places: In the opening days of Northern, Peter White provided the Art Department with a special stipend of $1,000 per year to purchase copies of art works. Eventually these reproductions were found through Kaye Hall. Today some of these prints reproductions of paintings are located in the Peter White Lounge.

Over the years, a number of plaster of paris statues were given to the University. From what can be learned there were the following in the Kaye Hall Auditorium: Abraham Lincoln and Donatello's Saint George located on either side of the stage; in the lobby landings there were: Venus di Milo and David which stood at the first landing facing the entrance of the building.

The Lincoln statue was a gift of the Class of 1916 and it was accepted by President James B. Kaye for the University in January 1917. Little is known of the Donatello statue's origins, although it was made by the same Ciprano Company in Boston. It, too, was probably a class gift. These statues remained in Kaye Hall until its demolition in 1972-1973. Three of them survived: Lincoln, Saint George and Venus di Milo. University officials placed the three of them in storage in the Birdseye Building along with many of the large reproduction paintings which lined the walls of the halls and classrooms. It should be noted that many of the other art reproductions were either removed by individuals or destroyed in the process of moving from the Kaye Hall complex.

Around 1984, the head of Art and Design, Michael Cinelli was contacted by Vice President for Financial Affairs, Lyle Shaw and asked if the Department wanted these items. The department accepted them. In time, Venus was destroyed. The Lincoln and Saint George statues were treated irreverently by students. They were covered with layers of paint which probably helped them to survive. By 1994 Lincoln had a hippie bow tie around his neck and a top hat while Saint George was decorated as Super Man. In April the University Historian, Russell Magnaghi identified their location and recorded their status on film. He was concerned that with the renovations of the Birdseye Building in the future, the statues would be finally lost. Over the months there were general conversations concerning the preservation of the statues. In March 1995, Professor Diane D. Kordich suggested that the statues be rehabilitated by Joann Rouen Laduke, an NMU alumna. This was completed in May 1995, and on May 30, the two statues were returned to "life" in prominent places in the University Center. The reaction from the faculty, staff and alumni who saw them was favorable. Those who remembered them from the past were nostalgic while others thought that they fit well in the Peter White Lounge.

The other additions to the University Center are a number of reproduction paintings. These included: "The Horse Fair" by Rosa Bonheur; "The Blue Boy" by Thomas Gainsborough; "The Sower"; and "On the Bank of the River" by Henri Lerolle Pinx. The frames on these works were dusty and the glass dirty. For the last decade they rested in an attic area of Lee Hall. These, too, were visited by the Historian in April 1994. Dr. Kordich and Professor John Hubbard restored the frames and made the paintings presentable. They, too, were brought to the building on May 30 and attached to the walls on May 31. The reactions by the first seers were similar to the viewing of the statues.

Some of the original paintings of Grace Spalding have been located and preserved and are in the University Art Collection. A Leon Lundmark (*See separate entry*) lakescape is also in the collection. On January 25, 1951, an oil painting of John M. Longyear was accepted by Northern from Mrs. Abby Roberts and hung in Longyear Hall. The portrait was removed from the university during a student sit-in during the late sixties and was never recovered.

In 1975, the Lee Hall Gallery was created and in 1996 its status was changed to University Art Museum (*See separate entry*). In the 1980s, Gallery 236, a student gallery was opened in Room 236 of the University Center. This gallery, funded with student monies, remained until it was replaced and moved to its present location on the main floor of the University Center in 1994.

Around the campus other pieces of sculpture have been placed. In late 1991, the piece "Flying Wild Geese" was donated by the friends of former Board of Control member, Edwin O. George. It is located at the east entrance of Cohodas. There is a sculpture in front of Lee Hall.

In the mid-1990s, Michael Cinelli, head of Art and Design developed a plan for the Sculpture Walk (*See separate entry*) located to the south of Carey Hall (*See separate entry*).

Arts and Sciences, College of: The largest college at Northern Michigan University, consisting of fifteen departments, the College of Arts and Science first became a distinct entity on July 1, 1962 with Luther S. West as Dean. In 1965 West retired, and the affairs of the College were taken over by Vice President Milton Byrd. The office was revived in 1966, with David Dickson as dean and Thomas Griffith as associate dean. Dickson resigned in 1967, in the wake of the McClellan affair (*See separate entry*), and Griffith became dean, with Eugene A. Whitehouse as associate dean. In 1967, the school underwent a major reorganization, and began the policy of writing open faculty evaluations. Griffith was succeeded by Robert B. Glenn as dean in 1971, who was succeeded by Donald D. Heikkinen in 1974.

The College presently consists of the following departments: Art and Design; Biology; Chemistry; Communications and Performance Studies (CAPS); Economics; English; History; Language; Mathematics and Computer Science; Military Science; Music; Philosophy; Physics; Political Science; (Criminal Justice and Sociology are no longer included). It also oversees three centers: Glenn T. Seaborg Center for Teaching and Learning Science and Mathematics; Native American Studies; and Upper Peninsula Studies. The Dean of the College is also the director of the NMU Press.

Deans: Luther S. West, 1962–1965; David W. D. Dickson, 1966–1967; Thomas Griffith, 1967–1971; Robert B. Glenn, 1971–1974; Donald D. Heikkinen, 1974–1990; Leonard Heldreth, (interim) 1991–1992; Michael T. Marsden, 1992–present. *Associate deans*: Eugene Whitehouse, 1967–1994 and Leonard Heldreth, 1994–present. (*The 1996–97 University Profile*, 1:52–60)

ASNMU: *See*: *Associated Students of Northern Michigan University*.

Assembly: Superintendent of Public Instruction, Delos Fall, and President Kaye were concerned about the character development of future teachers. On July 28, 1904, Fall addressed the Normal Executive Council and stressed the importance of religious exercises for the training of teachers and cultivating "a love for the institution and its traditions." In the fall he told principals of the Normal Schools, "I consider the religious exercise to be important, and more especially in a school for the training of teachers." As a result, Northern's assembly program was called "chapel" for several years. Students referred to missing chapel as "bunching." In October 1909 assembly exercises were referred to as "chapel exercises." As late as 1932, assembly continued to be referred to as "Chapel Hour" and missing assembly was considered similar to missing Sunday services.

When assemblies were held on a biweekly basis, classes and offices were closed. The programs consisted of travel accounts, faculty lectures, student presentations or visiting speakers. President Kaye was known for his high-minded presentations. After 1915, these assemblies were held in Kaye Auditorium.

The semi-required assemblies became rather voluntary in 1936–1937 and were described as "a course of musical entertainments and lectures open to students and to the public." Nine years later students were encouraged to keep 9:50 a.m. on Monday free in order to take advantage of "the broad cultural enrichment afforded by these programs." It was also seen as a time when the entire University community could come together. All programs were opened to the public. In the late 1940s some of the artists to appear on the Kaye Auditorium stage included, Cornelia Otis Skinner, the Chicago Symphony String Ensemble, The Don Cossack Chorus, Martial Singher (Metropolitan Opera baritone), and Dr. Rudolph Gantz. Prominent speakers included Norman Thomas, Senator Karl Mundt, and Dr. Bernard Iddings Bell. Despite these performers, in 1947 some students were critical of the assembly series and many thought that it was a waste of time. An editorial in the *Northern College News* commented on the benefits of such a cultural series. A decade later there was concern about the poor attendance at prepaid Assembly programs.

In the early 1950s the Marquette Community Concert Series was established. This concept was first organized in New York state and then spread across the country. The Marquette group sold subscriptions to the series and worked with Northern to make tickets available to students. This was at a time when the Assembly series began to decline in popularity. The Community Concert Series continues.

As late as 1968–1969 the University *Bulletin* listed a Lecture-Concert Series which was available to students. As with the original reason for holding assembly the *Bulletin* stated, "the lectures, concerts, drama, and foreign films help students understand the economic, social, and cultural background of people of the world and give students, faculty, and staff opportunities for experience in a variety of cultural and educational programs."

A number of programs operating on-campus bring fine entertainment and speakers to campus. This was true of the McGoff Distinguished Lecture Series *(See separate entry)* which existed from 1978–1988. In the decade of the 1990s this tradition continues. Platform Personalities sponsors speakers and entertainment as does the Performing Art Series (1990) under the direction of Wayne Francis. (NCN 05/17/1932, 03/12/1947; NN 10/21/1959)

Assistant to the President: Clair Hekhuis first came to Northern in 1957 at the behest of President Harden and first served as Director of Information Services. After a while since Hekhuis was a good writer, Harden tapped him as a speech writer and confidant. Later Hekhuis became secretary to the Board of Control.

The position of Assistant to the President was revived under the Jamrich Administration. R. Tom Peters served in this position. In 1991, his responsibilities included serving as the Director of Intercollegiate Athletics, Director of the Sports Training Complex, Overseer of Public Safety and Police Services, and Legislative Liaison to the State of Michigan. Peters retired in 1995 but continued to work for President Vandament in a decreasing capacity for a year. The President's Office took over many of the assistant's functions and the position was not replaced.

Associated Students of Northern Michigan University: The successor of the Student Council *(See separate entry)* the Association is more commonly referred to as ASNMU. The Student Senate (successor to the Council) of NMU reviewed the new constitution which had been proposed by the Senate Re-evaluation Committee. The Student Senate voted on March 25, 1969 to accept the new constitution and submit it for a student body ratification vote on April 22. The final vote was 927 to 698, and it was then submitted to the Board of Control. It was similar to the one in use at Michigan State University.

The organization met for the first time in the fall of 1969 under President Harry Campbell. In 1978, a revised constitution was passed by a student body vote. On February 17, 1999 proposed changes to the constitution were passed by a student vote. It separated the branches of student government, increased representation and provided the Governing Board with more control power the Student Finance Committee.

ASNMU provides an official voice through which student opinion is expressed. The organization is composed of three branches: Executive (President, Vice President, Chief of Staff, and Treasurer); Legislative (five representatives for Academic Affairs and seven representatives for Student Affairs); and Judicial (All Student Judiciary). There are a multitude of committees ranging from the Student Finance Committee (SFC) to the Service Charge Review Committee.

Presidents: Harry Campbell, 1969; Kevin O'Donnell, 1970; Ozel Brazil, 1971; Bonnie Jobe, 1972; Scott Phillips, 1973; Dennis Malaney, 1974; Frederick (Fritz) Mills and Jeffrey Watts, 1975; Christine Zeller, 1976; Joseph Sartorelli, 1977; Michael Frye, 1978; Carrie (Christensen) Anderson, 1979; Mark Strong, 1980; Steve Fawcett, 1981; Ed Buchynski, 1982; Matthew Wiese, 1983; Kevin Weissenborn, 1984; Jerry Cooney, 1985; Jane (Luft) Fonger, 1986; Dawn Danylczenko, 1987; Daniel Pilarski, 1988; Britt Lindholm, 1989; Alfred Keefer, 1990; Peter G. Drever III, 1991; Greg Rathje, 1992, 1993; Gregg Goetz, 1994, 1995; B. Allison Johnson, 1996; Ryan Weidner, 1997 (impeached); Chris Mann, 1998; Nicholas Vivian, 1998. (Hilton, p. 248; NN 03/14/1969, 03/21/1969, 03/28/1969, 04/25/1969, 02/18/1999)

Association for Childhood Education (ACE): ACE was originally established as the Kindergarten Club in the 1920s. By December 15, 1939 it was expanded and called the Kindergarten-Primary Club. It goals were "to promote professional spirit and to encourage closer social co-operation among its members." During the 1960s, it was renamed Association for Childhood Education and Sylvia Kinnunen was the faculty advisor. On February 4, 1968 it was replaced by Pi Omega Pi. This seems to be the oldest continuously active student organization on campus.

Association of Michigan Collegiate Faculties (AMCF): The AMCF was organized in 1971 by members of the faculties of Michigan's state supported institutions of higher education that awarded baccalaureate degrees. This was done prior to widespread unionization on campuses. John Watanen Jr. and Robert F. McClellan Jr. were the first delegates from Northern to attend meetings of the Association. John Watanen later became President of the Association. Later, David L. Carlson, who had served as vice president, turned down the presidency to work with the state AAUP office. Having little power, influence and resources the AMCF declined with the rise of unions on campus. (Association of Michigan Collegiate Faculties (AMCF), Records UA 100.1.1) Michael Fitzgibbon-Rhea

Athletic Administration: Prior to World War II, Northern did not belong to any national collegiate sports organizations. As a result there was little need or demand for an Athletic Director. The athletic programs during the early years were run by the coach who scheduled all the games and meets. The coaches were also faculty members and taught courses. There were a number of different coaches from the early 1900s to 1922 when C. B. Hedgcock was hired to coach all sports and teach classes.

The Athletic Director is an individual who is in charge of the entire athletic program at the university. Usually a coach was in charge of several sports and was the de facto AD. Hedgcock became Athletic Director in 1947 and continued through 1956. In 1947 C. V. "Red" Money was hired and for nearly a decade coached five sports, at times directed the intramural program and taught classes. In 1956 C. B. Hedgcock retired and President Tape made Money Athletic Director and Head of the Department of Health, Physical Education and Recreation. Then in 1957 Frosty Ferzacca became the head football coach and athletic director.

The college became a member of the National Association of Intercollegiate Athletics and remained a member through 1967 when the university joined the NCAA college division. Dr. Rico Zenti became the Athletic Director from 1966 through 1968. Rollie Dotsch, the head football coach, became director in 1968 and held the position for three years.

In March 1971 Gildo Canale became athletic director and remained in that position until January 1985. Many accomplishments and changes took place during this period: expansion of the women's program; hosting the national NCAA football playoff game and the national men's swimming and diving championships; joining the Mid-Continent Conference; and initiating the ice hockey program.

In recent years Jack Taylor was athletic director for about seventeen months. He was followed by Rick Comley who also serves as ice hockey coach.

Athletic Directors: C. B. Hedgcock, 1947–1956; C. V. "Red" Money, (interim) 1956–1957, 1957–1958; "Frosty" Ferzacca, 1958–1966; Dr. Rico Zenti, 1966–1969; Rollie Dotsch, 1969–1971; Gildo Canale, (interim) March 1971–July 1972, 1972–January 1985; Dr. Thomas Knauss, (interim) January 1985–June 30, 1985; Jack Taylor, July 1, 1985–January 12, 1987; Rick Comley, (interim) January 12–May 3, 1987, 1987–present). Gildo Canale

Athletic Council: This body is really the President's committee since he/she appoints its members. It is advisory to the Athletic Director and the President. The Council is responsible for student-athlete eligibility; monitors compliance to the National Collegiate Athletic Association (NCAA) and conference rules which keep the University out of trouble; advises the President on adding or dropping varsity sports; approves varsity awards for student-athletes.

The NCAA Manual directs each member institution to have an Athletic Council to govern intercollegiate athletics. Membership on the Council includes administrators (Registrar, Director of Financial Aid, and Athletic Director), faculty, and some student representatives. For many years the chair has come from the faculty.

Chairs: Henry Heinomen, Thomas Knauss, Hal Dorf, and James Suksi. Thomas Knauss

Athletic Directors: *See*: *Athletic Administration*

Athletic Fields: Over the years the University has had a series of athletic fields. Between 1899 and 1915 the field at the County Fair Grounds on Wright Street was used. In the summer of 1915 a piece of land behind Kaye Hall and now in front of the east entrance of the University

Center, measuring 200 x 300 feet was leased for five years for $5.00 with the option to purchase from the J. M. Longyear Company. Soon thereafter it was leveled, drained and surfaced, and a quarter mile running track circled the athletic field which was used for football and baseball. All of this was completed by the summer of 1918.

In early 1920 there were letters to the editor of the *Northern Normal News* and discussions about a "Memorial Field" honoring the veterans of World War I. Little seems to have come from these discussions and letters to the editor.

During the 1920s, numerous improvements were made to this field. When President Munson (a sports enthusiast) arrived in 1923 the finished site, adjoining the Normal gardens, consisted of a practice football field, a tennis court, baseball diamond, and a straight-away for the 100 yard dash.

By July 1927, additional improvements had been made. A 120-yard straight-away was located on the west side of the track. It was 21 feet wide and provided ample room for six hurdle lanes. The 240-yard dash and hurdles were run around the north and west sides.

The baseball diamond was located in the south end of the oval. It had a grass infield, while the lanes and midfield were constructed of rolled stone dust. The gridiron occupied the center of the oval slightly overlapping the baseball outfield. Hydrants were installed for watering the grass. In the winter the water was used to create an ice skating rink for the students and faculty.

On October 29, 1927, the State Board of Education passed a motion for the purchase of the parcel between Lee Hall and Kaye Avenue, which had been leased since 1915. Northern was the last Normal school in the state to be granted an athletic field-stadium.

The athletic field was opened on September 29, 1928, for the Northern-Stevens Point football game. "There will be no more of those cold tramps to the fairgrounds, no more rushes for a seat in the street cars, no more disappointments when your friend's flivver is filled. In the future, we shall find all the fun right at home in our own back yard." (NCN 09/25/1928). The reporter for the *Northern Normal News* noted that "there will be no parking problem at the new field because there is plenty of space around the old dormitory (vicinity of the northwest corner of Hebard Court and Kaye) and at the end of College Avenue."

The only thing that the field lacked was adequate bleachers, which made organized cheering difficult.

As the Northern athletic program expanded, there was a need for separate varsity and intramural fields. As a result, plans were developed to obtain the necessary land and develop a new stadium, which was known as College Stadium. The nine-acre site for the new stadium, at the end of Kaye Avenue, was purchased in February 1931. The site was nestled in a hollow which was open to the north. Work began in the spring of 1931 under the direction and plans of Luther Gant. Crews of men employed by the college graded, filled and built the new stadium. A steel fence, 578 feet long and 550 feet wide, running on a north-south axis enclosed the field proper. The terrain suited the construction of a natural stadium and it was not necessary to haul or place a single load of earth, as excavated loads were used to fill in the north end.

Two contracts were given out: one for hauling the gravel for the two-way drive from Kaye Avenue, and the other for constructing the bleachers. The bleachers were innovative. They were built in four sections on a natural slope facing the east of the grid and had room for 1,500 spectators. The seats were made of fir and fixed to concrete abutments. A road led around three sides of the hollow and allowed automobiles to park above the gridiron so spectators could watch events from the comfort of their automobiles.

Kaye Avenue was widened to its full extent of 80 feet at the expense of Northern. A two-way drive following Kaye Avenue circled the grid. A gate at the start of the drive, was a gift of the class of 1926. A type of brick, similar to that used on the John D. Pierce School, was used to build the six posts, each capped by a decorative concrete head, which supported three massive iron gates. The fence was concealed by a double row of lilacs, inside and out, and additional landscaping.

Care was taken in constructing the gridiron. First, it was spread with three inches of clay. Then, it was topped with two inches of loam. Finally, it was seeded with a mixture of bluegrass, red-top, and timothy. With the completion of this stadium, students were able to use the old field for intramural sports. The stadium was inaugurated on October 1, 1932, with a game against what is now University of Wisconsin at Oshkosh.

During World War II, the athletic field took on a somewhat different aspect when Victor Hurst "had a regular commando training set-up installed. It is so designed as to furnish a strenuous enough test to bring out the best there is in the toughest student."

On the low northeast part of the campus (vicinity of Waldo and Presque Isle) in the 1930s and 1940s, there were swings, teeter boards, and tennis courts. The University had six tennis courts that were used extensively and two backup courts.

In 1947 games began to be played on Memorial Field (north of Fair Avenue), although the field was used by the J. D. Pierce football teams. A decade later, there was talk of a "proposed football bowl" to the south of the present Hedgcock Fieldhouse. Prior to the start of construction of West and Gries Residence Halls, College Stadium was removed. In the summer of 1959 a new practice field was completed next to Hedgcock Fieldhouse. In September 1959 it was first used by the football team for practice. The Dallas Cowboys (*See separate entry*) in July–August 1962, trained on this field.

Memorial Field, once located to the east of the main campus was bound on the south by the standing iron fence and tall shrubs. The site was originally purchased for $7,000 in early 1940 by the Marquette Board of Education as the site of an athletic complex. On August 20, 1940, a $20,901 contract was awarded to L. W. Brumm, Inc. of Marquette to construct a football field, practice field, and an oval cinder track around the field for Graveraet High School. Beside providing the city schools with athletic facilities, the Board wanted to give the city a public recreation center for general use. Woven wire fencing was completed by the spring of 1941 by Lake Shore Engineering Company. By the summer a steel picket fence had been ordered.

The stadium plans were developed by Chicago-based architect, F. A. Cushing Smith & Associates, who had served the city of Marquette for several years. By May 1941 the initial bids were drawn to provide for construction of the stand, without exterior finishing, and for concrete walks from the gates to the stand. The stand was located on the west side of the field and included an enclosed broadcasting booth and press box.

The construction bid ($31,836) was awarded to A. H. Proksch, an Iron River contractor on August 1, 1941. The stand had a seating capacity of 1,600. It measured approximately 131 feet long, 52 feet at the base, and

26 feet high. Seats were built of specially treated redwood with a hard varnish finish.

The field was first used for a full season of football games in the fall of 1942 with a game between the Graveraet Redmen and Ishpeming Hematites. In February 1946 the Board of Education named the field, Memorial Stadium after veterans killed during World War II. An elaborate dedication was held on Memorial Day 1946.

Later, when money was available, the School Board enclosed the rear and sides of the stadium with cinder block. The area was used for storage, restrooms, and dressing rooms. In November 1961 the school board bought a Butler building as federal surplus to be used as a storage structure.

Following World War II, there were enough men on campus to have a football team. In 1947 Northern signed a contract to play its games at Memorial Field. Lights had been installed in 1946 and night games were popular. For a number of years afternoon games continued to be played at College Stadium. This continued until 1949 when all games were played in Memorial Field.

Memorial Field and Stadium were purchased in November 1965, from the Marquette Board of Education by Northern for $135,000. At the time, the 13.95 acre site consisted of a football field and track with substantial bleachers, press boxes, locker rooms on the west side, and a set of large metal bleachers for student use on the east side. In 1968 and 1969, new bleachers were installed, the press box was extended, the parking lot enlarged, and the public address system improved. The field was used for football games until the completion of the Superior Dome in 1991. The field was maintained as a practice field and in the summer of 1996, the east bleachers were sold, dismantled, and shipped for reuse in Oklahoma. In mid-March 1998, the old stadium was demolished and a few artifacts saved from the ruins. The Berry Events Center *(See separate entry)* constructed in 1998–1999 is located on the site of Memorial Field.

In late 1983, a 400-meter oval Olympic speed skating rink was constructed on the site of the Superior Dome. It was created to provide additional training space for the projected Olympic training program. It was removed with the construction of the Superior Dome.

The original tennis courts were located on the south side of the modern parking lot between the Cohodas Building and Lee Hall Drive, bound on the south by Kaye Avenue. In 1922, with the construction of the John D. Pierce School, they were removed to an area immediately to the south of the Sculpture Walk. In 1927, a new program called for one tennis court per every 100 students. At the time, there were two cinder courts which were in great demand. They were described as "the most modern and permanent courts possible." By 1935, a second set of cinder and asphalt tennis courts were constructed near the present east entrance to the Don H. Bottum University Center. As new building and parking spaces were needed, the courts were moved to the present parking lot between the Learning Resources Building and Hedgcock Fieldhouse. Both sets of tennis courts were removed when the new courts were constructed southeast of the PEIF Building in 1975. With the development of the Berry Events Center, the tennis courts were relocated to the western end of campus, at the site of the Green Barn in September–October 1997. They were first used in the fall of 1998. Indoor tennis courts are also located in the Superior Dome.

The Superior Dome (*See separate entry*) has become the home of the football Wildcats. Its bleachers can accommodate some 5,000 spectators, and with additional seating, more than 8,000, away from inclement weather. The outer area of the Dome is used for winter walkers. After football season, basketball, tennis and volleyball courts are set up for use by students. The football field in the Dome was named the "C. V. Red Money Field" on September 12, 1998 in honor of the former athletic director and head of HPER.

With the successes of the Women's Volleyball team (*See separate entry*), plans were developed in the mid-1990s to renovate the indoor playing field of PEIF. At that time, a new floor was laid and the volleyball court established, where national championships have been held. On November 9, 1997, with former president William Vandament and his wife Margery (*See separate entries*) present, the facility was dedicated as the "Vandament Arena." (NNN 12/12/1922, 07/26/1927; NCN 09/27/1928; MJ 10/1/1932, 10/4/1932; NCN 07/25/1933; NW 11/10/1983, 12/01/1983; MJ 08/21/1940, 01/21/1941, 05/16/1941, 07/12/1941, 08/02/1941, 09/26/1942, 05/31/1946; NN 10/16/1957, 07/28/1959).

Athletic Scholarships: In the early days, Coach C. B. Hedgcock found athletic scholarships limited to jobs that could be found, such as peeling potatoes and washing dishes in local restaurants or performing janitorial work. They were known as "work-or-no-scholarship" according to Don H. Bottum. After World War II football players were provided with quarters in Vetville "Barracks." As the athletic program developed and expanded, especially after 1963, so have the number of scholarships that are given out to student-athletes. Today NCAA rules regulate the scholarship program.

Athletics: Organized athletics at Northern prior to 1968 consisted of men's teams: Football (1904–present), Basketball (1906–present), Gymnastics (1966–1980), Swimming (1966–1980), Wrestling (1966–1988), Track (1928–1992), Golf (1948–1971, 1992–present), Skiing (1967–1980), and Tennis (1934–1985). In 1968, women's sports were added. Some of these sports had breaks in their existence over the years.

Changes to the Athletic Program at Northern are as follows:

YEAR	WOMEN	MEN
1968	add Field Hockey	
1970	add Basketball	
1971	add Downhill, Nordic Skiing	drop Golf, Track
1974	add Volleyball	
1976		add Ice Hockey
1977	add Gymnastics, Swimming	
1978	add Tennis	drop X-Country
1980	drop Tennis, Alpine, and Nordic Skiing	drop Swimming, Gymnastics, and Ski Jumping
1982	add Cross Country	
1984	drop Field Hockey	
1985		drop Tennis
1986		drop Alpine Skiing
1987	add Track, Nordic Skiing	
1988	drop Gymnastics	drop Wrestling
1992	add Tennis, drop Track	add Golf, drop Track
1996	add Soccer, Alpine Skiing	drop X-Country

Current women's sports at Northern include: Basketball, Swimming, Volleyball, Tennis, Soccer, Alpine and Nordic Skiing, and Cross Country Running. Current men's sports at Northern include: Ice Hockey, Football, Basketball, Golf, and Nordic Skiing.

The Department of Athletics is under the President's Division and seeks excellence through service in harmony with the overall mission of the University. The department strives to serve the entire University community. Northern is affiliated at the NCAA Division II level for all sports except ice hockey, which is supported at the Division I level, and abides by all the NCAA rules and regulations governing intercollegiate athletics and the ethics and principles of fair play. The department recognizes the importance of academic excellence, integrity, and strength of character in its athletes and the staff strives to project the best possible image. *See*: Individual sports.
(Sports Information Office) Michelle Kangas

Audio-Visual Services and Instructional Media Services: Roy McCollum had been in charge of the AV Department for many years, prior to his retirement in 1962. In the late 1950s, audio-visual services and carrier current WNMC were housed in the projection booth of the old Lydia Olson Auditorium. Two RCA 16mm projectors were housed in the booth in the rear of a 200 seat auditorium. There were additional projectors available for use in the Kaye Auditorium and elsewhere.

In 1962 Dr. S. Kenneth Bergsma headed Instructional Communications which included radio, television and audio-visual services. In October the State Board of Education gave Northern permission to acquire and operate an FM radio station "in connection with its educational program."

Now the staff began to form and take its positions. John Turner who had come to Northern in 1959, became the head of Audio-Visual Services and Chief Engineer for radio and television. Bruce Turner, who joined the staff in May 1963, acted as architect and carpenter and with electrician Jim Marietta converted Lee Hall Ballroom into a radio and television facility.

After this development Audio-Visual Services became part of the radio and television stations and continued to support University services.

Aviation, Department of: Prior to the development of the Department of Aviation, there were aviation training programs during World War II. An aviation flight school program was initiated in 1976, which gave students the opportunity to qualify for a Federal Aviation Administration commercial class or private aircraft license. Unfortunately, liability and cost factors closed the program in 1984.

In 1986, Richard J. Retaskie, director of the Vocational Skills Center, along with associate director Thornton D. Routhier and Paul H. Kaminen, heavy equipment instructor, joined forces with Representative Dominic Jacobetti to realize an aviation program which was not a flight program. Between 1987 and 1988, Retaskie, Kaminen, and Rothier wrote a grant and curriculum proposal. This ultimately led to a $4 million Training Development Grant from the governor's office through the Job Training section of the Michigan Department of Labor, with $1.2 million for the new Department of Aviation.

Space was renovated in the Jacobetti Center. A new overhead door wide enough for aircraft connected the interior tech training rooms with the exterior storage area. New equipment and tools were purchased. In May 1989 three associate professors were hired. They took the position that the quality of student education was directly related to the "life-like" atmosphere. As a result, in the summer and fall of 1989 six planes: three Cessena 310s, a Cessena 150, one Beechcraft-Duke, and a Mitsibushi MUZKD 1 were purchased, flown to the Marquette County Airport, inspected and certified, and transported to the Jacobetti Center.

The initial class entered in 1990, but there were some problems with decreasing enrollments and loss of faculty. Corrections were instituted and by 1998 the program is flourishing as there is a constant need for aviation technicians. An active program in recent years, numerous students have graduated and received FAA certification. In 1999 the department moved to the former K. I. Sawyer Air Force Base with its expanded facilities. (Sean J. Dieleman. "The History of Northern Michigan University's Aviation Department" (1995), UA; MJ 05/01/1969; NW 02/15/1990; *The 1996–97 University Profile*, 1:288–294)

Ayer, Frederick: (December 8, 1822–March 14, 1918) Mr. Ayer, a resident of Lowell, Massachusetts was a partner with John M. Longyear. He was a Boston millionaire and the founder and director of numerous industrial enterprises in New England. He was one of the organizers and for several years treasurer of the Lake Superior Ship Canal and Railway and Iron Company. The Ayers were the in-laws of General George Patton. In 1899 he and his wife, Ellen Banning along with the Longyears donated the first 20 acres of Northern's campus. Ayer also financed the construction of the original dormitory in 1900. (*See separate entry*) (*New York Times 03/15/1918*)

Baccalaureate: The baccalaureate was a religious service which was held in conjunction with commencement. This ceremony saw clergymen or the college president present a religious sermon to the graduates. The ceremony can be traced back to the first Northern commencement in 1900. Talks to end the ceremony probably were associated with the June 25, 1962 Supreme Court decision to end prayer in public schools. The last "official" baccalaureate was held on June 3, 1962, at 9:30 a.m. in the Hedgcock Fieldhouse, while the commencement took place at 2:00 p.m. The following year the *Northern News* noted that baccalaureate service would be held "as in former years." The difference was that it would be done on an individual basis with Marquette churches sending special invitations to graduates. (NN 07/24/1962; 06/04/1964)

Bachelor's Degree: Northern was authorized to grant a Bachelor of Arts degree in 1918. Requirements were established and courses developed for it. In 1926, the Bachelor of Science degree was added.

Bailey, Jr., Brendon S.: (August 1, 1945–) Mr. Bailey was born in Providence, Rhode Island. He received a B.S. in Mechanical Engineering from the University of Rhode Island, Kingston in 1967 and did additional work in education at American University, Washington, D.C.; George Mason University; and the University of Maine, Orono. He served in the U.S. Army Corps of Engineers at Fort Belvoir, Virginia and under combat conditions in Chu Lai, Vietnam (1967–1971). He separated from the military with the rank of captain. The Baileys were married on June 8, 1968.

Over the years, Bailey has taught mathematics and physics in middle and high schools in Virginia and Maine. He has written articles for model aviation magazines and state educational journals. Presently he is an adjunct faculty member in Northern's Physics Department and a full-time graduate student.

His memberships include: Kiwanis, Tau Beta Pi (National Engineering Honor Society), Phi Delta Kappa (professional fraternity in Education) and honorary membership in the American Society for Testing and Materials. He serves on the Board of Directors of the Lake Superior Hospice Association.

Bailey, Judith I.: (August 24, 1946–) The eleventh and first female president of Northern Michigan University, Judith Irene Hege was born in Winston-Salem, North Carolina. She received her B.A. in English from Coker College, Hartsville, SC (1968), M.A. Ed. in Administration (1973), and Ed.D. (1976) in Administration and Supervision from Virginia Polytechnic Institute and State University, Blacksburg, VA. She married Brendon S. Bailey, Jr. on June 8, 1968.

Dr. Bailey began her career in education as an English teacher and a secondary school administrator. After completing an Ed.D., she began her administrative career in higher education. At the University of Maryland, College Park she held an appointment as assistant professor and human relations coordinator in the Maryland Cooperative Extension Service, teaching in the adult and extension education division in the College of Agricultural Sciences. Her administrative appointment focused on affirmative action programs for Cooperative Extension. After four years, she went on to become the deputy director of cooperative extension for the University of the District of Columbia. She had administrative responsibilities over urban cooperative extension programs in forestry, health and nutrition, youth programs and small business management.

At this time she felt that she wanted a more rural environment if she was going to make a university career in the field of cooperative extension. Dr. Bailey served on several national cooperative extension task forces, including co-chairing a study of northeastern trends in food, fiber and forestry for the year 2005. Because of these experiences and her administrative abilities, she was selected as the first woman director for cooperative extension at the University of Maine, Orono. There were five women in the nation at that time who headed state extension programs. She served in various capacities in her nine years at the University of Maine, Orono. In 1992 Dr. Bailey was named the first woman Vice President at the university, overseeing the areas of research and public service. From July 1995 until July 1997 she served as Vice President of Academic Affairs and Provost. While at the University of Maine, Dr. Bailey learned about Maine's culture, economy and employment base, one that is very similar to that of the Upper Peninsula.

The Board of Control offered her the position of president of Northern which she accepted on May 7, 1997 at 6:45 p.m. Dr. Bailey began her tenure on July 15. As she took the presidency, a special focus of the Board was on increasing enrollments and securing state and private funds, leading to Northern's first endowment fund campaign.

The first thing President Bailey did when she came to the Upper Peninsula was to get a sense of place by traveling the region and meeting the people, especially school superintendents. She stretched out a hand of leadership and friendship to everyone she visited. This experience gave her a sense of how to deal with the enrollment question and the need to be better partners with businesses.

With projected declining numbers of graduating high school seniors, Dr. Bailey saw the imperative of dealing with the development of the region economically so that new families are attracted to the area.

One of the greatest challenges Northern faced was continued strong state funding. The university had to face the fact that the enrollments at some Lower Peninsula academic institutions were growing and legislators were pressured to allocate additional funds to growth institutions. A term-limited legislature meant the loss of long-time relationships and a need for continual work with state legislatures to tell Northern's story. The challenge for the entire university community was how to increase enrollment without growing cost.

The first year moved along in an orderly fashion. President Bailey took time to visit the campus and with academic departments. Here she talked with faculty and learned of their dreams and aspirations. Then on October 3, Dr. Bailey was installed in a ceremony in the Superior Dome. Dr. Bailey served on the state president's council (in 1997–1998 the only female public university CEO in the state). Dr Bailey also met with state legislators and the congressional delegation in Washington, D.C. In 1997 she also became involved with the Lake Superior Jobs Coalition. During her term as co-chair, the LSJC became the Lake Superior Community Partnership, an organization focusing on community economic development of the area. She saw building strong relationships with alumni in the Upper Peninsula and throughout the country as an important part of her presidency.

Dr. Bailey's administration focused on the five principles which she stated at her installation. They included: student access; student success; building and learning community; building partnerships with the community, business and industry; and moving the agenda in a timely fashion respecting the shared governance process. (Interview, 09/11/1998, UA)

Baseball: In the summer of 1915, baseball was started on campus and Northern, was first represented by an organized baseball team. Despite this early development, baseball has been a rare sport on Northern's campus over the years. In 1920 the Industrial League formed in Marquette and there was talk of organizing summer teams.

In March 1921 it was noted that Northern had several uniforms or suits and the equipment to start a team. However the team would be faced with a very short season. Snows lasted until late May and they had one month to practice and play. Coach Luther Gant pointed out that the team could get a head start by practicing indoors.

President John Munson, who came in 1923, was a baseball fan and when Victor Hurst came to Northern it was decided to have baseball on the athletic program. New uniforms were bought. Unfortunately there was only one season because of bad weather and the fact that by the time the city teams were organized, the college was closed. (*The Quill* October 1915, 18; NNN 03/22/1921)

Basketball (Men's): Men's varsity basketball began in 1906 with Charles H. Estrich serving as the first coach. The program remained low key until 1922 when C. B. Hedgcock took over the reins as head coach. He served until 1947 with a win-loss record 162–38.

During these early years the players practiced in the Peter White Annex gym. Their plain uniforms were green and gold, and some players wore kneepads. In 1920, "NSN" was printed on the uniforms. Ward M. Mills coached the team between 1908–1909 and was followed by DeForest Stull who coached until 1915. W. B. McClintock coached from 1915 to 1917. Luther O. Gant coached from 1917 to 1921. Charles B. Hedgcock came to Northern in 1922 as head of the Physical Education Department Team. He served as coach for 22 years. In 1947, he became the athletic director. Before Hedgcock's tenure, the team played local teams: Legion, YMCA, and All-Stars teams. In the 1920s, the great rivalry with Michigan Tech developed. In 1922, the NSN team was the first to leave the U.P. for a game.

After World War II, the program began to accelerate. Red Money was the coach from 1947–1956 and had a record of 87–69. Burt Gustafson, a former 12 letter winner at Northern, coached the following year.

Northern enjoyed a number of great years under the guidance of Stan Albeck (1957–1968). Northern lost the NCAA quarter final to New York Tech in Marquette with a score 58–57. In 1960–1961, Northern finished fourth in the nation in the NAIA National championships. The team which had been playing in the Kaye Hall gym (*See separate entry*) moved to the Hedgcock Fieldhouse (*See separate entry*) in 1958. During these years the team placed third one year, beat Michigan State University in another, and suffered a close loss to Air Force Academy. Glenn Brown, former assistant coach took over the head coaching duties. Northern played in the Mid-Continent Conference and in its first year (1978–1979) came in second place. In 1979–1980 Northern won the Mid-Continent Conference and won the Great Lakes Regional at Dayton, Ohio by beating Eastern Illinois University (58–56). Brown remained as coach through the 1986 season when he died from heart bypass surgery. While coach, the team became a member of Great Lakes Intercollegiate Athletic Council (GLIAC). Between 1978 and 1986, the team was out of GLIAC, until rejoining again in 1986. Brown was followed by the present coach Dean Ellis. (*Bulletins*; Frederick Nault, "NMU Men's Basketball") Gildo Canale

Basketball (Women's): Women's basketball flourished when the gymnasium addition to Peter White Hall of Science was completed in 1904. DeForest Stull, a geographer coached the first teams and encouraged spectators to give their support. In 1911, Grace Stafford became Northern's first full-time teacher of physical education. She coached women's basketball team and in the winter of 1912 sent teams to play in the Copper Country. Since 1912, women have been participating in basketball competition at Northern.

In 1975, women's basketball was accepted into the Great Lakes Intercollegiate Athletic Conference (GLIAC), making it an official varsity sport. Del Parshall started the program until resigning at the end of the 1976 season. In 1980, NMU women set the record for the most wins, 17, and played in the Division II national championship in 1980 and 1981. In 1998, the team made it to the Final Four.

Coaches: Dell Parshall, 1975–1976; Lu Darr, 1976–1977; Anita Palmer, 1978–1984; Paulette Stein, 1985–1989; Michael Geary, 1989–present. (*Bulletins*; Jeff Mitchell, "NMU Women's Basketball" UA) Alisa Koski

Beanies: Beginning in 1925 school spirit was encouraged by the Color Day Parade when everyone wore the school colors and every freshman was expected to appear in a green and gold cap called a "pot." The following year a faculty member noted "that the student body looked and acted like a real college group." By 1931 the use of the frosh class pot had become well-established tradition. This cap was used by many colleges throughout the country to identify freshmen students during their first few weeks on campus. In a series of questions a *Northern College News* editorial asked why frosh wore them and what was their ultimate purpose and benefit? Its original purpose was to identify freshmen students first entering Northern. At the time, there was some question if the "Frosh Pot" would be continued.

In 1954 Freshmen were required to wear beanies for initiation during homecoming week. After the snake dance, frosh competed with the upperclassmen; the consequence of losing was that freshmen had to wear their beanies until the end of football season. Kangaroo Court was formed for freshmen who disobeyed the beanie law.

The beanie tradition continued into the 1960s. In 1964 they were worn during Homecoming week. However the fact that the Student Council only had 1,000 beanies for 1,600 students indicates that they were not truly a requirement. One of the traditions was that if the freshman-constructed bonfire did not exceed the 31-foot mark, the frosh would have to wear the beanies for an additional week. If freshmen did not wear their beanies, it was implied that they could have their heads shaved. In the fall of 1968 the tradition was attacked by Professor William Cooper of the Economics Department, who seriously questioned the "herd mentality" of wearing beanies. Quickly some students complained of the tradition and the fact that the wearing of beanies was not closely monitored. In October 1970 the *Northern News* carried an editorial, "Beanie Boloney". Soon after, this Northern tradition came to an end. (NNN 11/02/1926; NCN 06/02/1931; NN 10/02/1964, 11/01/1968, 11/15/1968, 10/09/1970; NW 10/02/1975; Hilton, p. 73)

Behavioral Sciences, Human Services, and Education, College of: In 1959, the School of Education (*See: Education, School of*) was created. Over the years, it has dramatically changed. Today, the College consists of the departments of Criminal Justice; Education; Health, Physical education, and Recreation, Psychology; and Sociology and Social Work.

The development of the College has been one of constant evolution. It is a combination of several departments formerly housed in Northern's original School of Education and two departments formerly in the College of Arts and Sciences (*See separate entry*). Education (*See separate entry*) and Health, Physical Education and Recreation (*See separate entry*) were departments in the School of Education in the early 1960s. In the early 1970s, Psychology (*See separate entry*), which had been a part of a combined Education and Psychology Department from Northern's earliest days, became separate. In the early 1980s, the College also included the Departments of Home Economics (*See: Department of Consumer and Family Studies*) and Industrial Technologies (*See separate entry*).

In 1985, the Department of Criminal Justice (*See separate entry*) and the Department of Sociology and Social Work (*See separate entry*) formerly in the School of Arts and Sciences, were added to the School of Education to form a new unit, which was called the School of Behavioral Sciences, Human Services, and Technology. Earlier departments which were dropped in 1985 included Home Economics, Industrial Education, and Library Science (*See separate entries*).

In 1986, Industry and Technology was combined with several other programs to form the School of Technology and Applied Sciences. With the exception of nutrition and dietetics, the Home Economics became Consumer and Family Studies in 1988 and with its Fashion Merchandising and Child/Early Childhood Education programs moved to Technology and Applied Sciences. The Nutrition and Dietetics program of Home Economics was taken over by the Department of Health, Physical Education and Recreation. At this point, the School's name became Behavioral Sciences and Human Services. In 1989, it was changed to Behavioral Sciences, Human Services and Education. On July 1, 1992 the School, like the others at Northern, was renamed a College.

In addition to Criminal Justice, Education, HPER, Psychology, and Sociology and Social Work, the College houses the Upper Peninsula Center for Educational Development. The UPCED, a consortium of the University, the seven intermediate school districts of the Upper Peninsula, and the Michigan Department of Education, provides professional development services for educational personnel in all parts of the Upper Peninsula. The College also houses the Center for Research and Evaluation in Human Services and Education. The Center is a consulting operation which provides program evaluations and design for other agencies and organizations.

Deans: J. Wesley Little, 1984–1988; Lowell G. Kafer (Interim 1988–1990; Steven Christopher, 1990–present. (*Bulletins*; *The 1996–97 University Profile*, 1:177–185) Michelle Kangas and Alisa Koski

Benediction: *See*: *Invocation*

Bennett Collection of Asian Art: A collection of Asian art gathered by Captain Arthur and Jo Bennett while in Asia. He donated the collection to the University in 1983. It is part of the University Art Museum permanent collection. (NW 09/15/1997)

Berry Events Center: The Center is named after the Berry family. John Berry is a 1971 graduate of Northern who donated $2 million for the construction of the structure in 1998–1999. Upon completion the building will be equipped with movable theatrical rigging and lighting position, and an Olympic-sized ice surface which can be covered for University and community events. The sports areas will include a hockey area with weight room, trainer room, meeting rooms, locker rooms and support areas; designated locker rooms and support areas for male and female basketball teams and USOEC speed-skaters; four general use locker rooms; and skate rental and changing areas. There will be a 400 square foot, two-level press area, four large concessions areas at the perimeter of the arena, and fifteen private suites as well as a President's Suite. The exterior features of the Center will include a 30-foot high center glass entry facing south, sub-entry point at the perimeter of the building, and a pedestrian drop-off at the main entrance.

The general statistics of the Center: 60,000 square feet on two levels; 230 by 266 feet; height: 35 feet; exterior finish material: decorative precast concrete panels; 265 new parking spaces; and a seating capacity of 3,809 fixed seats with standing room for an additional 400. The contract manager is Oscar J. Boldt Company of Iron Mountain, MI and Appleton, WI and the architect is Integrated Design, Inc. of Marquette.

The Board of Control approved the construction project on October 2, 1997. Site prep work began in mid-March 1998 with the demolition of Memorial Stadium (*See: Athletic Fields*). On May 15, students, coaches and dignitaries led groundbreaking ceremonies and President Bailey announced a $1 million gift from Mr. Berry. Footings were poured and steel framing began in May/June. By October the exterior walls and roof were in place so that winter construction on the interior could continue. During the spring and summer of 1999, the finishing work and landscaping will be completed. Project completion is scheduled for August 1999.

The cost of the structure is $10 million. It is to be funded through a combination of bond sales, private fund-raising from individuals and corporations, and revenue from operations. (NN 10/02/1997; "NMU Events Center, Fact Sheet," (1998)

Bibliography: The following is a list of some of the major works dealing with Northern: Anonymous. "Academic Freedom and Tenure: A Successfully Resolved Case at Northern Michigan University." *AAUP Bulletin* 55:3 (September 1969): 374–85; Don H. Bottum. *Happened Long Ago, Like 1899*. Marquette: Privately Published, 1971; Francis R. Copper. *Northern Michigan University: A Personal History 1899–1943*. Russell Magnaghi, ed. Marquette: Center for Upper Peninsula Studies, 1999; Miriam Hilton. *Northern Michigan University: The First 75 Years*. Marquette: NMU Press, 1975; Russell M. Magnaghi. *Student Organizations at NMU, 1907-1999*. Marquette: Center for Upper Peninsula Studies, 1998; Magnaghi. "Folklore and Northern Michigan University." *Faculty Guide, College of Arts and Sciences*. Marquette: CA&S, 1997; Magnaghi. *Northern Michigan University Book of Days*. Marquette: Center for Upper Peninsula Studies, 1998; Magnaghi. "The Past and Future of Longyear Hall." *The Round Table* 1:4 (February 1992): 1–2;

William G. Mitchell. "Communication of an Educational Innovation [Common Learning] in an Institution of Higher Education," Ph.D. dissertation, Michigan State University, 1970; "Northern Michigan University, Educating Generations." *The Mining Journal* 09/19/1998 (Special supplement); Suzan Travis-Robyns. *Northern at 100: Celebrating Success . . . Embracing Change.* Marquette: NMU Communications and Marketing, 1998.

Bicentennial Committee of the U.S. Bicentennial, 1976: Northern's involvement with the Bicentennial celebration began with President John X. Jamrich being named the only Upper Peninsula member on the 26-member Michigan American Revolution Bicentennial Commission. In October 1973 and then again in March 1974 meetings were called by President Jamrich to get the public's input into the celebration.

On September 4, 1975 Northern was given state and federal recognition and workshops were held. Northern's Bicentennial Committee met for the first time on October 1, 1975 to begin exploring possible projects that might be undertaken in conjunction with NMU's celebration of the U.S. Bi-Centennial. The committee eventually developed three Sub-committees-(1) Heritage (2) Festivals and (3) Horizons. One suggested project was to set up exhibits in a museum of the Upper Peninsula which sponsors were seeking to establish in Lee Hall under a U.P. Institute for Cultural, Environmental and Heritage Studies. Projects eventually undertaken included the airing of historical vignettes over WNMR-FM (*See separate entry*), a political cartooning conference which brought nationally recognized cartoonists to campus, and the bringing of two respected Michigan historians to campus to give addresses. Other projects included tree plantings sponsored by the University Women's Association, the mounting of a native timber wolf for permanent display in the Luther S. West Science Building, and Northern's cooperation with the City of Marquette in sponsoring a town meeting at the Marquette High School. The one lasting result of the Bicentennial Committee on campus was the establishment of the University Art Museum (*See separate entry*). (NMU Archives: Records, UA 107.2.1; NW 03/27/1974, 09/11/1975, 10/02/1975)

"Billy Favorite": The Whisker Burger served at Whiskers Spirits and Eatery on Presque Isle Street was named after President William Vandament.

Biology, Department of: From 1899 to 1911, Biology was located in the Department of Physical Sciences, along with Chemistry (*See separate entry*) and Physics (*See separate entry*). In 1911, it was separated and labeled the Department of Natural Science.

In the 1940s, the department offered some interesting courses, such as "Land Use Problems of the Upper Peninsula." This class included a two-week tour of Michigan's Northern Peninsula. Camps were established at the Lake Superior State Forest, Porcupine Mountains, and the Keweenaw Peninsula. In each area there were studies of the geological history of the region, the nature of the soil, the flora and fauna, and the various uses humans had made of the area's biological resources. During this same time, Northern's *Bulletin* began listing requirements for a Forestry and Conservation major.

By 1955, Northern offered various courses in Biology, Botany, Zoology, and Specialized Biology. All these courses fell within the teaching of the Biology Department. The Department of Conservation and Agriculture (*See separate entry*) offered courses in Forestry, Wildlife, Soils, Dairying, and Horticulture.

With the expansion of Northern in the late 1950s and early 1960s, there was a demand for updated, modern facilities. In 1961, Dr. Emerson Garver conducted experiments in a makeshift hut behind Kaye Hall. At this time, Dr. Roy Heath, the first Research Coordinator, secured funds for scientific equipment. Plans were drawn for a new science building (*See: West Science*) and its completion greatly aided attracting new faculty to campus.

By 1964, Biology had become "one of the strongest departments" and continues in that status in 1999. The department of Biology offers programs for undergraduate majors and minors, as well as graduate students. The programs complement those in Nursing and Allied Health, Liberal Studies, Physical Education, and Conservation. The department aims to provide an education that leads to professional careers in Medicine, Dentistry, Veterinary Medicine, Allied Health, Wildlife Biology, Wastewater Management, Environmental Control, Teaching, and Research. In the beginning there were only eight courses offered by the Biology department. Today, over 30 courses, Bachelor of Art or Science, and Master of Science degrees are offered.

The department has three major collections which are used for instructional purposes and research. They include; the Herbarium, Insect Collection, and the Study Skins (*See separate entries*).

Department chairs or heads: Elliot R. Downing, 1901–1911; Samuel D. Magers, 1911–1918; John N. Lowe, 1919–1938; Luther S. West, 1939–1946; Gordon D. Gill, 1946–1962; Lewis E. Peters, 1962–1966; Thomas G. Froiland, 1966–1997; Ronald A. Parejko, (acting) 1997–1998; Neil Cumberlidge, (interim) 1998–present. (*Bulletins*; Francis Copper manuscript, UA; *The 1996–97 University Profile*, 1:68–74) Michelle Kangas and Alisa Koski

Birdseye Building: This cinder-block structure was constructed in 1946, covering 35,613 square feet. It was used by the Birdseye Veneer Company as a sawmill which processed birdseye maple and was located on County Road 510 a half mile north of campus. In 1966, it was purchased by the University to house the Job Corps (*See separate entry*). After the departure of the Corps in 1969, the building was used as the site for Art and Design (*See separate entry*) art studios, Military Science (*See separate entry*), archaeology (*See separate entry*) lab and Central Receiving. In 1995, renovation on the site began. It involved adding important additions to the original structure. During the summer of 1996, the equipment from Art & Design was stored in semi-trucks in the Summit Street parking lot. In 1996, Campus Security moved to its new location and in October, Engineering moved to the building from Cohodas. The original portion continues to house Central Receiving and the storage facilities for the Archives. *See: Services Building*

Black and White Bi-Weekly: This bi-weekly news publication's purpose was to "inform and educate" the campus community.

Several copies of the publication are on file. Dr. John Vande Zande of the English Department was the advisor. It had a short-lived history beginning in late 1972.

Blue Jeans Day: First held in 1994, the day is sponsored and organized by the Gay/Lesbian/Bisexual Student Union. Individuals wear blue jeans to show that they support equal rights for gays, lesbians and bisexuals. (NW 03/23/1995)

Blue Line Club: A core-support group for the hockey program which was formed in 1982. Members' donations help the hockey program with scholarships, recruiting and equipment support. The Blue Line Club is vital in keeping the NMU hockey program competitive in Division I.

Board of Control: The Board is the legal owner of Northern Michigan University. With the adoption of the new state constitution, conditions were established to give Northern Michigan College University status. This occurred on March 13, 1963 through a bill co-sponsored by Representative Dominic Jacobetti and signed by Governor George Romney. Prior to University status, the State Board of Education (*See separate entry*) was the legal body that governed Northern.

Members of the first Board of Control were appointed by Governor Romney on January 16, 1964. The first meeting of the Board was held on Thursday, February 13, 1964 in Lee Hall. At this first meeting, President Edgar Harden began the session by talking about the University's financial situation, the future and the "right-to-try" philosophy. The consensus among the Board members at the time was to make Northern into a University equal in stature to the downstate universities.

The first function of the Board was to create Bylaws which outlined the procedures and powers of the Board. These include: control over the selection of the president, the chief financial officer and the faculty and staff. It also controls the admission standards, the tuition rate and the bestowing of degrees. The Bylaws also contain the mission of the Board: "The Board of Control of Northern Michigan University reaffirms its obligation to the people of the state of Michigan to provide a high quality education to people from all walks of life. It pledges itself to the wisest use and distribution of resources at its disposal to meet this objective."

The Board's basic function is overseeing administration policies and staying informed on University business in order to make wise decisions. Although policies have to be approved by the Board, the administration has freedom to maneuver as the Board does not get closely involved in day-to-day operations of the University.

Over the years, the Board of Control has had to face vexing problems. These have included the struggle over the "right-to-try" policy of President Harden (1965); the McClellan controversy (1967–1968) *(See separate entry)*; student protest (1969–1970); the demolition of Kaye Hall *(See separate entry)* complex (1972); the McGoff *(See separate entry)* controversy (1978–1988); the demolition of Longyear Hall *(See separate entry)* (1991–1994) to name a few of the more prominent problems.

The Secretary of the Board is "subject to the President and the Board, he/she shall keep minutes of each meeting; showing the date, time, place, members present and absent, any decision made at a meeting open to the public, and the purposes for which a closed session was held." There have been three Secretaries: Clair Hekhuis, 1964; Jack R. Rombouts, 1964–1978 and Matthew J. Surrell, 1978–present.

The eight members of the Board are appointed by the governor of Michigan with state Senate approval for seven year staggered terms. Every other year the terms of two members of the Board expire.

Board members since 1964: Robert O. Berube (1991–); Sandra B. Bruce (1993–); Richard J. Celello (1989–1997; term expired 12/31/1996); James M.Collins (05/31/1983–01/16/1991; term expired 12/31/1990); Daniel G.DeVos(1995–);WalterC.Drevhadl (01/24/1964–12/31/1974); AlbertJ.Dunmore(02/13/1985–02/01/1989);LeoF.Egan (03/24/1987–04/17/1995; term expired 12/31/1994); John L. Farley (10/19/1965–12/31/1975);ThelmaH.Flodin (01/16/1964–12/31/1972); Lincoln B. Frazier (01/16/1964–04/1965); Edwin O.George(01/16/1964–03/23/1987; term expired 12/31/1986); JosephJ.Gross(04/07/1966–05/16/1973);EdwardF.Havlik (03/24/1987–04/17/1995;term expired12/31/1994); Ralph E. Huhtala (02/13/1973–04/26/1977,deceased);HughJarvis(02/13/19- 85–12/31/1992); Ogden E.Johnson(01/16/1964–09/01/1967); Barbara B. Labadie (1995–); Samuel Logan, Jr. (10/17/1989–12/31/1992); James T.Malsack (07/06/1977–04/30/1989; term expired 12/31/1988); BellaI.Marshall(05/31/1983–05/1988);resigned-termexpires 12/31/1990); John P.McGoff (01/16/1964–01/01/1972; resigned; first term, four years; second term expired 12/31/1976); Ellwood A. Mattson (1991–); Glenn G. Moreau (01/16/1964–12/31/1972); Dr. Jacquelyn R. Nickerson (09/10/1973–05/31/1983; term expired 12/31/1982); Susan D. Nine (12/12/1988–01/16/1991; term expired 12/31/1990); E. Harwood Rydholm (02/10/1972–02/13/1985; term expired 12/31/1984); Fred C. Sabin, MD (09/20/1967–02/13/1985; term expired 12/31/1984); Ellen G. Schreuder (1989–1997; term expired 12/31/1996); Dr. Larry J. Sell, MD (02/12/1975–05/31/1983; term expired 12/31/1982); John C. Walch (01/12/1976–03/23/1987; first term 2 years; second term expired 12/31/1986); Willis F. Ward (01/16/1964–03/08/1966); G. Katherine Wright (02/13/1973–04/30/1989; term expired 12/31/1988); Gilbert L. Ziegler (1993–). (Myron L. Johnson, Jr. "A Brief History of the Board of Control of Northern Michigan University" (1995), UA)

Board of Control Student Achievement Award: The Board of Control Award was first presented to a graduating senior in December 1983. Recipients have included: Lynn Marie Barrette (5–92); Eric Brooks (4–90); Sarah Caudill (5–93); Alicia Chenhalls (5–93); Gina M. Comensoli (5–91); R. Gregory Corace (5–93); Kristine Day (4–94); Treacy Duerfeldt (4–88); Alphonso Eason (4–89); Marianne Erickson (4–89); Natasha M. Gill (5–98); Chad M. Gross (12–83); Keith Hug (4–94); Dan Jutunen (4–89); Greta Keplinger (4–96); Kendra Knox (4–94); Terri L. Laitinen (4–95); Linda Luft (4–90); Polly Luomi (4–95); Jason Maki (4–96); Allen P. Mott (5–98); Christy Osborn (5–97); Marc A. Raslich (5–91); Scott A. Rice (5–92); Toby Rickett (5–97); Cara Sjoholm (4–88); Loren Snyder (4–96); Victor Somme (4–88); Jennifer Storey (5–97); Heidi VanDeHey (5–98); Kim M. Weinfurter (5–92); Paul M. White III (5–91); and Jeanette E. Zalba (4–95). (University Relations Office)

Bookstore: Prior to the development of a bookstore on campus students purchased their supplies and jewelry at local shops in Marquette. The first bookstore, called "The Normal Book Store" was organized early in President Munson's administration in 1923. It was located in the basement of Longyear Hall and measured 24 x 24 feet. It sold textbooks and supplies and was described as "an emporium of every school need." President Munson, the father of the store was hailed as a "problem solver." One of the early managers was Dr. Oscar Mattson, who was a member of the Mathematics Department. In the beginning, some of the ten per cent margin charged funded a football field located on the site of the University Center parking lot. This bookstore remained in Longyear Hall until the completion of the Lee Hall complex. President Tape investigated the relocation of the bookstore into Lee Hall in March 1952 and it was relocated soon after.

During this time managers, like Catherine Quarters and Ella Christian operated out of the Lee Hall location. In the summer of 1960, Ms. Christian resigned and she was replaced by Don Potvin. Potvin had an assistant and some student help during book rush. At this time, the bookstore was the only source of supplies and books for students.

Soon after the completion of the west portion of the Don H. Bottum University Center, Lee Hall was renovated and the bookstore was moved to the present location of the University Art Museum. At this time orders were made by telephone, six week delays were common, and it was not the purpose of the bookstore to make money. In 1966, Potvin resigned from his position as manager.

This was a turning point for the bookstore. Richard Harbick became the fourth manager and the store was relocated in the University Center in the spring of 1964. Over the years, the bookstore has expanded and moved within the University Center (*See separate entry*). In 1966 the bookstore consisted of 4,000 square feet of space and in 1993 it had expanded to 20,000 square feet. Major expansions took place during the summers of 1973 and 1984. In 1994 with the renovation of the University Center the bookstore moved to its present location.

Harbick retired on December 31, 1993. He was replaced by Mike Kuzak as acting manager on July 1, 1993 and as manager on June 22, 1994. Today, the Bookstore is under the Vice President for Student Affairs.

Over the years the bookstore has undergone significant change. The student buy-back program has expanded since it began in the 1970s. In 1973 a special window was constructed for this purpose and buy-back really took off. (*The 1996–97 University Profile*, 2:191–196; Nicole Turek. "Bookstore Evolution" UA; NNN 11/06/1923; NN 04/24/1-964)

Bottum, Don H.: (January 9, 1896–January 1, 1995). Mr. Bottum was born near St. Johns, Michigan. He attended St. Johns High School and received his bachelor's degree from Central Michigan University, and a master's degree from the University of Michigan.

After serving in the U.S. Army in World War I, he began his teaching career in Lake City, Michigan where he was principal and superintendent for four years before joining Northern in 1923.

He was principal of the John D. Pierce Laboratory School at Northern for 20 years, and served as dean of men for 16 years until becoming the first dean of students in 1957. He also directed the office of housing for off-campus and married students and veterans. Bottum was the author of: *It Happened Long Ago; Like 1899* (1971), *The Bottum Line* and *The Nothing Book* (1994).

Bottum retired in 1959 and lived in Marquette until 1973, when he became a seasonal resident of the city until 1984.

Bottum was married twice; his first wife was Laila and his second wife was Marian Roger whom he married on June 20, 1941. He has one son, John. The Don H. Bottum Memorial Scholarship was established at NMU. The University gave him an honorary doctorate of Laws in 1960. The Don H. Bottum University Center *(See separate entry)* was dedicated to him on September 10, 1966. (NCN 07/11/1941; MJ 01/04/1995).

Bowling: Interest in bowling was high in the late 1950s. The leader, of the bowling development was Dr. Rico Zenti *(See separate entry)*, who attracted other members of the faculty. The Bowling Club was established in 1958 and within a year such teams as the Bums, Oddballs, and Five Kegs were active on campus. The teams "rolled" at local alleys such as the Shoreland and the Elks Club. In 1966 when the new addition was constructed onto the south end of the University Center, so were several bowling lanes for use by the campus community. The Bowling Club remained active until 1992–1993.

Over the years, students won a number of awards for their skill. Six members of the Northern Bowling Team participated in the Individual Collegiate Games Competition held in Chicago in April 1960. Northern's bowling team led by Mike Bauman won the 1969 National College Team Championship held in Chicago by amassing a score of 7,683 to win the team event over the University of Tennessee.

As the years passed, interest in bowling declined. When the University Center was renovated in the early 1990s, the bowling lanes were replaced by the Bookstore *(See separate entry)*. (NN 05/06/1969, 05/20/1969, 05/16/1969)

Branch Prison: *See*: *Marquette Branch Prison*

Bright Lights Variety Show: The Tri Mu fraternity first performed this show in 1936. It was suspended between 1941 and 1948 and then resumed. In 1957, the performance contrasted Northern of the "Roaring Twenties" and Northern of the "Atomic Age." It consisted of skits, pantomime, silent scene changing and musical numbers. (NN 05/07/1957)

Buick Marquette: On November 3, 1993 John Peterson the owner of a 1930 Buick Marquette placed it on temporary display in the Superior Dome. After completion of the renovation project, the Buick returned to the Dome for a lengthier display. The project was initiated by President Vandament.

The Buick was produced by the Buick Motor Company of Flint, Michigan. Production of the 1930 model was begun on June 1, 1929 with an ambitious plan of six body styles. It was considered a "Baby Buick" and its prices ranged from $990 for the business coupé to $1,060 for the sedan. Built as Buick's answer to the depression slump, it became a victim and was taken off the market by 1931.

Louis G. Kaufman (1872–1942) a resident of Marquette played an important part in American financial circles and at General Motors Corporation in particular. After 1910 he was simultaneously president of the local First National Bank and the Chatham-Phenix National Bank of New York. He joined forces in 1913 with William C. Durant, and three years later Mr. Kaufman was largely instrumental in the reorganization of the General Motors Corporation which established itself as the dominant manufacturer of American automobiles. Mr. Kaufman was named chairman of GMC in 1929 and the Buick Marquette was named in honor of his hometown.

Bullpen: The large area in the Great Lakes Rooms in the University Center or in the Hedgcock Fieldhouse where students registered for classes was nicknamed "The Bullpen." The bullpen was usually the scene of chaos and frustration as crowds grew, lines formed, and frustrated students watched as classes closed on them as they waited in line or changed their schedules. This system ended with computerized registration which began in early 1983. (NN 02/24/1983)

Bureau of Business and Economic Research: The Bureau was created by the Board of Control on February 17, 1995. Its purpose is to develop and maintain a comprehensive data base describing conditions and trends of business and economic activity in the Upper Peninsula.

Between 1997 and 1998, Dr. Harry Guenther conducted a study on the economic impact of NMU on the local economy. Dr. Guenther, a faculty member of the Walker L. Cisler College of Business, was the first director and continues in that capacity. (MJ 02/18/1995)

"Burma Road": With the opening of Spalding and Gant Residence Halls in 1964, students had to walk from the northwestern end of campus to Kaye Hall on the southeastern side of campus. They followed a route which passed alongside a grove of trees, in front of West Science, Jamrich Hall, Thomas Fine Arts and along Spooner, Lee and Carey Halls to their final destination. It was named by groundskeeper, Elwin Bell because originally it was a rough trail strewn with rocks and reminded him of the Burma Road of World War II fame. With the growth of trees, paving, and the construction of new buildings the route is not as bleak as it once was and thus the name is a historical curiosity and little used today.

Bus: In October 1951, a reconditioned bus was purchased for $6000. Over the years, Northern has maintained its own buses. In the late 1990s, there was talk of selling the university-owned buses and leasing them when necessary. To date this has not occurred.

Bush, George H.W.: President Bush of the United States (1988–1993) was a recipient of an honorary doctor of laws degree from NMU in December 1973. At the time he was chairman of the Republican National Committee and gave the commencement address.

Business, Walker L. Cisler College of: By 1906, high schools in the Upper Peninsula were offering Commercial Training, including courses such as Typing and Shorthand. Private business colleges were being operated in major communities. At Ypsilanti in 1913, Michigan Normal College (now Eastern Michigan University) worked out a cooperative arrangement whereby students taking courses at Cleary Business College received certification as teachers of Commercial subjects.

In 1914, President Kaye appointed Casey C. Wiggins, a Commercial teacher in Negaunee and graduate of Ferris Institute (now Ferris State University), to teach Typing, Shorthand and the required Penmanship course for teacher certification. He expanded his offerings to include Commercial Law to assure that students had the skills to enter local business. By 1919, the department was offering Commercial courses in Accounting, Advertising, Arithmetic, Commerce, Commercial English, Finance, Geography, Penmanship, Salesmanship, Shorthand, and

Typing. There was a teacher education program in place as well. In the academic year of 1933–1934, Commercial Courses were renamed Commerce Courses.

In 1944, the State Board of Education authorized Northern to give a Bachelor of Science degree in Commerce and provided funds for additional staff and new equipment. In the late 1940s and early 1950s, courses in Accounting and Retailing were introduced.

The Business Education Department became the Department of Business in 1947, and offered Bachelor of Science degrees in Accounting, Retailing, or General Business Administration for the first time. By the time Mr. Wiggins retired in 1951, the department had grown significantly.

Prior to 1965, the Department of Business consisted of the following disciplines: Accounting, Business Education, Business Services, Insurance and Real Estate, Management, Marketing, Retailing, and Secretarial Services. After that time the major areas were Business Administration (Accounting, Commerce and Industry), Business Education, and Special Business Programs which included 1-2 year programs.

In 1967, the Department of Business became the School of Business and included the following departments: Accounting and Finance, Business Education, and Commerce and Industry. The school offered two distinct types of programs, Business Administration and Business Education, as well as Certificate and Associate Degrees in Secretarial, General Business, Accounting, and Retailing and Sales. On June 3, 1967 the Board of Control named the School the Walker Cisler School of Business Management.

The first two acting deans of the School of Business were Ronald J. Lewis and George Carnahan. Then in the fall of 1970, Donald Hangen was the first permanent dean. During his term the School saw a number of changes. In December, 1970 the Department of Commerce and Industry was changed to the Department of Management and Marketing. In 1973, the Board of Control established the Walker Cisler Fund (endowment) to support the School. The name of the Department of Business was altered to Office Administration and Business Education and in use on July 1, 1973.

Under Dean Robert Hanson (1977-1984) the Business Development Center was established (1979) and the Executive-In-Residence Program began in March with Robert E. Hunter (General Motors) as the first participant. In the Fall 1982 semester, Dean C. Carson was appointed the first visiting Distinguished Professor of the Cohodas Chair of Banking. In 1983, the School of Business Management consisted of three academic department heads (Accounting and Finance, Management and Marketing, and Office Administration and Business Education) and the School Advisory Council played an important role in the operation of the School.

Although the School was named after Walker Cisler in 1967, it was not until January 1, 1987 that the title was officially used. In 1992, the title for all University schools was changed to college. By the mid-1990s, the individual departments of the College had been ended as individual entities.

Over the years, students in the field of Business have developed numerous organizations. The first was the Commercial Club and later the Business Administration Club. In 1965, George Carnahan initiated a chapter of Alpha Kappa Psi, honor society for students in Commerce, Accounting and Finance. James Camerius formed a branch of the American Marketing Association in 1966. The faculty have and continue to take students on field trips to large urban and commercial centers.

As of 1999, the Walker L. Cisler College of Business offers baccalaureate degrees in: Accounting, Business Teacher Education, Computer Information Systems, Entrepreneurship, Financial Management, Management, Marketing, Office Systems and Ski Area Business Management. Associate degrees are offered in: Computer Information Systems, General Business, Office Information Services with legal and medical options; and a certificate program in Office Services. In 1994, the college's namesake, Walker L Cisler died at age 97.

Department chairs or heads: Casey C. Wiggins 1914–1951; W.Donald Nelson 1951-1958; James R. Wilkinson (acting) 1960–1961, Charles Pappas 1962–1965;   *Deans*: Ronald Lewis (acting) 1966–1968; George R. Carnahan (acting) 1968-1970; Donald H. Hangen 1970-1977; Robert Hanson 1977-1984; Brian Gnauck (acting-1984) 1985-1999; James Scheiner 1999-present.(Northern Michigan University Records, UAS 79; *The 1996–97 University Profile*, 1:221–236)

Cafeteria: See: Food Service

Calendar, Academic: The Calendar is developed by the Academic Senate (*See separate entry*) several years in advance. Originally classes began in mid-September with a Christmas break and a return to classes in January ending with final exams. Classes then resumed in early February, continued with a break at the Easter holiday, and ended in mid-June. The first academic year ended with commencement on July 3, 1900.

This traditional academic year was changed by President Jamrich beginning in 1972, giving students a jump on summer jobs. Classes began in early September and a few years later were moved up to late August. Commencement is in mid-December and the new semester starts in January with a mid-semester break. Commencement takes place in late April or early May.

Campus Commons Committee: In the late 1980s, there were complaints from students that there was no location on campus where they could relax. In 1988 the Campus Commons Committee was formed and headed by Donna Pearre, Vice President for Student Affairs. The Committee looked into the situation. By October 1990, it was found that the renovation of the Don H. Bottum University Center would cost $12 million and the Committee looked elsewhere. A number of possible plans and sites for a new Commons building were discussed. One suggestion was to place it in the area between West Science and Olson Library. In the spring of 1991, when the students defeated a referendum for $3 per credit hour fee to pay for the new Commons, the work of the Committee ended. It was at this time that plans for the renovation of the University Center went forward.

Camp Cusino: See: Field Stations

Campus, Evolution of the: NMU's ecological history began when the last glacier retreated into Labrador. The hill that NMU's campus rests on is actually part of a beach-head from the ice age. The area was inhabited by Paleo-Indians after the glacial retreats. Between the mouth of the Chocolay River and Presque Isle, there were at least 6 Indian villages.

The land on which NMU sits was first explored by William Burt in 1844. William Ives, who accompanied Burt, recorded field notes on the area. He mentioned that much of the area was a swamp, especially where Married Housing is presently located. An old 1857 map shows that an Indian trail passed from downtown Marquette, probably along the high ground of the campus, and then headed north.

Several people owned land which later became University grounds. John Outhwaite, mayor of Ishpeming in 1851, owned 640 acres. 199 acres were bought by David Nickerson in 1852. In 1855, the Sault Canal Company became landowner of most of NMU's property. In 1859, James Pendill, who later served as mayor of Marquette, purchased 59.25 acres. In 1899, 20 acres were donated by John Longyear and Frederick Ayer to build Northern State Normal School. Longyear, Dwight Waldo, and the State Board of Education decided to build the first buildings out of Marquette sandstone. Sidewalks were not built until 1905. In 1914, a gardener planned landscaping. In 1924, there was still wildlife on campus. During this time, however, thoughts were that wilderness was for use, not preservation.

The original site of Northern is located on a hill, known in the past as "College Heights," overlooking Lake Superior. It was a heavily forested area located at the northern limits of Marquette. As a matter of fact, when plans were being made for Northern, the city provided extension of water and sewer lines. When South or Longyear Hall was constructed in 1899–1900, the land was disrupted for the first time. The building was connected with the Dormitory by wooden walks.

When the original buildings were constructed on campus (1900–1902), between three and four feet of the original elevation were removed. The Heart (*See separate entry*) of Northern was the only evidence of the original elevation.

In July 1901, the president of the State Board of Education was in correspondence with Professor L. H. Bailey of Cornell University with reference to laying out the grounds. By 1902, a good portion of the campus had been graded and seeded with lawn.

The year 1903 saw a continued interest in the environment of the campus. Land clearance and additional grading was done on the north side of the campus and a fence constructed. A deposit of 5,000 cubic yards of clay was found on campus and was mixed with sand to created a better plant soil. The city put in new sidewalks around the campus that were partially paid for by the State Board of Education. On October 29, 1903, the Board of Education authorized the purchase of trees, plants, and shrubs not to exceed $200 for ornamentation purposes. These were to be planted in the 1904 season.

The State Board of Education on June 30, 1906 authorized President Kaye to have a permanent walk, nine feet wide, constructed to connect the street car tracks on Presque Isle Avenue to the building. At 13¢ per square foot, it cost $340. He was also authorized to spend $100 for shrubbery around the grounds.

In the fall of 1906, R.J. Coryell, landscape gardener of Birmingham, Michigan was engaged to create plans for beautifying the campus. A contract was signed with the State Board of Education in which Coryell, in the spring of 1907, would plant shrubs, plants and flowers on the campus. Execution of the plan began in April 1907, with the arrival of the vegetation and Coryell and his crew. During the first two weeks of May, Coryell busily landscaped the grounds, but there was a worry that the leaves and buds might be hit by a frost. A journalist from the *Mining Journal* hoped that this project would "make this campus one of the most beautiful of all those belonging to the state institutions of Michigan." It was also noted at this time that most of the landscaping was done close to the buildings and the majority of "the campus itself provides samples of dozens of native trees, hundreds of different plants, and a pond that teems with the abundant animal life."

When construction began on the John D. Pierce School in late 1922, the Pierce school garden and the old tennis courts were destroyed. New macadam tennis courts were constructed on level land north of the buildings.

The school garden had been a campus feature since 1908, if not earlier. At the end of summer school, a prize was given for the best flower garden cultivated by the training school students. The school zoo consisted of rabbits, pigeons and guinea pigs.

At this time, improvements were being made on the athletic field (*See separate entry*). Plans for improving the running track's shape were made. The baseball diamond and the football gridiron were given a covering of clay.

In the summer of 1933, the North Gate (*See separate entry*) was constructed at the northeast entrance to campus at the corner of Presque Isle and Waldo Streets. The area was landscaped by Hugo Muelle, who planted cedars and shrubs. He continued the work along Waldo and Presque Isle. Cedars for the work were hauled in from Chatham. A cinder path led from the gate to the steps near Peter White Science Hall, which marked the shore line of glacial Lake Algonquin. Other cinder paths intersected the walk at various points. The main path led through the training school playground, west of the lower tennis courts. Travel ditches were dug for surface draining and piping was laid to take care of the landscaping water supply.

During the 1920s, the athletic field (*See separate entry*) was renovated and expanded. Then in the early 1930s, a football stadium at the end of Kaye Avenue was constructed. In the 1940s land was purchased from the Catholic diocese to provide room for Carey and Lee Halls. Soon after, construction began on Carey Hall (*See separate entry*) which eliminated portions of the woods in that area.

Until the late 1940s, the campus was basically the original twenty-acre site with some additions. Then under President Harden (1956-1967), the campus began to move into the woods to the northwest and took on its present shape. Farm land adjacent to Fair and Lincoln Avenues was purchased along with the old County Fair Grounds along Wright Street. Much of this area would become the site for residence halls constructed in the 1960s and 1970s.

In the spring of 1960 Wilcox & Laird, of downstate Birmingham, was hired to develop a campus plan and conduct landscape work. A year later, the grounds around the new University Center and dorms were landscaped by James Plesscher of Marquette. Within the decade, the campus grounds department was in charge of campus renovations and landscaping.

Beginning in the 1970s the people in the grounds operation, especially under Max Muelle, began to develop a nursery where plants and trees could be grown for use around the campus. It was at this time that an active tree planting project was begun which continues to the present.

Today, the university plans structures and development with the intention of preserving the natural beauty of the campus. (Daniel Gocella, "The Ecological History of NMU" UA; Map of a Portion of Marquette County. New York, 1857–1861; MJ 09/23/1903; 04/20/1-907; 05/18/1907; 06/22/1908; NNN 12/12/1922; NN 07/25/1933)) Alisa Koski

Campus, Location of the: During the spring of 1899, the State Board of Legislature sent a Committee to various locations throughout the Upper Peninsula seeking a desirable location for the projected normal school. On April 28, 1899, when Northern was established, it had been decided that Marquette would be the location of the institution.

The first question for the Board of Education, after the establishment of Northern State Normal School, was the location of the campus in Marquette. On May 11, 1899, the Board reviewed the map and plat of the desired location in Marquette, but took no action. Eventually, there were two possible campus locations. One was on the south side of Marquette, promoted by Peter White and his associates, and the other was the present campus site promoted by John M. Longyear and Frederick Ayer.

In Ypsilanti, where the Board met on June 20, 1899 a delegation led by Peter White appeared in reference to a location in south Marquette in the vicinity of Division and Adams Streets. White stated that probably 90 per cent of the people of the city wanted this site. In a previous letter to the Board, Dr. James H. Dawson noted that the north side was adjacent to "marsh ground, saturated with cold spring water. This land is enveloped in fog almost every summer evening." Furthermore, it would "menace those inclined to bronchial and neuralgic difficulties." Finally, there was a problem with insects in this area. After this and other letters and telegrams, the Board decided on the south side location "on condition that a clear title could be given to all the territory offered by Mr. White and others."

This decision did not last long. When the Board met in Marquette on July 14th, members found that the White property title was not clear and unencumbered. It seems that Clark Young held claim to lot 18 of block 11 of White's Addition. The earlier resolution was rescinded and the north-side, or Longyear-Ayer site was accepted. Thus, the new campus was located on the north side of Marquette along the street car line. The legal description of the property is: "the northeast quarter of the southwest quarter of section fourteen (14) and the southeast quarter of the northwest quarter of section fourteen (14) north of range twenty-five (25) west."

Campuseer: The *Campuseer* was a hardcover yearbook published in 1941 and dedicated to President Webster H. Pearce and Dean of Men Harry D. Lee, both of whom had died in 1940.

Caps and Gowns: *See*: *Academic Apparel*

Carey, Ethel: (September 27, 1889–April 15, 1962) Ms. Carey attended Alma College and received a bachelor's degree in 1911. She took graduate work at Columbia University. In 1953, she received an honorary doctor of laws degree from her alma mater. Before coming to Northern Michigan University, she taught at Fenton and Harbor Springs high schools and at Central Michigan University.

She came to Northern as Dean of Women in January 1924, at the invitation of President Munson. In those days, to be dean of women, was for all practical purposes, to be dean of the college. Over the years, she played an important role in the development of the administration of the institution. Ms. Carey became legendary for her conservative stand in relation to student dress, personal grooming and social behavior generally. In most cases, she was merely implementing Board of Education or college regulations.

In September 1934, while driving with her mother to Grace Spalding's summer home on Middle Island Point, she was involved in a serious accident which took her mother's life. In the fall of 1934, she was on leave to recuperate, and this continued into 1936.

Throughout her career, Carey was concerned with the living conditions of the students who had to live in rooming houses and private homes throughout Marquette. Her dream was to have a dormitory on campus. This was realized when Carey Hall opened in September 1948. The hall was dedicated to her on June 18, 1949.

Ms. Carey retired from Northern in 1956. Upon her death, funeral services were held in Saginaw and she was buried in Fenton, Michigan. (Minutes SBE 11/03/1934, 12/21/1934, 03/07/1935; NN 05/0-9/1962)

Carey Hall: Funds for a dormitory were appropriated by the state legislature and were available in the summer of 1941 along with $20,000 for the purchase of a site. The college first looked to land immediately to the south, but this was unavailable. As a result, a parcel of land was purchased in the summer of 1941 to the northwest of the campus. With the coming of World War II, plans were scrapped. With the end of the War, the state of Michigan was in a position to entertain the idea to construct a dormitory on campus. On January 16, 1946, plans were reviewed by the State Board of Education. Soon after, trees were cut to start construction. The second women's dormitory on campus was completed in 1948, and opened to female residents on September 12, 1948. The structure had been the dream of Dean of Women, Ethel Carey, who lived to see the building open and its dedication to her on June 18, 1949 as part of Northern's semi-centennial anniversary.

The 58,712 square foot dormitory had an original capacity of 193 residents, living on three floors in suites and a few additional quarters on the ground floors. Here, laundry rooms, a recreation room with a tile floors and fireplace, kitchenette, storage rooms, and the health center were located.

When one entered Carey Hall through the double doors, there was an airy, well-lighted foyer. At the right was the reception desk, switchboard, and student mail boxes. There was also a small reception room in this area. At the extreme right of the foyer entrance, double doors led to the student quarters. The suite of furnished rooms consisted of a combination living-study room and a bedroom for the director.

Opposite the entrance adjoining the foyer, three-steps descended into a comfortable lounge which was originally furnished with blue and red leather upholstered chairs and divans. A fireplace added a cheerful atmosphere to this wood-lined room which faced a garden. At the left of the foyer another set of doors led to the dining room in the Union. This dining room was solely used by women. Later, when Spooner Hall was constructed, there was a special all-male dining room.

The Health Center was located in the east wing of the building at the ground level and opened in January 1949. It continued to be used until the opening of Gries Hall in 1961 when the Health Center moved out.

The dormitory was used by students until 1966 when the Job Corps took over the building. The building ceased to be a dormitory in the spring of 1982 as the rooms were converted to faculty and administrative offices. For a number of years, it was used as a faculty office building by the Head Start program, and the old Health Center became the office of the Department of Communication Disorders and the location of the Speech and Hearing Clinic. In late 1995, the last departmental offices in the building—Philosophy, Psychology, and Sociology—were moved to Gries and Magers Halls. For a brief period, the building was used by the Police Academy, Public Safety and Police Services. This ended when the Police Academy moved to K. I. Sawyer and Public Safety moved to the Services Building in the fall of 1996.

In 1996, a special committee, chaired by Carl Holm, discussed the future of the building. Student, staff and faculty input brought forth a number of ideas, but the major factors were age of the structure and cost for renovation. Discussion on future uses of the structure continued. Some thought of using it for the Centers for Upper Peninsula Studies and Native American Studies. In the winter 1997 semester, some parts of the building were used for classes, by skiers waxing their skis, and miscellaneous others. (MJ 07/04/1941;NCN 07/22/1948, 12/01/1948; NW 04/08/1982)

Carillons: Northern has had a number of carillons in its history. In 1951, some $3,437 had been left by graduating classes. Part of this amount was used for the purchase of "carillonic bells." These bells were located on the roof of Kaye Hall. The carillon was removed with the demolition of Kaye Hall in 1972–1973.

A few years later, Board of Control member John McGoff and his wife Marge donated funds for new carillons. The castellated effect of Kaye Hall was replicated, using some sandstone from the old structure. Two low-elevation towers were created with programmed taped music. The carillon was dedicated on August 8, 1980.

The carillon is operated by a computer system. Music is placed on chips and consists of generic and specialty selections. The carillon rings at 8:00 a.m., noon, 1:00 p.m. and 5:00 p.m. In late 1998, plans were developed to place a series of songs on the chip which was written by Northern students and faculty.

Catholic Nuns: The first nuns, or sisters, attended Northern during the summer of 1921. The following summer, 46 attended from Michigan, Wisconsin and Indiana. They represented the: Franciscans, Dominicans, and the Sisters of St. Agnes, Notre Dame, and St. Joseph. In 1923 some 71 nuns attended. Most of them received teaching certification and a few received bachelor degrees. By 1924 they had many friends among the faculty wives, and President Munson and Dean Carey organized a reception for them. Local orders of nuns like the Sisters of St. Paul of Chartres continue to send their sisters to Northern. (NNN 07/15/1922, 07/21/1923, 09/23/1924, 10/14/1924)

"Celebration of Student Research and Creative Works": This celebration was first held in April 1996, under the direction of Dr. David Prior. It consists of a symposium and includes oral presentations, readings and displays. This continues on an annual basis. (*Campus* 03/18–22/1996).

Centennial Celebration: Plans for the Celebration were begun in April 1994, with the creation of the Centennial Committee (*See separate entry*). The philosophy of the Committee was to guide and promote activities conducted by separate groups.

Some of the early activities included a dinner and oral history series. In April 1995, the first Founders' Day dinner was successfully held with a World War II theme. The 1996 dinner had to be canceled due to a lack of interest. In September 1996, the Committee started the "Centennial Memories" series (*See separate entry*). The Centennial Year runs from September 19, 1998 to September 19, 1999—the day the first classes were held.

During 1998, the following events have been held celebrating the Centennial: Centennial Art and Design Alumni Exhibition (08/22–09/26); Business after Hours (08/24); opening of the Presidential Memorabilia and the "NMU Dollar" display (08/26); premiere of the "Centennial Suite" composed by President Jamrich (08/29); All-Student Rally (08/30); dedication of C. V. Red Money Memorial Field (09/12); Student Alumni Project-Paint campus manhole covers (09/13–14); ASNMU Leadership Dinner (09/15); Centennial Opening Banquet and Ball (09/19); publication of *Educating Generations*, *Mining Journal* Supplement (09/19); publication of Suzan Travis-Robyns' *Northern at 100* (09/19); Centennial Alumni Awards Dinner (09/24); Homecoming '98 (09/24–26); Native American Writer-in-Residence Ray Young Bear Reception (09/25); rededication of the Veterans Memorial (09/25); Vital Issues Forum (*See separate entry*) "Investing in Diversity" (09/25); dedication of the Rico N. Zenti

Instructional Wing of PEIF (09/26); dedication of "Northern's Original Campus" historical marker (10/16); Student Centennial Bash (10/31); Holiday Kickoff (12/03); premiere of the video, *Northern at 100: A Century of Memories* (12/04); Centennial Commencement Ceremony (12/19).

For 1999 the planned events include: Vital Issues Forum: "Geopolitical Forces" (01/28–29); publication of Russell Magnaghi's *A Sense of Time: The Encyclopedia of Northern Michigan University* (04/1999); Vital Issues Forum: "Sustainable Environments" (03/25–26); Historical Candle Light Tours (04/06); Time Capsule Ceremony (04/07); Centennial Charter Luncheon (Lansing, 04/28); Centennial Gala (04/30); Centennial Commencement Ceremony (05/01); U.P. Conference of the Historical Society of Michigan (06/18–19); Summer Centennial Reunions/Picnic (07/08–10); Vital Issues Series: "Sports in Society"; Centennial birthday of the departments of Art and Design, Education, English, Geography, History, and Political Science (07/14); dedication of the permanent historical photograph exhibit in the History department (07/14); Closing Centennial Celebration (09/19). Throughout the year special exhibitions were mounted in the Peter White Lounge such as "Presidential Memorabilia," "Celebrating the Holidays," "The Developing Campus," "Student Life," "A Century of Publishing," "Celebrating Jubilee and Centennial," "Centennial Departments."

Centennial Committee: A committee of some 30 people from the University and community held its first meeting on April 20, 1994 to prepare for the Centennial celebration in 1999. The chair was alumnus Dr. Richard Peura, and the first co-chair was Dr. Lulu Ervast. With her death in June 1995, Dr. Russell Magnaghi assumed her position. The secretaries of the Committee were Janis Book (1994–1995) and Janet Laitinen (1995–1999). Business was conducted at monthly and then bi-monthly luncheon meetings held in the Charcoal Room. Over the years, the composition of the Committee changed due to retirements and deaths but the same areas were represented. The Committee encouraged various departments and offices to develop projects celebrating the Centennial which was successfully carried out.

Centennial Memories Series: A lecture series under the direction of the Centennial Committee which brought Northern old-timers to the Wild Cat Den Food Court where they told of their experiences at Northern. Dr. James Rapport began the series in September 1996, followed by Dr. Earl Hilton (09/24/1997).

Center for Economic Education: This Center was first administered under Continuing Education and was started with grants under Glen Stevens. Today it is operated by the Department of Economics, and is housed in Magers Hall. Its goal is to promote economic education among teachers throughout the Upper Peninsula.

Center for Native American Studies: See: *Native Americans*

Center for Research and Evaluations in the Human Services. See: *Behavioral Sciences* . . .

Center for Teaching Effectiveness and Improvement: The Center for Teaching and Learning Advisory Committee, consisting of twenty faculty and staff, began meeting in the fall of 1989 to discuss how to improve teaching and learning on campus. Its goal was to provide consulting services for teaching. This Center, officially titled Center for Teaching Effectiveness and Improvement, was proposed to the Board of Control on February 16, 1990.

Center for Upper Peninsula Studies: On May 10, 1974, the Board of Control approved the concept for Cultural, Environmental and Heritage Studies. Other than a report on the proposed Institute to consist of a museum, no action was taken in 1975.

Under different circumstances, Dean Michael Marsden, President Vandament, and other administrators began to discuss a similar center in 1993. The Board of Control approved the Center on August 16, 1996. On November 4, Russell M. Magnaghi was named director of the Center. The first summer program was instituted in 1996 and continues.

The mission of the Center is to facilitate teaching and research about the geographic, economic, political, social, and cultural aspects of the Upper Peninsula of Michigan. Housed within the College of Arts and Sciences, the Center focuses on the Upper Peninsula as a classic region defined and delineated by both its location and its distinctively rich and varied culture. The Center will help focus the resources of the University and the region on the serious scholarly study of the area.

The Center has co-sponsored a number of publications: *A Sense of Place* (1997), and *World War II Comes to the Upper Peninsula, 1939–1945* in Publications of the Center for Upper Peninsula Studies (Vol. 1, No. 1) in 1997.

Director: Russell M. Magnaghi 1996–present. (*The 1996–97 University Profile*, 2:172–176)

Championship Teams: In September 1995, this exhibit was opened in the Superior Dome. The display consists of trophies and related artifacts and photographs of the individual sport champions and teams. The National Collegiate Athletic Association championships include, Football, 1975, NCAA II; Skiing, 1987 and 1988, Men's Nordic Combined National Champions; Skiing, 1991, Women's Nordic Combined National Champions; Hockey, 1991, NCAA I Champions; Women's Volleyball, 1993 and 1994, NCAA II Champions. In May 1969 the Northern bowling team won the National College Team Championship.

Chapel: The Reynolds family donated money for a non-denominational chapel or meditation room which is located in the University Center. It was dedicated on October 1, 1977. (Minutes of the State Board of Education, 07/28/1904; NCN 05/17/1932)

Charcoal Room: This room located on the second floor of the University Center was opened on April 20, 1964. Overlooking the campus, it was designed to incorporate the tie between history and the major industries of the Upper Peninsula. Emphasis was placed on the charcoal industry as depicted in the name of the room, by specializing in charcoal cooking and by charcoal sketches on the walls. At first the room was a part of Northern's program for preparing students for future work in the food service industry. The room could handle 105 people at one time.

In 1993, with the complete renovation of the University Center, the Charcoal Room was closed as an extension of the dining room. Its characteristic decorations were removed and today only its name remains. (NN 04/24/1964)

The Charles B. Hedgcock Health and Physical Education Building: *See: Hedgcock Fieldhouse*

Charter Schools: A concept developed and promoted by Republican Governor John Engler (1990–present). The idea is to charter non-public schools. Northern signed a letter of intent with two Native American tribes to establish charter schools in February 1995: 1) the Nah Tah Wahsh school in Hannahville, which has been open since 1975 as a K–12 school, 2) the Bahweting Anishnabe Academy in Sault Ste. Marie, a K–6 school which opened in September 1994. In May 1997 it chartered the North Star Academy (alternative school), located in Ishpeming. NMU's Department of Education works closely with the faculty and administration of these schools. (MJ 02/18/1995).

Chase, Lew Allen, Outstanding Senior Award: This is an annual award given by the Department of History to the outstanding senior. It is based on grades and history-related activities. It is named after Lew Allen Chase (1879–1953) who came to Northern in 1919 and retired in 1944. He was head of the History Department and a prolific writer though handicapped by poor eyesight.

Cheerleading: In the late 1940s cheerleading became popular and nearly every college and university in the country had a squad. The cheerleaders were usually women who were considered, "pretty, peppy, and popular."

In 1947, the Physical Education Club created the "Roaring 40's" cheering section. In the same year, a cheerleading contest was held, sponsored by the Physical Education Club. Before an actual squad was formed, Northern had two or three "cheerleaders" who attended all home games and led the school in yells. In the 1949 *Peninsulan* appears a picture of seven females posing in cheerleading uniforms. The 1950s is considered the Golden Age of Cheerleading at American colleges and universities.

Men were added to Northern's cheerleading squad in 1978. The first co-ed team consisted of five male and eight female cheerleaders. Cheerleaders are an integral part of sporting events on campus, assisted by Wildcat Willy (*See: Mascot*). (NCN 03-18-42; *Kawbawgam, Peninsulan*) Michelle Kangas

Chemistry, Department of: As a subject in the Physical Sciences Department, Chemistry was one of the first subjects taught at the Normal School. William McCracken established the Physical Sciences Department in 1899.

The department became independent in 1962 and was initially located in the Peter White Science Hall. Four years later, the department moved from Peter White Science Hall to West Science. The introduction of the Nursing program at Northern greatly increased the number of students taking Chemistry. In 1967, there were 51 students. By 1974, this figure had risen to 381.

There have been concerns for safety in the vicinity of the Chemistry labs. In 1976, the department established standards for protecting students from carcinogens in the labs. There were also security problems in the labs, and measures were taken to secure them.

Over the years, the department has received numerous donations and financial awards. In the 1980s, Uniroyal Tire and private individuals donated a variety of equipment.

The department is accredited by the American Chemical Society. The Chemistry program emphasizes preparation for professional careers in Chemistry, Biochemistry, and related sciences at the undergraduate and graduate level. The department offers Bachelor of Art or Science degrees. The department also offers a Master of Arts degree, and the M.A. in education. In terms of service, the department offers numerous courses for the Liberal Studies requirement in Natural Science/Mathematics.

Department chairs or heads: Lucian F. Hunt, 1962–1965; Roy E. Heath, (acting) 1965–1966; Thomas Griffith, 1966–1967; Gerald D. Jacobs, (acting) 1967–1968, 1968–1989; Roger Barry, 1989–1994; Jerome A. Roth, 1994–present. (*Bulletins*; Francis Copper manuscript; *The 1996–97 University Profile*, 1:75–81) Jay Brennan and Michelle Kangas

Chez Nous: This model restaurant, located in the Jacobetti Center, is operated by the Restaurant and Institutional Management students. In the first year, students concentrate on the culinary arts of cooking and baking. The second-year students research and compile recipes, formulate production schedules and analyze the financial aspects of the menu. They also gain supervisory experience in the kitchen and dining room. For short periods during the academic year, Chez Nous is in operation. The students are supervised by the culinary arts faculty.

Chicken Head: This involves a faculty member, Sgt. Maj. Jimmy A. Powell of the Military Science Department. In September of 1983, in an over zealous moment, Powell brought a live chicken to class and bit off its head to show the students how they could live off the land. He was summarily transferred to another program. This incident made national news coverage and has been used by the U.S. Army as an example of what to avoid in class. (NW 09/15/1983)

Child Care Scholarship: The scholarship was established in 1994–95 by the ASNMU Governing Board. The $200 scholarship is funded from recyclable cans. When the amount is reached, the scholarship is announced and awarded. Recipients are chosen on the basis of need and whether or not they use a day-care service. (NW 01/23/1997)

Child Development Center: In the early 1960s, a Child Development Center was set up by Northern in the Thomas Fine Arts Building. The Center was designed to provide a laboratory experience for Northern students enrolled in the Pre-School and Family Life program. Northern provided funding for the physical space and staffing of the Center.

When the Center opened, child care services were free. The children enrolled in the Center were often children of faculty members, along with children from the Marquette community. Before the Center closed in 1995, cost of services had risen to approximately $5.00 per child per hour.

As Marquette General Hospital expanded, the Center moved into the Becker House on Wilkinson Street from Kaye Avenue in 1978. The Center moved again to the lower level of the Hedgcock Fieldhouse. In the fall of 1988, the Center was moved from the College of Behavioral Sciences to the College of Technology and Applied Sciences. The Center closed in 1995 due to discontinuance of the director's position.

Currently, Northern students enrolled in the Pre-School and Family Life program complete their laboratory experience at one of the area's nationally funded Head Start Programs. There are over ten centers in Marquette alone. Two Head Start facilities are located on Northern's campus: one in Carey Hall and one in the Jacobetti Center. (NN 06/30/1966; NW 10/19/1978) Michelle Kangas

Children's Playground: The playground located at the northeast corner of the campus in the vicinity of Waldo and Presque Isle was opened in 1924. It was operated by the John D. Pierce School as a recreational facility for the students and as a teacher laboratory.

City Hall: Known today as "The Old City Hall" the building was home to Northern State Normal School from September 19, 1899 through June 1900. On September 5, 1899 the common council gave its permission for several rooms on the second floor of the city hall to be used. By November 1, the school was using the entire second floor for office space, a tiny library and classrooms. Northern also hired its own janitor as required. With the completion of South or Longyear Hall in the spring of 1900, classes were permanently offered on campus.

Class Gifts: *See*: *Gifts, Class*

Clinical Laboratory Sciences, Department of: In 1979, a Clinical Science major was introduced under the Department of Medical Technology. The curriculum was designed for certified Medical Laboratory Technologists who desired to continue for a Bachelor's degree and certification as a Medical Technologist. After completion of the academic requirements and three years of clinical experience, the student would be qualified to become a medical lab technician after taking a test from the American Society of Clinical Pathologists. In 1973, Clinical Science became a part of the Allied Health branch of the Nursing Department. The name Department of Medical Technology was changed by the Board of Control, effective January 1, 1995, to the Department of Clinical Laboratory Sciences.

Allied Health majors are prepared for careers as technical and professional clinical laboratory personnel, such as Medical Technologists. Programs are offered from the Certificate to Baccalaureate level.

Coordinators: Mark McFadyen, 1973–1976; Lucille Contois, 1976–present. (*Bulletins*; *The 1996–97 University Profile*, 1:246–252) Michelle Kangas and Alisa Koski

Closure of Northern: The question of the possible closure of Northern during the 1950s is one that provokes some controversy among friends and alumni of the University. During the mid-1950s, there was talk among state legislators that Northern should be closed because of the small number of students attending and the fact that the resources could be used in expanding downstate institutions. For instance in June 1955, Northern graduated 21 students while Eastern graduated 126, Western 117 and Central 78. During these years the local economy was also in bad shape.

When President Harden was selected as president of Northern in 1956, he was told to either expand the institution or close it. He met the challenge and Northern remains a vital institution in the Upper Peninsula. (Russell Magnaghi. "Report on the Possible Closure of NMU in the 1950s," (1997), UA)

Cluster Minors: Some departments have approval to customize a "cluster" of courses in lieu of a minor for their major programs of study. For further information concerning this minor consult the latest *Undergraduate Bulletin*.

Coaches: See: *Individual sports*.

Cohodas, Sam: (September 10, 1897–April 1, 1988) Mr. Cohodas was an entrepreneur and philanthropist of the Upper Peninsula. He was born in the village of Kobylnik in modern Belirus. His father, Aaron emigrated to America in 1900. Sam emigrated to the United States in August 1903 along with his mother and siblings. The family settled in Marinette, Wisconsin. Unfortunately, his father Aaron died in August 1904, leaving his mother Annie to raise the family.

Sam Cohodas and his brother Harry, first became partners in the produce business. They started small in the Copper Country. Eventually, he had 19 warehouses, several canneries and packing houses and a number of orchards in Michigan, Washington and Arizona. Cohodas Brothers became the third largest fruit and vegetable company in the nation. During the Depression his business thrived.

In 1929, Cohodas married Evelyn Tourville. They resided in Ishpeming and later constructed a summer lodge on Lake Michigamme.

During the Depression, the Miners National Bank of Ishpeming closed and needed to be reorganized before the Federal government would approve its reopening. In April of 1933, Sam Cohodas called a public meeting and discussed why Miners National Bank should be publicly owned. At the session, citizens of the community agreed on and subscribed to a capitalization of $150,000 with Cohodas pledging $15,000, or 10 per cent. On January 2, 1934, the bank reopened its doors. From 1960 to 1981, Cohodas expanded his banking empire to include communities in the western Upper Peninsula and eventually there were over thirty banking offices.

In December 1973, he tendered a gift of $250,000 toward the administration building, which was the largest gift ever given to the University until that time. As a result, the Board of Control named the new administration building in his honor.

In the area of scholarships, Sam Cohodas played an important role. He set up a scholarship for the Accounting Department for $100,000 and started Cohodas Scholarships in most high schools across the Upper Peninsula. He also raised $1,100,000 to endow a Chair of Banking at Northern.

"Mr. Sam," as he was known, started the Presidents Club at Northern and was its president for several years. He was responsible for over 300 memberships. He was also one of the founders of the Golden Wildcat Club. In general he was a great supporter of all Northern activities—radio, television, UP North Films, and the Great Lakes Intercollegiate Athletic Association.

Besides this involvement, Mr. Cohodas aided Northern with other donations. Every five years he would have one of his famous birthday parties. The monies generated at these parties were donated to Northern and other charities. Finally he encouraged other members of the Cohodas family to make donations to Northern Michigan University.

The Cohodas Administrative Center (*See separate entry*) was named after him. Between 1975 and 1995, there was a Cohodas Room in the building titled with his memorabilia. Between May and September of 1995, this collection of materials was organized into a special exhibit located in the Cohodas Room in the Superior Dome which is open to the public for viewing. (Wilbur Treloar. *Cohodas: The Story of a Family*. Marquette: NMU Press, 1977).

Cohodas Administration Building: Located on the site of the original campus buildings, construction on the six-story Cohodas Building began in October 1973 and work was completed by the end of July 1975.

Most major administrative offices are located in the building. Data processing originally occupied the basement and in the fall of 1997 was relocated to the 5th floor. The main floor housed the business offices, mail room, central receiving, information office, building manager's office, and campus monitoring system.

The second floor contained the counseling center, placement and career office, institutional research and non-academic personnel office. Graduate studies, research and development, registrar's office, admissions, and financial aid were located on the third floor. The fourth floor held the vice president for student affairs, office of the dean of students, auxiliary enterprises, continuing education, and extension staff lounge. The fifth floor had the vice president for business and finance, office of the controller, purchasing, operations and maintenance, and budget director's office. On the top floor was the office of the Board of Control, President, communications and marketing, alumni relations, internal auditor, campus development, provost, vice president for academic affairs, and vice president for continuing education.

The building is decorated with dark brown brick and tinted thermal glass. Originally, the building was to be the same color as its neighbors. However, when the brick company was plagued by Environmental Protection Agency regulations, it had to change from coal to natural gas for its kilns. This changed the color of the brick. In 1990, Dow Chemical replaced the facade material of Cohodas because of the fear that it would fall.

The walls of the offices are movable. They extend from the floor to the ceiling and were constructed to facilitate easy removal. The offices range in size depending upon the rank of the occupying person or agency. The single offices range from 100 to 200 square feet for department heads, 225 square feet for vice presidents, and 300 square feet for the president. There are four conference areas, one each on the fourth to sixth floors. These are for use by all departments in the building, and possibly for outside organizations. The total cost of the building which covers 1,360,000 cubic feet was $4,032,639. The breakdown amounts to $37.73 a square foot.

The building is designed to be economical, attractive, and functional. To this end, windows are tinted and insulated. They open inward to allow washing them from the inside rather than from the outside.

However, the windows are washed from the outside. The heat is controlled by thermostats that regulate each wall, independent of the other three. This means that when one side of the building is away from the sun and colder than the other sides, the thermostat turns on the heat while the other side remains off.

The fifth and sixth floors of the Sam M. Cohodas Administration Building were occupied during the second week of July 1975. Over the years, changes have been made to the building. Offices have been moved out and others have returned. In 1997, several years of renovations were completed. In 1997–1998 the porticos over the east and west entrances were constructed for protection against falling ice.

The structure was named after Upper Peninsula banker, produce entrepreneur, and philanthropist, Sam. M Cohodas (*See separate entry*). Originally, a museum honoring Northern's benefactor was located on the first floor. It was originally called the Sam M. Cohodas Room and on October 16, 1987 changed to the Sam M. Cohodas Library by Board action. Between May and September 1995, the artifacts were moved and reestablished in the Cohodas Room in the Superior Dome. (NW 03/20/1975, 04/17/1975, 06/26/1975)

College Advisory Council: Each college of the University has a popularly elected council whose members are drawn from representative areas of the college. For instance, the Arts and Sciences Council consists of representatives from the arts, humanities, natural sciences, social sciences, and an at-large-member. The council advises the dean on a variety of matters.

College Woods: In 1935, the woods were identified as the area in front of, and on the site of, modern Lee-Carey Halls. The land is bounded by Wilkinson and Summit Streets, Elizabeth Harden Drive, and the Art Annex. Clearing of the section where Carey Hall is located began in 1946. In the mid-1950s more woods were removed to provide space for Spooner Hall. In 1956 the area to the northwest was cleared for the construction of student and faculty apartments. Eventually one faculty and eight married student apartment structures formed the complex located on the site. Remnants of the College Woods remain with groves of trees. (NN 01/28/1959)

Colleges and Divisions, Creation of: In the late 1950s, the college began to develop divisions which were quickly followed by schools. This helped to lead to the change from a college to a university in 1963. Continuing Education and Extension Division was originally established as the Public Services Division in 1956; College of Behavioral Sciences, Human Services and Education in 1959 as the School of Education; College of Graduate Studies, followed in 1960; College of Arts and Sciences in 1962; College of Business and Management in 1967; and the College of Nursing and Allied Health Sciences in 1968. All of these were called schools until July 1, 1992, when Board of Control action went into effect renaming them colleges.

Color Day: This special day of school spirit was started in 1925. Through the 1930s, school spirit was encouraged by the Color Day Parade. Everyone wore the school colors and every freshman was expected to appear in a green and gold cap called a "pot."

During homecoming week in 1952, students were asked to dress up. Wednesday was gold day and Thursday was green day. In September 1998, the Student Alumni Association, promoted school spirit. First they organized a pep rally for the students and followed this with painting golden Ns at strategic locations around campus. At this time President Bailey, declared every Friday with home athletic events, Green/Gold Day when the community should wear green and gold clothing. *See: Beanie* (Hilton, p. 73)

Color Guard: NMU's Color Guard was organized in December 1974, "to design and put forth a competent, competitive, marching color guard unit which will be able to represent NMU at the highest possible levels in Midwest competitive sessions." The Color Guard continues to march with the band.

Colors: The traditional colors of Northern Michigan University are "old gold and forest green." Over the years, the shades of these traditional colors have changed with the times. The first mention of colors was made at the first graduation in July 1900, when the assembly hall was decorated in green and gold, which were the class colors at the time.

The lyrics of a number of Northern songs from 1901 through 1919 give some indication of why these colors were selected. The colors selected were symbolic of Northern's environment. The green represented the rich foliage of the forests, especially the pines. Following through on the foliage theme, gold may well have symbolized the autumn colors of the region, particularly of the colors of beech and birch leaves in autumn.

In 1902, lyrics referred to the golden sands of time and the olive branch of victory. By 1915, when ivy was covering the buildings, the green was symbolic of the vines and the gold of the sunshine. Four years later it was written that olive was symbolic of honor, and gold of worth.

As the University Archivist wrote in 1986, "Obviously [the colors mean] different things to different people. Still most frequently they are interpreted as symbolizing the nature of Northern's environment and particularly its foliage. If one has to hazard a guess . . . the latter is the safest assumption."

R. Tom Peters recalled that in the early 1960s, he was talking over the matter of changing colors with President Harden because olive was getting more difficult to obtain from suppliers. Also, the olive they were getting was not a very attractive hue. Consequently, the decision was made to use the dark, forest green and gold-yellow used today.

In 1986, Peters concluded that Northern did not really have any officially approved colors. The olive and gold were all but abandoned. They were called back into service for Northern's 75th anniversary celebrations. Through constant use since 1964, the forest green and yellow have been established in practice as the University colors.

Around 1990, a booklet on the standards for use of the official NMU signature noted that "NMU gold and green colors represent warmth and new growth and, with the symbol's design, suggest elements of the University's surrounding environment." Today the Northern colors are PMS 335 green and PMS 116 gold. PMS equals Pantone Matching System, a printing industry standard for classifying ink colors. Note was made that PMS 116 used on a coated or enamel paper will appear too light. PMS 123 gold must be used in this instance. Anyone who plans to use the signature (*See separate entry*) or colors should refer to *Northern Michigan University Graphic Identity: Standards for Use of the Official NMU Signature* (c. 1990).

In the mid to late 1990s, the original shades of green and gold were used by the basketball and football teams for their uniforms. (MJ 07/05/1900)

Commerce, Department of: *See: Business, Walker L. Cisler College of*

Commencement: The first academic year ended on July 3, 1900, with the first commencement exercises. Three students who had entered Northern with advanced standing from other institutions were graduated. The ceremony was held on campus.

Between 1899 and 1958, there was only one commencement, in June, held on campus. This changed in 1959, when the format of three commencements was introduced. That year commencements were held on January 30, June 5 and July 29. This format continued until 1989 when the summer commencement was ended.

Over the century, spring commencement has moved from early July to late April. In 1972 a major changed was made to the academic calendar by President Jamrich. In that year, for the only time in the history of the university, there were four commencements (January 15, June 4, August 5, December 23). Since 1972 mid-year commencement has been held in December. In 1973 commencement was held on May 12 and since that time commencements have been held in late April or early May.

The early ceremonies involving few students were to be held on campus. With the graduation of larger numbers of students, the ceremony was held in the Marquette Opera House on Washington Street. With the completion of Kaye Hall in 1915, commencement moved to the 1500-seat auditorium. The last commencement was held in the auditorium on January 21, 1967 when the largest mid-year commencement to date was held. On June 4, 1967 the ceremony was first held in Hedgcock Fieldhouse where 494 students graduated. Seeking a larger space, the ceremony was first held in the Superior Dome on May 1, 1993, and continues to be held there.

Commencement was first televised in the winter of 1963 while WNMU was still on cable. It has proved to be a popular program. During the Jamrich administration when a televised summer commencement was dropped due to budgetary concerns, it was brought back by popular demand. Color broadcasting was introduced in 1976. Televised commencement is one of the longest running programs on WNMU-TV.

Commission for Women: The Commission for Women was established in 1990 by President James Appleberry. He urged the Commission to explore issues in working, learning and living which affected women at Northern. The Commission was also to advise the University President annually on the major concerns of NMU women and to make recommendations to address these concerns.

President Appleberry appointed thirteen women to the Commission. Soon after taking office, President Vandament made the group a standing Presidential Commission of fifteen members: two from the AAUP faculty, one from the NMUFA faculty, two from the management group, one from the administrative/professional employee group, one from the clerical-technical employee group, four students, and three at-large members.

Since its formation, the Commission for Women has provided educational programs on such topics as pay equity, sex equity, sexual harassment and women's health and well-being. Working together with other groups, special speakers have been brought to the campus. The Commission has also provided opportunities for women to network on campus through luncheons, colloquia, coke and conversation get together and other activities.

An annual event sponsored by the Commission for Women is Women's History Month which is celebrated each March. The Commission sponsors posters, displays, colloquia, speakers and fall and spring luncheons.

Many women have attended these various functions. Even more important is the fact that women on campus can feel that the Commission for Women provides them with a "voice," a group that listens to their concerns and tries to help. Women working together are much stronger than just one individual alone. (NW 02/13/1997) Jean Choate

Commission on the Future of Northern Michigan University: The University established the Commission as the initial step in developing an appropriate and useful planning process; one that would lift sights to opportunities as an institution, and build a cadre of external support persons to assist the University in achieving its goals. The strategic planning process was begun in 1985.

The Commission was composed of approximately 250 distinguished individuals from the corporate world, labor and the professions. Commission members were from 17 states and the District of Columbia, and were organized into 12 task forces.

The Commission was chaired by Michigan Supreme Court Justice Robert P. Griffin, former United States Senator from Michigan who guided the deliberations of the task forces. The campus liaison was Dr. Ruth D. Roebke-Berens, Assistant to the President for Strategic Planning.

The Commission on the Future met three times during 1986: January 23–25 in Marquette, June 13 in Detroit, and October 31 in Marquette. The 12 task forces: External Environment; Academic Excellence and Program Needs; Enrollment and Service to Special Constituencies; Olympic Training, Sports Training, and Intercollegiate Athletics Opportunities; Electronic Teaching and Information Services; Human Resources Development; Young Adult Students; Northern's Cultural Responsibilities; Applied Research; Physical Plant and Space Utilization; Public Service Responsibilities; and University Development and Private Giving met from four to eight times with many individual subcommittee meetings. These deliberations resulted in the 169 recommendations contained in a report presented to the Board of Control on February 19, 1987. The report triggered an internal planning process which was reviewed in detail in a special report, *Commission on the Future One Year Later*, issued in May in 1988. It concluded that the major of recommendations had either been implemented or were acted upon.

(UA: *Commission on the Future of Northern Michigan University* [Marquette, 1987]; *Commission on the Future One Year Later* [Marquette, 1988].

Committee A: Originally established in 1963, Committee A consisted of five members who dealt with the graduate and undergraduate programs. Under ex-officio member, Vice President Milton Byrd, Committee A created the Common Learning and Four-Course programs. Edward Pfau of Education was the chair most of the time and it was composed of: David Dickson, Art Pennell, K. Wahtera and Richard Wright. In 1966 it became the Committee on Undergraduate Programs (*See separate entry*)

Common Learning Program: Milton Byrd became Vice President for Academic Affairs in 1962 and was interested in developing a strong liberal arts program. He introduced the "Common Learning" courses that comprised the "Four-Course Plan." This was done to provide the students with general education.

A number of faculty committees spent many hours working out the content of the courses in order "to provide each student with basic learning skills, to awaken his intellectual curiosity and develop his concern for contemporary issues, and to help him understand the relationship of man and his environment." New courses to meet these goals were given the title of "Common Learning" and listed under the headings of Humanities, Social Science, Mathematics and Natural Sciences. The proposal for the Common Learning Program came from Committee A and it was approved by a faculty vote after several informational sessions.

The Common Learning courses were designed to include contributions from different areas and many were taught by interdisciplinary faculty teams. During the first year, many of the 45 minute lectures were presented to large sections by television. Because many students disliked this system, Vito Perrone (appointed Associate Dean for Common Learning in 1966) reported to the Board of Control in 1967 that no more than 20 minutes of class time would be used for televised lectures and demonstrations. Eventually there were mass lectures presented by faculty followed by smaller discussion sections also conducted by faculty.

The Four-Course Plan (*See separate entry*) and Common Learning (*See separate entry*) were both designed to unify a student's educational experience. The "Book of the Semester," was devised to unite the academic community. Students and faculty were invited to nominate books which would be interesting and valuable to everyone, and student votes decided which one would be read each semester. From fall 1965 to spring 1967, everyone was expected to read and discuss *A Canticle for Leibowitz,* Walter M. Miller; *The Immense Journey*, Loren Eisley; *Notes of a Native Son*, James Baldwin; and *Up the Down Staircase*, Bel Kaufman. All of this was aimed at promoting liberal studies and making full use of faculty skills.

In terms of reality vs the ideal, many of the older faculty avoided teaching in this Program. As a result, new and younger faculty were hired by departments to teach in this Program. Eventually there was a two-tier faculty structure at Northern—one to teach departmental courses and another to teach in the Common Learning Program.

Due to this and other problems, the Common Learning Program was modified in the early 1970s. It became known as the Liberal Studies Program (*See separate entry*) in 1974.

Communication and Performance Studies, Department of: The Communications and Performance Studies department had its origins in 1906 when Northern offered a course titled "Expression." Eulie Gay Rushmore aimed to teach students to "develop mind, voice, and body, and to rouse the student to a consciousness of himself and to bring him into confidence and power." Ms. Rushmore retired in 1925. In earlier years, Speech was part of the English and Expression Department. In 1958, the Speech Department separated from English. General and Public Speaking, Interpretive Reading, Radio and Television, Speech Science and Correction, and Theater were the different areas within the department. Until 1966, Forest Roberts headed the Department and played an important role in its continuing development.

Dr. James Rapport, who succeeded Roberts, was instrumental in increasing the prominence of the Speech Department. He helped design the Little Theatre, which was renamed the Forest Roberts Theatre (*See separate entry*) in 1969. Before this theatre was built, productions were held in the Kaye Hall auditorium where acoustics were poor. 1962 marked ground-breaking for the Fine and Practical Arts Building and the Little Theatre. Dr. Rapport retired in 1998 but volunteers his time in the Department.

In 1973, the department split again. Pathology became Communication Disorders while the other areas of study remained in the Speech Department. By this time, Bachelor degrees were offered in Speech Education, General Speech, and Drama. Between 1973 and 1980, Broadcasting, Public Address, Mass Communications, and Theater majors were offered. From 1984 to 1986 the department was called "Speech Communication, Theater, Broadcasting, and Mass Communications." The name was changed by Board action on July 31, 1992 to the Department of Communication and Performance Studies, or CAPS.

During the academic year 1994–1995 the Department reported the following level of activity: a) 300 (approx.) national play writing award scripts were reviewed; b) 200 (approx.) members in the First Nighters Club; c) 1,800 (approx.) Roberts Theatre season ticket holders; d) five main stage productions; e) nine student one-act laboratory productions; f) planned and hosted a regional media conference; g) received Michigan Association of Broadcasters Awards for three audio production students; h) four student papers were presented at Central State Conference; i) thirteen students attended the National PRSA Conference; j) "Haywire" (*See separate entry*) was invited to American College Theater Festival regional and national competitions; k) a sound track album for "Haywire" was produced by audio production class.

Department chairs or heads: Forest Roberts, 1958-1966; James Rapport, 1966–1993; Donald Rybacki, 1993–present. (*Bulletins*; Francis Copper manuscript, UA; *The 1996–97 University Profile*, 1:82–88; Jennifer Strand, "Haywire," UA) Alisa Koski

Communication Disorders, Department of: In 1965, Communication Disorders was listed as an experimental major in teacher certification programs. By 1973, Speech Pathology and Audiology had become its own department. It had been a part of the Speech department which included Theater, Speech, Interpretation, Broadcasting, and Speech Education. The Speech Pathology and Audiology Department has always been located in Carey Hall. In 1975, a name change occurred when Speech Pathology and Audiology became known as Communication Disorders.

The department aims to prepare graduate level Speech Pathologists to assume professional responsibilities in a variety of clinical work settings and meet all certification requirements of the American Association of Speech and Language Pathology and Audiology. The department also prepares undergraduate students to enter graduate programs. Both undergraduate and graduate programs are accredited by the Council on Academic Accreditation, something the department is proud of.

Department chairs or heads: Peter Smith, 1973–1977; Curtis Hamre, (acting) 1977–1978; James Davis, 1978–1994; Russel Davis, (interim) 1996–1997; Roger Towne, 1997–present. (*Bulletins*; Telephone Interview with Lon Emerick, retired, UA; *The 1996–97 University Profile*, 1:253–259) Alisa Koski

Communications Office: *See*: *Communications and Marketing*

Communications and Marketing, Office of: Prior to the Harden administration (1956–1967) information to the media was done in an ad hoc fashion. In the spring of 1949, Aurele Durocher was appointed to head the "Public Relations Project." Its two-fold purpose was to acquaint people in the Upper Peninsula with the accomplishments of Northern students and the general activity of the institution.

When President Harden came to Northern in 1956, he was a public relations type of individual who saw the need to put Northern on the media map. As a result, in 1957 he encouraged Clair Hekhuis, a UPI correspondent in Lansing, to join the Northern staff as Director of Information Services.

Hekhuis worked alone at first, gathering news and taking photographs. He did the sports news and got releases out on the faculty. The public throughout Michigan had to be told the Northern story. Hekhuis was soon assisted by Paul Suomi and then Paul Ripley and the *Mining Journal* worked closely with them. By the time Hekhuis left in 1966, the Office of Information Services had been firmly established on campus.

The office was known as the News Bureau until 1985 when it became the Communications Office. On July 24, 1997, the name was changed by the Board of Control to include Marketing. This office is a part of the University Relations and Development Division. The office exists to promote public understanding and support of NMU by planning, coordinating and facilitating effective two-way communications between the University and its many constituencies, both internal and external. The office provides public relations, communications, marketing advice and counsel; plans and executes programs; coordinates and clears information for release to the media; provides official spokespersons; prepares and places releases; manages the University relations with the mass media outlets and their representatives; produces periodicals and publications; develops and promotes compliance with publication standards; and provides still photographic support to the University community. Publications the office has been involved with include: *The Northern-News Review, Campus, Horizons* and *Horizons Extra*.

Directors: Clair Hekhuis, 1957–1966; Paul Suomi, (news Director) 1966–1967; Earl McIntyre, 1967–1985; Michael Clark, 1985–present. (NCN 03/16/1949; *Bulletins*; Communications Files, UA; *The 1996–97 University Profile*, 2:210–215.) Michelle Kangas and Alisa Koski

Community College at NMU: In 1966, Act 331 of the Michigan State Legislature defined community college as "an educational institution providing, primarily for all persons above the 12th-grade age level and primarily for those within commuting distance, collegiate and non-collegiate level education including area vocational-technical education programs which may or may not result in the granting of diplomas and certificates including those known as associate degrees, but not including baccalaureate or higher degrees."

In 1969, Northern received a letter from the State Board of Education to review programs consistent with the development of a community college. President Jamrich determined the legal designation of NMU's role as a community college in an agreement with the Michigan Board of Education in 1972. The program was initially under Continuing Education. Vocational education funding came from the state and supported many one-and two-year programs.

Programs at NMU include: 1. Vocational-technical education programs which may result in diplomas, certificates, or associate degrees; 2. A program of collegiate and non-collegiate level, credit and non credit developmental education opportunities for enrolled students; 3. Services to facilitate the enrollment and transfer of enrolled students seeking to complete a baccalaureate degree; 4. A program of community service, non-credit education, and continuing education opportunities for individuals living in the region.

In 1994, a task force was formed to define the above roles of community college at NMU. By the 1994–95 academic year, the ideas were being implemented. Plans to hire a Dean for Community College and Public Service Programs were dismissed in 1995 and the program was transferred to Dr. Virginia Slimmer, Dean of the College of Technical and Applied Sciences. In 1998 Dr. Brian Gnauck took over the Program upon Dr. Slimmer's retirement. (*Task Force on the Study of NMU's Community College Report to President Vandament March 16, 1994*; Telephone interview with Michael Marsden, Chair of 1994 Task Force) Michelle Kangas

Community Service & Distinguished Citizenship Award: This award is presented to a NMU alum whose volunteer service to her/his community has been outstanding for a minimum of 10 years.

Recipients: Joe Schmidt and Joe Konwinski.

Commuter Student Services: Commuter student services were available by the 1979–80 Academic Year under the Assistant Dean of Students. Services include tenant assistance and information about security deposits, leases, landlord relations, small claims court and other related topics. The office also assists in forming car pools, finding housing, and encouraging commuter students to participate in campus events. Michelle Kangas

Compass Campuses: The term used to describe Northern's sister institutions: Central, Eastern and Western Michigan Universities.

COMPACT: Also known as the Campus Compact. In 1989 Northern became a new charter member in a consortium of universities and community colleges aimed at promoting voluntary service among the students. At the time, Ruth Roebke-Berens was the campus liaison.

Components, Establishment of: Besides the Colleges at Northern, components have been developed since 1963 which provide both academic and non-academic credit for their programs. These include: Northern Michigan School of Banking, 1964-1995; Regional Criminal Justice Training Center, 1967; Great Lakes Sports Academy, 1983; Great Lakes Sports Training Center, 1983; U.S. Olympic Training Center, 1985; Glenn T. Seaborg Center for Teaching and Learning Science and Mathematics, 1985; Center for Native American Studies, 1996; Center for Upper Peninsula Studies, 1996. *(See separate entries)*

Computers: The first University Computer Center was opened in 1963 through the encouragement of the University Registrar, Harry A. Rajala, and Vice President of Business and Finance, Leo M. Van Tassel. In January 1963, authorization was given to purchase a 1620 Data Processing Machine from International Business Machines (IBM). The Data Processing Center, was initially staffed by only three operators under the direction of Robert Aikala, who took the position in July 1963. The Center was located in the basement of Longyear Hall. For many years, it conducted operations on unit-record tab equipment, storing administrative and accounting records on hundreds of 50-81 keypunch cards.

The Center added a IBM 1401 CPU, coupled with numerous interpreters, collators and printers to keep all University bills, files, and records in their proper order. By today's standards, these machines were bulky, slow, and horribly inefficient. The main responsibilities of the Center were: admissions, registration, tuition/billing, printing/mailing, test scoring, accounting, and record keeping.

The Center grew, updating equipment and adding personnel, until several keypunch machines were moved into West Science in the early 1970s. These terminals were used by students using computer programming packages, as well as package programs from geography, chemistry, statistics and physics. In 1975, about 20 terminals were added, allowing students better access.

At this time, the academic support area of the Computer Center came into being. This small division still worked with administration, but also lent support to academic mainframe applications. In 1975, with the opening of the Cohodas Administrative Center, the Computer Center was moved to the new location in the basement. In the fall of 1997 the Center was relocated to the fifth floor of Cohodas.

The microcomputer became a reality in 1975. At that time, Dr. William Ralph of the Physics Department was the pioneer faculty member in this field. The first student to own a microcomputer was Terry Horton of Marquette. Students and faculty had to build their own computers from a kit, and the Altair 8800 was popular; the 80-80 processor, which was an Intel product and the Z-80 Xitan were available. Each computer had to be hand-programmed and the disks were as large as eight inches, but gradually became smaller. Today there is talk of micro disks and CD ROMS.

By 1979, the microcomputer had become popular. The Apple, which was easy to use was introduced and IBM came out with its own computer. In the beginning it was a design disaster.

In the early 1980s several Radio Shack TRS-80 PCs were introduced which ushered in the microcomputer age on campus. In 1983, 25 new IBM PCs were installed in a lab location in Jamrich Hall. Three years later, the first MAC lab was opened in Thomas Fine Arts Building.

With the exception of supplying network access for the campus and beyond, the Computer Center has the same responsibilities as it did 30 years ago. However, its equipment has radically changed. From the IBM

1400 and 1600 generations, through the 360/370 generations, to the 9000 generation of today, hardware has improved exponentially in speed and efficiency over the years.

In 1997, the Center employed about 20 staff, senior computer operators and a number of professional programmers. The crew handles financial resources, human resources, payroll, student records and the alumni system. The Computer Center is under the Financial and Administration Division.

Academic Computing has changed since its inception in the mid-1980s. Headquartered in West Science, there was a micro-repairman and a PC support position. In 1989, Academic Computing was formalized. The PC/software support position was combined with the original academic main frame support position from the Computer Center and micro-repair was moved to Telephone Systems. This shift marked the formal creation of Academic Computing, as well as giving it an operational center in West Science. In 1993, the facility was moved to the Harden Learning Resources Center.

Over the years Academic Computing has changed its areas of support. Originally there were MAC labs in West Science and Thomas Fine Arts, PC labs in West Science and Jamrich Hall, and Computer Assisted Drawing and School of Business labs in the Jacobetti Center. In late August 1996, a consolidated computer lab with nearly 300 stations and several classrooms was opened in the Harden Learning Resources Center.

Over the years there have been updates and replacements across the campus. In the late 1980s, a Learning Technology Fee was introduced so that equipment could be updated. A four-year replacement cycle was introduced later. In March 1996, the Computer Center received a new IBM 9162 CPU server to replace the old campus main frame. The 1996 consolidations of lab space has been noted. As the use of computers continues to evolve in 1998, there has been ongoing discussion over the question of the University supporting both a MAC and DOS system on campus. There is also the development of a policy to encourage or require students to have laptop computers for class use in the near future. In the fall of 1998, the distribution of laptop computers to faculty was begun on a voluntary basis. Internet service is available. (Abe M. Voelker. "The Computer Center" (1995), UA; Interview with Dr. William Ralph 11/13/1998, UA; *Popular Electronics* 01/1975, 11/1975).

Conferences: Public Service and Conferences developed a sizeable staff during the Harden administration (1956–1967) By 1960 Northern had become the "Conference Center of the Upper Peninsula." The National Association for Student Teaching held the largest international workshop in its history on Northern's campus during the summer of 1961. Over the years it remained under Academic Affairs.

In January 1994 Public Service and Conference was transferred to Student Affairs and Auxiliary Services. At this time it was also given a new title, the Conference Department.

Today, Judith L. Place and her staff operate out of the Don H. Bottum University Center. During the conference year July 1, 1997–June 30, 1998, 304 conferences were held which attracted 29,854 participants. These conferences generated $301,633 for University Departments and had a $498,077 economic impact on the Marquette Community.

Connector Link: This 225-foot link was the idea of President Vandament who was seeking ways to physically unite the campus. The $700,000 project created an enclosed heated walkway which connects Gries Hall and the University Center. When it was opened in 1995, many complained about the extravagance. Once they used the link, they were appreciative of its existence, especially in the winter months.

Conservation and Agriculture, Department of: As early as 1905, Northern offered courses in Agriculture at first through the Biology Department and as special courses. Samuel D. Magers, Dr. Elliott Downing's successor in the Biology Department, was given the responsibility for developing a course that would teach Northern students to assist their pupils in planting and cultivating school gardens and beautifying the areas around their homes. Members of his agriculture classes planted gardens with regular and experimental crops and supervised the children in the training school in planting flowers and vegetables. He told *The Quill* reporter in November 1914, that "I shall refuse to pass any girl who fails to develop blisters on her hands." The school garden at this time was located to the southwest of Cohodas in the vicinity of Kaye Avenue. It was removed in 1922 with the construction of John D. Pierce School.

In 1912, the State Board of Education, in an attempt to improve education in the rural schools, required that all applicants for certification as rural school teachers complete a course in Agriculture. By 1914, courses in Practical Agriculture were added to the Rural and

Graded School courses. Every student had to become proficient in the use of the Babcock milk tester, the testing of seeds, work in the school gardens and regular textbook work.

The Department of Conservation and Agriculture was organized to fill requirements for teaching in rural schools, obtaining a major or minor for the purpose of teaching in a high school, and gaining experience so students could assist in the program of integrating conservation activities in a school system or go into professional training.

The short course in agriculture was canceled by the State Board of Education in 1924 because enrollment was low. But Michigan's rural school teachers were required to take agriculture, and the federal government paid the salaries of teachers of agriculture whose training met the requirements of the Smith-Hughes Act.

George Butler, Superintendent of Schools at Grand Marais who met the requirements with his degree from Michigan State University, joined Northern's summer faculty for several years before making the move to Marquette as a permanent member of the staff in January 1935. He was convinced that the Upper Peninsula was good country for potatoes, apples and dairying and took his students on trips to the Chatham Agricultural Experimental Station and local dairy farms to prove his point. He taught forestry, botany, soils, animal husbandry, field agriculture and agricultural economics. He also trained teachers of agriculture who qualified for employment under the Smith-Hughes Act. His courses were approved for transfer credit by Michigan State University.

In 1938, Butler worked on a project of his own, improving the supply of low-bush blueberries. Two years later, visiting professors from Michigan State and Western complimented him on his courses.

Over the years, various locations in the Peter White Hall of Science served as growing rooms and a greenhouse. In 1910, the growing room was located on the second floor. During a renovation of Longyear Hall in 1929, a room was provided for soils and a plant laboratory. In 1941, a greenhouse was added to the west end of the Peter White Hall of Science.

In 1956, the Department of Conservation and Agriculture was housed in new quarters in the Peter White Hall of Science. The quarters consisted of two labs, a classroom and some new pieces of equipment.

Nine courses were taught; credits could be transferred to other universities such as Michigan State.

Over the years, Butler encouraged Northern students interested in agriculture to attend the Conservation Training School at Higgins Lake sponsored by the Michigan State College Department of Conservation and the four Colleges of Education. It was Butler who encouraged President Tape to obtain the State Camp on Munuscong Bay in the eastern Upper Peninsula in 1948.

Northern had much to offer students who wished to get pre-professional training in the field of Conservation and Agriculture. The department carried on soil testing programs for farmers and other interested people in the Upper Peninsula. Students helped carry out these programs.

After Butler, the head of the department retired in 1959, Roger Norden and Alfred Niemi, both Ph.D.s in agriculture, taught in the combined Department of Geography, Earth Science and Conservation. The agricultural portion was discontinued in March 1963.

Department chair: George Butler, 1935–1959.

(MJ 05/19/1912; NCN 01/23/1935, 10/19/1938, 02/28/1940; NN 03/05/1956) Miriam Hilton

Consumer and Family Studies, Department of: In April 1910, Northern's faculty established requirements for a life teaching certificate in Domestic Science and Domestic Art. The first instructor was Margaret Buchly who began teaching in the fall of 1910. She introduced her department to catering banquets on campus. A tradition continued until the opening of Lee Hall in 1948.

In 1912, Buchly left and was replaced by Della McCallum, a Northern graduate, who remained until 1924. She developed a strong bond with her students who served some elaborate meals to the college community. During World War I, she taught summer classes in canning and preserving: first as a means of assisting the war effort, and later as a means of combating the post-war high cost of living.

The department was called Home Economics until, by Board action on October 16, 1988, the name was changed to the Department of Consumer and Family Studies.

At this time, the department was transferred from the College of Behavioral Sciences to the College of Technology and Applied Sciences. It was physically moved from Thomas Fine Arts to the Jacobetti Center in the early 1990s. Today, its descendent is the Department of Consumer and Family Studies. The Department is committed to offering quality undergraduate education from the certificate to the baccalaureate degree.

Department chairs or heads: Margaret Buchly; Della McCallum; Olga M. Hoesly; Helen Bosard; Jane Bemis; Joan Mattias; Mohey Mowafy; Walter Anderson.

(DMJ 12/10/1910; Hilton, p 23; *The 1996–97 University Profile*, 1:295–301)

Continuing Education and Sponsored Programs: Extension work can be traced back to the spring of 1904. Teachers who had taught at least six years under one of the Northern professors could enroll. Extension courses were given in Marquette, Negaunee and Ishpeming. This was extended to sites throughout the Upper Peninsula.

Correspondence courses go back to the 1920s. In 1922, some 62 courses from twelve academic disciplines were available by correspondence. In a campus newspaper article in December 1923, it was noted that there were many students getting credit who did not appear on campus—from New York to Kansas. The majority of students were from Michigan, Wisconsin, and Illinois. In the Lower Peninsula there were students from Grand Rapids, Cadillac, Saginaw, and Detroit. The program was directed by G. L. Brown, chair of the Extension Committee. Evelyn Verran was the secretary who oversaw the program.

During World War II there was an interest in developing vocational teachers' certification and adult education which was soon mandated by the state. After a special meeting with Governor Harry Kelly, President Tape and other educators, Northern worked through an adult education committee and developed courses for this program. The Office of Instruction and In-Service Education (*See separate entry*) was created under Max Allen in 1947. Correspondence and extension courses and in-service courses were offered to help teachers develop their skills in vocational training and provide classes for individuals seeking certification.

Under President Harden in 1956, the Instruction portion was separated from In-Service Education and Claude A. Bosworth was made the new dean of Public Services (*See separate entry*). While on campus the Women's Job Corps (*See separate entry*) was under this office. By 1963–1964 the position of dean was upgraded to a vice presidency. At that time the following were included in this office: Business and Industrial Programs; Business and Labor consultants; Field Courses; Public Health; Conferences; Area Training Center (later to emerge as the Jacobetti Center); and Practical Nursing.

In the administrative reorganization in August 1970 under President Jamrich, the Public Services Division became the Division of Continuing Education and Extension. After Bosworth's sudden death in 1969, the programs were directed by J. Donovan Jackson until Roland Strolle was named to head the Division in 1972. Jackson was instrumental in fostering the Women's Center. At this time, the community college initiative was placed under this office.

By 1973, the Division was in charge of training in criminal justice under Art Neiger as well as offering certificate and associate degree programs in that area. This served as an incubator for the Bachelor degree programs in law enforcement, security administration and corrections. The other programs directed by this division were: labor education, off-campus education credit classes, adult non-credit courses, independent study, management development, conferences, the evening college, community services and the Program of General Studies. The latter program offered 27 one and two-year programs under the directorship of Neiger. The division also directed the Northern Michigan Skill Center, which for many years was under the leadership of Richard J. Retaskie; the Northern Michigan School of Banking and the Bureau of School Services. The Bureau was under the supervision of J. Willis Owen and Neiger.

A Continuing Education Advisory Committee was formed in 1971 to keep the Division in closer touch with the academic community. Credit courses for inmates and custodial staff at the Marquette State Branch Prison, courses at the K.I. Sawyer Air Force Base, the Iron Mountain-Kingsford and Eastern Upper Peninsula centers, and a number of other cities continued to take Northern faculty to classrooms all over the region. The Program of General Studies offered one and two-year Certificate and Associate Degree programs, evening college classes and a number of adult non-credit courses to the general public.

In the late 1970s Jack Rombouts was appointed Vice President for Continuing Education. After his retirement in 1978, Continuing Education was placed under the Provost's Office, which later became the Office of the Vice President for Academic Affairs. At one point, non-credit was reported to one individual and credit courses to another. On December 18, 1987, Graduate Studies and other duties were combined to form the Dean of Continuing Education and Graduate Studies. Dr. Roger Gill was hired as the first dean under this designation on February 15, 1988. This situation continued until 1996 when the functions were split when Dean Gill left.

From the 1920s, correspondence courses on a fluctuating basis were available until 1992–1993 when the offerings were greatly expanded and advertised. In 1995, the name changed to Continuing Education and Sponsored Programs and some 17 correspondence courses were being offered.

The extension program was a different story. It began in the 1920s and flourished through the 1980s and went into decline. After the opening of K.I. Sawyer Air Force Base (*See separate entry*) in 1956, undergraduate and graduate courses were offered at the Base which attracted a large number of students. There were also extension courses offered at the Marquette Branch Prison (*See separate entry*) beginning in 1972 and lasting into the late 1980s. Prior to the mid-1980s, Northern had an extensive program located in communities throughout the Upper Peninsula. By 1998, only the Education Department offered extension courses on a regular basis. Two centers are currently open in Iron Mountain and Escanaba. Plans call for a number of other centers to be located around the Upper Peninsula.

By 1996, Continuing Education and Sponsored Programs were divided into non-credit and credit programs. The non-credit programs consist of Continuing Education units, Institute of Continuing Legal Education, Motorcycle Rider Safety, Professional and Personal Development, School Bus Driver Certification and Labor Education Program. Its credit programs include Extension Courses, Weekend College Program, Correspondence Courses and the Summer Session. (NNC 12/04/1923;Hilton, p. 222; (*The 1996–97 University Profile*, 1:22–26) Portions by Miriam Hilton

Controller: The position of comptroller was held by Leo Van Tassel in the late 1950s when there was no vice president for finances. Today the Office of the Controller is under the Finance and Administration Division. The Controller provides administrative support by accurate recording and reporting of financial information so that the University is in compliance with laws, regulations, and University policy and by providing accounting services to University students and departments. (*The 1996–97 University Profile*, 2:52–57)

Copper, Francis Roy: (May 1, 1882–January 8, 1949). Copper came to Northern in 1918 as principal of the John D. Pierce School and then joined the Department of Education. In preparation for the celebration of Northern's semi-centennial in 1949, Copper was appointed University Historian whose task it was to write a history of the institution. Given his long service and experience at Northern, he was able to write a history using personal recollections and those of his colleagues. Several drafts of the history were written, but when death intervened six months before the June celebration, the manuscript was abandoned and not published until 1999. The F.R. Copper Scholarship was named after him. (NN 04/16/1947; MJ 01/10/1949)

Correspondence and Extension Courses: See: *Continuing Education . . .*

Council of State Teachers College Presidents: The Council was created in 1928 and was an advisory body composed of the presidents of Eastern, Western, Central, and Northern. The presidents worked collectively through the Council and were concerned with matters of common interest to all the colleges which required uniform practice. The secretary of the Council was the assistant superintendent of Public Instruction. With these institutions going to university status, the Council was disbanded.

Counseling Center: When Northern was a smaller institution with an enrollment of several hundred students, counseling was usually taken care of by Deans of Men or Women. In many cases, deans took a personal interest in students and their problems. However, as Northern expanded, the Counseling Center took over student development.

Under the Student Affairs Division, the Counseling Center facilitates student development and the attainment of institutional goals through leadership and services which address psychological, emotional, behavioral and social factors. The Counseling Center provides, or assures and directs, the provision of a variety of services including personal and career counseling, crisis management and consultation regarding emotionally distraught or high risk students, training for students and NMU personnel who in turn serve students, programming in residence halls, classrooms, etc., substance abuse, prevention and early intervention services, and psychological consultation for a variety of NMU personnel and decision-making bodies. (*The 1996–97 University Profile*, 2:113–118).

Cox's Inn: Located on the outskirts of Marquette at 405 Brookton Road, it was popular with Northern students in the 1920s. Many of them went there a majority of nights of the week. It was also used for faculty parties as well. The modern Moose Lodge is on the site. (NNN 07/29/1921)

Credit and Debit Cards: Credit cards have been popular on campus since the 1970s although students were warned to be careful about how they used the cards. In the 1980s, a debit card was created for the Olson Library. In the early 1990s, a Dina-Val card was credited for the Wild Cat Den Food Court and could be used on specially rigged vending machines. In 1995, First of America Bank introduced the Wild Cat Express card which did much the same. This card also acted as official identification. A special outlet for the bank was created in the University Center to service these cards.

Criminal Justice, Department of: When crime rates began to increase in the 1960s and 1970s, the federal government responded by increasing education and licensure of law enforcement personnel. The Law Enforcement Assistance Administration (LEAA) provided funding for enhancement officer training and education. In the early 1970s, Arthur Neiger, director of the Bureau of School and Community College Services, received an LEAA grant to conduct a two-week training academy for working police officers. Eventually, the Northern faculty took the training program across the region as a 16-week Regional Training Academy. In 1962, Neiger developed an associate degree program in Law Enforcement and a two-year police science curriculum was developed. When administrators in corrections, security, and conservation caught on to the trend, a curriculum was created in these aspects of Criminal Justice, and two and four-year degrees were offered in Law Enforcement or Corrections/Private Security. The Michigan Board of Education approved the four-year Criminal Justice program in the fall of 1974.

By the spring of 1977, Criminal Justice was named a department in the School of Arts and Sciences. Later it was attached to the College of Behavioral Sciences, Human Services, and Education. In 1992, the department was renamed Justice Studies, only to return to its original name in 1995.

Northern is currently the headquarters for the American Association of Correctional Officers who publish a quarterly newsletter, *The Keepers Voice*. Each summer the Regional Training Academy and the American Legion conduct a summer cadet officer program, a police academy simulation for U.P. high school students interested in law enforcement careers.

Department chairs or heads: Ken Fauth, 1977–1981; Richard Johnson, 1981, one month; Robert Barrington, 1981–1987; Donald Lee, (acting) 1987–1989, 1989–1991; David Kalinich, 1992–1997; Paul Lang, 1997–present.

(*Bulletins*; Matthew Krok, "Department of Criminal Justice" UA; *The 1996–97 University Profile*, 1:186–192) Michelle Kangas

Cuban Crisis: The crisis was based on the fact that the Soviet Union had been building missile and bomber bases in Cuba. The crisis lasted between October 22 and November 2, 1962. The crisis had a temporary impact on classes taught at Sawyer Air Force Base. At the height of the crisis, when Robert Bordeau went to the Base to teach a political science class, he was escorted to the Base classroom and found that all of his students were gone. They had been repositioned to bases in the South. Students who were mobilized during the crisis were refunded their tuition.

Cuban Refugees: In 1963, the Catholic church under the direction of Msgr. David Spelgatti brought 25 Cuban children refugees to Marquette. They were both high school and college age and were housed in the Holy Family Orphanage. On October 30, 1963, the Gries Hall Association held a dinner for them. Afterwards there was a speech and questions and answers which made Northern students aware of Cuban issues. (NN 10/24/1963)

Cusino Station: *See*: Field Station

Dallas Cowboys: Through the efforts of President Harden, Northern's campus was the site of summer training for the Dallas Cowboys. Between July 13 and August 24, 1962 the team quietly practiced in Marquette, attracted by the facilities and the climate. A special training field was located in the vicinity of Russell Thomas Fine Arts Building. The coach was Tom Landry who was building this expansion team from scratch. Two of his more famous players were Don Meredith and Bob Lilly. Meredith was on the Monday night Football telecast for several years, along with Howard Cosell. Lilly was just starting out and became one of the all-time greats at defensive tackle. (NN 07/24/1962; Hilton, p. 191)

The Dark Tower: *See*: *The Thaw*

Dean of Students, Office of: Soon after NMU opened in 1899, it was seen that an individual was needed to regulate the behavior of the students. This was true of women living in the dormitory. Sophie Linton supervised the girls in the dorm and taught classes. From the beginning, the State Board of Education was concerned about the morals of the students in all normal schools under its control. Future teachers could not be "guilty of ungentlemanly or unladylike conduct." It was the purpose of the school "to constantly lead the students to higher and better ideals of character and public service." Those found unfit were requested to leave. These regulations can be found in all of the *Bulletins* from 1908 to 1939, when they were slightly altered.

The official deanship dates back to 1904 when Northern hired a history instructor and a "preceptress." Catherine E. Maxwell was appointed to fill the position which she held until her death in 1918. Lilian Swan was

Maxwell's successor who supervised the girls in the dorm and taught classes. She was known for entertaining students at her camp at Middle Island Point in the summer, her storytelling ability and sense of humor.

In 1923, President Munson invited Ethel Carey, who had previously held a similar position at Central State Normal School (now Central Michigan University) to join the Northern staff beginning on January 1, 1924. Carey was known for the enforcement of the many rules and regulations set by the Board. She was also known for promoting a high level of social life. Female students were warned not to wear the color red, short skirts or tight sweaters, for example. Dancing was highly regulated with Dean Carey and faculty acting as pro-active chaperons. Over the years, Carey promoted the construction of a dormitory which she saw completed in 1948 and dedicated to her a year later. She held the position until her retirement 1956. For a short time, Anne Thompson was the Dean of Women.

The position of Dean of Men developed later. Harry D. Lee was superintendent of the John D. Pierce Lab School and served as the first dean (1922–1940). He saw to it that the men maintained high moral standards. Periodically, he would assemble the men in the gym for a session of "fatherly" advice, ranging from table manners to getting along with custodians in the field. Lee also watched over the teachers at the college.

The second Dean of Men was Don H. Bottum, who came to Northern in 1923. He served as dean from 1941 to his retirement in 1957. Bottum was known to have dismissed a student for excessive use of alcohol.

In 1957, the offices of Dean of Men and Women were combined as the Dean of Students, with Bottum as the first dean. The former tight hold on student social conduct was loosening. The office functions of withdrawing students from school, verifying class absences and handling veterans affairs continued.

During the decades of the 1950s and 1960s, attitudes definitely changed. Women successfully protested the requirement to keep special hours, and regulations on the use of alcohol on campus were loosened. In 1969, Dean Norman Hefke played a large role in the development of the *Student Code*. It set forth the rules and regulations for the first time in print and also outlined procedures of due process, where students would be tried by their peers. In 1994, a revised code was approved by the Board of Control and published.

In 1970, the Office of the Dean of Students was formally assigned responsibility for student conduct, assistance to student governing programs and personnel, student leadership training, student organization advisement, student development programs, handbooks, identification cards and withdrawals from school.

By the 1990s, the main function of the office was to provide general assistance to all students. Staffed by highly trained professionals and paraprofessional students, the office is known as a "clearing house for all student concerns, questions, and problems." The office offers detailed assistance in specific areas and offers a wide variety of special opportunities. Some of the services and programs offered by the office include the Dean's List, withdrawals from the university, coordination of the Student Activities and Leadership Programs, Commuter Student Services (*See separate entry*), child care information, and freshman studies counseling, to name a few. Other offices that work under and in close contact with the Dean's office are: Educational Development Services, Academic Advising, Student Supportive Services, and Diversity Student Services.

Dean of Women: Sophie Linton, (unofficial) 1900–1904; Catherine E. Maxwell, 1904–1918; Lillian E. Swan, 1918–1920; Gladys L. Gray, (acting) 1920–1922; Lydia Olson, (acting) 1922–1923; Ethel Carey, 1924–1935; Irene Morris, (acting) 1935-1936; Carey, 1936–1956; Anne G. Thompson, 1956–1957; *Dean of Men*: Harry D. Lee, 1922–1940; Don H. Bottum, 1941–1957; *Dean of Students*: Don H. Bottum, 1957–1959; Wilbur West, 1959–1960; Dr. Allen Niemi, 1960–1968; Dr. Lowell Kafer, 1968–1979; Dr. Norman Hefke, 1979–1984; Dr. Karen Reese, 1984–1987; Dr. Alexandra Michaels, 1987–present. (Amy Henderson. "History of the Office of the Dean of Students," (1995), UA; *The 1996–97 University Profile*, 2:125–130).

Debate: *See: Forensics*

Dedication Dates of Buildings:

Namesake	Date	Facility
Don H. Bottum	09/10/1966	D. H. Bottum University Center
	09/23/1994	Renovated and re-dedicated
Ethel G. Carey	06/18/1949	Carey Hall
Sam Cohodas	05/22/1976	Cohodas Admin. Center
Luther O. Gant	11/22/1964	Gant Residence Hall
Walter Gries	10/13/1961	Gries Hall
Lynn H. Halverson	10/03/1965	Halverson Res. Hall
Edgar L. Harden	08/11/1973	Harden Learning Resource Center
Elizabeth C. Harden	10/04/1975	Circle Drive
C. B. Hedgcock	12/06/1958	Hedgcock Fieldhouse
Lucian F. Hunt	06/09/1968	Hunt Residence Hall
Dominic Jacobetti	05/02/1981	Jacobetti Center
John X. Jamrich	12/19/1975	Jamrich Hall
James B.H. Kaye	06/18/1949	Kaye Hall
James B.H. Kaye	11/15/1979	Kaye House
Harry D. Lee	06/18/1949	Lee Hall
Mildred Magers	10/16/1966	Magers Hall
Wayne B. McClintock	04/25/1965	McClintock Industrial Arts Building
John & Marge McGoff	08/08/1980	McGoff Carillon Towers
Gunther Meyland	10/16/1966	Meyland Hall
C. V. "Red" Money	09/12/1998	Stadium in Superior Dome
Lydia M. Olson	10/19/1951	Olson Library (Demolished)
Lydia M. Olson	08/08/1975	Re-dedicated as Lydia M. Olson Library (LRC)
Lucille M. Payne	10/03/1965	Payne Residence Hall
John D. Pierce	05/25/1927	J.D. Pierce Lab/School (Demolished)
Max & Phyllis Reynolds	10/01/1977	Meditation Room (UC)
Harvey G. Ripley	06/27/1975	Ripley Heating Plant
Forest Roberts	05/31/1969	Forest Roberts Theatre
Grace A. Spalding	11/22/1964	Spalding Residence Hall
Charles C. Spooner	06/13/1965	Spooner Residence Hall
Russell Thomas	10/10/1965	Thomas Fine Arts Bldg
Maude Van Antwerp	06/09/1968	Van Antwerp Res. Hall
William & Margery Vandament	11/09/1997	PEIF, Vandament Volleyball Arena
Ada B. Vielmetti	10/16/1976	Vielmetti Health Center
Luther S. West	08/20/1966	West Science Building
Wilbur D. West	10/02/1960	West Residence Hall
Peter White	12/08/1995	Peter White Lounge (UC)
Rico N. Zenti	09/26/1998	PEIF, Instructional Wing

Degree Programs: The Bachelor of Arts Degree Program started in 1918, followed by the Bachelor of Science, which was established in 1926. Although a Master's Degree was initiated in 1938, in conjunction with the University of Michigan, it was not until 1960 that it became independent. *See: Graduate Studies, College of* and *Graduate Programs.*

Demonstrations, Student: The rise of student demonstrations on NMU's campus began in the late 1960s, but it was less frequent and violent than on other campuses. The reasons are varied according to different opinions. Some said many professors were committed to their work and life in the community and did not take active radical positions. Others noted that the students, most of whom come from the Upper Peninsula, had been socialized not to get involved in major conflicts with authority groups. Part of the reason, others said, laid in the fact that conflict in the past was unsuccessful and also protest or conflict could mean the loss of a job. There was also the role of religion. Furthermore, there were always few minority students who might be concerned with change. In 1970, out of 7,800 students, 161 were African Americans or 2.24%. Twenty-five years later, out of 7,442 students, there were: 136 Native Americans, 87 African Americans, 37 Asian, and 31 Hispanic.

The first student protest took place on April 1, 1965 when President Harden abruptly resigned his office over a conflict with a member of the Board of Control over his right-to-try philosophy. Over 2,500 students and faculty appeared at the President's home with signs of support. Eventually, this student support got President Harden to withdraw his resignation.

In 1967, the McClellan controversy (*See separate entry*) developed. It basically involved the termination of history professor Dr. Robert McClellan over his academic freedom. Students marched, boycotted classes and protested, demanding that McClellan be reinstated. Eventually the faculty and students sued the Board of Control. The matter was eventually settled out of court.

The assassination of Dr. Martin Luther King, Jr. in April 1968 led to serious unrest throughout the country. Violence was not the response at Northern. Between 350–400 students held a peace vigil in Dr. King's memory. The following night 230–300 students from the Campus Christian Ministry and Alpha Phi Alpha marched in a candlelight procession from the campus down North Third Street and back.

The Jobs Corps came to campus in 1966, the only one in the country on a university campus, and involved numerous African American students. Some 400 students at Northern protested its closing in April 1969. A large group of students boycotted and held a sit-in against history professor, Dr. Richard O'Dell.

The Vietnam War caused years of intense protest throughout the United States. However, early in the war years, Northern students took a pro-government approach to the war. In November 1965 some 200 students marched through Marquette supporting the war. A few months later, Chi Sigma Nu fraternity erected a veterans memorial on campus.

One of the early antiwar protests took place against the presence of the Military Science Department being on campus in early 1967. During the Vietnam Moratorium on October 15, 1969, protests took place on campus which included a flag burning incident. The National Guard shootings at Kent State University on May 4, 1970 and shootings at Jackson State University in Mississippi had a reaction on campus. African American students were challenged, and for a number of days there was unrest on campus. Throughout the war, speeches and protest marches were held on campus. In April 1972 a radio marathon on WBXX was held on a strike over the bombing of Hanoi.

Although African Americans were a minority in the student body, they actively and militantly protested. A sit-in occurred on December 17, 1969, when some seventy Black students seized the dean of students office and held it for nineteen hours. During the demonstration, Vice President for Student Affairs Dr. Allan Niemi was threatened and held captive for 30 minutes and President Jamrich was refused entry. The office was ransacked and damages amounted to $395. This happened after the All-University Student Judiciary voted to suspend Charles Griffis, a Grand Rapids senior, for two semesters. Griffis had been accused of having a woman in his Spooner Hall room, in violation of University regulations. During the occupation, Griffis was acquitted after an appeal to the University Student-Faculty Judiciary.

After the event, the University and the Marquette city police investigated the incident. By early January 1970, the University was considering charges against 24 Black students and the Black Student Association. On February 10–11, 1970, the Student-Faculty Judiciary acquitted five Black students (Joe Davis, Linda J. Martin, Michael Gains, Gary Bolden, and Jesse Allen). There were others acquitted, and finally

President Jamrich in consultation with staff and faculty recommended the dismissal of the remaining charges against the five students.

Since the end of the Vietnam War, protests on campus have been few in number. In 1996 students marched on Cohodas over a new fee structure and the matter was discussed with President Vandament. When students were upset over a faculty member striking a student, a march was held by a small number of student on Cohodas and a community forum defusing the situation was called by President William Vandament to publicly discuss the matter. (MJ 05/25/1966, 01/27/1967; NW 11/05/1965, 02/28/1967; MJ 04/05, 06, 10/1968; NN 10/24/1969, 01/09/1970, 02/06/1970, 02/13/1970, 02/20/1970, 04/24/1970, 04/21/1972)

Departments, Original: On July 14, 1899, the State Board of Education created the following faculty positions which can be viewed as the earliest departments: Art and Design, Education, English, Geography, History, Mathematics, Political Science and the Sciences.

Depression: The Great Depression of the 1930s began with the stock market crash in October 1929. The effects slowly spread across the nation and eventually were felt by the Northern community. In the Upper Peninsula, the mines (the producers of taxes) were closed or operated intermittently. As a result, the counties lost revenue and suffered.

In April of 1933, President Munson returned from Lansing fearful that the legislature would cut Northern's budget from $238,000 down to $128,000 even after operating expenses had been made. At the time, $212,000 was used to pay salaries. By 1932–1933, faculty salaries were cut by 15 percent and were further reduced by the legislature by one-third. Northern escaped the "necessary curtailments" which saw faculty let go at sister institutions. There was even talk of closing two state teacher's colleges because of the overabundance of teachers on the market. In March 1935, the State Board of Education requested "that the $1,506 unencumbered in the Personal Service Account be spread on the salaries of the personnel during the months of March, April, May and June."

The WPA (Works Progress Administration) would have contributed 45% of the cost of a girls' dormitory if 100 girls promised to live there for $3.00 a week. There were neither enough girls nor funds available and the option lapsed.

In 1934, each teachers college was allowed to give two scholarships awarded on the basis of need. Three years later, ten students at Northern used State Department of Public Instruction scholarships to earn rural school teaching certificates. Students were also assisted by the growing loan funds on campus from which they could borrow.

Federal funds available to Northern through the Federal Employment Recovery Act and the National Youth Administration program paid students 30¢ an hour for cleaning, painting, repairing, and doing research. During these years, using federal funds, Lew Allen Chase (History) supervised the indexing of the *Mining Journal* at the Marquette County Historical Society. By careful distribution of the monthly $960 allotment, L.O.Gant arranged for 86 of Northern's 354 students to receive some federal aid in 1935. Many high school graduates enrolled in local freshman courses, where unemployed teachers, approved by Northern, taught college classes. In 1938, the editor of the *Northern College News* wrote that there were many students benefitting from the NYA and some 40 others were employed by Northern. The coming of World War II brought an end to Depression conditions. (NCN 04/18/1933; MJ 01/28/1935, 11/11/1935; NCN 06/15/1938)

Development Fund: A Michigan non-profit organization organized on March 19, 1968 with IRS Section (501c(3) standing and is the fund raising/endowment entity for the University.

According to its mission, it plans and implements an annual fund campaign to generate undesignated monies for Northern to be utilized as directed by the NMU Development Fund Board of Trustees. It also provides fundraising implementation services to constituents on campus through telemarketing, direct mail, personal solicitation, training and advice. Scholarships are developed and maintained as funded through private sources. As of December 31, 1997, the fund had assets of $9,161-,561.

Components of the Development Fund include: 1) The Edgar L. Harden Century Club (donation of $100,000 cash or securities or pledges of $10,000 a year for 10 years, or have given $200,000 in planned or deferred gifts, including Charitable Remainder Trusts, Life Insurance, Wills, or Living Trusts); 2) The Kaye Society (minimum contribution for membership is $20,000 over a ten-year period; 3) The Presidents Club ($5,000 or more); 4) The Waldo Society (alumni joined at $500 level); 5) The Superior Society ($250 gift); 6) The First Nighters Club (theatre); 7) Friends of NMU Art Museum Club; 8) The Blue Line Club (hockey); 9) The Golden Wildcat Club (all intercollegiate sports); 10) The Gridiron Club (football); 11) The Alumni "N" Club (former student-athletes, $50 membership); 12) Locker Room Projects; 13) The Great Lakes Training Center Association.

The Fund supported the following programs in 1997: Student Leadership Fellowship Program (*See separate entry*), Student Travel Grants, Faculty Travel Grants, and the Washington Internship Program.

Originally, the Fund was under the Vice President for University Advancement and was officially called Institutional Development. When this Division was eliminated in mid-1995, the fund was relocated under the University Relations and Development Division. In April, 1998, LoriLee Rebhan was named Executive Director of Development at Northern. She is responsible for planning and execution of capital campaigns, and annual giving programs, corporate and foundation relations, major gifts, and planned giving. Since the mid-1990s, the annual report of the Fund is published under the title, Premier.

Directors of Development: R.Thomas Peters, 1969–1977; Joseph Skehan,1977–1986; Bruce Anderson(VP for University Advancement/ Director of Development) 1987–1997; LoriLee Rebhan, 1998–present. (*The 1996–97 University Profile*, 2:216–221; AS 04/15/1998)

Discovery Daze: A program started in the fall of 1998, which provides the Northern campus with positive healthy activities that expand the mind and heighten awareness of what can be done in the Marquette area. It is based on the Free University (*See separate entry*) concept of the late 1970s. Some of the 25 activities included aquatic fitness, bass fishing, historical walk of campus, massage therapy, sea kayaking, model aviation and song writing. The program is under the guidance of Student Activities and Leadership Programs.

Discipline: *In loco parentis* is a Latin term meaning "in place of a parent." It was a long-held doctrine that an educational institution can and should act in place of the parent. Since 1900, the State Board of Education and the Northern administration and faculty were concerned about discipline and morality among students. These were teachers who were going out into the world and would be role models. Over the years there were written and unwritten rules and regulations which the institution enforced on students. There could be little argument with many of the rules, but others were intrusive: regulating the distance between dancing couples and the type and color of clothes to be worn were just a few. Most of the regulations were directed toward female students.

By the 1960s the concept of "in loco parentis" began to be modified in some schools and rejected in others. At Northern, Dean of Students Allen Niemi lamented the demise of this concept. Historically, most of the intrusive "in place of the parent" rules and regulations were eliminated.

Today the Dean of Students office monitors and regulates student conduct guided by the published *Student Code of Conduct* (*See separate entry*).(NN 06/03/1959, 02/09/1968, 02/27/1970;Magnaghi, "Student Discipline at Northern," (1999), UA)

Distance Learning: Over the years, Northern has had television courses transmitted across the Upper Peninsula and to Lower Michigan. The early programs were not interactive and faculty went on site several times a semester and held classes.

Beginning in 1992 a new Distance Learning initiative was established. Special classrooms that allow interactive class experiences were established across the campus. Today there are such classrooms in the Harden Learning Resources Center, Jamrich Hall, the Superior Dome and the Jacobetti Center. In the contract (1997–2000) between NMU and the AAUP, special funds were set aside for faculty to develop distance learning courses.

This system has also been used to interview prospective faculty members. Beginning in the winter of 1996 with 13 interviews, the process increased to over 40 by the spring of 1998. On August 25, 1998 a special hook-up linked Northern with the University of Natal for a conference.

Distinguished Alumni Award: The Award was established in June 1964 to honor alumni who are outstanding in their professions and have made significant contributions to society and/or professions. Other requirements include demonstrated leadership and/or honors received that clearly set them apart from their peers. The intention is to honor a person who is distinguished by her/his achievements.

Recipients: Carl R. Anderson (6-68); Robert R. Archibald (12-98); Thomas L. Baldini (12-90); Dr. John Beaumier (12-88); Matthew C. Bennett (6-67); John W. Berry, Jr. (12-98); Elizabeth E. Binda (8-80); Robert M. Bordeau (10-87); Jeanette S. Bowden (8-71); Mr. and Mrs. Roy Brigman (8-810; Dennis Callahan (12-97); Gustav G. Carlson (8-81); J. Walter Carlson (8-85); Charles C. Carpenter (6-72); George R. Cavender (8-82); Pak-Wing Steve Chum (12-96); Rodney D. Coe (8-78); Margaret A. Coughlin (12-98); Joseph L. DeCook (5-74); Priscilla Densmore (6-66); Carl A. Erickson (6-69); Kenneth R. Erfft (8-79); Irene M. Finnegan (6-70); Richard J. Finnegan (8-77); John C. Fleming (12-94); Olive G. Fox (6-64); Ruben Franco (12-92); T. Dennis George (12-96); Gerald M. Glanville (12-91); Ira L. Griffin (8-85); David Hart (12-93); Frank Hartman (6-71); Edward F. Havlik (8-83); David S. Haynes (12-88); Janet A. Haynes (12-98); W. Lawrence Hebbard (6-68); Henry S. Heimonen (6-70); Jerry J. Herman (8-74); Francis Hetherington (6-71); Michael P. Hocking (12-93); Melvin G. Holli (8-85); Scott Holman (12-89); William K. Jensen (5-76); Aili I. Johnson (12-74); Milton A. Johnson (8-74); Hugo E. Kilpela (6-71); Thomas Klei (12-90); Stephen Klinker (12-91); Thomas L. Knauss (8-84); Clyde F. Kohn (6-72); George E. Koskimaki (4-80); Edward H. Kukuk (8-77); Norman E. Kukuk (5-74); Dale M. Larson (12-94); Harriet T. Latimer (5-76); John E. Lautner, Jr. (5-75); Patricia A. Lewis (8-80); Grant U. MacKenzie (6-64); Lowe S. MacLean (8-86); Charles T. Mangrum (8-86); Ellwood A. Mattson (6-69); Malcolm McNeill (12-89); Keith E. Molin (6-73); Carl A. Moyer (6-66); Mary Nash (12-93); William H. Nault (8—78); Bruce K. Nelson (6-73); D. Neil Nystrom (8-79); John R. Ogren (8-86); Edwin B. Olds (6-69); Edward L. Pearce (6-66); Claudius G. Pendill (11-84); R. Thomas Peters, Jr. (5-75); Patti L. Peterson (12-95); Edwin C. Peterson (8-81); Roy Peterson (12-90); Earl O. Phillips (5-76); Leonard F. Picotte (12-92); Clifford E. Puckett (8-82); Harry A. Rajala (8-82); Taimi M. Ranta (6-67); Hamilton Robichaud (6-67); Wilbur H. Schenk (12-80); Dorothea J. Schlechte (5-75); Howard Schultz (5-98); Gordon H. Seger (6-65); Larry J. Sell (12-97); Roland S. Strolle (6-70); Cornelius J. Sullivan (6-72); Paul Suomi (12-87); James A. Surrell (12-96); Louis F. Taccolini (12-79); Dale R. Tahtinen (8-79); Rollin K. E. Thoren (5-74); Roger Budd Tompkins (8-84); Albert I. Treado (8-77); W. H. Treloar (6-65); Sylvester W. Trythall (6-65); Edmund F. Vandette (6-73); Dan B. Walsworth (6-64); Jean K. Weston (6-68); Kathleen E. Weston (8-83); David Williams, II (12-98); James Wills (12-89); Rico N. Zenti (6-66); Gilbert L. Ziegler (8-83).

Distinguished Citizenship, President's Award for: The award was created in 1974 for NMU's 75th anniversary to honor Upper Peninsula residents with outstanding citizenship qualities, who have provided unselfish support of civic, social or cultural activities. It is presented to recipients at a special dinner held in the fall.

Recipients: Busharat Ahmad (8-87); Elinor Benedict (10-91); Samuel S. Benedict (12-85); Roy T. Bergman (8-87); Guido J. Bonetti (5-75); Douglas R. Bovin (10-95); David R. Boyd (10-90); Burton H. Boyum (8-80); Raymond J. Buchkoe (7-75); Ruth G. Butler (8-78); Rev. Louis Cappo (8-81); Willard M. Carne (10-90); Moses Cooperstock 8-87); Herbert W. Corey (8-79); Geraldine DeFant (7-92); Harold H. Derusha (12-80); Nancy A. Douglas (7-88); Donald R. Elzinga (5-76); Frieda Engblom (4-77); Paddy Fitch (4-83); Lincoln B. Frazier (5-76); Albert J. Gazvoda (5-75; Marian Gibson (12-74); Margaret C. Goldthorpe (10-95); William Gregory (10-91); Peter C. Grieves (12-92); Elsie Guimond (12-74); Fred H. Hahne (5-74); Norma J. Harger (8-86); Perry Hatch (12-74); Jayne Hiebel (4-77); Ralph J. Jalkanen (10-90); William K. Jensen (8-82); Margaret Johnson (7-74); Rev. D. C. Kalweit (7-74); Robert V. Langseth (10-93); Harlan J. Larson ((12-81); John L. Lehtinen (10-96); John A. Lemmer (8-79); Robert Ling (4-83); Waino A. Liuha (10-96); Malcolm McNeil (5-75); Ellwood A. Mattson (7-75); Wesley H. Maurer, Sr. (10-94); Daniel S. Mazzuchi (7-92); Patricia L. Micklow (10-95); Benjamin J. Myler (7-75); Wesley W. Myllyla (5-81); Robert Neldberg (10-91); Barbara Nemacheck (10-93); Geraldine Noyes (5-75); Helmi Osterberg (12-74); Carl V. Pellonpaa (10-96); Ann Pratt (5-74); Maxwell and Phyllis Reynolds (12-82); Moira D. Reynolds (8-79); Clifton F. Rogers (8-84); Ernest Ronn (12-74); Kenneth D. Seaton (7-89); Raymond L. Smith (5-75); Earl St. John, Jr. (8-87); Lois G. Tucker (10-94); John A. Vargo (10-93); William Veeser (5-74); June Waisanen (7-89); Merle E. Wehner (4-77); Jean Worth (5-75). (Source: University Relations Office)

Distinguished Faculty Award: It was the wish of the President and the Board of Control "to recognize and honor full-time teaching faculty, including academic department heads, who have made a significant professional contribution(s) to Northern Michigan University and to their professional area." The monetary award is $1000 net after taxes to each recipient. Up to three faculty members are selected, and are typically senior faculty. Faculty who have previously received this award are also eligible for consideration, based upon the record of achievement since the time of nomination for their last award. The screening committee is composed of the academic deans and the Vice President for Academic Affairs. The Committee bases its decision on the faculty member's record of significant contributions to his/her professional discipline in all three of the following: 1) teaching or other assigned responsibilities; 2) research, scholarship, creative or other appropriate professional activities; and 3) university or professionally-related community service. The Awards are usually announced and presented at Spring Commencement. The office of the Vice President for Academic Affairs administers this Award.

Recipients: Roger B. Barry (5-85); Ramachandran Bharath (4-90); Sandra Lee Briggs (12-79); George R. Carnahan (5-86); Sara L. Doubledee (4-90); Fillmore C. Earney (12-81); Lon L. Emerick (12-81); J. Patrick Farrell (4-89); John Frey (4-90); James L. Godell (4-83); David Goldsmith (4-94); Richard K. Gorski (12-82); Thomas Griffith (12-83); Harry Guenther (5-93); Robert N. Hanson (5-87); Leonard G. Heldreth (5-87); Roberta M. Henderson (4-88); Earl R. Hilton (12-79); Lois A. Hirst (4-96); John Hubbard (4-84); Gene D. L. Jones (4-89); Alfred N. Joyal (4-88); Sylvia Kinnunen (12-80); Diane D. Kordich (4-95); Kurt Kynell (5-93); Philip Legler (4-84); Charles Leith (5-92); Russell M. Magnaghi (4-96); Fred Margrif (5-91); Robert McGinty (5-91); Mohey Mowafy (5-85); James Panowski (4-94); Katherine Payant (4-94); Arthur E. Pennell (12-81); Steve A. Platt (12-79); James L. Rapport (4-83); John Renfrew (12-82); D. Sue Rigby (4-84); William H. Rigby (5-86); William L. Robinson (12-80); Jon L. Saari (5-85); Bruce C. Sherony (4-88); Thomas J. Sullivan (5-87); Zacharias P. Thundy (4-89); John VandeZande (5-91); Phillip Watts (5-92); J. Kirwin Werner (5-86); Marvin Zehnder (5-93). (University Relations Office)

Diversity Student Services: The unit had its origins back in the early 1970s with Black Student Services. Over the years there were employees in this area in the Dean of Students office. It eventually evolved into Multicultural Student Services and Multicultural Affairs. In May 1998 it was renamed Diversity Student Services. The office is focused on student concerns and working with NMU's various ethnic components. Workshops are held to improve cultural sensitivity of students and others. Director: Pamela Motoike, 1998-present.

Dogs: Prior to an ordinance passed in December 1971, students brought their dogs to campus and left them, summer or winter, at the doors to class buildings and the Olson Library. There was little concern for the icy conditions and the unprotected paws of the animals. After several years of discussions, Northern's Board of Control passed a new regulation on pets on August 3, 1984. Today cats and dogs are not allowed in University buildings except under special circumstances (such as leader dogs) and must be leashed on campus.

Dome-Mania: Superior Dome director Ken Godfrey said the event was created by adding summer fair activities to the basketball event, Superior Slam Three-On-Three Basketball Tournament. The all-day event was held on February 11, 1995. It included family picnic games, summer carnival games, an arts and crafts fair, basketball, live music and catered food. Between 6,000 and 8,000 people were estimated in attendance. The event was sponsored by NMU and local businesses.

Domestic Arts and Science Department: *See: Consumer and Family Studies, Department of*

Domino's Pizza: *See: Franchise*

Dormitory: Financed by John Longyear and Frederick Ayer, this four-story private structure, called The Dormitory was located on the corner of Hebard Court and Kaye Avenue. Construction began in early April 1900. C.C. Van Iderstine signed a contract to provide a rush job on the construction and have it ready for occupancy by June 15. Work on the structure progressed at a fast pace. The first floor consisted of the dining room, kitchen, pantry, and steward's quarters. Leading off the east entrance were wardrooms for both men and women, and a reception room along with a few dorm rooms. The second and third floors were given over to "sleeping apartments." Some additional rooms could be created in the garret. The structure could accommodate 100 students in sleeping quarters and double that number for board. Edward Quarters and his wife were the first stewards for the dormitory and had an apartment in it. For a number of years, it served as home to Principal Waldo and his family.

During these years, the structure fell into disrepair. By 1918, it was sold by Longyear and Ayer to the Catholic Diocese of Marquette. In 1918-1919 members of the Student Army Training Corp were housed there.

During the 1920s, it was used to house Catholic nuns who attended to summer school at Northern. Then, the building was abandoned for many years. In 1943, the Catholic diocese created St. Michael's parish. The top two floors were removed, having suffered water damage. The bottom two floors were used as a school, convent and church. This use continued until the school and church were completed. The building was demolished in late April 1963. (MJ 04/10/1900)

Doxiades Plan: Constantinos A. Doxiades (1913–1975) was a world renowned Greek architect. He was regarded as a visionary city planner whose concepts touched the lives of millions of people. He sought to make the city into a civilized habitat.

During the early to mid-1960s, Northern's enrollment greatly expanded and there was talk of a campus with possibly as many as 20,000 students and even doctorate programs. In order to realize this, a plan was created by Doxiades Associates and announced in October 1966. The Plan emphasized the proximity of the campus to the water. "To the Sea" became the theme. The basic idea was that learning resources and administrative buildings would be concentrated on lands already owned by the University. Housing facilities would be expanded into North Marquette on land which the study called "a low-density area of sporadic residences." The people living in the area bound by Presque Isle, Wright, Waldo Center, and Tracy streets were naturally worried about the encroachment of the University.

The city of Marquette was also concerned about the implementation of the Doxiades Plan. Meetings were held between NMU administration and members of the City Commission. Minor details were worked out. A minority on the City Commission went so far as to attempt to get the city to appropriate funds to retain an attorney for the homeowners to stop the University expansion. Robert Bordeau, city attorney at the time, had to advise the Commission of the illegality of such an action. In response to citizen concerns in December 1966, an organization of North Marquette residents, "Citizens for Marquette," was formed. Its steering committee, which included faculty member Dr. Robert McClellan, met with University officials and was promised all possible consideration.

In an attempt to alleviate the hostile situation, a group of community leaders, including Ellwood Mattson, organized a non-profit corporation to acquire land north of Wright Street to provide locations for homes that were moved at little or no cost to the residents. Only a few of the houses were moved onto these lots.

By August 1967, Northern had purchased 23 of 181 lots needed for the first stage of its expansion program and the first houses were moved out of the area. Most of these houses were located in the vicinity of Tracy and Wilkinson Streets. Unfortunately, the involvement of Professor McClellan in this protest caused President Harden to fire him and this action was backed by the Board of Control. This led to the McClellan controversy (*See separate entry*). Due to the controversy, the retirement of President Harden, and changes in funding, the Doxiades Plan was shelved and the vacant lots in North Marquette remain today. Most of the land north of Wright Street ultimately became part of the City's low-cost housing project. This was a very tense time between the City and the University. (Hilton, pp. 162–163; MJ 09/12/1966, 10/20/1966; *Horizons* 06/1966)

Earth Day: Earth Day was first celebrated in 1970 and evolved from the work of Senator Gaylord Nelson of Wisconsin. The day is celebrated on campus during April. (NW 04/21/1994)

Eateries on Campus: *See: Food Service*

Ecology: *See: Campus, Evolution of the*

Economic Impact: In 1899, Northern had a small economic impact on Marquette and the Upper Peninsula, but this changed over the century. Between 1997 and 1998, Dr. Harry P. Guenther, director of Northern's Bureau of Business and Economic Research, conducted a study on the economic impact of Northern Michigan University on the community. NMU, its students, university-generated visitors to the region and affiliated organizations spent nearly $148 million during the year analyzed by the study. Using appropriate regional multipliers provided by the U.S. Department of Commerce, this spending translates to a total economic impact of $239 million.

In a talk to the Marquette County Economics Club in January 1999, President Judi Bailey noted that nearly 2,600 of the 5,800 students living off-campus during the last school year reported home addresses outside the Upper Peninsula. By themselves, these non-U.P. students spent more than $13 million on room and board, along with goods and services from area businesses. Estimated expenditures by NMU-generated visitors to the Upper Peninsula totaled $3.4 million. This covers lodging, food and miscellaneous spending. By conservative estimates Northern provides 5,900 jobs and $239 million in economic revenue. (*Impacting the Upper Peninsula: A Summary of the Economic Impact of Northern Michigan University* (1999) Kristi Evans

Economics, Department of: The Economics Department offers courses for Economics majors and minors as well as courses supporting other majors, general electives, and liberal studies. The first Economics class was offered in the Fall of 1918 and was taught by John E. Lautner. He also taught Languages, Economics and Sociology at Northern for 36 years. Until 1963, Economics was a subject taught in the History or Social Science departments. In 1963, Economics and Sociology shared a department. Three years later, the departments became separate. Three economics alumni at the time, Arnie Aho, Neil Carlson, and Tom Holmstrom went on to teach in the department until their retirement in 1996–1997.

Two-thirds of Economic sections (EC 101, 201, and 202) and approximately 95% of its total student credit hours are devoted to service courses. The department provides a major and minor in Economics for students who desire a liberal arts degree for work or entry into graduate or professional schools. It also trains teachers of economics and social studies in grades K–12. Through the Economic Education Center, teachers are assisted in workshops and in-service programs.

Department chairs and heads: Jean Pearman, 1963–1964; Kenneth Parkhurst, (acting) 1964–1965; Neil Carlson, (acting) 1965–1966; Phillip May, 1966–1970; Howard Swaine, 1970–1997; David Prychitko, (acting) 1997–present. (*Bulletins*; Francis Copper manuscript; *The 1996–97 University Profile*, 1:98–95) Michelle Kangas

Edgar L. Harden Learning Resources Center: The concept of a structure housing a library and associated information services was first developed by President Harden. He fought to have the necessary appropriation passed when the University of Michigan tried to out-maneuver him and have the first learning resources center in the state.

Ground breaking took place on June 14, 1967. The building was completed in February 1969, and opened for use in the Fall. Construction cost $5.5 million. The top two floors of the center house the Lydia M. Olson Library, which has a 300,000 book capacity. When it originally opened, the first floor housed 220 faculty offices. Although they were to be temporary and lacked privacy, they continued to be fully occupied until September 1989. President Appleberry was instrumental in relocating some of the offices to Magers Hall. The office space continued to be used by faculty as departments moved to Gries Hall (1995) and the last department, Communications and Performance Studies (CAPS) moved to the Russell Thomas Fine Arts Building in the summer of 1996.

This former office space went through a reuse in the summer of 1996. Offices for WMNU-FM are located there, along with the University Archives, Academic Computing (offices, classes, and lab), Bookbinders Snack Shop and other offices and meeting rooms.

The lower level houses the offices and studios and WNMU-FM and WNMU-TV. Audio visual and other offices and repair areas are located here as well.

The Center was dedicated to former President Harden on August 11, 1973. A memorial plaque honoring President Harden was set into the building in April 1997. (NN 06/30/1967; 03/28/1969)

Education, Department of: Northern was one of four normal (*See separate entry*) or teachers' training schools in the state: Eastern (1849), Central (1892), and Western (1904) created by the state legislature. Northern State Normal School began in 1899 with the principle mission of training new and continuing teachers primarily for positions in the Upper Peninsula. Properly educated teachers were in severe demand throughout the region. Without certification, county boards gave tests to prospective teachers and then hired them. Due to this mission, the development of teacher education and the Department of Education was and is integral to the development of the University.

It should be remembered that between 1899 and 1963 Northern was controlled by the State Board of Education. Only teacher certificates were given to two-year graduates until 1918, when the bachelor of arts degree was authorized.

The Department of Pedagogy and Psychology, as it was then called, was created by the State Board of Education on July 14, 1899. The first instructor, Lewis F. Anderson, was hired at $1,200 annually.

The history of the Education Department is anchored in the requirements set by the state legislature and the State Board of Education. In July 1900 the state authorized limited or three-year certificates. In September the curriculum was expanded and two-year courses could lead to life certificates in both general and specialized fields. However there were contradictory problems on the state level that resulted in Northern not giving life certificates until June 18, 1902.

Northern offered varied programs for its student teachers. In September 1900 the training school was opened in rented property on North Third Street and later it returned to campus. Summer school, which has been a feature since 1900, was always well attended with teachers returning to improve their qualifications. It was a highly developed program, with visiting educators, and fit the needs of the students. There were concerns that teachers be trained to help immigrant children adjust to American life. Courses were offered in the field of psychology or mental hygiene and statistics. Even former Principal Kaye taught Philosophy and Ethnics for many years after his retirement. In 1916 a new course, Educational Administration, was first offered for principals and superintendents. With all of these new services and programs developed by Northern, a study made in 1922 showed that conditions in rural schools had improved, and many high schools in the Upper Peninsula were offering vocational training.

In 1933, the State Board of Education abolished the two-year teaching training programs. As of September 1, 1936, all teachers were required to have completed four-years of work. As a result, beginning in 1938, Northern in cooperation with the University of Michigan offered summer and Saturday graduate programs which were in demand. Through the decade of the 1930s, the Department of Education offered extension work, graduate and correspondence courses, and workshops to assist students with their requirements. Individual faculty members like Gilbert Brown and F. Roy Copper actively published and were engaged with professional organizations. Maude Van Antwerp was a specialist in children's literature and taught reading. Harry Lee, who was in charge of preparation and placement of teachers, was highly regarded for his concern for student teachers and job placement.

The decade of the 1940s brought substantial change to the Department of Education. Teachers continued to be trained in educational theory and supervised in practice teaching. The Michigan Legislature and the enlarged Department of Education established stricter requirements for course work and practice teaching. After 1939, a candidate had to successfully teach three out of five years after receiving the provisional certificate.

During World War II, when there was a tremendous need for teachers, the state legislature reintroduced the Limited Certificate. In response, President Henry Tape encouraged Upper Peninsula high school graduates to come to Northern for the two-year course.

Dr. William C. Hoppes became Director of Student Teaching and Placement in 1945 and suggested a number of innovations in the teacher curriculum. Off-campus courses were arranged at Bay Cliff Health Camp, Indian Lake and at Munuscong Conservation Camp (*See: Field Stations*). The use of audio visual materials created during World War II was encouraged, and in 1948 a driver training program was introduced.

On-campus students could keep abreast of educational developments through various professional organizations. Northern's Kindergarten-Primary Club became a branch of the American Childhood Education Association. The Don Bottum chapter of the Future Teachers of America was organized in 1952, and there was also the honorary society, Kappa Delta Pi.

With the coming of President Harden in 1956, Northern began to take on a new emphasis, away from the traditional focus on education. Despite this change as the enrollment grew, so did the number of students enrolled in teacher education. In 1957, there were 490, and in 1972 the number peaked at 713 only to decline to a low of 114 in 1993.

These increased enrollments called for an expansion of the administration of the department. Back in 1945, Dr. Hoppes was the department head, director of student teaching and director of placement. By 1964 his position was divided among five people: Dr. Edward Pfau was Dean of the School of Education, Dr. Wilbert Berg was head of the Department of Psychology and Education, Dr. Jack Rombouts was principal of the Training School, Dr. Edward Ruman was director of Professional Laboratory Experiences and Keith Forsberg was director of Placement.

The School of Education became a separate administrative unit in 1963, the year Northern was given university status. The Department of Psychology and Education was part of the school, along with the Office of Teacher Placement. Psychology became a separate department in 1968.

In 1961 the state legislature closed the high school in the John D. Pierce School. Given the fact that the laboratory school could not accommodate the growing number of student teachers, by 1964 they were all sent into the field and trained under 164 supervisors on the faculty of eleven public school districts in the Upper Peninsula and Northern Wisconsin.

The Community school movement brought adult education courses to public schools from 1964 to 1980. The Education Department became responsible for Northern's community school program in 1970, along with programs in vocational-occupational and career education. Community schools were funded by the Mott Foundation and related programs received funding from the Michigan Department of Education vocational division.

Special education, first funded by federal grants began in 1965 with a course in "exceptionalities" offered by Dr. Jean Rutherford. School Counselor Training Program was combined with Human Services Agency Counseling in the Education Department. It was cut in the 1980s, but was reestablished in fall 1997. In 1995 and 1997 the Department of Education chartered three schools. (*See: Charter Schools*)

In 1999 the Department of Education offers professional studies courses leading to the Michigan Professional or Provisional Teaching Certificate at the elementary and secondary levels as well as courses for continuing professional development through the master's degree. The department also offers selected courses as a service to majors in the preschool/family life services program.

Department chairs or heads: Lewis F. Anderson, 1899–1910; George C. Fracker, 1910–1913; Gilbert L. Brown, 1913–1946; Dr. William C. Hoppes, 1946–1959; Dr. Edward Pfau, 1959–1960; Dr. Wilbert A. Berg, 1960–1966; Dr. Elmer Schacht, 1966–1978; Dr. James Hendricks, 1978–present.

(Lynne Churchill, "The Education Department, The Early Years," (1995) and Lori Glaser, "The Department of Education, The Later Years," UA; interview with James D. Hendricks (6/23/97); Hilton; interview with Marjorie McKee by Lynn Churchill, 2/17/95); interview with Elmer Schacht 6/20/97; *The 1996–97 University Profile*, 1:193–199)

Education, School of: Education played a critical role in Northern's history and was the reason for its creation in 1899. In July 1959, William C. Hoppes became the first dean of Education and four years later the School of Education appeared. At that time the School was composed of the Departments of: Education and Psychology, Industrial Arts, Home Economics, Physical Education, Professional Laboratory Experience (Student Teaching), and the John D. Pierce Laboratory School. The first significant change came in 1968 when the Department of Education and Psychology was divided into two separate departments. Eventually the Professional Laboratory Experience was merged into the Department of Education. In 1985 the School of Education became the School of Behavioral Sciences, Human Services and Technology. Education was left out of the title. A year later it was called the School of Behavioral Sciences and Human Services. Then in 1989 it was renamed the School and later College (1992) of Behavioral Sciences, Human Services, and Education. (*See separate entry*)

Deans: Dr. William C. Hoppes, 1959–1960; Dr. Edward Pfau, 1960–1966; Dr. Wilbert A. Berg, (acting) 1966; 1967–1981); Dr. Elmer J. Schacht, 1981–1984; Dr. Alson I. Kaumeheiwa, (acting) 1984;
J. Wesley Little, 1984–1988. Continued under *College of Behavioral Sciences* . . .

Educational Policy Committee: The EPC consists of seven faculty, the five academic deans and two administrators appointed by the President. The EPC advises the Vice President for Academic Affairs and keeps the American Association of University Professors (AAUP; *See: Unions*) informed on academic program planning, curriculum and academic policy matters. It also makes recommendations on budgetary support for academic concerns, staffing requirements and new degree programs.

Electric Car: In 1981, Professor Robert Evans and his students in the transportation and heavy power department of the Jacobetti Center developed a plan for an electric car. Working with a 1974 Chevrolet Vega, they developed an electric engine. The biggest problem was trying to find batteries that would make the electric car viable. (NNR 11/1981)

Electronics, Department of: The Department is a part of the College of Technology and Applied Sciences. Before becoming a department in 1991, electronics courses were offered through Industrial Education programs. The first electronics courses were listed in 1963 under the heading "Electricity and Electronics." Two classes were offered: Basic Electronics and Advanced Electronics. Today, two Baccalaureate degree programs are offered in electronics. The Electronics Engineering Technology Program is designed for students who desire electronics courses with an emphasis in mathematics and science. The Electronics Technology degree is intended for students who desire electronics courses in an algebra-based curriculum. Associate degree programs are offered in Electronic Servicing Technology, Electromechanical Technology, and Electronics Technology. (*Bulletins*; *The 1996–97 University Profile*, 2:302–308) Michelle Kangas

Elizabeth Harden Circle Drive: Originally called the University Drive, Circle Drive was developed with the northward expansion of the campus in the early 1960s. For many years, it was a two-way street. In 1974, for a short period, controversial traffic bumps were installed. On October 4, 1975 it was dedicated to Mrs. Harden, former first lady of Northern. During the summer of 1996, portions of the drive were closed for a massive pipe laying project.

Employee of the Quarter Program: The program was initiated in October 1989 to recognize employees, who demonstrate through the performance of their responsibilities and other campus involvements, laudatory effort in terms of quality of service, concern for others, initiative, safety, etc. which promotes the image of Northern. John H. Hammang, director of Human Resources was one of the originators of the program. It operated under Robert W. Herman, director of the Personnel Department and was first given in December 1989 and continues to be awarded. In recent years it has not been given every quarter.

Recipients: David Adams (07-09/1991); Gail Anthony (10-12/1995); Michael Bath (04-06/1992); Beverly Boyer (01-03/1992); Sharon Carey (01-03/1995); James Carter (10-12/1992); Janet Coller (07-09/1993); Arlene Dorf (07-09/1996); Michael Fields (04-06/1995); Betsy Jaakola (01-03/1997); Muriel Kangas (01/03/1991); Joan Kendall-Rozman (10-12/1994); Genette Kluckner (04-06/1990); Steven LaFond (04-06/1994); JoDee Larsh (07-09/1990); Steven Lasich (04-06/1991); Diana Malouf (10-12/1990); Diane Mankamyer (10-12/1989); Sara Niemi (04-06/1993); Nicole Norman (07-09/1992); Tim Schmeltzer (01-03/1990); Russell Tarris (07-09/1994).

Employees: Over the last century, several thousand people have been employed by Northern. In 1899 six people, including the principal, constituted the faculty. In 1956 Northern listed 133 full-time employees, and in 1961 the number had grown to 222. Today Northern employs over 1,000 people.

Records of their employment can be found in the minutes of the State Board of Education (1899–1963) and the Board of Control (1964–present). The NMU Archives has a rather complete file on personnel consisting of news clippings to the 1960s and the file continues in a new format after 1994. Obituaries can usually be found at the Marquette County Historical Society. No attempt has been made to list all of the employees hired at Northern.

Energy Conservation: Throughout Northern's history, administrators have been concerned about heating bills. New heating plants (*See*: *Heating Plants*) were constructed and pipe lines were laid to be more efficient. However, since the oil crisis of 1973, the administration at Northern has been conscious of the importance of energy conservation. As early as December 1973, thermostats were turned down, paper saved, and state automobile drivers told to keep speeds at 50 mph. Studies were made to upgrade windows and heating systems. In 1981, residents were assessed $10 per semester for window replacement. A year later, the heating system was tied into a computer to regulate all systems on campus. Energy conservation continues to be an important concern.

Engineering and Planning Departments: As Northern developed and expanded, there was a growing need for this department. The mission of Engineering and Planning is to provide the expertise and resources necessary to meet the engineering, architectural and planning needs of the University's facilities. The department is concerned with all campus construction and renovation which will lead to attractive, functional, safe facilities for the University community. This department is under the Financial and Administration Division. (*The 1996–97 University Profile*, 2:64–75)

Engineering and Services Department: A part of the Learning Resources Division, this department provides administrative and technical support for the instructional and public service mission of Northern. The Engineering Department is responsible for a wide range of equipment campus-wide. These operations include, but are not limited to, WNMU-FM, WNMU-TV, Learning Resources Production/Operations, Audio Visual Services, the instructional closed-circuit campus cable Channels 8 and 10, the University cable access Channel 12, the broadcast laboratory administered by the Communications and Performance Studies Department and other instructional and administrative electronic systems, both on and off campus. This responsibility extends to the approval of specific equipment for purchase, writing specifications for purchase, installation and maintenance of equipment.

The division maintains all public broadcasting transmission facilities to FCC legal standards without interruption of service to the peninsula-wide audience. It also maintains FM translators in Marquette, Manistique, Newberry, Escanaba, and Marinette to FCC legal standards. (*The 1996–97 University Profile*, 2:228–233)

English, Department of: The English Department, established on July 14, 1899, educates students in composition and liberal studies, and provides advanced instruction for undergraduate and graduate students of English. Northern's first English teacher was Flora Hill, who taught until 1905. The Department of Language and Literature was created in 1920 and James C. Bowman was appointed its chair. Under Bowman, the study of English at Northern expanded from its focus on teacher training. He became the Director of Debate, Drama, Forensics and Student Publications. Bowman resigned in 1939 and Dr. Russell Thomas became Department Head. The Department of Speech (*See: Communications and Performance Studies*) was split from the Department of Language and Literature in 1957. Early in 1967, the foreign language component was separated and became its own department (*See: Languages, Department of*).

133

Some significant teachers in the department included: James Bowman, Mildred Magers, Earl Hilton, Aurele Derocher, Gunther Meyland, and Ellsworth "Dutch" Barnard. Dr. Magers was the first female professor at Northern to receive a Ph.D. in 1944.

The English Department offers four undergraduate majors and four minors. The four major tracks of study are Liberal Arts, Graduate-Bound, Writing and Secondary Education. There are six minor tracks: Writing, Journalism, Liberal Arts, Teaching, and Gender Studies (the latter two are interdisciplinary programs).

The department oversees the University writing requirement. Incoming freshmen take the Placement Exam in Composition which places them in an appropriate course according to their writing ability. EN 111, College Composition, is the first course taken in the series followed by EN 211 which is divided into Writing and Literature, Narrative and Descriptive Writing or Technical and Report Writing.

The Writing Center began in 1971 as the Writing Workshop. In 1978, the English Department became responsible for administering the Writing Proficiency Examination, which all bachelor's degree students must pass in order to graduate.

The graduate studies program began in the mid-1970s, at first offering a master's degree in literature. Since 1985, graduate students in the English Department have been able to study writing as an emphasis in their master's degree program. At the current Masters level, the writing and literature tracks are intended for students interested in careers in writing, publishing and secondary and college teaching, and for students planning to pursue the Ph.D.

The Eta Phi chapter of Sigma Tau Delta, the international English honor society was started at Northern in 1986. The chapter sponsors the English Faculty Colloquium Series. The Society was preceded by two literary societies, Osiris and Ygdrasil (1907–1925) and the English Club, which was started in 1922.

The English Department has produced several publications featuring student or faculty writing: *The Quill*, 1914–1918; *Comment*, 1961; *Driftwood*, 1964; *Horizons*, 1964; *The Intruder*, 1972; *Mandala*, 1971, 1972; *The Golden Fern*, 1981; *The New Yooper*, 1983, 1984; *Limited Space*, 1984; *Engrams*, 1985; *Revisions*, 1985; *AG-Student Writers and Artists*, 1989, 1990; *The Dark Tower*, 1990–1996; *Thaw*, 1996–present, and *Hartley's Review* (not dated). Since 1996, the English Department has been the home of *Passages North*, a biannual literary magazine of national reputation. The exact beginning and ending years are uncertain because complete runs of these publications do not exist.

Department chairs and heads: Flora Hill 1899–1920; James C. Bowman 1920–1939; Russell Thomas 1939–1962; Ellsworth Barnard, (acting) 1963; David Dickson 1964–1966; Arthur E. Pennell 1966–1971; Robert Glenn, (acting) 1972–1973; Daryl Davis 1974–1978; John Kuhn 1978–1985; Rowena R.Jones, (acting) 1985–1987; Leonard G. Heldreth 1987–1998;Teresa Kynell & Darryl Davis, (interim co-heads), 1998-present.

(Hilton pp. 172–74, 229–30; Sally VanDenburg, "Northern Michigan University's English Department: An Overview," (1996), UA; *The 1996–97 University Profile*, 1:96–102; English, Department of, Northern Michigan University, Records, UA 67.)

Enrollment Figures: These figures are about as accurate as they are available. They all are from the fall semester as a base except for those marked with ★ which are for the academic year. Beginning with 1980, enrollments from the Jacobetti Center were included.

1899: 61; 1900: 130★; 1901: 198★; 1902: 210★; 1903: 258★; 1904: 284★; 1905: 334★; 1906: 179; 1907: 188; 1908: 225; 1909: 266; 1910: 266; 1911: 268; 1912: 278; 1913: 258; 1914: 297; 1915: 385; 1916: 441; 1917: 383; 1918: 388; 1919: 403; 1920: 423; 1921: 566; 1922: 519; 1923: 563; 1924: 625; 1925: 664; 1926: 750; 1927: 711; 1928: 749; 1929: 713; 1930: 774; 1931: 717; 1932: 592; 1933: 492; 1934: 507; 1935: 546; 1936: 535; 1937: 549; 1938: 654; 1939: 641; 1940: 679; 1941: 522; 1942: 374; 1943: 210; 1944: 230; 1945: 281; 1946: 930; 1947: 1,101; 1948: 1,102; 1949: 1,022; 1950: 847; 1951: 655; 1952: 586; 1953: 604; 1954: 735; 1955: 888: 1956: 1,090; 1957: 1,277; 1958: 1,628; 1959: 1,792; 1960: 1,876; 1961: 2,405; 1962: 3,061; 1963: 3,551; 1964: 4,291; 1965: 5,561; 1966: 6,897; 1967: 7,085; 1968: 7,286; 1969: 7,839; 1970: 8,272; 1971: 8,167; 1972: 8,053; 1973: 8,208; 1974: 8,437; 1975: 8,826; 1976: 8,864; 1977: 8,977; 1978: 8,845; 1979: 8,756; 1980: 9,376; 1981: 9,046; 1982: 8,465; 1983: 8,229; 1984: 7,869; 1985: 7,702; 1986: 7,916; 1987: 8,000; 1988: 8,260; 1989: 8,511; 1990: 8,700; 1991: 8,722; 1992: 8,897; 1993: 8,729; 1994: 8,057; 1995: 7,593; 1996: 8,040; 1997: 7,826; 1998: 7,826. (*Development Plan 1968/1980* (1969), p. 12; UA).

Environmental Changes to the Campus: *See: Campus, Evolution of*

Epidemics: Over the years, the personnel and students of Northern have been affected by epidemics. The most serious to hit the campus was the Spanish influenza of 1918–1919 which sickened many and took the life of Dr. Samuel Magers. During this epidemic, Northern was closed for several weeks in the fall semester as were other public facilities throughout the nation. A number of alumni died due to the flu, both in the Upper Peninsula and around the nation.

One year, students were kept on campus due to a typhus outbreak down-state during the Thanksgiving break. In 1930, there was a fear of a smallpox epidemic and the entire student body was vaccinated. A variety of flus constantly plague the campus during the winter months and personnel and students are encouraged to take flu shots. Polio shots were administered in 1957 as part of a national immunization program. In April 1957, a smallpox prevention program was initiated on campus. Twenty years later, in November a "mild epidemic" of stomach flu sent 133 students to the health center and 23 to the hospital. In December 1968 an outbreak of viral illnesses sent 400–500 students to the Health Center in four days. HIV infection and AIDS are current problems of epidemic proportions which are monitored by the Health Center along with other diseases. (NCN 04/04/1957; NW 11/10/1977; MJ 12/13/1998)

Ethnics on Campus: The University was created to provide teachers to the Upper Peninsula and later to serve a wider interest group. As a result, the institution attracted the sons and daughters of immigrants from its earliest days. In the early graduating classes, Charlotte and Bessie Preston (*See separate entries*), the daughters of a Jamaican immigrant, were enrolled. In 1919, the first foreign student, a Japanese women, Zendya Krihara, came to Northern. (*See: Foreign Students*)

A survey of the freshman class of 1934 filed in the Registrar's office showed that one-fifth of the students had parents born outside the United States and that most were descended from English immigrants. Swedish, German, and Finnish descendants ranked next. President Pearce told an assembly of Finnish campers in 1936 that Northern had a larger enrollment of Finnish students than any other school in the state. The 1937 Senior Booklet announced that among the graduates there were "57 Finns, 41 English, 27 Swedes and a few others."

Several hundred African Americans (*See separate entry*) were attracted to campus by the mid-to late-1960s. During the mid-1970s, there were some 30 Micronesians (*See separate entry*) on campus. Native Americans (*See separate entry*) came in the late-1960s and early 1970s. Hispanic Americans (*See separate entry*) were on campus in small numbers.

In 1978 when the Federal government required that all ethnic groups be counted, the figures were as follows: Non-Resident Aliens: 60; Black Non-Hispanic: 216; American Indian or Alaskan Native: 78; Asian or Pacific Islander: 33; Hispanic: 39; White Non-Hispanic: 8,486. These figures included all full-time and part-time students.

Beginning in the 1970s, various ethnic celebrations were held on campus for African Americans, Native Americans, Hispanic Americans and Finnish Americans. The International Food Festival (*See separate entries*) was begun in 1990. (MJ 07/21/1936)

Evangelists: Although Northern is a state institution, evangelists have the right to preach on campus. By the late 1990s, two campus evangelists, Rick Warzywak from downstate and Tim Timbrook from Marquette County were a common sight in front of Jamrich Hall. Student reaction to this form of "street preaching" was generally negative. (NW 12/10/1998)

Events Center*: See: Berry Events Center*

Evergreen Ceremony: The class of 1910 established Evergreen Day, with ceremonies imitating the "Chains" in Eastern colleges. Part of this ceremony included the "daisy chain" which at Northern was made from ground pine since it was too early for daisies at graduation. The chain was made by the graduating class and carried around the campus and to the dormitory as they said their farewells. As part of this ceremony, evergreens were planted with song and ceremony. Unfortunately, over the next eight years, the trees consistently died. In 1919, the seniors, dressed for the occasion in caps and gowns, planted ivy against the main building and began Ivy Day (*See separate entry*) (NCN 10/23/1935; Hilton, p. 42)

Student Activities

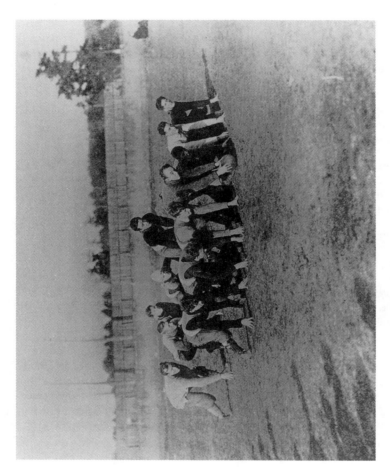

NMU football team practicing, 1910

NMU women exercising, ca. 1910

NMU women's basketball team, 1915

Summer faculty picnic Presque Isle, 1919 UA

Theater production, 1920s

"In India," an outdoor pageant in the 1920s

Rush Day, June 5, 1931

Students registering for classes in the "bull pen," held in Hedgcock Field House

Snow sculpture in front of Don H. Bottum University Center, 1964

NMU cheerleaders, 1979

Forest Roberts Theater production, 1979

149

The University

Kaye Hall foyer, looking toward main entrance

West side of Kaye (l) and Longyear Hall (r), tennis courts on the site of the future John D. Pierce School, ca. 1915

John D. Pierce School wood shop, 1927

Northern Michigan University, ca. 1935

Memorial Field, 1946

A view of Vetville and original cafeteria (lower right), 1948

Family in Vetville apartment, ca. 1948

Lunch time in the Army surplus cafeteria. Mildred Magers second from left, 1948

Aerial view of the campus, looking north with Lee Hall in center, 1958

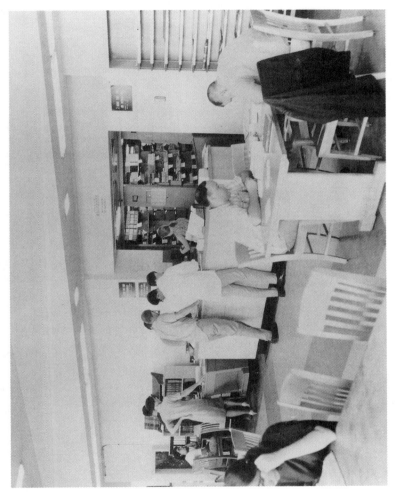

Old Lydia Olson Library, 1960s

Northern Michigan College campus, 1961

Superior Dome under construction with PEIF and old Memorial Field above, September 10, 1990

The Presidents

Dwight B. Waldo:
1899–1904

James H. B. Kaye:
1904–1923

John M. Munson:
1923–1933

Webster H. Pearce:
1933–1940

Henry A. Tape: 1940–1956

Ogden E. Johnson, interim:
Sept 1967–June 1968

L–r: Edgar L. Harden (1956–1967),
James B. Appleberry (1983–1991, and
John X. Jamrich (1967–1983)

William H. Vandament:
1991–1997

Judith I. Bailey: 1997–

Excellence in Service Award: The Award established in 1984, recognized staff members of the University community for excellence in service. All full-time University employees, other than teaching faculty and academic department heads, were eligible. The a screening committee for the ESA consisted of employees from across the campus. The award winners were annually honored at the Retirement and Service Awards Luncheon held in April. The award was discontinued in 1993.

Recipients: Grace E. Albert (5-91); Jacquelyn Andersen (87); Elwin L. Bell (86); David L. Bonsall (84); Margaret M. Britton (85); H. Robert Constance (85); Darlene D. Frazier (4-88); Marjorie R. Fries (86); Kathleen G. Godec (5-91); Kenneth G. Godfrey (5-91); Sharon I. Harr (5-92); Gilbert J. Heard (4-88); Robert W. Herman (85); Carol S. Huntoon (5-92); James A. Inch (5-92); Lowell G. Kafer (87); Michael Kuzak (4-90); Marjorie G. Leffler (4-88); Robert H. Manning (85); Carol Marjomaki (89); Kristine Martin (89); Susan Menhennick (87); Mary L. Nault (84); Robert Nystrom (4-90); Joyce L. Peterson (86); Earl Polkinghorn (84); N. Jane Potvin (4-88); Jacqueline G. Richer (5-91; Gloria Slade (4-90); Mary E. Steadman (86); Thomas J. Taylor (89); George W. Tomasi (89); Donald Wierzbicki (4-90); Gerald Williams (87). (Source: University Relations Office)

Expansion of the Campus: See: *Campus, Evolution of the*

Expression and Physical Training, Department of: This department was created in the fall of 1905 and Eulie Gay Rushmore was placed in charge. Beginning that fall, all Northern students were required to take physical training in order to "correct abnormalities, develop physical strength and increase the elasticity of the muscles." Two years later, it was noted that "the work is arranged to be in harmony with the voice and body training of the expression class." Ms. Rushmore sought to get her students to express their emotions. When Longyear Hall was rebuilt in 1907, Ms. Rushmore had a special room created with seating for 100 students and had a platform for a piano.

Between 1905 and 1911 Ms. Rushmore also taught Physical Training for Women. At the latter date, Grace Stafford joined the faculty as the first full-time physical education teacher.

Under Ms. Rushmore, early student theater productions were presented. In the years following 1906, Ms. Rushmore directed "As You Like It", "The Merchant of Venice", "Twelfth Night", "Midsummer Night's Dream" and the opera, "A Bohemian Girl." In 1911, the students and faculty produced "The Drama of Michigan." Two years later, Gertrude Mossler, Rushmore's temporary replacement wrote and directed Northern's first musical comedy, "In College Days." Choruses sang Northern Normal songs, and the dancers performed two of her compositions, "the Snake Dance" and "the Dance of the Vestal Virgins." In the fall of 1913, Ms. Rushmore's class presented "Land of Heart's Desire" by W. B. Yeats, reflecting their teacher's concern over the Irish question. The 1917 senior play was "The Melting Pot," which sought to end Old World prejudices and feuds.

Other plays directed by Ms. Rushmore included: "The Rivals" (dramatization of Monsieur Beaucaire), "Jayville Junction" (1918; a student farce), "Marquette" (1919; town and gown pageant), A.A. Milne's "Mr. Pim Passes By" and "Captain Apple." Her students assisted high school productions and performed in light comedies and one-act plays that were "the basis of the Little Theater movement found in most large cities." Ms. Rushmore was also in charge of a number of Spring Pageants held on campus during the 1920s.

Ms. Rushmore presented plays at the Marquette Branch Prison. After a particularly outstanding performance, an inmate, Charles Meyers, composed a melody, "The Normal Girl's Dream," which he dedicated to Ms. Rushmore. The music was published and all profits went to the Student Girls' League.

The department was in existence for nineteen years. When Ms. Rushmore left in 1924, the Department of Expression became the Speech section of the Department of English. At this time, the Physical Education portion developed into its own department.

Department chair: Eulie Gay Rushmore, 1905-1924. (Hilton, pp. 25–26, 53; DMJ 01/26/1907, 12/05/1908, 06/21/1906, 06/22/1910, 06/24/1913; NNN 04/15/1922)

Extension Courses: *See: Continuing Education*

"EZ Tickets": A computerized system whereby tickets for NMU activities can be instantly purchased began in 1995. The system has outlets at the Superior Dome (Central Office), Forest Roberts Theater, Lakeview Arena, and the University Center's Willy's Snak Shak. The system greatly facilitates the purchase of tickets for all events.

Facilities: The origins of this department go back to the early years of Northern. At that time one individual was in charge of buildings and facilities or grounds. By the 1950s it was called the Maintenance Office and later in 1960 Maintenance and Operations.

Over the century as the University grew, especially during the era of President Harden (1956–1967), the department became more elaborate. In 1968 David H. McClintock was made the coordinator of Campus Development and Capital Outlay.

The Facilities Department is under the Vice President for Administration. It consists of Engineering and Planning and Plant Operations (*See separate entry*). Its mission is to maintain and upgrade buildings, grounds, and equipment with a high level of proficiency, so as to provide the proper environment for the University community. In its effort to meet its mission, the Facilities Department stresses the protection of property and investment in the continued long-range use of facilities. The major concerns of the Department are the attractiveness of the campus, healthful conditions, safety and economy of operation.

Directors: Alfred M. Barry, 1901–1909; Harvey Ripley, 1909–1945; Frank H. Schwemin, 1945–1970; Ernest L. Neumann, 1970–1977; Bruce Raudio, 1977–1999; Carl Pace, 1999–present. (*The 1996–97 University Profile* 2:58–63)

Faculty, Original: Dwight Waldo (*See separate entry*), principal, teaching history and civics; Martha Ackermann: geography and drawing; Lewis F. Anderson: pedagogy; Flora E. Hill, "lady principal" and English; Edward G. Maul: mathematics; William McCracken: science. These departments were established on July 14, 1899. (MJ 08-31-1899).

Faculty Council: The original Faculty Council first existed in 1901 and consisted of the faculty meeting with the President. The Council was a smaller version of the modern Academic Senate coupled with the President's Council. In August 1904, President Kaye had the faculty create permanent committees: advanced standing, course of study, board and rooms, extension work, athletics, teachers bureau, and commencement arrangements. It continued to operate until the faculty got too large. By the 1920s, there were over twenty faculty members meeting. Attendance was marked on a sheet.

Northern's Faculty Organization in 1947 voted to form a modern Faculty Council and on April 9 the first regular meeting was held. The faculty created the Council for the general welfare of Northern, to present faculty positions on institutional policy to the administration, and as an avenue of communication. It consisted of eight members (six elected by the faculty and two chosen by the president) who met regularly with the president and to appoint faculty members to committees.

The Council was active from 1947 through 1963 when the Academic Senate was created by the Faculty Organization. Minutes of both Faculty Councils can be found in the University Archives.

Faculty Reception: In the early days of Northern the faculty gave elaborate receptions for students, complete with receiving lines, refreshments, and a dance orchestra. In 1902, the faculty limited expenses to $20, or one fifth of the average monthly salary. In return, each class put on a formal reception annually for all the students and faculty at Northern. As the college expanded, this tradition ended. (NCN 10/23/1935; Hilton, p. 40)

Faculty Wives: *See: University Women*

Fantastics: A popular entertainment group considered "NMU's Entertainment Ambassadors" was known as the Fantastics, composed of 14 full-time Northern students. The Fantastics performed everything from big band to choral arrangements and comedy. The group was formed in 1970 and first performed in December 1970 and within three years gave over 100 performances. Later the Fantastics were directed by Delmar "Del" Towers who came to campus in July 1974. Stylistically, they were all rolled up in one enthusiastic explosion of the finest in the sounds of the 50s, 60s, and 70s.

In January 1973, the Fantastics entertained American forces in the Caribbean, as USO representatives selected through the Department of Defense and the National Music Council. The group performed at Northern on April 30, 1976 for two hours. They made a 29-day USO tour which took them through military bases in Alaska. Over the years, they cut several records which are available in the University Archives.

Never a part of the Music Department, they were an adjunct musical group funded by a special appropriation of the State Legislature. In the late 1970s, when the funding was cut, this popular group ceased to exist. (CR 09/1974; NW 04/08/1976, 04/29/1976; NN 10/23/1970)

The Federal Men: In 1920 there were three students attending Northern under the direction of the Federal Board of Vocational Education. A year later the number had grown to 24 students. These men organized to improve their own conditions and promote Northern's interests. They organized a chapter of the Disabled American Veterans of the World War. The chapter was organized on March 23, 1921, and named the Northern State Normal Chapter of the Disabled American Veterans of the World War.

Female Firsts: Some female firsts in Northern's history: class of 1899 was composed of women; first commencement was composed of women (1900); first woman instructor was Martha Ackermann who taught drawing and geography (1899–1905); first female librarian was Minnie Waldo (1900–1903); first official dean of women and history professor was Catherine Maxwell (1904–1918); first female producer of theatrical productions at Northern was Eulie Gay Rushmore (1905–1924); first women's basketball team played in 1912; Mary E. Moore was the first woman to finance the student loan fund (1914); Zenya Krihara was the first foreign student from Japan who attended Northern in 1919; first well-known art teacher was Grace Spalding (1904–1938); first Catholic nuns came to Northern during summer school in 1921 for their teaching certificates; the first meeting of the University Women took place on March 18, 1926; first female professor to received a Ph.D. was Mildred K. Makers (March 1944 from the University of Michigan); the first building on campus named after a woman was Carey Hall (1949) after Ethel Carey, the longest serving dean of women (1924–1956); first female cheerleading squad was formed in 1949; first female intercollegiate sport-field hockey (1968–1984) was coached by Barbara Patrick; the founding dean of the College of Nursing and Allied Health Sciences was Margaret Rettig (1968–1982); she was also the first female to serve as an academic dean; the first female member of the Board of Control was Thelma H. Flodin (1964–1972); first women's volleyball NCAA championship title was won in 1993; first female president of Northern is Judith I. Bailey (1997-present).

Field Hockey: A game played on a turfed field between teams of 11 players each whose object is to direct a ball into the opponent's goal with a hockey stick. Started at Northern in 1968, Women's Field Hockey was under the direction of Barbara Patrick. This was the first women's varsity sport and pre-dated Title 9 requirements creating equality in all sports. The training program for the women was extensive and complete. Three days a week, a weight-training program was held with emphasis on the wrist and arm muscles (besides the entire body) with weekly maintenance following. The women practiced six days a week, three hours daily. The home games were free and were played in a field east of the Events Center. This sport ended in 1984. (NW 09/15/1977)

Field Stations: Northern has had a number of educational field stations located across the Upper Peninsula. In the early days, students used the surrounding woods and an experimental garden on campus to conduct field research for the sciences. George Butler, professor of agriculture, encouraged interested students to attend the Conservation Training School at Higgins Lake sponsored by the Michigan State Department of Conservation and the four colleges of education. Butler's classes regularly visited the Chatham Agricultural Experimental Station, a silver fox farm and the Seney and Cusino wildlife refuges.

In July 1948, Northern leased for one year with the option to renew from the U.S. Forest Service, the Clear Lake Camp in Chippewa County to be used for an outdoor education program.

The future Munuscong field station was originally a state camp on Munuscong Bay along the St. Marys River, 25 miles south of Sault Ste. Marie and seven miles northeast of Pickford. Munuscong had been owned by the Dodge Motor Company as a hunting and fishing camp. The Dodge Motor Company turned the property over to the state for use as a state park.

In 1948, Butler heard that the site was available for a conservation laboratory. President Henry Tape, who visited the site, was interested in the project. On July 23, 1948, the Board of Education approved the policy whereby the State Department of Conservation could either lease or give the Munuscong Group Facility for use by Northern. On October 19, the 59.1 acres were transferred from the Department of Conservation to Northern for the consideration of $1.00.

In the summer of 1949, the first classes in outdoor education were held there. By 1956, two summer sessions beginning in June and August were offered by the Department of Conversation and Agriculture. Due to the distance, it was decided to relinquish the Munuscong Bay property. On October 19, 1960, the Board returned the property to the Department of Conservation.

Interest in such a facility was revived in the 1960s. There was property at Lake Cusino, located northeast of Munising. In 1966, the property was transferred from Western Michigan University to Northern. Between 1966 and 1980, the camp was extensively used by Northern faculty for classes. In early 1982, there was talk of closing the facility as a cost-cutting measure. As a compromise, it was advertised in the *Wall Street Journal* as a "conference-seminar retreat." August 31-September 1, 1988, a two-day seminar was held to discuss uses of the NMU Field Station. In a report of January 2, 1990, it was noted that it would take $190,100 to bring about the necessary improvements and code upgrades.

Soon after, this report was sent to President Appleberry who concluded that its operation was a drain on the budget during a time of serious financial strain. As a result it was returned to the Department of Natural Resources. There were many people on campus who had hoped that it could remain part of the educational experience. In October 1997, the DNR indicated that the property was up for sale, but no action was taken by Northern.

Located in the immediate vicinity of the University are the Longyear Forest (*See separate entry*) and the Greenwood Nature Center (*See separate entry*). Both sites have been used by science students on a day basis. The former has been allowed to return to nature while the latter was returned to Cleveland Cliffs Iron Company. (NN 03/05/1956; 07/24/1957)

Financial Aid: In 1998 approximately 75 percent of the students attending Northern receive some form of financial aid, including student employment. Financial aid in the early years of the school often came in the form of donations from Marquette citizens and organizations. During the Depression, the state permitted Northern and other colleges to employ needy students as janitors, using federal funds. Soon, Northern was able to arrange part-time work for students throughout the university and the community. The Federal

Employment Recovery Act and the National Youth Administration in the 1930s paid students 30 cents per hour for various campus jobs. In 1934, the state permitted teachers colleges to give two scholarships per year on the basis of need, instead of athletic or extracurricular achievement. In 1937, ten Northern students used state scholarships to earn rural teaching certificates. During this period, the availability of loans also increased. The G.I. Bill for veterans followed World War II and other conflicts.

A $215.00 increase in the cost of tuition and fees in 1958 challenged Northern's financial aid sources, which by then included around 100 State Board of Education scholarships. That year, the Federal Student Perkins Loan Program (formerly the National Defense Student Loan) began, as did several substantial private scholarship funds. In 1960 the federal government began guaranteeing low-interest student loans from local banks. In 1965, the Federal Work Study Employment Program began, followed by the Federal Supplemental Educational Opportunity Grant Program, the Federal Stafford Loan Program (formerly the Guaranteed Loan Program), and the Michigan Competitive Scholarship Program. Robert L. Pecotte, was the first and longest (1965-1997) serving head of the Financial Aid office.

In 1966, the Michigan Tuition Grant Program started; in 1970, the Federal Nursing Scholarship and Loan Programs; and in 1972, the Federal Pell Grant Program Aid from these programs grew rapidly. The Academic Achievement Awards Program or "Triple A" scholarship program also began in the 1970s. Between 1976 and 1986, a number of other student financial aid programs were added, including student wage classifications, the Michigan Indian Tuition Waiver, the Federal Parent Loan Program, the Michigan Work Study Program, the Michigan Adult Part Time Grant Program, and the Michigan Educational Opportunity Grant Program. These were followed by the Michigan Tuition Incentive Program in 1988, the Michigan loan and the subsidized Federal Stafford Loan Program, now called the Ford Direct Lending.

Today an office of the Student Affairs Division, its mission is: 1) to obtain and distribute financial resources on a financial need basis to enable those students who, without financial assistance, could not attend Northern; and 2) to utilize financial resources, particularly University-provided funds, to recognize, attract, and retain talented students in a number of areas who will enhance the NMU community.

Directors: Robert Pecotte, 1967–1997; Shirley Niemi, 1997–present. (*The 1996–97 University Profile*, 2:155–160; Mark Crist, "A History of Financial Aid and Student Employment at Northern Michigan University," 1995, UA)

Finance and Administration, Vice President of: When Northern State Normal School opened in 1899, a secretary handled finances and administration. The first secretary was Lydia Olson who remained until 1905. As enrollment increased, there were committees which handled some of these tasks. By 1937, there was a faculty committee for administration. Leo Van Tassel, an experienced bookkeeper and public accountant came to Northern in 1945 and for many years served as the comptroller. In July 1964 he became the first vice president for Business and Finance. By 1983, the office was called Finance and Administration.

The Vice President of Finance and Administration provides financial and administrative counsel to the President and other units of the University, and serves as the treasurer of the Board of Control while managing the financial and administrative departments in the division in conformance with University policy. Under this Division are: Planning & Analytical Studies, Director of Personnel, Director of Sports Training Centers, Director of Facilities, Director of Business Services, Director of Financial Services, and Administrative Information Technology.

Vice Presidents: Leo Van Tassel, 1964–1976; Lyle Shaw, 1976–1993; Michael Roy, 1993–present. (*Bulletins*; *The 1996–97 University Profile*, 2:42–45) Michelle Kangas and Alisa Koski

Financial Services: A unit of the Financial and Administration Division, this office provides administrative support by accurately recording and reporting financial information so that the University is in compliance with laws, regulations, and University policy. It also provides accounting services to University students and departments. (*The 1994–95 University Profile*, 2:67)

Finnish American Studies: Northern lies in the midst of one of the largest concentrations of Finnish Americans in the United States. From Northern's earliest days, there has been a connection with this ethnic group. A survey of the freshman class of 1934 filed in the Registrar's office showed that one-fifth of the students had parents born outside the United States and that most were descended from English immigrants. Swedish, German, and Finnish descendants ranked next. President

Webster Pearce told an assembly of Finnish campers in 1936 that Northern had a larger enrollment of Finnish American students than any other school in Michigan. The 1937 Senior Booklet announced that among the graduates there were "57 Finns, 41 English, 27 Swedes and a few others."

Starting in the 1970s, a number of Finnish American faculty on campus began to promote a Finnish American focus. In 1974, Finnish Culture Week was celebrated. At this time Professor Jon Saari introduced a new course, "The Finnish Immigrant in America" which is still taught. Finnish language courses continue to be offered on demand. A minor was discussed, but never materialized due to insufficient courses. The International Food Festival (*See separate entries*) was begun in 1990 and involves Finnish students.

On February 3, 1977, a short-lived institute was created and placed under the Provost's office. However on January 12, 1978 the Board of Control dissolved the institute at the request of Suomi College.

A number of faculty members have directed their research towards Finnish and Finnish American topics. Some have traveled to Finland and taught and studied there. Since the 1960s, Professors John Watanen (Language), John Kiltinen (Mathematics), and Michael M. Loukinen (Sociology) have received Fullbright-Hays Fellowships to Finland.

In the 1980s, Dr. Michael M. Loukinen (Sociology) began directing a series of movies—*Finnish American Lives* (1982), *Tradition Bearers* (1983), *Good Man in the Woods* (1987) which deal with the Finnish immigrant experience in the Upper Peninsula. These are available in video format.

In the 1970s for their promotion of Finnish studies on campus, President John X. Jamrich and Professor Watanen were invested with the award, Knight First Class of the Order of the White Rose by the Finnish ambassador. This is the highest decoration that Finland can award to someone not a Finnish citizen.

FinnFest was held on campus, among other venues around Marquette, in August 1996. President William Vandament served as honorary chair of the organizing committee. Several thousand Finnish-Americans from around the nation visited the campus and hundreds stayed in University housing. Many lectures, exhibits and shopping areas were presented or located on campus. It was one of the most successful FinnFests held to date.

As part of the ongoing interaction with Finland in January 1999, Northern hosted six young ambassadors from Finland, under the coordination of Dr. Jon Saari. The ambassadors hailed from Tampere, Finland and started a one-month tour of Midwestern colleges and universities at NMU. The purpose of their visit was to acquaint the public with Finland and its connection with the New Europe. ((MJ 07/21/1936; NW 01/21/1999)

Fire Safety and Fires: Over the century, there have been concerns for fire safety on campus. On October 29, 1903, Principal Waldo requested that the Board of Education purchase a fire hose for adequate protection of Longyear and White Halls. He also asked that there be a meeting with the city water commission to immediately lay a sufficient amount of pipe for the protection of the growing campus. No action seems to have been taken on this matter.

On December 18, 1905, the worst fire in Northern's history struck Longyear Hall (*See separate entry*). Members of the State Board of Education thought that the fire was caused by a powder mill explosion which took place earlier in the day along the Dead River. The explosion jarred the chimney on the hall and led to the fire which destroyed the building.

The Longyear fire was the only one that burned student records. Grades had to be reconstructed from professors' grade books. The Registrar's Office has old record cards that say "Before Fire." Today these records are kept in multiple copies at several locations for security purposes.

Over the years, minor fires have taken place in the dorms without extensive damage or loss of life. Public Safety maintains a fire prevention unit. The Marquette City Fire Department services the campus.

First Impressions: A student organization which was founded in the autumn of 1987 to promote the development of traditions on campus. Two of their newest traditions are the Holiday Dinner and the President's Ball held in March.

First Nighters Club: The Club was established in 1984 to maintain the artistic quality of Forest Roberts Theatre Productions. The contributions also promote the various activities in which the Forest Roberts Theatre is actively engaged in the areas of acting, directing, designing, costuming and management. Membership is open to all interested people and organizations.

First Students: In the 1899 class students were: Grace E. Bay; Alda J. Bertrand; Olive Blanchard; Catherine W. Carey; Ella A. Erickson; Teresa Hennesey; Harold L.S. Johns; Maggie M. Layne; Sarah MacLeod; Nellie W. McKnight; Irene F. McNuity; Ida A. Mitchell; Lydia M. Olson; Charlotte M. Preston; Eugenia A. Primeau; Anna M. Richardson; Fannie Russell; Bada Schmidt; Mary M. Wallace; Anna Zerbel. (MJ 08-31-1899)

First Year Experience: The FYE concept began over 20 years ago at the University of South Carolina. At Northern this program goes back to Fall 1995, and was established to track incoming freshman students in order to see how well they do as college students. It is open, on a self-selected basis, to any regularly admitted students and those students admitted to the Freshman Studies Program. A special course, UN 100, Freshman Seminar, is used to help track students and compare their success rate with students who did not participate in the program. An Advisory Board oversees the program. By 1998, the data showed that there were improvements among FYE participants statistically through retention and higher Grade Point Averages. Laura Soldner and Yvonne Lee between 1995 and 1998 guided the program and then in the fall of 1998 Steve Oates became the first director. (*Campus* 05/22–26/1995)

Flag: In 1961–1962, President Edgar Harden and Kevin Sheard, associate professor of Business Administration, discussed the development of a master's degree academic hood. The flag concept was a secondary result. There seems to have existed what Dr. Sheard called a "floating billboard," that is a flag on which someone had appliqued the name of the college, its location, the name of the team, and telephone number. Dr. Sheard designed a flag which can be described in vexillogical terms as "Olive, the College seal in the hoist and two chevrons, point to fly, gold." Possibly the only prototype was made by Sheard, who gave it to President Harden. Harden presented a recommendation for approval of the flag to the State Board of Education on March 28, 1962, and approval was given on April 11, 1962.

In February 1996, the University Historian, Russell Magnaghi uncovered the fact that the University had a flag. It was not until August 1 that Magnaghi found the description at the State Board of Education office in Lansing. The information was passed on to President Vandament, who in turn brought it before the President's Council which discussed protocol. By coincidence, Sheard visited the campus on an unrelated matter in August and indicated that he had designed a flag. Magnaghi was soon in touch with him and obtained all of the historical and design details about the flag.

At the same time, the President's office received word that Astronaut Jerry Linenger wanted an item to take aboard the space shuttle on January 17, 1997. Magnaghi was put in charge of obtaining the item and had Melinda Stamp (WNMU-TV) make a cloth version of the flag which was presented to the President on September 26. A model flag was presented to the Board of Control on October 4. In the following month two standard size flags were prepared by a commercial company. One is kept in the Board of Control meeting room and the other is held by the Military Science Department. The flag was officially used for 1997 commencement which Sheard attended.

There were other flags used on the campus. The Military Science Department has three flags which represent its mission at Northern. The newest version was issued by the U.S. Army in the summer of 1996.

Between 1977 and April 1979, the University had its own lake-going vessel, the *Spruce Hill*, captained by Robert Manning. Captain Manning, a former Coast Guardsman, felt that the ship needed an ensign and June Jamrich created one which had a gold field and the old pine tree logo in the center. Neither the original nor a copy is in existence.

There are also a number of flags which have either and "N" or "NMU" on a field of green. These flags and windsocks are sold in the bookstore and have been used at games and by local businesses. These flags are unofficial. (Minutes of the State Board of Education 04/11/1962, UA; Sheard to Magnaghi, 09/08/1996; MJ 09/27/1996)

Flu: *See: Epidemics*

The Food Court: *See: Food Service*

Food Service/Dining Facilities and Programs: The earliest food service facility on campus was located in the private dormitory operated by Longyear and Ayer between 1900 and 1917. After that time until the opening of Carey Hall in 1948, students resided in rented rooms in homes and took their meals in the homes or at special private dining facilities. There were a few restaurants like the College Inn, located in the vicinity of Northern.

In the early years of Northern's existence, receptions and banquets were held in local hotels. In 1910, Margaret Buchly was hired in the Department of Domestic Science. She began to use the department to provide the institution with on-campus banquets. With the completion of Kaye Hall in 1915, its large foyer allowed these banquets to be held in this location.

With the end of World War II, President Henry Tape saw that the enrollment would suddenly increase due to the G.I. Bill, and additional dining facilities would be needed. In early 1946, he negotiated a deal with the U.S. Army to obtain a temporary dining room structure. It consisted of a dining room, kitchen, and its own heating plant to accommodate as many as 200–400 students. The cafeteria, measuring 80 by 40 feet, was located 100 feet to the east of the entrance of the University Center and was built by the end of October 1946. It was ready for students in January 1947 and was located close to the barracks-style dorms. This cafeteria was in use until the opening of Lee Hall in 1948.

In 1967, the old cafeteria became the home to workshops for ceramics and metal working. A roof fire caused the condemnation of the structure and the workshops were then moved to the Birdseye Building. After that date, the cafeteria had a variety of uses until it was demolished in 1970.

The Lee Hall cafeteria was opened for use in late December 1948. Located on the main floor of the Union building, where the University Art Museum is presently located, it was accessible to the residents of Carey Hall. It was available to small groups by partitioning the room, which held 175 guests. By 1958 this was known as the Wild Cat Den.

The Lee-Carey Hall complex also had separate dining facilities for men and women students serving Carey and Spooner Halls.

When the University Center opened in 1960, it had residence hall dining facilities and the cafeteria, known as the Wild Cat Den on the first floor. Its characteristic feature was wooden booths which had names, etc. carved into them. With the eastern extension of the UC in 1964, the Charcoal Room (*See separate entry*) was opened which originally served grilled food. It became a favorite dining room for faculty, staff and administrators.

All of these facilities continued to operate until the UC was renovated in the early 1990s and its was decided to consolidate all of the food service operations. The Charcoal Room and the Wild Cat Den were closed. The old residence hall dining room on the second floor became the central dining facility on campus serving the entire community. It was originally called The Food Court. In response to student opposition to the name change, in 1994 the Board of Control officially named it the Wildcat Den Food Court.

The area below the dining room in the Magers-Meyland complex developed into a variety of student recreation areas. In 1975, it became the down campus equivalent of the Wildcat Den. It was known as the Lower Deck, Golden N and the Ancient Mariner Galley. For a number of years, prior to 1998, the second floor was an empty space used for meetings of the Academic Senate and Catholic religious services. In March 1998, the area became the two-year temporary home of the Peter White Public Library, as the facility was being totally renovated.

Today, there are meal plans for students. Accounts are set up and are accessed by using a student I.D. card. Students residing both on and off campus can set up an account plan which is appropriate for their needs. Before 1987, Housing and Food Service were one department in the Finance and Administration Division. Now, both Housing and Food Services are separate departments in the Student Affairs Division.

Current locations of Food Service outlets include: Quad I Dining Hall in the Gant/Spalding-Payne/Halverson complex which provides daily buffet menus; Bookbinders Eatery in the lower level of the LRC which provides fast meals and snacks; the Wildcat Den Food Court in the University Center which provides a "shopping mall style" dining experience with a Domino's Pizza, salad, deli, and taco bars; and the Convenience Store Plus in the Gant/Spalding-Payne/Halverson complex which provides fast meals and snacks, along with convenience products. For one month out of each year, the Restaurant and Institutional Management students operate the Chez Nous Restaurant (*See separate entry*) in the Jacobetti Center (*See separate entry*). A full menu and service are offered. (NCN 10/30/1946, 12/01/1948; MJ 01/15/1949; *The 1996–97 University Profile*, 2:161–166) Alisa Koski

Football: Men's varsity football began in 1904 under the direction of William McCracken when Northern had enough male students to organize a team. The first game was played on Saturday October 15, 1904 against Hancock High School, and the score was 14 to 5 in favor of Hancock. At the time, Northern was known as the Teachers.

Due to the fact of distance to similar schools and travel costs in the early days, the Northern team played local high schools, YMCA and city teams. The number of games played greatly varied, and between 1913 and 1915 no games were played. In 1916, six games were played for the first time; in the past only three were played per year. St. Norberto's College in DePere, Wisconsin was the first collegiate school Northern played in 1916. World War I disrupted football games in 1918. The following year, two games were played. Three games were played in 1920: Michigan Tech twice, and St. Norbert. It was after this year that Northern started playing other colleges such as Michigan Tech, Central Michigan, and Wisconsin colleges. After that time until the disruptions created by World War II (no games were played between 1943 and 1945), six or seven scheduled games were played each year. In 1947 Northern began to play its games at Memorial Field (*See: Athletic Fields*).

The football program began to accelerate in 1956 when Northern went undefeated (7-0-1) under coach Lloyd Eaton. Frosty Ferzacca was hired in 1957 and remained football coach through the 1965 season. Northern participated in the National Association of Intercollegiate Athletics (NAIA) playoff in 1960 tying Lenoir Rhyne College (North Carolina) 20-20. The game was decided on the team with the most yardage and Northern lost. During Rollie Dotsch's tenure as coach (1966—1970) Northern went undefeated in 1967 and participated in the NAIA playoffs, losing to Fairmont State College (Virginia) 21-7.

In 1974, Gil Krueger became the head coach and remained through the 1977 season. In 1975 Northern won the NCAA Division II National Championship defeating Western Kentucky 16-14 in the Camellia Bowl at Sacramento, California. The following year Northern was defeated in the National semi-finals by Akron University 29-26 in overtime. Northern lost to North Dakota State 20-6 in the quarter finals in 1977.

A former Wildcat Great, Bill Rademacher became head coach in 1978. Northern participated in the NCAA playoffs in 1980–1981–1982. Herb Grenke, an assistant coach took over as head coach in 1983. The team participated in the NCAA playoffs in 1987 losing in the semi-finals to Portland (Oregon) State 13-7. In 1991 former player Mark Marana became coach through 1994. The following year Eric Holm was hired as head coach and remains in that position.

Football coaches: William McCracken, 1904;Charles E. Estrich, 1905–1906; Ward M. Mills, 1909; Deforest Stull, 1912; W. B. McClintock, 1916–1917; L. O. Gant, 1919–1921; C.B. Hedgcock, 1922–1933, 1936–1937; R. Victor Hurst, 1934–1935, 1938–1942, 1946; C.V. "Red" Money, 1947–1955; Lloyd W. Eaton, 1956; Fausto L. "Frosty" Ferzacca, 1957–1965; Rollie Dotsch, 1966–1971; Rae Drake, 1971–1973; Gil Krueger, 1974–1977; Bill Rademacher, 1978–1982; Herb Grenke, 1983–1990; Mark Marana, 1991–1994; and Eric Holm, 1995–present. (MJ 10/16/1904)

Ford, Henry: (1863–1947) The automotive giant who spent his summers in Big Bay. At one time, he tentatively planned to discuss an ethnomusical study or program with Lew Allen Chase of the History Department. Unfortunately, nothing came of this idea.

Foreign Languages, Department of: *See: Language Department*

Foreign Students: The first foreign student, Zenya Krihara from Japan, enrolled at Northern in 1919. In January, 1921, Ramon Quinit, a resident of San Quentin, Luzon, Philippines, attended Northern. Later, there was a student from Mexico.

By 1995, there were 112 international students studying at Northern: Canada (37); Japan (17); China (10); Malaysia (5); three each from Brazil, Germany, India, Mexico, Pakistan, the Philippines and Sri Lanka; two each from Austria, the Bahamas, Finland, Indonesia, Kenya, Liberia, Hong Kong, Switzerland, and Vietnam; one each from Bulgaria, Iran, Jamaica, Laos, the Netherlands, Norway, Portugal, Russia, Serbia, Spain, Sweden. They are assisted by the Office of International Student Services. (NNN 01/25/1921; Laura D. Wiesmann, "The International Affairs Department." (1995), UA)

Forensics: This is the art and study of argumentative discourse which in the old days was called debate. In the 1926 there was a paragraph in the *Bulletin* stating that there were "excellent opportunities to students who are interested in debating." In the 1920s, James C. Bowman was Director of Debate, and the drama societies met each week to "train young men and women to prepare arguments logically and to present them effectively." The Girls' Affirmative Debating Team and the Mens' Affirmative Intercollegiate Team were formed in 1927, along with the Negative Intercollegiate Team. The Webster Debating Club and the Haynes Debating Society were men's organizations organized in 1927 and started debating in 1928. The Minervan Debating Society consisted of women and formed in 1926. The women's Forum Debating Society formed a year later.

In 1955–1959, the team was active and Forest Roberts was the coach. Northern's team competed in national tournaments at the University of Wisconsin-Madison, Northwestern University, etc. The team continued into the early 1960s and proved to be very successful, winning many trophies. At the time of Roberts' retirement (1966), the debaters had a reunion-recognition dinner for their former coach at the Northwoods.

In the spring of 1965, NMU competed in a national tournament in Tacoma, Washington. Coach John Monsma, working with other coaches, chartered a train which left from Chicago and stopped all across the country picking up other coaches and teams. Pi Kappa Delta was the honorary debate society on campus.

Northern's forensics team was awarded top honors in the Michigan Intercollegiate Speech League Novice Division held by Ferris State University in the fall of 1972. The team chalked up a perfect 6-0 record, the only team out of twenty-five remaining undefeated throughout the competition. In 1973, coached by Barry Spiker, they walked off with the MISL varsity debate title from a competition held in Ann Arbor. In 1975, Northern was ranked 11th nationally. A few years later during a financial crisis, money for this successful program was abruptly removed and the program terminated. (Sources: *Bulletins*; *Kawbagam 1926–1928*) Michelle Kangas

Forest Roberts Theatre: The Little Theatre was part of a three-unit complex which was completed in 1963. The complex includes Russell Thomas Fine Arts Building and the Wayne McClintock Building (formerly the Industrial Education Wing).

The Little Theatre was dedicated and renamed for Forest A. Roberts, on May 31, 1969. In the summer of 1997, during a memorial service, a special bronze plaque and painting honoring Mr. Roberts was placed in the lobby of the theater.

The Forest Roberts Theatre has been described by visiting artists as one of the finest theaters of its kind in the world. It accommodates 550 people in a continental seating arrangement and has its own storage areas, shops, make-up and costume facilities, and dressing rooms.

Over the years renovations and improvements have been constantly carried out on the structure. During the summer of 1969, the final phase counterweight units, drapes and shop equipment were installed. This made the facility a totally complete and extremely flexible staging area. The Theater is particularly noted for its remarkable acoustics.

In 1995, a $320,000 project renovated the lobby and addressed several accessibility concerns.

Fort Wilkins Historical Complex: Since 1987 Northern has received a number of contracts from the Michigan Bureau of History whereby the History Department selects and trains student role players. They spend the summer in the Copper Harbor facility, recreating life in the summer of 1870 at the fort.

Four Course Plan: In January 1965, Northern Michigan University faculty adopted a "four-course" curriculum plan, to become effective on a university-wide basis in September, 1966. Under the new curriculum, the traditional credit-hour as a unit of academic measure was abandoned. In its place appeared the course, which represented the acquisition of a skill and/or a body of knowledge engaging approximately one-fourth of the formal academic effort of a student during one semester. The plan called for all courses to be equal in credit; most full-time students enrolled in four courses each semester; the successful completion of 32 courses was required for a baccalaureate degree.

During 1965–66, the faculty developed new curriculum offerings within the general pattern of the plan. The faculty believed that the new curriculum would afford students an opportunity to explore subject matter in greater depth, to pursue more easily the general arrangement of degree requirements, and to benefit from improved academic advisement.

The problem with the Plan was that it did not include credits. Under it, the Registrar's Office had no way of accepting transfer credits. As a result it had to be abandoned. Four-credit courses are retained by the University. Some departments offer varied credit for courses, but four credits remains the norm. (Source: *Bulletin* 1965)

Founders Day Banquet: First held in April 1988, sponsored by Phi Alpha Theta, the banquet drew over 200 people to the University Center Explorer Rooms. The program consisted of an exhibition honoring Northern's involvement in World War II. Earl Hilton was the guest speaker, and Cliff Maier received the Phi Alpha Theta Award or later Waldo Award (*See separate entry*). The second annual dinner in 1989 was held at the Bonanza Restaurant, due to a lack of space on campus. At this time Martin Dolan (Admissions) was presented with the Waldo Award for his work to bring a Phi Alpha Theta chapter to campus in the spring of 1969. The next banquet was held in early April 1995, and its theme was World War II. The 1996 dinner had to be canceled due to a lack of interest. On April 30, 1999 the Centennial Gala will be held on campus in the Superior Dome continuing this tradition.

Franchise: The first franchise on the NMU campus was Domino's Pizza, which is located in the Wildcat Den Food Court. According to Dick Wittman, director of Food Services, this was done in response to students who "wanted the franchise or brand names that they grew up with." Operated by Domino's employees, the station caused concern for the union workers. Numerous articles appeared in the *North Wind* beginning on 01/12/1995.

Fraternities: *See: Greek Organizations*

Free University: Also known as "Free U," The Free University or "alternative university" concept began at Northern in the fall of 1976. Classes and workshops were taught by NMU faculty, students and local residents. Topics ranged from "Investing for Pleasure and Gain" to "Appalachian Clog Dancing." Interest in these informal classes went from seven classes with 85 participants in the beginning to 50 classes and 1,000 participants per semester by the fall of 1983. There was no academic credit given for these classes. Registration was $1 for a student with a valid ID and $3 for a non-student. The program was one of 25 in the nation run solely by students. Interest in this program waned among students in the late 1980s and the program was terminated. The concept was revived in the fall of 1998 with Discovery Daze (*See separate entry*) developed by the Student Activities and Leadership Programs. (NW 09/28/1983)

Friday's Fairest: A weekly photo feature of an attractive female student in the *Northern News* which ran from 1965 into the early 1970s. It was a take-off on *Playboy*'s "Playmate of the Month." (NN 12/12/1969)

Friends of Lee Hall Gallery or Friends of the University Art Museum: *See: Art Museum, University*

Frog Pond: A low lying area "behind the tennis courts," which would now be on the south side of the Sculpture Walk, the pond was filled with standing water and had a frog population. It was filled in the summer of 1934, along with other ponds in low lying areas in the vicinity.

Gallery 236: *See: Art Works and Places*

Gannon Lumber Mill: A large milling complex which was located off the Big Bay Road. The site was purchased by the University and became the site of the Jacobetti Center which opened in 1980. Prior to building construction, tons of saw dust had to be removed.

Gant, Luther O.: (September 23, 1888–November 8, 1971) Born in Hancock County, Indiana, Mr. Gant was a graduate of Fortville High School, Indiana and DePauw University, Green Castle, Indiana. He did graduate work at the University of Chicago and taught in the French Lick, Indiana High School.

From 1913 to 1917 he taught at Ishpeming High School. From there Gant came to Northern as coach and mathematics teacher. Gant served as Northern's football coach from 1919 to 1921. In 1926, he was appointed Registrar and 30 years later he became Director of Admissions, a position he held until his retirement in 1959.

In recognition of his service to the University, he was awarded an honorary Doctor of Laws degree in 1959 from Northern. Gant Hall was dedicated to him on November 22, 1964.

He was a member of the First United Presbyterian Church, Michigan and National Retired Teachers Associations, and a life member of the Fortville Lodge (Masonic) and Ahmed Temple Shrine. Gant was also an honorary member of the Michigan Association of Collegiate Registrars and Admissions Officers. (MJ 11/08/1971)

Gant Residence Hall: *See: Quad I*

Gender Studies: This interdisciplinary minor, evolved from feminist women's studies, explores the significance and meaning of gender in human experience, including the roles, status and accomplishments of women and men within a number of academic fields. The minor is considered particularly appropriate for students majoring in humanities, social science, counseling, or communication. For specific information consult the latest *Undergraduate Bulletin*.

Geography Department: One of the original departments created by the State Board of Education on July 14, 1899. The first geography courses were basic and were taught by Martha B. Ackermann. The program included Physical Geography, Meteorology and a general course for teachers of geography. There were also drawing courses that included cartography. In 1903, General Geography (human geography) replaced the course for teachers and Commercial Geography supplanted Physical Geography and Meteorology.

The Geography Department was officially created in 1905, with Frances Martin Kelsey as its head. Many changes in course offerings and department heads soon followed. Among these changes were the increase in the availability of text materials. Such materials reduced the department's emphasis on the use of maps, models, laboratories and field trips that were used to teach geography early in the century. New offerings included courses in geology and continental geography, which were fields of knowledge being developed early in the Geography Department's history.

The department's course offerings in conservation in the 1960s attracted some of the transient, environmentally attuned members of the nation's burgeoning counterculture known as "the backpackers." They would attend Northern courses for one or two semesters, then move to another college town. At one point in the mid 1960s, there were over 600 students majoring in geography.

Most graduates of the department in the first half of the century became teachers, but jobs for geographers in government and industry increased in the second half of the century. By the early 1970s, the geography department had eleven full-time and two part-time professors. Courses were often revised as specific needs of employers were realized. Diverse course offerings included recreation planning, bio-physical systems and environmental studies.

By the mid-1990s, the Department was committed to offering programs in applied geography, teacher education and preparatory work for graduate study. The department was also committed to offering quality courses that satisfied the Liberal Studies requirement in the areas of social science, natural science/mathematics and world culture. The department's liberal arts majors are land use planning and management, conservation, geography and earth science. These majors prepare students for a variety of careers and professions ranging from government service to private industry to research. The secondary education program prepares students for teaching careers in geography, earth science, social studies and general science.

The department's Laboratory for Mapping is one of the best cartographic labs in the country. The Global Position System (GPS) operates via satellite and is in place to accurately locate and map campus buildings, roadways, and other physical features. Graphic Information System (GIS) provides documentation and expands management information data on all campus buildings and grounds.

As the department grew and expanded, its name did as well. In 1960 the Department of Conservation and Agriculture was altered and became a part of the Geography Department. In March 1963 Agriculture was discontinued as a part of Geography. The name of the Department of Geography was changed to the Department of Geography, Earth Sciences, Conservation and Planning, effective July 1, 1986. This reverted back to the Department of Geography in 1998.

Department Chairs and Heads: Frances Martin Kelsey, 1905–1906; Charles H. Estrich, 1906–1909; Ward Magoon Mills, 1909–1910; Theodosia Hamilton Hadley, 1909–1911; DeForest Stull, 1909–1923; J. Russel Whitaker, 1924–1930; Lynn Halverson, 1930–1962; Henry Heimonen, 1962–1972; John Hughes, 1972–1978; Jarl Roine, 1978–1988; Alfred Joyal, 1989–1992; J. Pat Farrell, 1992–1997; Alfred Joyal, (acting) 1997; Michael Broadway, 1997–present.

(J. Pat Farrell, interview 7/11/97, UA; Hilton, pp. 169, 231; Nathan P. Mellott, "History of the Geography Department," UA; *University Bulletins*; *The 1996–97 University Profile*, 1:103–109)

Get Fit Program: The Get Fit Program is a professionally supervised adult physical fitness program tailored for each individual. Participants are required to pre-register, go through an initial physical fitness assessment which includes a "resting" electrocardiogram, body composition analysis, lung function, and a graded exercise test. Based on this assessment, the participant's exercise prescription is carried out within exercise sessions available. There is a fee and the exercise sessions (aerobic, muscular endurance and exibility exercises) take place in the PEIF building.

Gifts: A lost tradition at Northern is the presentation of a class gift to the institution. Some of the gifts have included the statue of Abraham Lincoln (1916), $50 from the Ygdrasil Literary Society for two student loans, the entrance gate (class of 1926) for the 1932 football field at the end of Kaye Avenue and the Northeast Gate at the corner of Waldo and Presque Isle, which served as a memorial to the class of 1932. The class of 1935 donated the flagstone for the gate entry. By 1951, $3,437 had been collected from several classes. The money was used to purchase "carillonic bells" and amplifying equipment for the auditorium. In the 1950s gifts included a television, a 35-mm camera, and a whirlpool for the Health Center. As Northern grew the class gift was dropped as a tradition.

Girls' League: *See: Student Girls' League*

The Glenn T. Seaborg Center for Teaching and Learning Science and Mathematics: *See: Seaborg, Glenn T.*

Glenn T. Seaborg Science Complex: *See: Seaborg, Glenn T.*

Global Position System (GPS): *See: Geography*

Golden Fern: A literary magazine produced during the late 1980s by students with a faculty advisor.

Golden N: *See: Food Service*

Golden Wildcat Club: A dedicated group of alumni and friends created the Club in 1969 to promote and financially support the University's total athletic program. As an example of their work during the 1995–1996 school year, the Golden Wildcat Club assisted athletics with at least $135,000 for scholarships and recruiting expenses. The Club is part of the NMU Development Fund.

Golf (Men): As early as 1936, golfers from Northern played matches against golfers from Michigan Tech. Men's varsity golf was introduced as an official intercollegiate sport for the first time in 1948 and continued through 1972 when the sport was dropped because of budgetary constraints. The highlight of the varsity golf program was in 1965 when Northern won the State NAIA championship defeating Central Michigan University by 16 strokes. Members of the team coached by Gildo Canale were Ken Hurska, Garrett Leffter, Jim Powell, Richard Lehto and Peter Zenti.

In 1993, the men's golf team was reinstated to fulfill the number of sports required by the NCAA Division II membership. The 1993 golf team consisted of six players, four being from the Upper Peninsula. The head coach of the team is Dean Ellis, who is also the basketball coach.(NCN 05-20-36, 04-07-48; Sports Information Office) Michelle Kangas

Graduate Council: *See: Graduate Program Committee*

Graduate Program: The graduate program can be traced back to March 1935, when the State Board of Education opened negotiations with the University of Michigan to give graduate courses on Northern's campus during the summer. Beginning in the summer of 1938, Northern offered graduate courses under a cooperative plan with the University of Michigan. Under this program, approximately one-half of the members of Northern's faculty were approved by the University of Michigan to teach graduate courses and some 100 courses were offered. Courses were offered at Northern by its own faculty and Michigan faculty. Students were required to spend a summer on the Michigan campus. For this work they received a master's degree from the University of Michigan.

Authority to establish an independent program was granted by action of the State Board of Education on October 12, 1957. This authority went into effect on September 1, 1960. By the same action, Central, Eastern and Western Universities were authorized to set up autonomous programs.

Drs. Harold M. Dorr and Edgar G. Johnston provided the first graduate training. Dr. Albert H. Burrows was the chair of the Departments of Social Sciences and Graduate Studies (1944–1957). In 1957, Burrows was removed as head of the former department and devoted full time to expanding the program of graduate studies. (MJ 06/19/1957; NN 02/25/1959); *The 1996–97 University Profile*, 1:18–21).

Graduate Program Committee: Commonly referred to as the GPC, this Committee had its origins in the Graduate Council of Northern's Graduate Program, which was created in 1960. It was responsible for the formulation and supervision of all policies pertaining to this program. It was later replaced by the Graduate Program Committee which continues to guide the graduate program.

Graduate Studies, College of: The Graduate Studies Program came under the sole control of Northern in June 1960 (*See: Graduate Program*). In August 1960 the first master's degree was awarded to Olive Atkins. During the 1960s, graduate courses were offered in such fields as education, biology, English and history. Many of these courses were taught in the summer, with fall and winter courses most often taught by professors to individual students. Graduate degree programs in chemistry, mathematics, secondary education, and physical education were authorized in 1968. The chemistry graduate program closed during the 1980s, but was reborn in 1990. The Art and Design Department's graduate program began in 1970 and ended in 1993 due to funding. The graduate English program began in 1970.

The College of Graduate Studies provides degree programs for teachers, school administrators, public administrators, and other professionals; Master's degrees in selected academic departments; and post-degree professional development and enrichment opportunities. Graduate degrees currently exist for the following departments: Administrative Services, M.A.: Public Administration, Administrative Services; Biology, M.S.; Chemistry, M.S.; Communication Disorders, M.A.; Education, M.A.E.: Educational Administration, Elementary Education, Special Education, Secondary Education in major disciplines; Education

Certification Programs: State Professional Education Certificate, Secondary, Elementary Provisional, Secondary Provisional, Additional Endorsement, Professional Personal Development; English, M.A.: English, Writing; Exercise Science, M.S.; Individualized Studies; Mathematics Education, M.S.; Nursing, M.S.N.: Advanced Adult Health Nursing, Nursing Administration, Advanced Practice Nursing; Public Administration, M.P.A.: General Administration, Health Care Administration, Personnel and Labor Relations, State and Local Administration, Community Planning, Financial Administration; Administration Certification Programs: Personnel Administration, Budget Administration, Health Care Administration, Public Program Evaluation and Analysis.

Deans: Albert Burrows, 1960–1962; Vito Perrone, 1962–1969; Lloyd Swearinga, (acting) 1969–1970; Roland Strolle, 1970–1975; Roy Heath, 1975–1980; Jane Swafford, 1980–1985; Peter Smith, (interim) 1987–1988; Roger Gill, 1988–1992; Peter Smith (interim) 1992–1995; David J. Prior, 1995–1998; Sara Doubledee, (acting) 1998–present. (Joshua Crane, "Graduate College," (1995) UA; College of Graduate Studies, 1997; Hilton p. 232; *The 1996–97 University Profile*, 1:18–21)

Grand Rapids Rampage Arena Football: The game is played on turf placed in an ice arena and used as the field. There are eight players on the field and it is a fast action, high scoring game. The Arena Football League, or AFL bills itself as "the 50-yard indoor war." The season runs from April through August.

Dan DeVos, vice president for corporate affairs for Amway Corporation and member of the Board of Control owns the team. It came to the Superior Dome for pre-season practice from March 28 through April 14, 1999.

Graphic Identity Standards Task Force: *See: Signature*

Graphic Information System (GIS): *See: Global Positioning System*

Great Lakes Sports Academy and Outreach Programs: *See: Olympic*

Great Lakes Sports Training Center: *See: Olympic*

Great Lakes State Games: The first State Games were held between July 31 and August 2, 1987 on campus and at facilities throughout Marquette County. This Olympic-style festival of competitions brought participants from throughout the state of Michigan. It was an official Sesquicentennial (of Michigan Statehood) event.

3,602 athletes attended and registration had to be cut off. The event had a $3.6 million economic impact on the Marquette economy. The Games received extensive television coverage.

A Commission recommended to the Governor that the Games be held again in 1988 in Marquette and $350,000 was appropriated. However, the Games were held downstate.

Greek Organizations or Letter Societies: The earliest Greek society, Sons of Thor, dates back to 1914. Over the years, but especially in the 1920s, numerous Greek societies developed and expanded. Tri Mu, one of the earliest NMU fraternities, having started around 1922, was the first fraternity to buy a house for its members. Theta Omicron Rho and Alpha Delta (organized 1924) bought houses in 1927. Three sororities were established in 1923: Cegmer Seg, Delta Sigma Nu and Beta Omega Tau. By 1930, three other sororities were added: Phi Kappa Nu, Tau Pi Nu and Gamma Phi Alpha.

In 1963, there were twenty Greek organizations on campus; in 1966 there were thirteen: two local and two national sororities, five national and four local fraternities. Several local Greek organizations affiliated with national fraternities during the 1960s. Tri-Mu became a chapter of Tau Kappa Epsilon in 1961, the first national fraternity on Northern's campus; the Theta Omicron Rho fraternity joined Delta Sigma Phi; in 1962, Sigma Rho fraternity joined Phi Kappa Tau and Delta Sigma Nu sorority joined Alpha Xi Delta, becoming NMU's first national sorority; and Beta Omega Tau sorority joined Delta Zeta.

During the period from 1969–1973 there were 15 social fraternities and nine sororities active on campus. During this heyday, the societies provided social activities and some of them provided community service. The Greek Rush held in the spring was a major event on campus. Many of the members of the Greek societies played an important role in campus political life.

By the end of the 1970s, the Greeks had declined to eight organizations, and in 1983 there were six: five fraternities and one sorority. These included the fraternities: Alpha Phi Alpha, Alpha Sigma Phi, Lambda Chi Alpha, Phi Kappa Tau, Theta Chi, and the sorority Alpha Xi Delta. Many of the older societies which dated back to the 1920s were disbanded.

In 1983, there was serious talk of reviving the Greek system, but little had come of it a decade later. The plan was to establish a "fraternity row" in the vicinity of Tracy and Wright streets. By 1997–1998 the Greek organizations included: Alpha Gamma Delta, Alpha Kappa Psi, Alpha Phi Omega, Alpha Xi Delta, Delta Chi, Greek Council, Lambda Chi Alpha, Panhellenic Council, Phi Kappa Theta, Phi Kappa Tau, Phi Sigma, Tau Kappa Epsilon.

The departmental honorary societies are: Alpha Kappa Psi (Business), Kappa Delta Pi (Education), Gamma Theta Upsilon (Geography), Phi Alpha Theta (History), Sigma Tau Delta (English), Sigma Theta Tau (Nursing). (NW 02/24/1983, 10/20/1983; Hilton, pp. 73, 184)

Greek Row: During the winter of 1987, discussions about a Greek Row were begun when Mayor Michael Coyne created a Greek Row Committee composed of representatives of the City Commission, NMU administration, students and home owners. An ideal location was Tracy Street, which was closed off at Wright Street. The funding was to come from the national and local organizations through loans. After the initial concerns and interest, the project was not realized. (NW 09/26/1991)

Green Barn: This metal structure was located on the west edge of campus and originally was the livestock barn for the Marquette County Fair. It consisted of 13,340 square feet of space and was used for storage. By the 1990s, the roof needed repairs and leaked. Items stored in the structure were easily damaged by the elements. In September, 1997 the structure was demolished to make way for a new tennis court complex.

Greenwood Nature Center: A proposal to establish a Regional Environmental Educational Center (REECUP) at Cleveland Cliffs' Greenwood Reservoir was reported to the Board of Control on July 17, 1975. The Center was created in 1976 on land leased to the University by Cleveland Cliffs Iron Company. It consisted of 160 acres of sphagnum bog, tag alder swamp, open marsh, upland deciduous forest and a lake, Greenwood Reservoir on the Middle Branch of the Escanaba River. The site was located eighteen miles west of Marquette in West Ishpeming.

The site was administered by REECUP, a unit of the University. The professional consultant and advisor of the Center was Dr. Donald A. Snitgen. It was a designated ecological study area, and inter-disciplinary learning activities were planned for the site. Plans called for a nature center, trails, and a variety of activities and workshops for university students, area schools and the general public.

It operated through the decade of the 1970s. In December 1982, the University signed an annual lease with Cleveland Cliffs from $1 to $10, effective January 1, 1983, for the remaining nine years of the lease. Unfortunately, due to budget cuts which followed, the site was closed soon after. (David Kronk. "A Proposal to Develop the Greenwood Nature Center," (1979); "Master Plan for the Greenwood Nature Center," August 1979. UA)

Gridiron Club: The Club was organized in 1996 to encourage, promote and support football at Northern. Membership is opened to anyone interested in the sport of football.

Gries, Walter (October 1, 1892–November 8, 1959) Mr. Gries was a civic-minded and prominent citizen who served in numerous public capacities over the years. He was born in Lake Linden, Michigan and began his career in education after graduation from Calumet High School in 1912. Gries taught in a rural school in Houghton County before he entered the University of Michigan. He received his bachelor's degree in education in 1923 after attending summer sessions and an interruption by World War I when he served on the Houghton County Draft Board. He was married to Velta and they had one daughter.

Later he served as principal of the Tamarack School in Calumet and a grammar school in Ishpeming. For seven years, he was superintendent of schools in Marquette County (1927–1935) and president of the Michigan County School Commissioners Association and vice president of the Michigan Education Association. He taught three summer sessions at Northern during the 1930s.

Gries was a member of the Michigan Prison Commission and was appointed warden of the Marquette Branch Prison, 1935–1937. He became affiliated with the Cleveland Cliffs Iron Company in its Welfare Department in 1937 and assumed the superintendent's position in 1938.

He was known as a gifted after-dinner speaker and was in demand throughout the Upper Peninsula. Gries also was a folklorist of Cornish dialect stories that were used in folklore collections, especially those of Richard M. Dorson.

Long interested in Michigan education, Gries was a trustee of the State Board of Education from 1953 to 1957. He was president of the Board from 1957 to 1959 when he declined reelection. During this time he was a staunch supporter of Northern.

In the spring of 1954, when President Henry Tape was ill on Long Island, the Board appointed Gries acting president. On the afternoon of April, 29 he met with Northern administrators and created the Interim Administrative Committee which consisted of L. O. Gant (chair), Max Allen, Don Bottum, Ethel Carey, and Leo Van Tassel. Gries met with them on a weekly basis to administer Northern. Under these conditions, work proceeded on construction plans for Spooner Hall.

Gries was honored by Northern on two occasions. On June 13, 1953 he was awarded an honorary Doctor of Laws, and he received a Centennial Award from Michigan State University in 1955. Upon his death in November 1959, President Edgar Harden praised his worked with the youth of Michigan. On October 13, 1961 Gries Residence Hall, which has subsequently been converted into faculty offices, was named in his honor. The Walter F. Gries Memorial Fund was instituted at Northern.

His service and memberships included innumerable fraternal and welfare organizations throughout the Upper Peninsula and the state. (NCN 06/05/1953, 06/03/1959; MJ 08/28/1958, 12/10/1958, 11/23/1959, 11/27/1959; *Cliffs News* 08/1958, 02/1960; *Negaunee Iron Herald* 12/24/1954; *Harlow's Wooden Man's* 7:3 (Summer 1971)

Gries Hall: Named in honor of Walter Gries, the hall (52,482 square feet) was constructed in 1961 and dedicated on October 13, 1961. It remained a residence hall until the early 1990s when there were preliminary discussions to convert it to a faculty office building. In 1995, a $4.2 million project was completed which included renovation of the building for faculty offices, classrooms and laboratories. The building is also the location of the Upper Peninsula World War I Military Hall of Fame located in the Military Science Department. The Ada Vielmetti Health Center is located on the ground floor of the east wing. A plaque placed in December 1996 identifies Walter Gries.

Guest Day: The Home Economics Department sponsored an annual "Guest Day" in the spring. In April 1950, some 700 teachers and students of home economics from the Upper Peninsula attended the event on campus. The program consisted of a dance or mixer. On the following day, there was a university welcome, group singing, discussion of projects, luncheon and a style show in the afternoon. (NCN 04/26/1950)

Gulf War (1991): See: Persian Gulf War

Gun Storage: See: Weapons on Campus

Gymnasium, Original: The original gymnasium, completed in June of 1906 at a cost of $16,000, was an annex to the south of the Peter White Science Hall. The upper rooms of the building housed recreation facilities and the basement was a gymnasium which was first used in the 1906–1907 academic year. With the completion of Kaye Hall in 1915, all of the structures were connected. The gym was used as an auxiliary gym for a number of years and then it was converted into office space. The building was demolished in 1972. Alisa Koski

Gymnastics (Men): In 1926, a men's tumbling team was formed as a campus organization coached by Victor Hurst. Lowell Meier inaugurated men's gymnastics as a new varsity sport in 1966. Sophomore Glenn Wellman was the first to score points for Northern in a tumbling event. The team competed in the Great Lakes League and NCAA championships as well as the Lake Erie and Midwestern conferences. During the tenure of the sport, Meier coached three All-American athletes—William Summerhays, Richard Dahl, and Scott Winder—at the NCAA Division II level.

Meier served as coach until 1988 when the program was dropped because of financial constraints. Overall, the team posted 89 wins and 41 losses. (Sports Information Office file) Michelle Kangas

Halverson, Lynn H.: (1900–May 23, 1973) A native of Madison, Wisconsin, Halverson was graduated from the then Oshkosh State Teachers College in 1917 and later obtained bachelor's, master's and doctoral degrees from the University of Wisconsin, Madison.

A veteran of World War I, he served as a first sergeant in an Army machine gun company. His military career also included service as an officer in the Michigan State Troops, formed when National Guard units were called to active military service.

Prior to coming to Northern in 1927, he taught at the State College of Iowa, University of Wisconsin, and Joliet Township, Illinois high school and junior college. He was also on the summer session faculties of Northwestern University and Michigan State University.

Halverson was appointed by President Munson to head the Geography Department. For the next thirty years, he and Roy M. McCollum taught all of the courses in geography and earth science. He was known for trips to Presque Isle with students in the Geography Club to study the ancient Laurentian shield upthrust and young sedimentary rock. Halverson also lectured on utilization and rural zoning. Following his retirement on June 30, 1962, he was named professor emeritus. During his retirement, he spent the winters in Sarasota, Florida and his summers in the Beulah-Frankfort areas of Lower Michigan.

Active in civic affairs, Halverson was a member and chair of the first Marquette Planning Board established in 1946, was elected to the Marquette Charter Commission (1949), and was elected three times to the Marquette City Commission after 1952.

Interested in hunting, fishing and boating, he served as president of the Marquette Rod and Gun Club and was active in the Northern Michigan Sportsmen's Association. While in Marquette, he was also affiliated with the Rotary Club and the First Methodist Church. He was also an enthusiastic traveler, visiting all parts of the United States, several sections of Canada, and eleven European nations.

In 1964, Halverson was named recipient of Northern's Arts Recognition Award for contributions in language and literature. Halverson Residence Hall was dedicated on October 3, 1965.

Halverson Residence Hall: The three-story hall is located near Lincoln and Wright Streets. The architect was Swanson Associates of Bloomfield Hills, Michigan, and it was constructed by the Caspian Construction Company of Caspian, Michigan. Construction was completed in 1965 at the cost of $2,058,000. The building covers 55,935 square feet. The building was dedicated to Dr. Lynn Halverson on October 3, 1965. (NN 09/24/1965) Alisa Koski

Harden, Edgar L.: (October 31, 1906–May 2, 1996) Dr. Harden was born in Montezuma, Iowa. A graduate of Iowa State Teachers College in 1930, he earned his Master of Arts degree from the State University of Iowa in 1937, and his doctorate from Wayne State University. Dr. Harden began his teaching career in Iowa, served as principal of high schools in Iowa and Illinois, and came to Michigan in 1945 as principal of Battle Creek High School. Over the years he also coached both basketball and baseball, and as a high school principal encouraged participation on athletic programs.

In 1946, he joined the faculty of Michigan State University as associate professor of counseling, testing and guidance. Dr. Harden was promoted in 1950 to Director of Continuing Education at Michigan State University. In 1951, he helped break ground for the Kellogg Center for Continuing Education. Two years later, Dr. Harden was named Dean of Continuing Education, a position he held until 1955, when he resigned to enter the management ranks of industry as executive vice president of the Drop Forging Association. While at MSU, Dr. Harden represented the University on the Big Ten Conference Council.

Over the years Dr. Harden developed the Michigan State University idea that a university must be concerned with outreach to the people. He also had strong leadership skills and had a philosophy of education. Some people would criticize him for his paternalism but that was standard among college presidents at the time.

Dr. Harden was appointed by the State Board of Education to become the president of Northern Michigan College in 1956. When he came to Northern, the Upper Peninsula was in a precarious state with a poor economy and the small enrollments at Northern. This situation had caused some legislators to talk of closing the institution. As a matter of fact, Harden was told to either close the place or make it a better institution. (*See: Closure*)

Harden saw this as a challenge. He thought in terms of building broadly in order to serve more people and in the process to enlarge and enrich the region economically. He wanted to create an institution where people could learn and develop the skills to allow them to help themselves. This was a key ingredient in his philosophy, the right-to-try.

His administration (1956–1967) was taken up with developing this philosophy. First he quickly became acquainted with the people of the Upper Peninsula by traveling throughout the region and meeting them. He modernized the administration and brought in individuals who shared the Michigan State University outreach orientation. Clair Hekhuis was brought in to manage the News Bureau. Harold Sponberg became the first vice president in Northern's history and Claude Bosworth was placed in charge of the Public Services Division established in 1956. The radio and television stations were developed so that the University could serve the larger region.

Harden's right-to-try philosophy was part of an overall outlook that people should help themselves. Having experienced the terrible times of the Depression, he wanted to provide youth with an opportunity. Part of his view was that Northern should be a broad-based institution and not a prep school. Numerous students were attracted to Northern because of this philosophy, graduated, and have gone on to make their mark in the world.

Naturally, increased enrollments were important. He made sure Northern was constantly in the news and he, his staff and faculty visited schools and people throughout the Upper Peninsula. Music and theater programs were a way to advertise Northern. He even had the admissions staff go to distant places like Cleveland, Ohio to promote Northern. During his administration, the only Job Corps (*See separate entry*) program on a college campus was activated. Many of the trainees stayed and enrolled in regular academic programs. The result was that in 1955, the student body numbered 888, and when Harden left in 1967 the fall enrollment was 7,085. This proved to be an average annual increase of 8.4 per cent.

The curriculum was expanded as was the number of faculty members. He also oversaw the break-away of the graduate program from the University of Michigan and the development of Northern's own graduate program in June 1960. New departments and schools were created. Strong extension programs developed around the Upper Peninsula and K. I. Sawyer Air Force Base was a major off-campus site. As a result of this planning, Northern Michigan College became a University on March 13, 1963 and with that came its own Board of Control, seal and flag.

In the legislature he out-did his mentor, Dr. John Hannah, the president of Michigan State University, with his budgets. When questioned about their size, he said he was merely seeking what was best for the people of the Upper Peninsula. Dr. Harden maintained excellent relations with the two key Upper Peninsula legislators, Joe Mack and Dominic Jacobetti. As a result, during his tenure the budget went from $914,376 to $5,140,342.

The physical plant of the campus was radically expanded. The Don H. Bottum University Center (*See separate entry*) opened in 1960 and quickly expanded in 1964 and again in 1966. The Gries-West Residence complex was opened and Quad I and II along with student and faculty apartments were developed. The Luther West Science Building was constructed and opened in the mid-1960s. Plans were developed for Jamrich Hall for instructional purposes. President Harden was personally instrumental in developed the Learning Resources Center (*See separate entry*) which was dedicated to him. He wanted to have all of the learning facilities from books to television under one roof.

In his move to broaden the University, President Harden encouraged the development of the athletic program and the marching band. He felt that all of the parts made up the whole, broad university.

Harden was open to students and faculty. His office was on the first floor of Kaye Hall, and anyone could see him. He knew every faculty member and what they were doing. One time when the state could not meet the payroll, Harden took out a personal loan and the staff and students got paid.

One major problem-the McClellan controversy-(*See separate entry*) faced his administration in its closing days. Dr. Robert McClellan was a member of the History Department who activated students to warn people whose land the University sought that they had rights and did not have to sell their property. Dr. Harden saw McClellan as a challenge to the presidency and had the Board of Control not reinstate him. Dr. Harden had resigned and was gone, when the court challenge and campus protest broke out. This resignation had nothing to do with the controversy. The affair was resolved by court action, which saw McClellan reinstated during the Jamrich administration in 1968.

Dr. Harden received the Exceptional Service Award from the U.S. Air Force in recognition of distinguished patriotic service during the period 1953 to 1962 as Chairman of the Armed Forces Education Program Committee; as President of NMU, which developed an educational program for Air Force personnel at K.I. Sawyer Air Force Base; and as a civilian leader who made outstanding contributions to the military-civilian relationship. For his service to education, Dr. Harden earned numerous distinctions.

He resigned from NMU in 1967 to become president of Story Incorporated, an automobile agency in Lansing. Dr. Harden was presented with an honorary Alumni Citation in 1956 and was given the Distinguished Citizen Award in 1975 by the MSU Board of Trustees. In 1977, he was designated co-chairperson of the Mid-Michigan Committee for the University's $17-Million Enrichment Program. In 1977, the MSU Board of Trustees appointed Dr. Harden acting president after Clifton R. Wharton, Jr. announced his resignation.

At a later date, the Board took official action and dropped the "acting," making Dr. Harden the 16th president of Michigan State University until August 1, 1979. Upon his retirement, he was given the title president emeritus from MSU. In 1983, Dr. Harden retired as president of Story Incorporated and became vice chairman of the Board of Directors.

He was married to Elizabeth "Betty," and had two children, Pamela and Donald. When not living in Marquette, the family resided in East Lansing.

On campus, he is remembered with the Edgar L. Harden Learning Resources Center, dedicated on August 11, 1973 and a memorial scholarship in his name. In August 1980 he was awarded an honorary doctorate in Public Service. He ended his August 1994 interview summing his reason for doing what he did on campus with, "I like to help people." (*Towne Courier* (E. Lansing) 05/11/1996; Interview, 08/04/1994, UA)

Harden, Edgar L. Learning Resources Center: While Edgar Harden was president 1956–1967, it was clear that the Olson Library, which was built in 1951, needed improvements. The library was suited to accommodate 618 students and there were 1,876 students in 1960. In a 1962 report done by the State College of Iowa, Northern was ranked 23rd in population out of 46 Midwest state colleges. Of the 46 colleges, 75 percent had more library space per student than Northern did. President Harden had an idea that a new library should have all learning resources under one roof, creating the concept of the learning resource center. He said, "The learning resource center was something I dreamed about, because I think you should get faculty, students, and facilities close together." By 1967, ground was broken for the new Learning Resource Center. Though the structure was not complete until 1969, the name "Edgar L. Harden Learning Resources Center" was decided upon in 1968. The official dedication ceremony took place on August 11, 1973. Cost upon completion totaled $5.5 million. Today, there are no more faculty offices in the LRC; they were moved out by 1996. The building currently houses a computer lab with over 300 computer spots, the Bookbinders eatery, a distance learning classroom, the Central Upper Peninsula and Northern Michigan University Archives, the Library, the Connector Link tunnel which connects the LRC to West Science, and the Learning Resource Division which includes Audio Visual, Engineering, Instructional Development, Productions and Operation, WNMU TV, and WNMU FM. (Jonathan Kistler, "The LRC," UA; Hilton, pp. 212–213) Michelle Kangas

Harden, Elizabeth "Betty": The wife of President Edgar L. Harden. She acted as "mother" to many students who needed her help and intervention. The Elizabeth C. Harden Circle Drive (*See separate entry*) was named in her honor by the Board of Control on July 17, 1975.

Harlem Globetrotters: The Harlem Globetrotters professional basketball team came to Hedgcock Fieldhouse for the first time on February 26, 1959 and has made return engagements over the years. (NN 02/18/1959).

Haywire: In the fall of 1994, Dr. Shelley Russell-Parks wrote and produced, the musical "Haywire" (lyrics by Russell-Parks, music by Russell-Parks and Robert Engelhart, musical arrangements by Engelhart). It was first produced on Northern's campus and received rave reviews. In 1995 it was performed at the American College Theater Regional Festival at the Weidner Center in Green Bay, WI and later at the National Festival at the Kennedy Center in Washington, D.C.

Health Center: For the first 30 years of Northern's existence, limited on-campus health services were offered. Students were referred to city health officials in the *Northern Bulletin* in the 1920s. In 1922–1923, the City Health Officer provided physical examinations to students at the Normal school. In 1922, he gave 200 students heart and lung examinations to see if they were fit for taking physical training. In October 1927, Dr. W. L. Casler was appointed the school physician for women and Dr. H.B. Markham held a similar position for the men. Other physicians filled similar positions over the years. Northern's first nurse was Martha Hatch, who was listed in the *Bulletin* for 1944–1945. Her tiny office was in Kaye Hall.

Ailments treated by the nurse were most often colds, sore throats, anemia, headaches, earaches and menstrual problems. Worse ailments were treated at St. Luke's Hospital, and athletic injuries were handled by coaches. Health examinations were given to students at the beginning of the school year.

Hatch resigned to become an instructor for Northern's Licensed Practical Nurse program and Ada Vielmetti of Ishpeming was hired to replace her in 1948. Vielmetti was also an instructor for a course, "Effective Living," and she scheduled campus visits for several local doctors.

In 1949, with increased enrollment following the end of the war, a Health Center was opened in Carey Hall. It housed examination rooms, a nurse's office and emergency beds. Student health insurance began about this time with maximum coverage set at $40, an amount students felt was inadequate.

In late 1961, a new Health Center was completed by Miller-Davis & MacDonald, Inc. Construction Company at the cost of $131,650. In the summer of 1962, the Center opened its doors on the ground floor of Gries Hall with new medical equipment worth $200,000. The new facility featured a larger waiting room, solarium, a private room, five double rooms, two double isolation rooms, an ambulance entrance and a full-time doctor. By 1973, the center had grown to include the second floor of Gries Hall, three full-time physicians, ten nurses, eighteen beds, twelve examination rooms and a pharmacy. Vielmetti retired from nursing in 1968, and on October 17, 1975 the Board of Control voted to name the health center the Ada Burt Vielmetti University Health Center. Soon after, students and faculty began to complain that the center was overstaffed, over-charging and performing unnecessary tests. A 1978 study by consultants resulted in modifications to the center during the 1980s.

Today, the Health Center is part of Northern's Student Affairs Division, and it handles an array of services, from examinations, testing, and preventative health education, to primary care and referrals. Immunizations and prescriptions are also given. Its staff consists of two full-time physicians, Dr. Thomas W. Schacht, and Dr. Nancy Hamlin, two part-time nurse practitioners from the Northern nursing faculty, two nurses, a pharmacist, medical technologist, three secretaries and part-time custodian.

The Health Center started providing full primary care medical services to employees and families in 1992. In 1993 an extensive renovation of Gries Hall, including the Health Center was completed. In 1996, a plaque honoring Ada Vielmetti was placed in the entry area.

Directors: Peter J. Farago, 1967–1968; Ada B. Vielmetti, (acting) 1968–1969; Darrell P. Thorpe, M.D., 1969–1970; Barbara Lyons, M.D., 1970–1972; Robert White, M.D., 1972–1979; Barbara Lyons, M.D., 1979–1980; Gary J. Symons, (administrator) 1980–1990; Thomas W. Schacht, M.D., 1990–present. (Hilton, p. 221; *The 1996–97 University Profile*, 2:167–172; Alisa Koski, "A History of NMU's Health Service," 4/15/96; NN 07/03/1962). Alisa Koski

Health, Physical Education, and Recreation, Department of: The Department of Expression and Physical Training was formed in 1905. Beginning that fall, all Northern students were required to take physical training in order to "correct abnormalities, develop physical strength and increase the elasticity of the muscles." The men were taught by Ward M. Mills and the women by Eulie Rushmore. Two years later it was noted that "the work is arranged to be in harmony with the voice and body training of the expression class." Programs titled Physical Training for Men and Physical Training for Women were required.

In 1908 men were required to wear a regulation "gymnasium suit" and the women were required to wear bloomers, a blouse and tennis shoes.

In 1911 Grace Stafford became Northern's first full-time physical education teacher. A physical training department began to develop under Wayne McClintock in 1915. Charles Hedgcock strengthened the department during his career at Northern (1922–1956). By 1969, Varsity athletics were separated from the HPER department. In 1971, a major and minor in Recreation were approved. Eight years later, Dr. Jean Kinnear set up an outdoor recreation major. By 1984, the HPER department shifted from an emphasis on training educators to an emphasis on health and fitness.

As of 1997 the mission of the department is to prepare students for secondary education or liberal arts undergraduate degrees. Within this context, several programs are available. In Physical Education and Health Education, a student may elect teaching as a major. Both programs are approved by the National Council for Teacher Education (NCATE). Liberal arts degrees may be obtained in the following disciplines: Sports Science; Health Education; Management of Health and Fitness; Physical Education; and Outdoor Recreation Leadership and Management. Students may also major in the dietetics program, approved by the American Dietetics Association (ADA). Minor areas of concentration are available in health and physical education. A concentration in athletic training is also offered.

At the graduate level, a Master's degree is offered in Exercise Science which attracts those individuals preparing to work in industry, rehabilitation programs or education. Upon completion of the M.S. degree, some students enroll in Ph.D. programs.

The Department of HPER offers a health promotion program required of all students. The mission of this program is to provide educational background and knowledge which will enable students to obtain and maintain a desired level of physical well-being. Beyond the physical well-being course, students have the opportunity to select from various physical activity courses designed to promote an active lifestyle.

Department chairs or heads: C. V. "Red" Money, 1947–1967; Rico Zenti, 1967–1976; Robert Hockey, 1976–1978; M. Cameron Howes, 1978–present. (*Bulletins*; Francis Copper manuscript; Christi Nagy, "The Department of HPER," UA; *The 1996–97 University Profile*, 1:200–206. Alisa Koski

The Heart of Northern: The original Heart was a raised berm measuring 20 by 40 feet, three feet in height and shaped like a heart. A portion of it is located in front of the Cohodas Building. Francis R. Copper noted this was what remained after the ground had been lowered due to construction and landscaping. It first appears in photos around 1907.

The Heart was a romantic place on campus in the 1920s. It was the site for engagements, pinnings, May festivals and band concerts, "first kisses of coeds," photo location for the college band, studying, weddings and crownings. It was also known as "The King and Queen Knob." According to collegiate folklorists, such spots which attract couples are common, but this spot is unique because it attracted not only couples but groups of people.

After World War II as campus expansion moved towards the west, interest in the Heart languished and in many cases people began to forget about it. The final disaster to the Heart came during the summer of 1963 when two-thirds of the Heart was demolished during parking lot expansion.

The first discussions to reproduce the Heart were begun in 1994. Between the fall of 1996 and July 1997, earth was piled, shaped, the lawn seed sown and the privet hedge planted. The new Heart is located to the east of Jamrich Hall. (MJ 06/02/1924; NNN 08/03/1926; *The Quill*, 05/1915, p. 89;10/1915,p. 13;NN 05/07/1965;NW 04/20/1995, 02/16/1995, 10/10/1996; *Horizons*, Winter 1996)

Heating Plant: When the first structures were constructed on campus, namely Longyear Hall and the Peter White Hall of Science, each structure had its own furnace. As the institution grew and expanded, there has been a corresponding increase in heating capacity of the plants on campus. On July 22, 1907, the State Board of Education named D. F. Charleton as the architect for the first heating plant. It was constructed in 1908–1909 at the cost of $33,000 and was located midway between the University Center and Cohodas. The plant and the buildings it served were connected by underground concrete tunnels. A vacuum system and the Johnson system of heat regulation were installed in all of the buildings. Over the years, repairs and improvements were made to the building and equipment. Until the construction of Kaye Hall (1915), the open space between the two sets of buildings was dominated by the landmark smoke stack of the power plant. The stack was demolished during the summer of 1957.

In May 1957, the new heating plant (12,639 square feet) located to the west of the Service Building and north of Spooner Hall (*See: Art & Design North*) was made operational. With two boilers in use, a third boiler from the old plant was moved.

In December 1965 a heating plant located on a 5-acre tract of land at the corner of Wright Street and County Road 550 was completed. The brick structure was constructed by Howard Herrild Builders of Menominee at the cost of $1.2 million. This plant was dedicated on June 27, 1975 to Harvey G. Ripley (*See separate entry*).

Over the years, the heating pipes deteriorated and the state legislature provided monies for their replacement. The replacement project began in early April and was completed on September 11, 1996. In the afternoon, university and company officials celebrated the end of campus disruption with an on-site party.(NCN 04/04/1957, 05/29/1957; NN 09/17/1965)

Hedgcock, Charles B.: (1887–February 3, 1986). Mr. Hedgcock was born in Illinois, received his bachelor's degree from Knox College, Galesburg, Illinois and his master's degree from Harvard University. Before coming to Northern, Hedgcock had been a high school teacher and administrator and a member of the Knox College faculty.

He served as the head of Northern's Health, Physical Education and Recreation Department from 1922 until his retirement in 1956. Hedgcock compiled a 30-50-5 record as a football coach from 1922–33 and 1936–37; posted a 162-138 coaching mark in basketball from 1922–42 and 1945–47. He also directed the Northern track team. He was the longest serving coach in Northern's history and promoted a broad program in the field of health and physical education.

The C. B. Hedgcock Health and Physical Education Building (*See: Hedgcock Fieldhouse*) was dedicated in his honor on October 30, 1965. In 1974 Hedgcock was elected to the Upper Peninsula Sports Hall of Fame. (MJ 10/29/1965; 02/06/1986).

Hedgcock Fieldhouse: The C. B. Hedgcock Health and Physical Education Building was simply known as The Fieldhouse, this large structure served a great need. Prior to 1958, the college had to use an inadequate gymnasium constructed in 1915.

The tri-unit structure, completed in 1958, measures 128' x 234' and covers 92,606 square feet. It once housed a fieldhouse, gymnasium (90' x 122'), a gym for intramural sports, and natatorium. The building also included staff offices, classrooms, locker and shower rooms, a training room and other facilities. There were plans to use the balcony for table tennis, golf driving with nets, shuffle board and wrestling. It was designed by Warren Holmes and Co., Architects, Lansing. The general contractor was the Proksch Construction Co., of Iron River.

Over the years, the structure went by a number of names. At first the structure was unofficially known as the "Health & Physical Education Building." On May 13, 1957, the State Board of Education officially named it the Northern Michigan College Fieldhouse. Use of this name continued until the building was formally dedicated on October 30, 1965 to C. B. Hedgcock.

The fieldhouse, with a seating capacity of more than 5,000, was the largest indoor gathering site in Northern Michigan. Dedicated on December 6, 1958, with a basketball game against the University of Chicago, the fieldhouse quickly became familiar to Upper Peninsula residents as the home of NMU athletic teams and as the site of high school championship basketball tournaments and indoor track meets.

Over the years, the fieldhouse was also the home of NMU commencement ceremonies, concerts, lectures, and major events, such as political campaigning and the circus, since it as one of the largest structures in Marquette and could accommodate large audiences. Commencements were held in the structure from June 21, 1967 through December 1992. On October 14, 1969 the inauguration of President Jamrich took place here. The 75th anniversary banquet of the University was held in the structure in 1974. In the fall of 1992 and 1996, candidate and then Vice President Al Gore campaigned in the Fieldhouse. In 1996, it was the site of an extensive Finnish market during FinnFest.

With the opening of the PEIF structure in 1976, many facilities and services were moved to the new building. During the 1990s, the uses of the building changed. The natatorium was removed and replaced with a boxing arena used by Olympic aspirants. Offices and classrooms had moved, and the Head Start Program took over a portion of the building. In the spring of 1993, commencement was moved to the Superior Dome. The last varsity basketball game took place in the

Fieldhouse on Saturday February 20, 1999. Currently there are plans to renovate and convert it into a student services center. (NCN 03/20/1958, 07/21/1958; MJ 10/29/1965; MJ 02/21/99)

Heimonen, Henry S., Award for Excellence in Geography: This award is given annually to a student for outstanding work in geography. Professor Heimonen was a Northern graduate who after getting his Ph.D. from the University of Wisconsin returned to his alma mater in 1948 where he served as professor and department head (1962–1972).

Herbarium: This collection of dried plant specimens, mounted and systematically arranged for reference and class use is located in the Biology Department in West Science. Although plants were collected earlier, the department received a foundation collection of some 700 dried plants from the Cranbrook Institute of Science, Bloomfield Hills, Michigan in 1948. For many years Dr. James Merry was curator and increased the collection. In 1969–1970 Dr. Maynard Bowers took over as curator, a position he held until his retirement in 1998.

Today the department has a modest collection of some 5,000 specimens which is continually added to by botanists in the department. The noted botanist Dr. Edward Voss of the University of Michigan consulted and cited items from the collection in his monumental, *Michigan Flora*. The Michigan Fern Society has consulted the fern portion of the collection. The collection is listed in Index Herbariorum, an international listing of herbaria. (Interview with Maynard Bowers, 12/14/1998, UA)

Hilton, Miriam: A Marquette resident since 1950, she received her B.A. from Wellesley College (1946) and a master's in education. Over the years she served as a faculty member at Northern. In 1972, she accepted President John Jamrich's invitation to write a history of the University. The result was the monograph, *Northern Michigan University: The First 75 Years*, published in 1975. Since 1994, she has served on the Centennial Celebration Committee (*See separate entry*)

Hispanic Students: Students from Latin America have come to Northern over the century. A number of them were teachers studying English on campus. In 1995 there were three students from Brazil and three from Mexico. Hispanic American students numbered only 39 in 1978 and that figure stayed constant between 1993 and 1998 with an average of 42 Hispanic students. In the mid-1990s, Hispanic students were celebrating September as Hispanic Month, participating in the

International Food Fest (*See separate entry*), and active in the Latino American Organization and the Spanish Club.

Historian, University: Over the years there have been two official University Historians. The first was Francis Roy Copper (*See separate entry*), who was appointed and wrote a history of the University. Unfortunately, he died in January 1949, prior to the celebration of the semi-centennial in June. His manuscript was not published until 1999.

In preparation for the Centennial Celebration, there were discussions about hiring an external historian, when Dr. Sara L. Doubledee promoted the idea of using a member of the faculty. In April 1994, President Vandament appointed Russell M. Magnaghi the second University Historian. The functions of the position are to collect and preserve artifacts and structures on campus, write a university history or encyclopedia, and act as a liaison between the university and external historical agencies. Under his supervision a historical marker program was begun, the Heart of Northern redeveloped, the NMU flag created, and *A Sense of Time: The Encyclopedia of Northern Michigan University* was published in 1999. (MJ 04/30/1994; *Campus* 04/25–29/1994; NN 10/04/1961)

Historical Markers and Plaques: The first historical marker located on the campus was the state marker located at the north entrance of the University Center, dedicated on May 19, 1966. The dedication ceremony was attended by University officials headed by President Edgar Harden; Donald Chaput, a member of the Michigan Historical Commission; W.H. Treloar, an alumnus and master of ceremonies; Ernest H. Rankin, executive secretary of the Marquette County Historical Society; Forest Roberts, faculty; and Mrs. Abby Beecher Roberts, guest of honor and John M. Longyear's only living daughter.

The marker reads:

NORTHERN MICHIGAN UNIVERSITY

Established by the Legislature in 1899 as a normal school to provide teachers for the Upper Peninsula, Northern opened with thirty-two students, six faculty, and Dwight B. Waldo as principal. A four-year colleague program was introduced in 1918, and the first bachelor of arts degree was conferred two years later. In the 1950s Northern became a multi-purpose institution placing emphasis on instruction, service, and research. In 1960 it established its own graduate program leading to the master of arts degree. Serving an ever-increasing student body, Northern in 1963 achieved university status through an act of the Legislature.

The first plaque honoring an individual was dedicated to Harry Lee and is located in the lobby of Lee Hall.

In late 1990 and into 1991, a committee formed consisting of Matt Surrell, Ruth Roebke-Berens, Gil Heard, Cliff Maier, Jim Carter, Larna Etnier and Veronica Graves which was called the Heroes Project. It was part of an effort to revive University traditions across the campus. One of the purposes of the Project was to develop plaques to honor individuals for whom buildings were named. Outside of developing an extensive file on the subject, the plaques were never created due to financial constraints.

In preparation for the Centennial Celebration, Vice President for Financial and Administration, Dr. Michael Roy developed a similar program in 1995. The process of creating and placing bronze plaques, honoring deceased individuals for whom buildings were named, was implemented by University Historian Dr. Russell Magnaghi. The first plaques highlighted Walter Gries, Ada Vielmetti, Don H. Bottum, and Wilbur West; the second set honored Harvey Ripley, Russell Thomas, Edgar L. Harden, and Forest Roberts, a third set honored C. V. "Red" Money and Rico Zenti, "Northern's Original Campus" and NMU veterans. Currently, the project continues. (NCN 05/20/1966)

History, Department of: The History and Civics Department was created by the State Board of Education on July 14, 1899 with Principal Dwight B. Waldo teaching both history and civics. The first female professor in the department was Catherine Maxwell, who taught from 1904 until her death in 1918. With the coming of Lew Allen Chase in 1919, there was an infusion of research and publications. He was one of the best-known professors in the department from the early days. Chase remained department head until retirement in 1944.

During these years, the traditional United States and English history courses were expanded with courses on Latin American history, Europe after World War I and others. The direction of the department remained constant until the 1960s. All during these years, the department never had more than 2–3 members.

The boom years of the 1960s brought changes. In 1962, the Department of History and Social Sciences was split up and the History Department became independent. The increased enrollment of these years caused a need for additional faculty to handle the large sections. Beginning in the mid-1960s, the number of faculty substantially increased. Faculty were hired to cover various geographical areas of history: Asia, Americas, United States, African, European, Middle East and others. The new faculty published more than in the past.

A number of organizations and a publication have been developed since 1969. In May 1969, the Omicron Mu chapter of Phi Alpha Theta was formed on campus. In the early 1970s, an NMU History Club was formed which ran in competition with Phi Alpha Theta. By the late 1990s, the latter organization dominated the scene. The journal *The Round Table* was published (1991-1993). It not only provided an outlet for student and faculty publications, but it also allowed students the opportunity to try their hands at publishing. In 1998, the NMU History Association was established by a group of enthusiastic students.

In the late 1980s, the department, in cooperation with the Michigan Bureau of History, developed a living history program at Fort Wilkins State Park Complex (*See separate entry*) in Copper Harbor. This has been a successful enterprise. In conjunction with this program, the department has also created internships to provide students with hands-on experience.

From the 1960s until 1994, the department had a master's program. In June 1967, Jim Carter, formerly of Communications and Marketing, received the first graduate degree in a straight history curriculum. In May, 1985, a Military and International Services Masters Program was established. The idea was to capitalize on the officers at K. I. Sawyer Air Force Base who would come into the program. The success of the Program was questionable, and it eventually declined. Inadequate funding caused it to fall into a state of disrepair. On April 29, 1994, the Board of Control approved the suspension of the M.A. degree in History. The Department approved a minor in Public History in 1999.

Department chairs or heads: Dwight B. Waldo, 1899–1904; Catherine Maxwell, 1904–1918; Lew Allen Chase, 1919–1944; Albert H. Burrows, 1944–1957; Richard F. O'Dell, 1957–1963; Eugene Whitehouse, (acting) 1963; Anthony Forbes, 1964–1968; Richard Sonderegger, 1968–1970; Stephen B. Barnwell, 1970–1975; Barry L Knight, 1975–1980; Ruth Roebke-Berens, 1981–1988; Knight, 1988–present. (NNN 02/03/1925; *The 1996–97 University Profile*, 1:110–116)

Hockey, Ice: Early mention of forming an ice hockey club can be found in the pages on the *Northern News* in December 1952. By the end of January 1953, the editor wrote that his proposal for an intramural team had met with "scant enthusiasm." Later, interest finally developed and hockey had its beginnings at NMU in the form of club teams. The Northern Quintet, which only lasted a few years, was a five-man squad which played local teams. During the 1959–1960 season, the Intramural Hockey League included the Copper Country Pioneers, Sigma Rho Epsilon, Theta Stickers, and the Tri Mu Snor-Kisas. From the 1950s into the 1970s, fans watched hockey games at the Palestra arena, which was also home to the Marquette Iron Rangers, a community team.

The varsity sport was inaugurated in 1976 and to this date has had only one head coach, Rick Comley. The program joined the Central Collegiate Hockey Association in 1978 and remained in the league through 1984.

In 1980 the team finished second in the nation in the NCAA Division I losing to University of North Dakota 5-2. In 1991 Northern joined the Western Collegiate Hockey Association (WCHA) and remained in the conference through 1996. Northern won the NCAA Division I National Championship beating Boston University 8-7 in three overtimes in 1991. Northern rejoined the CCHA in 1996 and remains as a member to this date. (NCN 12/17/1952, 01/28/1953; NN 01/13/1960; *Bulletins*; Kevin McCarthy, "NMU Ice Hockey,"; Yearbooks, UA) Michelle Kangas

Holidays: Over the century, Northern has celebrated a variety of holidays. As of 1999 the chief legal or public holidays observed or commemorated on campus are: January 1, New Year's Day; 3rd Monday in January, Martin Luther King Day; last Monday in May, Memorial Day; July 4, Independence Day; 1st Monday in September, Labor Day; 4th Thursday in November, Thanksgiving; and December 25, Christmas Day. Only Martin Luther King, Jr. Day is not celebrated with closure of the university. The one day event was first celebrated on January 15, 1986. The week-long celebration started from January 15 to 22, 1993. Today it consists of public lectures with guest speakers, movies and activities which commemorate and honor the man and his ideas.

The December holiday season has been celebrated over the years with a special choral concert which has been held either on campus or in town since the 1920s. Between the 1930s and 1950s, early December was a special time for proms, dances, dinners and parties. An old tradition was the Christmas party held in the atrium of Kaye Hall. Singing students stood on the various floors overlooking the event, amid garlands and green and gold lights. A faculty member (usually Forest Roberts) dressed as Santa Claus would appear. After 1949 when Lee Hall was completed, a Christmas party was held there, but at times would return to the Kaye Hall location. This tradition continues with the holiday celebration held in the atrium of the University Center in early December. There is also a special dinner served in the Wildcat Den Food Court available to the university community.

Since 1993, the African American celebration of Kwanzaa, honoring heritage, tradition and family has been held on campus in December. It is usually a small celebration and not as elaborate as Kwanzaa celebrated nationally. It has been held every year except 1997.

Prior to 1972, when the school year ended in mid-June, Easter was the time for a break in the semester. Afterwards, the holiday was not marked, except that until 1998, the University closed at noon on Good Friday.

Since 1987, Halloween has been celebrated with a special party and various activities in the University Center for the children of the parents of the university community. Thanksgiving Day in November has been celebrated by the university community in their homes. Classes are usually dismissed on Tuesday evening and do not begin again until the following Monday.

Homecoming: The first attempt at holding a homecoming was made in 1924. All alumni were urged to attend the Northern-Michigan Tech football game and make it "a homecoming game." It was hoped that this could become an annual event, but little came of this.

The first traditional homecoming celebration at Northern was held on October 25–26, 1935. President Pearce announced the first homecoming in his annual Fall assembly address. L.O. Gant was chairman of the faculty committee which arranged the program. A pep meeting and parade were held on Friday evening. A bonfire was ignited at the end of the parade, where students cheered for their football team which played Saturday afternoon. To finalize the weekend, a homecoming dance was held. Free tickets were sent to area high school students to attend the football game. The event was the beginning of a tradition meant to bring alumni and current students closer together. Through the years, homecoming has become an exciting tradition at Northern. Students dressed in green and gold participated in games such as tug-of-war, nominated homecoming kings and queens, and organized events for visiting alumni. The bonfire became a "mourning ceremony" where Northern students would burn the "coffin" of the opposing football team, which signified predicted victory. Homecoming has been held each fall, except between 1943 and 1947, due to World War II. On October 6, 1977 an attempt was made at holding a gigantic musical chairs (*See separate entry*) game to get into the *Guinness Book of World Records*. 1,674 people participated and temporarily broke the record. In 1978 the world's largest pasty (*See separate entry*) was baked and eaten. On September 24–26, 1998, a special elaborate homecoming was held in conjunction with the Centennial Celebration. (NNN 10/28/1924; NCN 10/23/1935, 10/3/01946; NN; NW, UA) Michelle Kangas

Home Economics Department: See: *Consumer and Family Studies, Department of*

Honorary Degree Recipients: Since 1949 Northern has given honorary doctorate degrees. The process is in the hands of a Committee. Abbreviations: Ed-Education, HL-Humane Letters, H-Humanities, L-Letters, Lit-Literature, PS-Public Service, SE-Science Education.

Recipients: Paul Adams (4-90, HL); Walter Adams (12-91, H); Durward L. Allen (8-71, HL); Charles Leroy Anspach (59, HL); Doris King Arjona (50, L); Robert H. Atwell (12-85, E); Richard H. Austin (12-89, PS); F. Lee Bailey ((12-77, Laws); Ellsworth Barnard (12-96, HL): Lynn Mahlon Bartlett (60, Laws); Terrel H. Bell (4-84, PS); Leon Bernstein (8-72, HL); Connie B. Binsfield (4-96, Laws); George E. Bishop (57, PS); Don Hollis Bottum (60, Laws); Paul F. Brandwein (74, SE); Jerome Seymour Bruner (6-69, HL); Margaret M. Bryant (12-79, L); Albert H. Burrows 8-72, HL); George H. W. Bush (12-73, Laws); Bruce Catton (8-75, L); Marjorie Bell Chambers (3-82, HL); Bernard Cherrick (8-77, HL); MayBelle H. Chitwood (8-77, Science); Walker Lee Cisler (6-65, Laws); Harlan Cleveland (12-80, PS); Wilbur J. Cohen (8-83, PS); Sam Myron Cohodas (62, Laws); Joe Lee Davis (6-71, Lit); Peter Dawkins (4-83, PS); Vine Deloria, Jr., 5-91, H and speaker); Helen DeVos (12-98, H); Richard DeVos (12-98, Business and speaker); Robert E. Dewar (8-77, Laws); Alice Dobie (53, SE); Lewis N. Dodak (12-92, PS); Constantinos A. Doxiadis (6-65, HL); Norman Drachler (8-70, Ed); Dwight Lowell Dumond (6-65, Lit); James L. Dye (12-92, Science); Loren Corey Eiseley (6-66, HL); Coy G. Eklund (12-79, HL); Harold L. Enarson (12-93, H and speaker); Nita Engle (5-86, HL); Kenneth R. Erfft (61, Laws); Elliott M. Estes (5-76, Laws); Sylvia Eskola (49, Master of Liberal Arts); William Faust (5-81, Laws); Robben Wright Fleming (6-68, L); Thelma H. Flodin (12-74, Ed); Gerald R. Ford (11-78, Laws); William D. Ford (4-80, Laws); Louis W. Foster (4-94, H); John Hope Franklin (8-78, L): Douglas A, Fraser (8-86, PS); Luther O. Gant (59, Laws); Harry A. Gast (7-88, PS); Clifford Geertz (5-75, HL); Ioannis Georgakis (5-78, Laws); Edwin O. George (6-66, Laws); Patricia A. Graham (8-87, HL); Andrew M. Greeley (5-93, HL and speaker); Walter F. Gries (53, Laws); Robert P. Griffin (5-70, Ed); Martha W. Griffiths (5-73, Laws); George E. Gullen (8-75, Laws): Oscar Handlin (6-69, HL); John A. Hannah (57, Lit); Edgar L. Harden (8-80, PS); LaDonna Harris (4-94, H and speaker); Patricia Roberts Harris (8-73, Laws); H. Stuart Harrison (6-67, Laws); Philip A. Hart (8-69, HL); William E. Harwell (12-90, H); Harlan H. Hatcher (6-64, Lit); John W. Henderson (12-73, Science); Peter J. Hilton (10-77, H); Richard M. Hoben (8-76, PS); Nettie Manthei Howe (52, Master of Liberal Arts);

Hubert H. Humphrey (5-66, HL); Andrew D. Hunt, Jr. (5-78, HL); Dominic J. Jacobetti (12-84, Laws); Ralph J. Jalkanen (12-74, Ed); John X. Jamrich (6-68, HL); Fred A. Jeffers (49, Laws); Edwin B. Johnson (8-84, Science and speaker); Clara Stanton Jones (5-78, HL); Phillip S. Jones (6-72, HL); Nancy Landon Kassebaum (5-86, Laws); Cornelia G. Kennedy (6-71, Laws); John E. King (6-66, HL); Harlan C. Koch (60, HL); John I. Kolemainen (12-74, L); Melvin Kranzberg (12-72, L); Adrian N. Languis (6-65, Laws); David Lawrence, Jr. (12-87, HL); Jerry M. Linenger (12-97, Science and speaker); Frederick M. Logan (5-74, Art & Art Ed); Maynard Mack (5-76, Lit); James T. Malsack (4-88, PS); Albert H. Marckwardt (8-73, L); William C. Marshall (5-82, Political Science); Martin E. Marty (4-89, H); Ellwood A. Mattson (5-82, Laws); Russell G. Mawby (12-81, PS); Paul W. McCracken (5-82, HL); Wade H. McCree, Jr. (5-85, PS); John P. McGoff (5-76, Laws); Mark T. McKee (7-71, Laws); Beatrice Medicine (8-79, HL); James W. Miller (1-72, H); William G. Milliken (6-69, HL); Glen H. Morey (61, Science); Elba Morse (55, Science); Charles S. Mott (8-70, Ed); William H. Nault (12-88, Laws); Harry K. Newman (57, HL, 8/66 speaker); Allan L. Niemi (5-93, H); Russell B. Nye (1-68, HL); Ernest C. Oberholtzer (6-66, HL); Walter J. Ong, S.J. (12-77, HL); Allan W. Ostar (12-78, HL); Gary M. Owen (12-83, Political Science and speaker); Gordon Parks (5-97, HL); Ernest L. Pearce (62, Laws); W. Leslie Pengelly (4-79, HL); Dick Posthumus (12-91, Political Science); William Proxmire (4-90, Laws); Ward L. Quaal (67, Laws); James H. Quello (12-75, PS); Dixie Lee Ray (8-74, Science); Margaret A, Rettig (12-94, Health Sciences); W. Ann Reynolds (12-95, H); John J. Riccardo (7-71, Laws); Abby Beecher Roberts (6-67, HL); Forest A. Roberts (5-87, HL); George Romney (5-75, HL); Lenore L. Romney (5-75, HL); Phillip E. Runkel (5-87, PS); Loret Ruppe (8-81, PS); Philip E. Ruppe (1-71, HL); E. Harwood Rydholm (5-85, Laws); Fred C. Sabin (12-84, Science); Paul A. Samuelson (5-73, L); Clarence N. Sayen (58, Science); James R. Scales (6-72, Lit); Harvey W. Schiller (12-92, H) and speaker); Howard Schultz (5-98, H and speaker); Thomas F. Schweigert (12-72, Laws); Leslie W. Scott (6-64, Laws); Glenn T. Seaborg (62, HL; speaker 5-92); Martha R. Seger (12-86, Laws); L. William Seidman (4-88, Laws); William E. Simon (8-82, Laws); Helvi Sipila (4-77, H); Bernard F. Sliger (8-85, PS and speaker); Raymond L. Smith (8-76, Laws); Ellen Solomonson (55, Science in Ed); Roland S. Strolle (12-90, H); Jessie Hilton Stuart (6-64, Lit); Eugene W. Surber (6-72, HL); Clifford A. Swanson (49, Laws); A. Alfred Taubman (4-95, H and speaker); Helen Thomas (12-89, L); Roy

H. Thomson (6-68, Laws); Leo O. Tuominen (12-74, HL); Arthur L. Tuuri (6-68, H); Jay Van Andel (12-76, Business); Margery R. Vandament (5-97, PS); William E. Vandament (5-97, L); Charles Van Riper (6-71, HL); Paul Van Riper (6-64, HL); John D. Voelker (58, Laws); Myron H. Wahls (4-96, Laws and speaker); Willis F. Ward (1-70, H); Edward W. Weidner (1-69, H); Luther S. West (8-69, Science); W. Donald Weston (8-86, Science); Clifton R. Wharton, Jr. (12-75, HL); Roger W. Wilkins (12-94, H and speaker); G. Mennen Williams (12-82, Laws); Jack Frederick Wolfram (60, Science); G. Katherine Wright (12-89, PS); Harold E. Wright (12-93, HL).

Honors Convocation/Banquet: The first Honors Convocation was inaugurated by the Student Council as the only official recognition given Northern's outstanding students. Its purpose was to recognize those students whose academic success, campus leadership and citizenship were distinguished. It was held on April 19, 1956 in Kaye Auditorium and honored 80 students. During the first decade, the convocation format was used and then switched to the banquet format. Besides the presentations of awards to individuals, there is usually a principal speaker.

A number of changes have been introduced over the years. The presentation of scholarships and awards has been ended. Departments present their outstanding senior award at this time. In 1987, the Outstanding Graduate awards were presented. The chairs for this event have included Dr. Eugene Whitehouse, Dr. John Frey, Dr. Pryse Duerfeldt and Dr. William Knox.

Honors Program: An early recommendation for an Honors Program came from the Committee on Undergraduate Programs and was presented to the Academic Senate in May 1967. At that time little was done to develop such a program. However over the years the idea was discussed by both the faculty and administration. Finally in the fall of 1998, the Honors Program was put into operation having been developed in the previous years. William L. Knox is the director.

Housing and Residence Life, Office of: With the opening of Carey Hall in 1948 and the expansion of residence halls and apartments in the 1960s and 1970s, there was a need to coordinate student residence life.

The mission of this Office is to provide on-campus residence hall and apartment facilities for students and to create physical and social climates in those facilities which contribute to their personal development. As a result, student residents are actively encouraged to become involved in the creation and maintenance of their environments. *(The 1996–97 University Profile*, 2:173–178)

HPER Building*: See: PEIF Building*

The Hub Student Resource Center*:* Located on the second floor of the Cohodas Administrative Building, The Hub was opened in the fall of 1997. Studies of retention and graduation rates showed that students need this support. The Hub encompasses: the Academic and Career Advisement Center (ACAC) and the Counseling Center. (Source: Brochure, [1997]).

Human Resources Office*:* This office is concerned with human resources on campus in terms of personnel. It consists of a director, benefits manager, employment manager, and payroll. (*The 1996–97 University Profile*, 2:76–81)

Human Rights Commission*:* This service was created in May 1969 and was designed to help disadvantaged students at Northern. The Commission had three main responsibilities: 1) to assist disadvantaged students regarding financial aid, 2) to help provide tutorial assistance, and 3) to settle cases of alleged racial discrimination.

Dr. Jack Rombouts, Northern's Vice President for Administrative Affairs, was head of the commission which consisted of five students, five faculty members and two administrators. The responsibilities of the Commission have been taken over by the Student Affairs Division. (NN 10/24/1969, 02/13/1970; *The 1996–97 University Profile*, 2:125)

Hunt, Lucian*:* (May 4, 1898–August 4, 1986). Hunt was born in Montezuma, Iowa and came to Marquette in 1927. He graduated from Coe College in Cedar Rapids, Iowa with a B.S. (1920), and received his master's (1922) and doctor's (1931) degrees from Ohio State University. Hunt was professor of chemistry at Northern from January 1927 to 1967 and had the longest years of service to Northern. He was promoted to full professor in 1927. Between 1947 and 1962, Hunt served as head of the Physical Science and Chemistry Department, and between 1962 and 1964 as head of the Department of Chemistry. He retired in the summer of 1967. Hunt Residence Hall was dedicated in his honor on June 9, 1967.

He was married to Myrtle on August 10, 1927, and they had a daughter, Catherine.

Hunt was a member of First Methodist Church and was an active member in Freemasonry. (MJ 08/04/1986)

Hunt-Van Antwerp Hall: See: Quad II

Ice Hockey: See: Hockey, Ice

Inauguration of the University President: Prior to Edgar Harden, presidents of Northern merely took office and did not go through an inauguration ceremony. For instance, in May 1904, with the departure of Principal Waldo and the arrival of Principal Kaye, the male faculty entertained both men at the Hotel Marquette. A similar procedure was followed with other presidents.

President Harden, who took over in 1956, was the first to have a formal inauguration on October 2, 1957. The ceremony was witnessed by students, faculty, business, industrial, labor and civic leaders, and delegates of eighty colleges and universities in the United States. It was the first inauguration in Northern's 58-year history and took place in the Kaye Hall Auditorium with an academic procession from Lee Hall.

The second president to be inaugurated was John X. Jamrich. His ceremony was "simplified and streamlined" and invitations were limited to individuals and institutions connected with Michigan. The televised event was held on the afternoon of October 14, 1969 in the Hedgcock Fieldhouse. At this inauguration, the medallion or chain office, and the mace and special green academic robe were used for the first time. Two members of the Board of Control placed the medallion around the president's neck.

President James Appleberry was installed during the regular commencement on December 17, 1983 without any fanfare. President William Vandament came to Northern on an interim basis and then remained. There was never talk of an installation.

The installation of President Judith Bailey was centered around the theme "A Celebration of Learning and Discovery." The festivities began on October 1, 1997, with an Academic Symposium which highlighted faculty research. Festivities ended with the installation ceremony on October 3, 1997 held in the Superior Dome. It was attended by the university and larger communities. Board chair Robert Buzz Berube and vice chair Ellwood Mattson placed the chain office on Dr. Bailey. A reception followed in the University Center. (MJ 05/22/1904; NW 10/02/1997; MJ 10/04/1997)

Inclement Weather Policy: See: *Snow Days*

Individually Created Program: In 1976, a non-teaching degree program was developed which was designed for students who did not have educational goals that corresponded with existing programs offered at NMU. Students and advisors developed the program following certain guidelines: 124 credit hours must be elected, including four P.E. credits and 16 foreign language credits for a B.A. Liberal studies requirements remain the same. Forty of the 124 credits must be from upper-level classes and students must complete 40 hours of the program after admittance. Individually-created programs contain no more than 80 percent of the courses required for an existing major. Applicants to the program submit paperwork and plans to the ICP committee.

The Chair of the Committee, which is a subcommittee of the Committee on Undergraduate Programs, seeks faculty members from each of the Colleges and an extra member from the largest College, Arts and Sciences. The Committee reviews the application and makes a decision.

Chairs: Russell Magnaghi, 1976–1983; Tom Skoog, 1983–1993; Grant Soltwisch, 1993–present. (NW, 09/09/76)

Industrial Arts, Department of: See: *Technology and Applied Sciences, College of*

Industrial Technologies Department: In 1990, the Board of Control changed the name from the Department of Engineering and Computer Integrated Manufacturing to the Department of Industrial Technologies.

The mission of the Industrial Technologies Department is twofold: 1) to serve undergraduate majors enrolled in technology-based associate degree programs, and 2) to serve undergraduate majors seeking baccalaureate degrees in Industrial Technology and Technology and Applied Sciences. Instruction at the associate degree level focuses on understanding the materials, processes and systems of the following technical disciplines: architectural technology and computer aided design-mechanical. (*The 1996–97 University Profile*, 2:309–315)

Insect Collection: The collection of several thousand specimens is a decent collection of insects given the size of Northern. They are identified and pinned and located in the Biology Department. The collection was started by Dr. Luther West prior to World War II, but really developed in the late 1940s. Dr. Gordon Gill became interested in the collection as a student in the late 1940s and became its curator in 1957. Upon retirement in 1984, Dr. Donald Snitgen took over as curator and remained in that capacity until his retirement in 1998.

The collection is used for class purposes, by researchers, and by agricultural and other agencies. Portions of the collection are shipped to qualified scholars throughout the United States for study. The department benefits from this by having the scientific information about the specimens developed by the researcher, added to its collection. (Interview with Gordon Gill, 12/14/1998, UA)

Inside View: The official newsletter of the Sports Training Centers at Northern, first published in 1994.

Institutional Research and Planning, Office of: See: *Office of Planning and Analytical Studies*

Instruction and In-Service Education: During World War II there was an interest in developing vocational teachers' certificates (07/31/1943) and adult education which was soon mandated by the state. After a special meeting with Governor Harry Kelly, President Tape and other educators in March 1944, Northern worked through an adult education committee and developed courses for this program which expanded. In 1947 the Office of Instruction and In-Service Education was created under Max P. Allen. Earlier-created correspondence and extension courses and in-service programs were conducted by this office. In the early 1950s, driver training instruction was given.

Allen, who taught history and political science, remained in charge of the program until 1956 when it was split. Allen remained director of the Instruction portion while newly hired Claude A. Bosworth was made dean of Public Services (*See separate entry*). In 1960 Allen left Northern to become president of McKendree College, Lebanon, Illinois. At this point Public Services (*See separate entry*) was an entity and would later emerge as Continuing Education. (*See separate entry*)

Instructional Facility: See: *Jamrich Hall*

Instructional Media Services: Instructional Media Services had its origin in1945 when Dr. William Hoppes, director of Student Teaching and Placement, encouraged his colleagues to study the classroom use of new audio visual equipment developed during World War II. In 1993, Audio Visual, Media Services and Instructional Media Services divided into their own separate divisions. Media services is located on the first floor of the Library and provides training in the use of classroom audio visual equipment. Instructional media services handles the Library's film and slide collections and also handles classroom requests for audio visual equipment. Audio Visual handles the distance learning classroom as well as non-academic audio visual requests, such as PA systems and headsets at athletic events. In the 1960s, the Audio Visual division operated a campus switchboard which handled long distance phone calls. Robert Manning was the Audio Visual director from 1965 to the early 1990s.

Directors: Audio Visual: Michael Bath; Media Services: Carolyn Meyers; Instructional Media Services: Keenan Tunnel and Bryant Varney. (Tom Collins, "Instructional Media Services," UA) Alisa Koski

Intercollegiate Debate Team: See: *Forensics*

Intercollegiate Athletics: See: *Athletics*

Interdisciplinary Programs: The following are programs offered at Northern: *Gender Studies Minor (See)*; General Science; *Individually Created Programs* (ICP; *See*); *Special Studies Program* (SSP; *See*); Special Studies Certificate Program; Native American Studies Minor; *Pre-Professional Programs (See)*; Social Science; Social Studies; Water Science. For further information on specific programs and their requirements see the latest *Undergraduate Bulletin*.

***Internal Audit*:** Under the President's Division, its main objective is to assist the Board Audit Committee, President and other University management in discharging their responsibilities by furnishing independent analyzes, appraisals, recommendations, and comments as part of the auditor's review of University units, systems and operations. In 1999, Matthew Riipi is the internal auditor. (*The 1996–97 University Profile*, 2:27–32)

***International Affairs, Office of*:** The program began in 1987 under the direction of Dr. Jon Saari who had helped start the Szechuan Province Exchange Program with China. At this time, there was a student interest in international study options. The program's goal is to help students and faculty to develop ties abroad through work, study and research. An interdisciplinary International Studies major was developed and went into operation in the fall of 1989. The broad liberal arts major provides students with a basic understanding of modern world history, international relations, world cultures and world religions. The program utilizes intensive language and general instruction abroad. There are NMU-sponsored and affiliated programs, directed studies and non-NMU affiliated programs. An original goal was to have 20 percent of the student body having an off-campus experience by the year 2000.

International Student Services recruits international students and monitors immigration and naturalization services compliance and records. The Study Abroad Program has a library which offers over 1,000 student-aboard opportunities and assists in the financial aid, identification, and travel planning for studying abroad. In 1994, the International Studies Program, International Student Services and The Study Abroad Program were united into one centrally administered program. The International Student Club facilitates social activities among the international students on campus. Its annual International Food Festival has become an autumn campus tradition.

Directors: Jon Saari, 1987–1994; Hal Dorf, 1994–1997; John Wetting, (acting) 1997-present. (*Bulletins*; International Affairs Office Mission Statement; NW 11/07/1991; Laura D. Wiesmann. "The International Affairs Department." 1995, UA; *The 1996–97 University Profile*, 1:25–26.) Michelle Kangas and Alisa Koski

International Food Festival: Started in 1990, it was first seen as a small event at which international students gathered. In 1994 some 400 people attended and four years later it had to be held in the Jacobetti Center. It consists of a series of buffet-style presentations so people can sample food from each region and return for more. Folk dancing is part of the festival.

International Relations, Office of: Established on July 1, 1966, its primary functions were: 1) to coordinate and support the international activities of NMU faculty and students; 2) to actively assist international students within all parts of the University community; and 3) to advise and assist the president and the University's administrative council concerning Northern's program commitments on campus and abroad. There was no faculty, nor curriculum of its own. Its programs depended on the effective interaction with the faculty and existing schools and departments. This office entered a period of dormancy and was revived by Dr. Jon Saari as the Office of International Affairs (*See separate entry*)

International Studies Major: See: *International Affairs*

Intramural Sports: Before organized intercollegiate sports were formed at Northern, students participated in intramural sports. Softball and tennis tournaments were held for students each spring. Other sports were also offered, depending upon student interest, and special athletic fields were created. Today, intramurals are still offered for students interested in participating in sports but who are not members of athletic teams. Michelle Kangas

Invocation: From the earliest days of the Normal School it was a tradition to have a member of the clergy give an invocation or benediction at University functions. In 1993, President Vandament concerned about the national trend against public prayer, decided to end invocations at university functions. The last invocation given at a commencement was by Lt. Colonel Theodore L. Wuerffel, Lutheran chaplain at K. I. Sawyer Air Force Base on December 17, 1994.

Ives, William: U.S. land surveyor of the Upper Peninsula who surveyed the campus in June 1846. The survey line follows Tracy Street and its north-south extensions.

Ivy Day: The first Ivy Day went back to 1919 as part of the commencement ceremonies. The Ivy Day ceremony continued until around 1928 when it ended. The ivy continued to grow and enveloped the buildings. Since it was destroying the buildings, it was removed in the 1960s much to the dismay of many on campus and many alumni. (NNN 05/12/1921; NCN 10/23/1935)

Izzo-Mariucci Academic Center: The academic center will be located in the lower level of the addition linking the Berry Events Center and the PEIF. The center, with study areas, will be open to all students. Funding for the center amounting to $150,000 was a joint gift from former NMU athletes-turned-successful-coaches, Steve Mariucci and Tom Izzo. Mariucci, who coaches the San Francisco 49ers is currently the youngest head coach in the National Football League. Izzo is the head coach of Michigan State University's men's basketball team.

The second level of the addition will include a large lounge area, called the Wildcat Room which will seat 150 people and will have concessions and ticket areas serving the Berry Events Center and PEIF. Funding for the addition, came from 1998 bond proceeds totaling $350,000; gifts from private donors: $300,000; general funds and investments: $200,000; and $150,000 from recreational facilities. Construction will begin in the spring of 1999. (NW 01/14/1999)

Jacobetti, Dominic "Jake": (July 20, 1920–November 28, 1994) The longest serving legislator in the Michigan legislature from Negaunee, Michigan. Mr. Jacobetti was born to Italian immigrants, Nicholas and Josephine (Sano) Jacobetti. The family had settled in the Patch Location in the early 1900s. Jacobetti said that it was here that he learned to be a fighter. He was a 1938 graduate of Negaunee St. Paul High School, where he was captain of the basketball team and captain and quarterback of the football team. His nickname, Puga, was given to him by childhood friend Jimmy Maino of Patch Location.

During the Depression Jacobetti learned how to survive under difficult conditions and decided to help people when he could. Jacobetti was hired at age 18 through President Roosevelt's National Youth Administration (NYA) as a school janitor. He went to work at the Athens Mine in 1940 and became a grievance chairman and president of the United Steelworkers Local 2867. Jacobetti was also the first president of USWA Local 4950.

Eventually, he became staff representative for the Steelworkers and held that position until he was approached by the local Democratic Party chair to run for the state House in 1954. Though Jacobetti was reluctant to run, he was convinced to give politics a try and won that first election by 162 votes. He won his seat 20 more times.

For eighteen years he was House Appropriations Committee Chairman, known as the "Godfather" for his ability to bring state funds to his district. Over the years, he provided strong support for education in general, and NMU in particular. Jacobetti had a great love for the Upper Peninsula, its people, and the role of education in helping children. On campus the Jacobetti Center was dedicated to him on May 02, 1981.

In 1993, he was stripped of the chairmanship of the Appropriation Committee in the wake of a scandal over the misuse of $1.8 million at the House Fiscal Agency, which the Appropriations Committee oversaw. While several others were charged and sentenced, investigators did not charge Jacobetti with any wrongdoing and he was steadfast in his denial of any involvement in the scandal. Eventually, he was exonerated of any blame in the scandal. Despite this situation, he won re-election over Republican Terry Talo on November 8, 1994 with 70 percent of the vote in the 109th District.

Jacobetti had a strong love for family. He and his wife, the former Marie Burnette, celebrated their 52nd wedding anniversary in February 1994. They have three children: Colin of Iron Mountain, Dominic "Dukey" Jr. of Negaunee, and Judith Jacobetti-Furey of Chicago.

Jacobetti was a Democrat and Roman Catholic. His memberships included Negaunee Eagles, Elks, Knights of Columbus, Rod and Gun Club, Marquette Moose Lodge, Druid Lodge, NMU's Golden Wildcat Club, Marquette County Historical Society and Young Democrat Club. He was an honorary member of the Veterans of Foreign Wars V.A. Romo Post 3165 of Negaunee and of AMVETS Post 124.

After his death, the Jacobetti family donated his papers and artifacts to the NMU Archives. In 1997, two tributes to him were developed and unveiled. One is in the Jacobetti Center and the other is in the Superior Dome titled, "Legends of the Upper Peninsula." In June 1997, he was inducted into the Labor Hall of Fame on campus. (Sources: MJ 11/28/1994, 11/29/1994) Portions by Renee Prusi

Jacobetti Center: The Center got its start as seven school buildings scattered throughout the Marquette area, known as the Area Training Center and NMU Skills Center. Today, the school has evolved into Northern's state-of-the-art College of Technology and Applied Sciences located in the Jacobetti Center.

The training center began in 1962 under President John F. Kennedy's Manpower Development and Training Act. It was part of JFK's New Frontier concept of government assisting people in more than basic, mundane ways. The idea of the Manpower Act was to retrain people who had lost their jobs or who were without skills for industry. After a while, the idea developed that some part of the community would take over the program and make it part of its system. "I believe" said Dick Retaskie, director of operations at the Center, "we're the only program in the nation that ever fulfilled the original intention of the act"

The Area Training Center's first building was an old railroad depot on Spring Street that became a stenography/data processing/machine tool classroom. At first students could enter the program at any time, but financial aid restrictions caused the program to develop a semester schedule.

The Area Training Center evolved into the NMU Skills Center, which offered classes not only to those pursuing a post-secondary degree, but also to some high school students interested in vocational training. Classes were offered at sites around Marquette.

After several years, it became obvious that all of these sites had to be located under one roof. Representative Dominic J. Jacobetti was interested in the project and plans were developed in 1977. Soon, construction began on a $16.5 million facility near campus on County Road 550. The building, with five aces or 225,000 square feet under one roof, was opened in 1980. On April 15, 1980, the structure was named the D. J. Jacobetti Vocational Skills Center by the Board of Control. It was dedicated on May 2, 1981. The Board changed the name to the D. J. Jacobetti Center effective January 1, 1987.

The Center serves people from 16 years of age and over and of varying abilities. It is constantly changing to remove and add programs which are demanded by the working world. (NW 11/10/1977; MJ 05/09/1993)

Jacobetti Center Property and Ruins: This area of campus has had a unique and exciting history and contains some interesting ruins. In 1870, the Lake Superior Powder Company, located nearby, manufactured gun and blasting powder. Between 1881 and 1905 there were a series of serious explosions with a loss of life. The last explosion in December 1905, destroyed 10 buildings, killed 5 and injured 10. Some say that this explosion jarred the chimney on Longyear Hall and led to the fire that destroyed the building. Later, the plant moved to the Copper Country. Eventually, Northern bought the site for the Center.

The concrete ruins that can be seen at the east end of the parking lot are the remains of the New Process Metals Company. These remains are the last of four furnaces built by John Tyler Jones to process low grade ore. Fearing the eventual depletion of high grade iron ore, he constructed an experimental furnace for the processing of low grade ore in 1909. Jones was encouraged to locate on the site by John M. Longyear on land donated by Longyear. Ore was recovered by burning it in a 120-foot revolving tube turned by an electric motor. Unfortunately, Jones did not live to see the end of high grade ore. Plagued by many problems, the plant closed around 1915 and was soon dismantled, leaving only the ruins seen today. This iron process became practical around 1947.

Jacobetti Center Storage: This 5,820 square foot structure was completed in 1989. It is located immediately to the northwest of the Center.

Jamrich, John X.: (June 12, 1920–) Jamrich was the eighth president of NMU. He was born in Muskegon Heights, Michigan, but during his early childhood, his family moved back to Czechoslovakia for several years. When they returned to the United States, they settled in Cudahy, Wisconsin. Dr. Jamrich received his B.S. from the University of Chicago (1943), M.S. Marquette University (1948), and the Ph.D. from Northwestern University (1951). During World War II (1942–1946) he was a captain in the U.S. Army Air Force where he specialized in weather forecasting. His knowledge of Slavic languages aided him in dealing with Russian airmen in Alaska.

Dr. Jamrich married June Ann Hrupka on June 26, 1944. They have three daughters: June Ann, Marna Mary, and Barbara Sue.

He came to Northern, having served as associate dean of Michigan State University's College of Education since 1963. He accepted the presidency on March 8, 1968. During his 15 year tenure, President Jamrich had to deal with the transition from a unilateral presidency, where all decisions were made from the top down, to one of shared governance. Thus he had to maximize the participatory activity of the university community.

President John Jamrich shared the educational philosophy of President Harden. Both men had been influenced by Michigan State University. As a result, the Jamrich presidency can be seen as a continuation of the Harden years.

When President Jamrich arrived in 1968, the university was in a period of turbulence, involving President Jamrich in the final resolution of the McClellan affair (*See separate entry*). Then there were problems with Black student protests, their "demands for justice," and demands for a Black Studies program, among other things, between 1969 and 1970. Higher education throughout the nation faced similar and more aggravated problems at this time as well. The controversy over the demolition of Kaye Hall (*See separate entry*) in 1971–1972 caused agitation with the community and alumni, but little could be done over a decision by the state legislature not to fund renovation of the historic building.

Despite this unrest, the university was going through a period of growth and expansion. Representative Dominic Jacobetti (*See separate entry*) provided the necessary clout in the State Legislature as the Chairman of the State Appropriation Committee. The President could go to the committee and point out that Northern was involved with the right-to-try program (*See separate entry*), community college initiative, labor education (*See separate entry*), and the skills center (*See: Jacobetti Center*) to train and retrain people. All of these programs, which affected a broad spectrum of the Upper Peninsula population, were looked on with favor by the legislators.

Besides these programs, academic programs were promoted that were in demand by students. As a result, programs were expanded, and new faculty and physical facilities were added. During these years, the first computer science program (*See separate entry*) was developed in the Mathematics Department. The College of Nursing and Allied Health Sciences was established in 1968 and proved to be popular with students. There was also the development of Criminal Justice, Business, Communication Disorders, Military Science and Anthropology (*See separate entries*). All of these developments needed a constant expansion of the library resources as well.

The community connection, first promoted by President Harden and continued under President Jamrich. The expansion of WNMU-TV and WNMU-FM (*See separate entries*) strengthened the ties between the University and the people of the Upper Peninsula. There was also interaction with Bay de Noc and Gogebic Community Colleges. The off-campus programs were flourishing at this time. Northern also developed ties with the Finnish American and Native American communities through a number of programs.

There were a number of areas which President Jamrich did not pursue. These included the Sea Grant and the development of a doctoral program. Concerning the latter, President Jamrich did not consider this a viable program for Northern.

The concept of shared governance came to a head with the organization of the American Association of University Professors (*See: Unions*) in May 1975. Over the years, the staffs in other areas of the University unionized as well.

Between 1980 and 1983 the University faced major budget reductions. State directives reduced revenues over $5 million which represented a 19.5 percent reduction of the University budget. At one point cuts were made by executive orders issued monthly. As a result it was impossible to implement a well developed plan of adjustment. This decline in funds also resulted in a decline in students from 9,376 in 1980–1981 to 8,229 in 1983. During these same years graduate assistantships dropped from 90 to only seven, with a 32 percent drop in graduate enrollment. These were difficult years for the Jamrich administration.

In the area of athletics, the Jamrich administration was active as well. Women's sports were developed with the introduction and expansion of field hockey (*See separate entry*) in 1968. Ice hockey (*See separate entry*) was added a few years later and the football team (*See separate entry*) won the NCAA II National Championship in 1975. It was during this time that the Physical Education Instructional Facility (*See separate entry*) was opened for use in 1976.

Two symbols of the Jamrich administration were the pine tree logo and the motto, "Working to Put Tomorrow in Good Hands." The logo showed a pine tree breaking through conventional restraints, a characteristic considered appropriate for Northern by President Jamrich.

In 1999, the Jamriches live in Florida and Dr. Jamrich remains active composing music. They started the Jamrich Endowment (*See separate entry*) On July 11, 1997, his "Centennial Suite" debuted in the Superior Room of the University Center. It was next performed by Pianist Nancy Redfern on August 29, 1998 at the opening reception for the NMU Art and Design Alumni exhibit at the University Art Museum. The Instructional Facility was named after him and dedicated on December 19, 1975. (Source: Oral interview, 07-25-1994, UA; MJ 08/26/1998)

Jamrich, June Ann Hrupka: A native of Wisconsin, Mrs. Jamrich married her husband on June 26, 1944 and they have three daughters: June Ann, Marna Mary, and Barbara Sue. In addition to her duties as first lady of Northern, Mrs. Jamrich held an appointment as Instructor of Figure Skating, the first wife of a president to be so employed by the University since Minnie Waldo (1899–1903).

Jamrich Endowment, John X. and June A.: The Endowment was started in 1973, when the Jamriches set aside personal funds because they felt "art and music are essential elements in education." Originally conceived to support a piano competition, after several years the fund was redesignated for visual arts exhibits at the University Art Museum. The endowment supports one exhibit a year that otherwise could not be mounted. The shows are designed to enrich the cultural life of the students and community. Past examples include: Latino Artists of Chicago; Art of Haiti; Masks of the World; Creation Cycle (Native American). (MJ 08/26/1998)

Jamrich Hall: Construction on the hall began in the summer of 1968 and was completed in the spring of 1970 at a cost of $2,790,000. Of this amount, $930,000 was provided by a Federal grant, and the remainder appropriated by the State Legislature. It was designed by the architectural firm of Swanson Associates Inc. of Bloomfield Hills.

Covering 97,850 square feet, it originally contained 28 classrooms and two learning laboratories on the second floor. Their sizes range from 32 to 94 student stations. On the first floor, there is a 500-seat lecture hall, two 300-seat and two 150-seat halls. Each lecture hall was originally equipped with a rear screen projection system, an overhead projector and integrated sound systems. The lower level has faculty offices, storage rooms and houses the Museum Collection. Over the years the structure has undergone a variety of renovations especially in regard to language and computer labs.

It was originally called the Instructional Facility or IF. On October 17, 1975, the Board of Control acted on a motion offered by Dr. Fred C. Sabin of Marquette who said the motion "reflected the Board's strong feeling for the superb job Dr. Jamrich has done for NMU." The Board unanimously voted to name the building after President Jamrich. The dedication took place on December 19, 1975. (NN 06/02/1967, 02/06/1970).

Job Corps Center for Women: The Job Corps Program was created as part of the Economic Opportunity Act of 1964. It was created for disadvantaged, poor youth 16 to 20 years of age. The program's plan was to educate youth in a healthy atmosphere, and thus promote vocational training for future employment.

President Harden was interested in bringing this program to campus and the final negotiations with federal officials were conducted by the University in January 1966. A month later, U.S. Representative Raymond Clevenger announced that Northern had received the largest federal grant to date, $2.7 million, to operate for one year the Job Corps Center for Women. This would be extended. This was the first time that such a contract had been made with a university.

The Center brought some 300 young women and a staff of 107 to campus. Many citizens were apprehensive about how Job Corps staff and enrollees would adjust to Marquette. About half of them were expected to be from minority groups. Their way was eased in Marquette by a Community Council chosen by the Center Director, Bert Jones, and was composed of men and women prominent in civic, religious, political, and commercial affairs of the city. Council members took a personal interest in the women and encouraged their friends to invite the enrollees to their meetings and homes.

At the opening of the Center in June 1966, Dr. Benetta B. Washington, national director of the Job Corps for Women, pointed out, "Women in the program get their first taste of what it's like to live an American life in the way we hope American life should be."

The Center, operating under the Division of Public Services, provided training for women between 16 and 20 years of age in occupational skills such a secretarial, graphic arts, drafting, tailoring, data processing and practical nursing. General education was also emphasized in oral and written communications, mathematics, home and family living and personal hygiene. The corps women lived in Carey Hall and their classes were taken in the recently acquired Birdseye Building.

During the heyday of the Corps, some enrollees went on to transfer into regular college programs while others continued their vocational training. Corps women built a float for Marquette's Fourth of July parade, formed their own choir and published their own newspaper.

In April 1969, the federal government gave notice to the University to immediately begin the process of closing the Center. This was part of a budget-saving move by the federal government to close sixty-five Job Corps Centers throughout the nation.

This federal edict brought signs of protest on campus. "Save the Job Corps" buttons were worn by many on campus, while Young Americans for Freedom Chair, Dean Carl carried a sign "Dick [Nixon] did the trick" and "Sock it to 'em President Jamrich." A referendum was held and students voted 1,322 to 791 in favor of closing down the center.

Although the notice called for "immediate closing," President Jamrich and the Board were successful in delaying this action until June 20, enabling seventy-five women nearing completion of their training programs to graduate on June 16. The other trainees, in various phases of their programs, were transferred to other centers. The Program benefitted many participants from not only Michigan but the nation. (MJ 02/11/1966, 06/28/1966; NN 07/28/1966; Marnie E. Foucault. "Controversial Job Corps Center Comes to N.M.U." (1995), UA)

JOBSearch Center: The Placement Office, the predecessor of the Center, has a long history at Northern. Until 1916, Northern would send job applications from its graduates directly to the superintendents and commissioners of schools. From 1916 to 1945, there was an Appointment Committee which was headed by the President of Northern and the principal or director of the training school. The committee handled placement of Northern graduates. From 1945 to 1949, there was a Placement Office with a director and staff.

From 1949 to 1960, there was simply a Placement secretary. Then Dr. Edward Pfau was the director of Student Teaching and Placement (1960-1961). Between 1961 and 1963, Pfau's title was changed to the Dean of Education and Teacher Placement and R. Thomas Peters became the director of Alumni Relations and non-teacher Placement. From 1963 to 1986, Keith Forsberg was the director of Placement. In August 1969, the name was changed to Office of Career Planning and Placement. The office has gone through recent name changes. In 1971, it was titled the Office of Placement and Career Planning, and in 1996 it was renamed the JOBSearch Center.

The mission of the Center, located in the Bottum University Center, is to assist current and former students and alumni with career exploration and job placement concerns. This is accomplished by providing resources and services focused on assisting the process of career exploration and decision-making, linking Northern students and alumni with potential employers, teaching effective job search strategies, providing supportive information and resources to faculty/staff in addressing career-related concerns of students and marketing the attractiveness of Northern candidates to prospective employers.

By 1998, the JOBSearch Center developed a program to work more closely with faculty who could advise students on career choices. The Faculty Guide to the JOBSearch Center pamphlet familiarizes faculty with the Center. The Center is located in the University Center.

Directors: The Appointment Committee: James Kaye and Steven Stockwell, 1916–1923; John M. Munson and Harry D. Lee, 1923–1929; The Placement Committee: Munson and Lee, 1929–1933; Webster Pearce and Lee, 1933–1941; Henry Tape, Joseph Dewey (Pierce Director), and Don H. Bottum (Principal of Pierce School, 1941–1945; Placement Office (Placement Committee still Present until 1945): Joseph Dewey, 1942–1946; William Hoppes, 1946–1949; Priscilla Densmore, secretary, 1949–1960; Director of Student Teaching and Placement: Ed Pfau, 1960–1961; Office of the Dean of Education and Teacher Placement: Ed Pfau, 1961–1963; Office of the Director of Alumni Relations and non-teacher Placement: R. Thomas Peters 1961–1963; Office of the Director of Placement: Keith Forsberg, 1963–1971; Office of Placement and Career Planning, Keith Forsberg, 1971–1986; Brian Enos, 1986–1996; JOBSearch Center, Brian Enos, 1996–1997; John Frick, 1997–present. (NN 03/28/1962; *Bulletins*; *The 1996–97 University Profile*, 2:179–184) Michelle Kangas

John D. Pierce Training School: Between 1900 and 1971, a laboratory school was operated by Northern. Student teachers were assigned to the lab school for their training. It was first organized and opened in September 1900, taught by five critic teachers whose pay was not to exceed $750 per year. The city of Marquette gave Northern the free use of an abandoned ward school located on North Third Street between Michigan and Ohio. From 1901 until 1925 when the John D. Pierce School opened, classes were held in Longyear Hall. In 1903 the superintendency of the training school was separated from the Department of Psychology and Pedagogy.

Plans for the new laboratory school were developed in 1922, and architects were Smith, Hinchman & Grylls. The Pierce School was first occupied on April 6, 1925, and was dedicated on May 25, 1927. It was named after the first State Superintendent of Public Instruction (*See*: Pierce, John D.). The school was a laboratory school where Northern students working toward teacher certification were trained. The school included grades K–12. Many of the instructors taught both in the school and at Northern. The state legislature closed the high school in 1961. However, that same year, the basketball team under coach Vic Hurst won the state "D" championship. The elementary grades ended in 1971. For a number of years, the remodeled building was used by the Psychology Department and other offices. Abandoned for several years, it was demolished in 1991–1992 by the Pitsch Company of Grand Rapids, Michigan.

Directors: Lewis F. Anderson, 1900–1904; Frances M. Kelsey, 1904–1911; Hugh S. Buffum, 1912; Steven S. Stockwell, 1913–1922; Harry D. Lee, 1923–1940; Joseph C. Dewey, 1940–1945; Don H. Bottum, 1945–1947; William C. Hoppes, 1947–1960.

Principals: Francis R. Copper 1918–1924; Don H. Bottum, 1924–1947; Evan H. Kelley, 1947–1958; Thomas A. Phillips, 1958–1959; Edward Pfau, 1959–1960; Allan Schwarz, 1960–1963; Jack R. Rombouts, 1963–1965; Thomas Culhane, 1965–1971.

(NNN 12/12/1922; MJ 07/04/1941, 05/08/1961, 08/19/1967, 10/16/1968, 11/25/1968, 10/17/1991, 01/07/1992; NN 10/11/1968; Hilton)

Johnson, Ogden E.: (November 1, 1901–October 16, 1969) Interim president of Northern Michigan University, Johnson was born in Wausau, Wisconsin and graduated from the local high school. He received his baccalaureate degree from Augustana College and master's degree from Boston University. He served as a teacher, coach and principal at Newberry High School before joining the Ishpeming school system. During his coaching tenure at Newberry, his 1926 team won the state high school Class C championship.

Johnson went to Ishpeming in 1929 and served as principal and superintendent of the Ishpeming public schools for 23 years. Johnson left the superintendency to join Cleveland-Cliffs Iron Company as director of industrial relations when that department was formed in 1952. He retired from the position on July 1, 1967.

In 1955, Johnson was a delegate to the White House Conference on Education. In 1959, he served as regional chair for the White House Conference on Youth.

Governor George Romney appointed Johnson a member of the Board of Control in 1964. With the resignation of Dr. Harden, the Board of Control met in August 1967 and named Johnson interim president. Governor Romney replaced him on the Board with Fred C. Sabin.

Johnson was interim president from September 1, 1967 to July 1, 1968. He was faced with the difficult and controversial McClellan controversy (*See separate entry*). Before Harden left office, the Faculty Senate had tried to reconsider his recommendation that the appointment of Dr. Robert McClellan of the History Department be terminated. He had refused, and in September the new Academic Vice President, at the request of the Senate, asked President Johnson to reopen the case. Again, he refused. As a result, there was general chaos and upheaval during the fall and spring semesters. The Senate resigned. There were class boycotts, resolutions, marches and pickets. The *Mining Journal*, owned by the Panax Corporation who had two members on the Board of Control, came out against the faculty and students. The Board reaffirmed its decision to dismiss McClellan on October 27. The trouble continued. On May 22, 1968, a suit for violation of the civil liberties of McClellan was filed against President Johnson and the Board of Control on behalf of 137 members of the faculty and the Student Government Association. On June 25, an out-of-court settlement was announced and McClellan remained on Northern's staff.

Despite the upheaval, Johnson oversaw the operation of the University. However, the experience had taken a toll on the man. In October 1969, he passed away.

Although busy with educational and industrial positions, Johnson found time to be active in many fields at the local, county, and regional and state levels. Locally, he was a member and past president of the Ishpeming Rotary Club and a member of the Ishpeming Town Club, and Chamber of Commerce.

In May of 1969, Johnson was presented with an outstanding achievement award by the Augustana College Alumni Association at its annual Alumni Day dinner. He was cited for his "significant achievement in educational administration and industrial promotion." (Hilton, pp. 199–204; MJ 10/17/1969)

Journalism: The first Journalism course was offered through the Language and Literature department in 1935. The course title was English 301. Students could earn up to three credits toward their degree, but Journalism could not be applied toward a major or minor. Students were required to work for one semester at the student newspaper.

Early in 1975, curriculum changes were aimed at improving the practical value of a number of journalism courses. At that time, Dr. Thomas Hruska, assistant professor of English, was NMU's only instructor of journalism.

Currently, journalism is offered as a minor. Students are still required to write for the *North Wind* as part of their laboratory experience. Non-journalism minors work at the paper, also. The *Detroit Free Press* has provided Northern with a scholarship for a student studying journalism. (*Bulletins*; NW 02/20/1975) Michelle Kangas

Jubilee Celebration: Plans to celebrate the 50th anniversary (1949) of the foundation of Northern were begun by President Tape in early 1948. The celebration consisted in a gigantic homecoming in the fall of 1948 and the commencement in the spring of 1949. At that time the Administration Building was renamed Kaye Hall and Carey Hall was dedicated (06/18/1949). This was followed by an afternoon luncheon in Lee Hall. A planned history of the institution by Francis R. Copper was never published due to his sudden death in January.

Judo (Men) and Taekwon-Do: These teams were listed as new sports in the *1975 Peninsulan*. Currently, there are student organizations for martial arts, Isshinryue Club and the North Korean Taekwon-Do Club. (*Peninsulan*; 1997–98 Telephone Directory) Michelle Kangas

"Junior Prom": A spoof prom-type dance was the brain child of Dale Wetig (Art & Design). It was first held by Art & Design students in the spring of 1984. At first, participation was limited to students in the Department of Art and Design, but as the popularity of "Junior Prom" expanded, it was opened to the public. Over the years it was held every year except 1998, in such varied locations as Birdseye, the University Center, Ramada Inn, Marquette Mountain and the Northwoods Supper Club.

Justice Studies, Department of: *See*: *Criminal Justice*

Kaufman Oratorical Prize: This cash prize was created by Nathan M. Kaufman in 1909. Orations on any subject were encouraged. In May 1909, the first contest was held and Ernest Roberts was the recipient of the $30 first prize for his speech on "Wendell Phillips," an American orator and reformer. Over the years, the topics of the speeches varied. Disarmament, divorce, and race relations were topics in 1912. Other topics included educational issues, student self-government, military training in the schools and the separation of the Upper Peninsula from Michigan. Women's suffrage in the United States, and particularly in Michigan, where it was on the ballot in 1914, was often debated. The Prize was last awarded in 1922.

Kawbawgam: *See Annual*

Kaye, Ina L. Tracey: (Died June 7, 1945) A native of Custer, Michigan, she married James Kaye on August 22, 1893. They had two children: John Tracey and Mildred (Richard Beldsoe). She died in Ludington and funeral services were held from the First Presbyterian Church.
(MJ 06/08/1945)

Kaye, James Hamilton Barcroft: (March 12, 1862–July 10, 1932) Second president of Northern (1904–1923) and also served as professor of philosophy and education. He was married to Ina L. Tracey (1893) of Custer, Michigan and they had two children: John Tracey who became a physician and Mildred (Richard Beldsoe). Kaye, who was born in Farnworth, Lancashire, England was educated there and came to the United States in 1883.

His father, John B. Kaye was deeply involved in the slavery controversy in America, which caused him to emigrate. He was a personal friend of Lord Tennyson and Charles Dickens and gave his son a rich heritage of personal and cultural associations.

President Kaye attended the University of Michigan where he was an instructor and fellow until he received his bachelor of arts degree in 1892. Kaye received his master of arts degree in 1912 from Albion College. While he finished his master requirements, he was an assistant instructor at Albion College.

Prior to coming to Northern, Kaye served in a number of educational capacities around the state. He taught in the public schools of Custer, Chase, and Ludington, Michigan. From 1892 to 1896, he was superintendent of schools in Reed City and superintendent in Cadillac from 1896 to 1904.

In July 1904, he became the second principal and later president of Northern State Normal School. Kaye proved to be an able leader. During his eighteen year tenure as head of Northern, the longest in the history of the institution, he oversaw the completion of the first physical plant and expansion of the campus. Annexes were constructed and by 1908–1909 a new steam heating plant was in operation. As early as 1912 President Kaye was promoting the completion of the physical complex as envisioned by Architect D. F. Charleton in 1899. In the summer of 1915, Kaye Hall, which was dedicated to him in 1949, was opened for use. He was also responsible for the development of the first athletic field on campus to the west of Kaye Hall in front of the present University Center.

President Kaye traveled around the Upper Peninsula and met with the people. Often he went on commencement trips where he gave two or three commencement addresses in as many days. His devotion and unselfish service to the institution gained him a host of friends and admirers throughout the region.

During his presidency student enrollments went from 284 in 1904 to 563 in 1923. Academics were important to him, but he was also concerned about the social and moral well-being of the students. He implemented many rules and regulations which were mandated by the State Board of Education.

His administration saw Northern go from a teacher's training school to a college. In 1918 the institution was allowed to grant the bachelor of arts degree. As a result of this action, students came to Northern to pursue a four-year degree as well.

In 1927, after he was out office, the State Board of Education retitled the institution as Northern State Teachers College to better identify the institution that he had worked so hard to expand.

On December 11, 1922, President Kaye announced to the Faculty Council, that due to poor health he planned on retiring on July 1, 1923. After his retirement, Kaye gained emeritus status and continued to teach at Northern for an additional nine years. He taught philosophy and education. He and his family spent the summers in Custer or at his country home at Scottville, seven miles east of Ludington, and returned to Marquette for classes in the winter.

President Kaye was a scholar who was interested in philosophy and the problem of human conduct and human relationships. He published numerous articles on the subject of education. He was also an omnivorous reader and developed a wealth of diverse knowledge. Kaye was a literary scholar who read widely in Latin, Greek, Old German and Anglo Saxon. He was an authority on Tennyson and Dickens and corresponded with a host of contemporary scholars.

His memberships included the National Education Association, National Society for the Scientific Study of Education, Michigan State Teachers Association (served as secretary and vice president), Northern Michigan Teachers Association (secretary and president), Upper Peninsula Educational Association, National Institute of Social Sciences (executive council), and the National Economic League (1929). Fraternally he was a Knight Templar and a 32nd Degree Mason.

During his later years Kaye became involved with Rotary International and its program for world understanding and the betterment of conditions for handicapped children. He was elected governor of the Fifteenth Rotary District at Wausau, Wisconsin in 1920 and during his year in office became affectionately known as "Governor Jim."

Both the city of Marquette and the University have memorialized him. In 1925 the City Commission renamed Hematite Street, bordering the southern boundary of campus after him. In June 1949 the original administration building was named in his honor. After the building was demolished, in November, 1979 the new president's residence was named Kaye House by the Board of Control. (MJ 07/12/1932; *Ludington Daily News* 07/11/1932)

Kaye Avenue: A street running from Presque Isle broken by the campus and then continuing to Lincoln Avenue on the west. It was originally named Hematite, but was renamed by the City Commission in 1925 honoring President Kaye. Prior to 1935, the section running from Presque Isle to Hebard Court was used as a parking area. It was narrow and rocky with telephone posts in the middle of the street and gullies caused by rain runoff. President Pearce did not like the condition of the street. In 1935, he made an arrangement with the city to clear and pave the street to the football field on the west. A smooth and broad thoroughfare was the result, with adequate parking for the time. Later, the street was widened to its present size. In the summer of 1996, Lee Drive was realigned and a new entry to the campus was opened onto Kaye Avenue.

Kaye Avenue Entrance Landmark: As part of the Centennial celebration, the idea of highlighting the main gateway to campus was discussed. In 1997, Michael Cinelli worked with Dale Wedig, both of the Art and Design Department, to develop this concept. Wedig proposed to construct stepped masonry walls mounted with a steel screen on either side of the Kaye Avenue entrance. Also masonry based, and located behind the west wall would be constructed a 35–40 foot clock tower clearly visible from a distance. Masonry for both structures would consist of sandstone remaining from former buildings (Longyear, Kaye, and Pierce) and feature architectural details from those structures. The screen would be constructed from half-inch painted steel plate.

The concept was presented to the Centennial Committee, the Board of Control and to a variety of groups on campus. Funding for the project is being considered.

Kaye Hall: The Legislature appropriated $150,000 for a new building and $10,000 for its equipment. The main building in the original Northern complex was completed and ready for occupancy in June 1915 for summer school. It had a front of 128 feet and a depth of 160 feet using a Tudor architectural style. Three stories in height, it had a central tower and was constructed of native teardrop sandstone to match the other buildings. Its gymnasium was the largest in the Upper Peninsula at the time and included a running track in the gallery which could be used by spectators during games. Connected with the gym were a large locker room, "shower baths," and modern equipment.

The large auditorium (*See: Kaye Hall Auditorium*) could accommodate some 1,500 people. It was also used by conventions, meetings of the Upper Peninsula Education Association, and for commencements between 1915 and 1967. The library (numbering 20,000 volumes) needed more room, which was found in the new structure.

As described in *The Quill*, "the central feature of the new building, from an architectural point of view, is the beautiful stairway around which are grouped the various rooms." There were 15 classrooms arranged in suites so that the faculty office was connected to the classroom. The administration offices were located here as well.

The building was formally dedicated on October 6, 1915, but not called Kaye Hall. From its completion until 1949 it was called the "Administration Building" and is best remembered for its famous and beloved atrium lobby. It was dedicated to the second president, James H. B. Kaye, on June 18, 1949. In July 1950, the Board authorized a remodeling project for Kaye Hall. It was at this time that a second story was added to the front wings.

For years Kaye Hall was the center of the campus. In the mid-1950s, campus buildings began to be built westward, and Kaye Hall (which was overcrowded) became irrelevant, though loved by generations of alumni. Its proposed demolition created the greatest historic preservation debate in Marquette's history. Unfortunately, despite the debate which involved alumni, city residents and university officials, the state mandate not to expend money on a condemned building caused its demolition which began on August 1, 1972 and continued into 1973.

The debris from the structure is located a few miles up County Road 550. The bitterness of its demolition has remained in the memories of many. The original campus buildings are remembered by a historical marker dedicated on October 16, 1998. (MJ 10/06/1915; NW 09/22/1983)

Kaye Hall Auditorium: The auditorium was constructed and opened in 1915 as part of Kaye Hall. It was located to the west of Kaye Hall and entered through the grand foyer. The auditorium was the largest structure in the Upper Peninsula with a spacious balcony. It could hold as many as 1,500 people and easily accommodated the entire student body for assemblies. It was also used by conventions and for meetings of the Upper Peninsula Education Association. The first graduation was held in the Auditorium on June 22, 1915. Due to expanding graduating classes, the last commencement was held in the Auditorium on January 21, 1967 and Hedgcock Fieldhouse became the new site for these ceremonies.

In July, during the first summer of its existence, the auditorium was used to comfortably seat a thousand to enjoy the concert by the fifty-voice Normal Chorus and Abby Beecher Roberts, John M. Longyear's daughter and to applaud Sophie Linton's performance on the orchestrelle. During World War I, numerous performances from the auditorium stage raised money for war relief. Some of the groups and people which appeared in the auditorium over the years included: the Marine Band, Mozarteum from Salzburg, Austria, and Eleanor Roosevelt (*See separate entry*), who presented a lecture there in 1956.

In the 1960s, the Fire Marshall found that the balcony was not properly secured to the south wall and the balcony could not be used. This led to the state condemning the structure and not allowing additional funding for its improvement. It was demolished with the rest of the Kaye Hall Complex in 1972–1973. (MJ 07/24/1915; Hilton, p. 51)

Kaye House: *See*: *Presidential Homes*

The King and Queen Knob: *See*: *The Heart of Northern*

Korean War: On June 25, 1950, war began when the North Koreans invaded South Korea by crossing the 38th parallel and refused to abide by the UN call for a cease-fire and withdrawal. Two days, later United States forces were committed by President Truman. The war continued through the armistice on July 27, 1953.

Colleges throughout the country were faced with the serious problem of decreasing enrollments. At Northern, the enrollment in 1950 was 847. There was a wave of student enlistments in preference to monthly draft calls in the last half of 1950. By enlisting, students could select the choice of their branch of service. In the winter 1951, most males remained through the semester until their deferments ran out.

As the war progressed, the decline in male students was obvious. In the winter 1951 semester, enrollment declined by 14 percent less than the fall 1950 semester. Between September 1950 and February 1951, eleven students were called back from inactive reserve to active status and most of the 18 that enlisted entered the Army Air Corps. Ruby Short, a W.A.C. reservist, entered active duty in February. Some 35 draftees remained in school because their induction status had been postponed.

Classes were noticeably smaller through 1951 and 1952. By the fall of 1952, the enrollment had declined to 586 which was the smallest since 1950. The athletic programs were hit by the decrease of male students. Two of Northern's 1950 grid-iron opponents—Gogebic Community College and Detroit Tech—had to drop football for the duration of the conflict.

With the armistice in June 1953, there was a small increase in the fall enrollment to 604 students. By the following fall, there were 735 students. In January 1954, there were 79 veterans attending college through financial aid offered by the G. I. Bill. Those under the Korean G. I. Bill received a monthly allotment of $110, which was increased if they were married and with children. (NCN 1/17/1951, 2/27/1951, 01/20/1954)

Krihara, Zenya: A student from Japan, she was the first foreign student to enrolled at Northern in 1919.

Kuralt, Charles: American newsman known for his television programs "On the Road with Charles Kuralt" and "Sunday Morning" on CBS. On January 29, 1975 he came to campus and presented a lecture, "America Behind the Headlines."

Labor Education Program: This Program was developed in the 1960s and was directed by Martin Duffy. It was funded as an extension service of the University of Michigan and Wayne State University. Northern's independent program was established in 1970, on the initiative of

Michigan State AFL-CIO President William Marshall and through the legislative efforts of Senator Joe Mack. Joaquin Gomez became the director at that time.

The Program provides training, consulting, and education resources to the members, officers and staff of Upper Peninsula and selected Lower Peninsula's counties' labor organizations. Program development reflects the active involvement of a Labor Advisory and Planning Committee representing sixteen national and international unions as well as the Michigan State AFL-CIO and the Michigan Building and Construction Trades Council. In 1997, the Upper Peninsula Labor Hall of Fame was created on the Northern campus.

Directors: Martin Duffy, early 1960s; Jack Meyers, 1964–1968; Joaquin "Keen" Gomez, 1970–1985; Fred Kotler, 1985–1995; Ted Balzarini, 1995–present.

Laboratory School or Practice School: *See*: *John D. Pierce School*

Lake Front Property: In the 1960s, Northern obtained the triangular piece of land bound by Pine, Fair, and Lake Superior. The land consisted of lake frontage and undisturbed ancient beaches covered with original trees and flora and inhabited by small animals and birds. For a number of years in the mid-1960s, the site was used by the biology faculty as an outdoor laboratory close to campus.

When Northern sought to construct the PEIF building in the early 1970s and the city needed a site for its convention center-ice arena, negotiations were begun for a land transfer. In 1971–1972, Northern's Board of Control and President Jamrich negotiated the transfer of some 2 acres of land upon which the Palestra was located at the foot of North Third Street with the city of Marquette. In return, the city received a parcel of land bound by Fair, Pine, Lakeshore Boulevard and Northern's property. The Lake View Arena was constructed on the southern portion of this site.

North of the Lake View Arena was approximately fourteen acres of land. As early as 1971–1972, two service organizations at NMU, Alpha Phi Omega (APO) fraternity and Gamma Sigma sorority first promoted the idea of establishing a student park on the site.

The site was dedicated by President Jamrich and student representatives in the last week of July 1972. Called University Harbour Park, it was designed to service NMU students with picnic sites and nature trails. The plans called for students in the fall to clear trails for botany and nature students, clean up the beach area, and construct picnic tables and barbecue pits for student outings. These plans were never realized and the land has remained in its natural state ever since. (NMUP 08/04/1972; MJ 07/28/1972) Emily Magnaghi

Landscaping: See: Campus, Evolution of the

Languages, Department of: The Department of Languages was formerly known as Foreign Language. Between 1901 and 1903, R. Clyde Ford taught German and French and was replaced by John E. Lautner. Lautner had broad interests which included economics and sociology. Other faculty joined the staff. Soon French, German, Latin (*See separate entry*) and Spanish were the main languages being taught on campus.

In 1916 during World War I, anti-German sentiment developed in the region and as a result German ceased to be offered. In order to assist students, there were numerous foreign newspapers and periodicals ordered for the library. As candidates for the bachelor of arts degree, students needed two years of a foreign language in high school and one year at Northern. The Foreign Language Department was merged in 1923 with the English Department which became known as the Department of Language and Literature. Prior to World War II, language instruction involved primarily grammar and reading. Afterward, communication became important as well.

During the 1960s, Flora Loubert and Madeleine Rubin de la Borbolla dominated the study of French and Spanish. In 1960, there was renewed student demand for German, which resulted in evening courses in German and even Russian. It was at this time that the first language laboratory was introduced on campus. The lab was opened in the fall of 1963 with 36 booths, sound-proof ceiling and an adjoining classroom to enable using the lab for half a class period. With the opening of Jamrich Hall in 1970, the Language Department had a new and expanded language lab.

In 1964, Helmut Kreitz was recruited to teach German. Three years later, he became the head of the newly created Foreign Language Department. Kreitz promoted travel abroad and the development of comparative literature. He also oversaw the expansion of the department during the late 1960s. By 1973, it was a six-person department. There were majors, minors, and a master's degree program in education in French, German and Spanish. Since 1980 there has been an interest in Chinese, Finnish, Japanese, Italian, Latin, and Russian, which have been taught on an ad hoc basis.

There was a period of controversy in the early 1990s with the introduction of Ojibwe. Since Ojibwe was not seen as a "foreign language," the title of the department was changed to the "Language Department." Ultimately, Ojibwe was housed in the Center for Native American Studies, but the title change remained.

The late 1990s saw the Department go through change. For a while the Department was headed by the dean of the College of Arts and Sciences. Although there was a growing interest in some languages with the development of an International Studies major and foreign study opportunities, there was also a decline in others. In 1998, due to a decline in students taking German, this language ceased to be offered as a major but continued as a minor. Now funding could be focused on Spanish which was more popular.

Over the years, there was always an interest on the part of students to form foreign language clubs. There were numerous French clubs dating from the 1920s, while in the 1970s and 1980s the German club was extensively promoted by Dr. Rudi Prusok. The origins of the Spanish club go back to 1948, although it was reactivated in 1989.

Department heads: Helmut Kreitz, 1967–1976; Rudi Prusok, 1976–1989; Rolande Graves, 1989–1996; Tim Compton, 1995 (acting department head while Graves was on sick leave) Fall 1995; (interim while Graves was on professional leave) Winter 1996; (program chair) Fall 1996–Winter 1998; Dean Michael Marsden, (interim) Fall 1996–Winter 1998; Tim Compton, (interim) 1998–present. (NCN 04/03/1939; Hilton, p. 174; Becky Berube, "History of the Foreign Language Department." 1995, UA; *The 1994–95 University Profile*, 1:101–104) Michelle Kangas and Alisa Koski

Latin: Following tradition, the Latin language and literature was taught for many years. The first Latin teacher was Belle Middlekauf who left in 1906 to continue her studies at Radcliffe. Principal Kaye persuaded Earle M. Parker to leave Marquette High School and come to Northern. He taught courses in Latin, English, and, for a brief time, Italian. In 1910 he organized the Latin Club. By 1931–1932 Parker oversaw a plethora of Latin courses, which included Caesar, Virgil, Livy, Horace, Latin comedy, classical studies, teacher training, Latin poetry, Roman literature and medieval Latin. By the 1940s, Parker's enrollments in college Latin classes declined. He then offered a new course, "Our Classical Heritage." When he retired in 1946, after thirty-six years at Northern, Latin was no longer listed in *Northern's Bulletin*. In the 1980s, Latin was offered a number of times by Dr. George Javor due to student demand.

Law Library: A special law library was created in 1957 on the Northern campus and was the first such library in Michigan. The concept was developed and promoted by State Supreme Court Justice John Voelker. Some 3,000 law books were housed in the Olson Library on campus. Although the idea was sound, it ran into a problem of distance from the court house and convenience. The Law Library was dismantled and returned to the Marquette County Courthouse in 1965. (NN 05/29/1957, 08/04/1967)

Learning Resources Division: Over the years, various areas of the University developed which would eventually comprise this division. They included the Audio-Visual and Graphics areas, WMNU-FM, and WNMU-TV. These various parts were united in 1962 under this Division and are currently housed in the Edgar L. Harden Learning Resources Center (*See separate entry*).

The mission of the Director's office of this Division is to administer the departments of LRC, including WNMU-FM, WNMU-TV, Engineering, and Audio Visual Services, and Productions Operations; to coordinate and monitor legal, legislative and FCC activities on behalf of the various departments; and to pursue a full range of fundraising activities to support operations.

Since 1972, the Division has had 100 percent compliance of FCC regulations each year. Both WNMU-FM and WNMU-TV receive Federal grants from the Corporation for Public Broadcasting. The fiscal year 1998 grant for television was $397,146 and for radio it was $130,682. During fiscal year 1997, WNMU-TV raised $527,300 and WNMU-FM raised $275,000. These fundraising campaigns have become even more necessary with the decline in federal monies. Beginning in 1992, the Division has been actively involved in the development of Distant Learning Facilities.

Directors: Ken Bergsma, 1962–1965; William Mitchell, 1965–1974; George Lott, 1974–1979; Ernest Phelps, 1980–1983; Scott K. Seaman, 1983–present. (*The 1996–97 University Profile*, 2:222–227)

Lee, Harry D.: (July 15, 1878–December 17, 1940) Mr. Lee was born in Decatur, Michigan, the son of Daniel and Sarah Lee, pioneer residents of that community. He graduated from Decatur High School in 1897 and from Michigan State Normal College (Eastern Michigan University) in 1901 with a life certificate. In 1913, he received an A.B. degree from the University of Michigan. Mr. Lee was awarded a M.A. degree from Teachers College, Columbia University, in 1926.

Between 1901 and 1908, he served in a variety of capacities in lower Michigan: as departmental superintendent in Frankfort (1901) and Shelby (1902–1903) and as principal in Holland (1904) and St. Joseph (1905–1909). In the Upper Peninsula, he was superintendent of schools at Lake Linden (1909–1913) and at Hancock (1913–1919). Between 1919 and 1922, he served as superintendent of schools in Waterloo, Iowa, where he oversaw the construction of a new high school.

Prior to coming to Marquette permanently, he taught summer school at Northern and at Western. He married Selma Knoche in September 1926, in Iowa. She was a former member of Northern's faculty.

During his 18 years of service at Northern, Mr. Lee had unusual success in placing graduates in teaching positions. As head of the placement bureau, he made an outstanding record, not only because of his wide acquaintance among school executives in the Upper and Lower Peninsulas, but because he gave the closest possible attention to his work and left nothing undone in his efforts to find employment for every graduate whose qualifications measured up to teaching standards. For a long period, the Northern placement bureau records show that Mr. Lee was successful in finding positions for nearly 100 percent of the graduates. Even during the hard days of the Depression, he found positions for students.

Many say that "he died with his boots on" since he was on his way home for lunch when his heart attack occurred. His associates at Northern felt that he had been overtaxed by the extra work he had been called on to do after the death of President Webster Pearce in October. During the period before President Tape's arrival on campus, Lee and L. O. Gant were placed in charge of Northern by Dr. Eugene E. Elliott, state superintendent of public instruction.

His memberships included Marquette Rotary Club, the Masonic Lodge, the National Educational Association, the Michigan Education Association and the Congregational church of Waterloo, Iowa. Lee Hall was dedicated to him on June 18, 1949. (MJ 12/18/1940)

Lee Hall/Union Building: This building, measuring 26,632 square feet was completed and opened in late December 1948. Through the 1950s, it was the social center of campus life.

One entered the building through the present doors. To the right of the foyer was the office used by the manager, secretary and bookkeeper. Further into the building was a faculty-student "living room," or lounge, with a comfortable fireplace (presently the Art and Design Department's main office).

In the center of the building was a large kitchen, a dining room for the women residents of Carey Hall to the rear (seating capacity 190) and a cafeteria and soda fountain in the front part of the structure (seating capacity 175) The cafeteria could be partitioned for small groups.

On the second floor of the building was the Ball Room, which had a capacity of 300. Contiguous with the ballroom, there was a conference room used for group meetings. Over the years, the ballroom and dining room were heavily used by the campus community. It was also rented to local groups and was very popular for proms and similar events.

The Union served as a center for student activities, organization dinners, conferences, faculty meetings, card games, movies, ping pong "and anything else." Some students found employment in the building while commuters used the handy dining room and cafeteria. Every year, the foyer was decorated with a Christmas tree and trimmings, followed by an annual Christmas party for the employees. The yule log was found burning in the fireplace and students relaxed in the lounge.

The Union proved to be too small, as the student enrollment dramatically increased in the late 1950s, and in 1959 construction was begun on the Don H. Bottum University Center (*See separate entry*). With the completion of the Center in 1960, Lee Hall was converted into a television and radio studio. Later in the 1970s, it became the home of the Art and Design Department (*See separate entry*), the University Art Museum (*See: Art Museum*), and the Department of Public Safety and Police Services (*See separate entry*). The latter department moved to the Services Building (*See separate entry*) in 1996.

Managers: Don H. Bottum, 1949–1950; Clyde C. Irwin, 1950–1952; Edward S. Woodridge, 1952–1953; H. Duane Plough, 1954–1958; Eldon E. Lawson, 1958–1960. (NCN 12/01/1948; NN 01/17/1951)

Lee Hall Art Gallery: *See*: *Art Museum, University*

Legislation Creating Northern: State Senator Peter White introduced a bill in the state senate to "established a branch of the State Normal School in the Upper Peninsula" in March–April 1875. Unfortunately this bill was not passed. The people of the Upper Peninsula continued to hope that a teacher's school would be established. In 1889, the issue was brought to the House of Representatives, but no action was taken. In February 1891, many groups of citizens from throughout the Peninsula petitioned the legislature to establish a school. A school was established in 1892, but it was Central Michigan University at Mount Pleasant.

Early in 1899, the question of a normal school in the Upper Peninsula arose again and petitions were sent to the legislature. On February 13, Fremont C.Chamberlain from the western Upper Peninsula, introduced the bill in the House of Representatives. During the following weeks, the Committee on Education visited various cities in the Upper Peninsula to decide on a definite location. John R. Gordon, the representative from Marquette managed the bill through the legislature. On March 30, the bill passed the House by a vote of 75 for and one against. It passed unanimously in the Senate on April 18.

The bill was enrolled, compared and presented to Governor Hazen Pingree on April 20. It was privately signed by Governor Pingree eight days later, along with six other bills. The governor sent notice to the Speaker of the House, that he had approved, signed and deposited the bill in the office of the Secretary of State.

Officially, it is Public Act No. 51, entitled "An Act to provide for the location, establishment and conduct of a Normal School at Marquette, in the Upper Peninsula of this State, and to make an appropriation for the same." The signed copy of the act is housed in the State Archives in Lansing and there are copies in the University Archives. (MJ 02/08/1899, 02/10/1899, 04/20/1899, 04/29/1899)

Legler, Phil, Poetry Prize. First given in 1993, the Phil Legler Poetry Prize commemorates the work of Professor Legler in the English Department. It is given annually ($100) for the best poem written in the department. (NW 04/21/1994)

Liberal Studies Program: Under President Jamrich, the Liberal Studies Program replaced the Common Learning Program (*See separate entry.* The Common Learning Program was instituted in 1962 by Milton Byrd, Academic Vice President.

The Liberal Studies Program was in effect by the 1974–75 academic year. Faculty designed the program based on the principle that "well-educated persons need to know more than can be learned from their areas of concentration." Originally the Program was divided into four areas: Composition, Humanities, Natural Science/Mathematics, and Social Sciences. In the late 1980s, Formal Communication Studies and Visual and Performing Art were added.

Today the Liberal Studies Program is divided into six areas, each requiring a certain number of credits: Composition(6 credits), Humanities (6 credits), Natural Science/Mathematics (6 credits), Social Sciences (6 credits), Formal Communications Studies (3 credits), and Visual and Performing Arts (3 credits). Students are required to complete 40 hours of Liberal Studies with at least three of the hours above the 300 level. No specific office or department administers the Liberal Studies Program. Students contact their advisors with questions.

While the program was being implemented, Dr. John Frey of the Chemistry Department was the Assistant Dean for Liberal Studies. Dr. Eugene Whitehouse of the History Department was the Associate Dean of Arts and Sciences assisting Dr. Robert Glenn (then Dean of Arts and Sciences) in the administration of the 16 departments offering Liberal Studies courses.

In the decade of the 1990s, there were various concerns raised about what was considered the overly-broad nature of the Program. A committee of the Academic Senate began to discuss the situation in the late 1990s and some embryonic plans for change were developed. Michelle Kangas

Library: The first library was located in a single room next to Principal Dwight Waldo's office in the city hall and consisted of a single bookshelf. The first librarian was William McCracken, the science teacher. He was followed by Minnie Strong Waldo, who held the position until her death in January 1903.

With the completion of South or Longyear Hall, the library under the direction of Grace E. Downing, found new quarters on the first floor, in the southeast corner of Longyear Hall in a small room. Within a few years, there was a demand for larger quarters for the growing library. In May 1904 construction began on this extension to Longyear Hall and was completed in September; the library was ready for occupancy by January 1, 1905. The cost for the annex was $12,500. It was called the Library Annex and was located in a north annex from Longyear Hall and eventually constituted the basement and first floor of the connector between Longyear and Kaye Halls. On December 18, 1905, Longyear burned to the ground. A stone fire wall and an efficient fire department saved the library. At the time, the library was considered one of the largest in the Upper Peninsula with over 12,000 volumes from the private collection of Moses Coit Tyler. A few books were damaged in the fire.

With the completion of Kaye Hall in 1915, the library was relocated in that building. As enrollment increased, so did the demand for adequate room for the growing collection. In the fall of 1951, the Lydia M. Olson Library was opened. Formal dedication ceremonies were conducted on October 19, 1951, and were in honor of Lydia M. Olson, an alumna of Northern and librarian from 1908 to 1941.

The new structure had storage space for 125,000 books and a seating capacity for 300 students. It was a closed stack system. By 1956, the collection consisted of over 50,000 books and bound periodicals. In addition, there was a picture file and pamphlet collection. The Moses Tyler Collection was housed in a special room on the second floor. It consists of books in the fields of American literature, biography, history and English. The collection was purchased for the University by E.N. Breiting, M.N. Kaufman and Peter White in 1904. Beginning in the summer school of 1954, library science courses were first offered. In May 1957, the Upper Peninsula Law Library (*See: Law Library*)—the first regional law library in Michigan—was established on campus. It remained here until 1965.

In the spring of 1969, with the completion of the Learning Resources Center, the Olson library was ready to move. Over the years, the library grew. By June 30, 1994, there were over a half million volumes under its care.

In the early 1990s, efforts began to unite the Lydia Olson Library, Academic Computing, the University and Area Archives, and Instructional Media Services under Academic Information Services (AIS). This was done and in operation in 1993–1994. Dr. Thomas Peischl was the first dean of this newly formed unit.

Librarians or directors: William McCracken, 1899–1900; Minnie Strong Waldo, 1900–1903; Grace E. Downing, 1903; Rena C. Miller, 1903–1905; Sarah McLeod, 1905–1908; Lydia M. Olson, 1908–1941; Frances Cook, 1941–1953; Harriet P. Wirick, 1942–1953; Taisto John Niemi, 1953–1960; Norman Bunker, (acting) 1960–1962, 1962–1963; Helvi E. Walkonen, 1963–1981; John Drabenstott, 1981–1983; Jane Swafford (acting) 1983; Rena K. Fowler, 1983–1992; John Berens, (interim) 07/01/1992–05/31/1993; Carolyn Meyers, (interim) 06/01/1993–06/30/1994; Thomas M. Peischl, 1994–1998; renamed Dean of Academic Information Services (*See*: *Academic Information Services*). (NN 03/05/1956)

Library Science, Department of: In the past the courses in library science prepared teachers in the elementary and secondary schools, or students who expected to enter a graduate program in another library school. Northern no longer offers a degree in library science. Since 1993 its courses are designated by "AIS" identifier. These are service courses for students to make them proficient in seeking information.

Loan Fund: In 1913–1914, a Students' Loan Fund was created through a gift by Mary E. Moore of Marquette and was known as the "Mary E. Moore Student Loan Fund." This fund consisted of $1,000 which was loaned to female students who would otherwise be unable to continue their work at Northern.

Over the years, other privately-contributed loan funds were made available to students. Today the Office of Financial Aid (*See separate entry*) administers the loan program.

Lock Shops: There are two lock shops on campus, one in the Housing Office and the other in Public Safety and Maintenance. The former is concerned with residence halls and the University Center and the latter with state sites.

Prior to the 1970s, keys were maintained by department chairs and their secretaries. New keys were made on campus. The Housing Office had always maintained its own keys and locks. In 1979, the lock shop was created for state sites and Sharon Harr was placed in charge, a position which she still holds. On February 2, 1988, Public Safety took over issuance of keys and announced the new policy. Today Harr deals with over 4,500 locks in doors throughout the campus and more than 17,000 key issuances.

Logo: *See: Signature*

Longyear, John: (April 15, 1850–May 20, 1922) Mr. Longyear was born in Lansing, Michigan, and was an iron mogul, two-time mayor of Marquette and president of the Marquette County Historical Society.

In the summer of 1899, he and his wife, Mary, along with their business partners, Frederick and Ellen Ayer, gave the first twenty acres of the original Northern campus to the State Board of Education. Longyear also contributed to furnishing the first building and his wife provided the salary for the first music teacher, Sophie Linton. He and Ayer built the first dormitory, which operated until 1917.

Northern has accepted a number of gifts from the Longyear family. In 1949, Mrs. Abby Beecher Roberts gave the Longyear Forest to Northern. Additional acreage was donated by the Longyear heirs in 1959. In January 1951, she gave an oil painting of John M. Longyear to the college. For the next twenty years, it hung in Longyear Hall and then was illegally removed and lost. (NN 01/25/1951)

Longyear Forest: In 1949 at the time of the semi-centennial, Mrs. Abby Beecher Roberts (John Longyear's daughter) gave Northern some 120 acres of land near Forestville Road for educational purposes. The heirs of John M. Longyear donated an additional forty acres of land to the University in 1959. The Shiras Institute contributed funds to develop it into an outdoor laboratory. This was done, and the site, which included Waldo Pond and Redberry Lake, was used by numerous science classes.

In the 1970s, the purpose of the Forest was changed. A difficult cross-country ski trail was cut into the land, along with a target practice area for biathlon. As the years passed, members of the Biology Department lost interest in the changing use of the land, which began to be invaded by people using it for target practice. By the late 1980s, Dr. Don Snitgen allowed the vegetation to reclaim the trails. It is used infrequently for some classes, but not as it had in the past. Any new redevelopment of the tract would have to depend on policing the site and keeping guns off the property. In the summer and fall of 1998, a new initiative began to see if there was a demand for educational and recreational use of the property. At the same time Ken Godfrey, director of Recreational Facilities, began negotiations to develop a cross-country ski trail through the property.

Longyear Hall: The State Board of Education contracted with Marquette architect, D.F. Charlton to develop plans for the Normal School complex, which he completed by October 1899. Construction on Normal Hall or South Hall began on August 25, 1899, when the site was staked out. The contractor was Lippsett & Gregg of Sault Ste. Marie. They were known for constructing the Newberry Hospital and a barracks wing at Fort Brady. The cost for the 25,048 square foot structure was $22,000, excluding the heating mechanism. Work continued through the seasons, and the building was completed and dedicated on July 3, 1900 and used for the summer session that year. On October 31, 1902, the State Board of Education voted to name it The John M. Longyear Hall of Pedagogy.

On December 18, 1905, it was destroyed by fire possibly the result of a chimney pushed ajar during a recent Dead River powder mill explosion. The bid ($38,000) for its replacement was awarded by the Board of Education to Northern Construction Company of Milwaukee on April 26, 1906. Lake Superior Steam Heating of Marquette received the contract ($3,460) for the heating and plumbing work. The modern fireproof replacement structure was completed in the fall of 1906. In the summer of 1907, E. W. Arnold was hired to develop plans for the third story of the structure and hoped to have it completed by the fall.

The State Board of Education signed a contract with Lippsett & Sinclair of Marquette in late 1909 to complete the addition and changes in the basement between Longyear and the Library wing. These were made in strict accord with the plans, specifications, and details made by Charleton & Kuenzli.

In July 1950, plans were adopted by the Board to remodel the structure. By the mid-1960s, the legislature decided against further renovations on the entire complex. As other buildings were constructed, there was a declining use of the building. The building was used until 1972 when it was condemned. Until 1994, it remained vacant and in deteriorating condition. Longyear Hall was demolished after an unsuccessful attempt to raise money to save the building. The site was covered with grass, and an historical marker unveiled on October 16, 1998, provides a history of the complex. (MJ 07/28/1899, 04/10/1900, 07/05/1900, 07/13/1907, 07/27/1907).

Losey Collection (Elizabeth and Everett): This collection of Native American Indian and Eskimo Art was donated to the University in late 1994 and is housed in the University Permanent Collection. The entire collection was placed on display between October 27 and November 21, 1995. In July 1998 a special exhibition area in Lee Hall was opened to display many of the items in this collection.

Lower Deck: See: *Food Service*

Lundmark, Leon: Lundmark was a nationally known seascape artist who frequently spent his summers during the 1920s and 1930s in Marquette. In 1954, retired professor James C. Bowman (1880–1961) presented an original Lundmark painting to Northern. It was an oil painting of moonlight on Lake Superior. Bowman gave it as a memorial to his daughter, Jeanne, who graduated from Northern and died a few years later. President Henry Tape placed the painting in a prominent location for public view. Lundmark died in 1942. Today the Lundmark painting is housed in the University's Permanent Art Collection. (MJ 08/01/1923, 05/05/1942)

Mace: First developed from the war-like medieval mace, this piece of academic regalia represents the authority of the University. Northern's first mace was designed and developed by Kauko A.Wahtera of Industrial Arts and his students in 1968–1969. It was first used at the inauguration of President John X. Jamrich on October 14, 1969.

The mace is usually carried by the oldest faculty member marching in the academic procession who is considered the grand marshall. At that time, it was carried by Dr. Henry Heimonen who also wore a special green academic robe and sash. The robe was specially created to be worn by the marshall by De Moulin Bros & Company of Greenville, Illinois.

Over the years, senior faculty refused to carry the mace for a variety of reasons and it fell into disuse and then into disrepair. In September 1998, the renovated mace was placed on display in the Peter White Lounge. A new era began in the December 1998 Centennial commencement when carrying the mace was reintroduced into the ceremony. Plans are underway to create a new mace for Northern's second century.

Magers, Mildred K.: (June 10, 1896–January 28, 1958) Dr. Magers was born in Houston, Texas and came to Marquette when her father Samuel had a position at the Northern in 1911. In 1920, at the University of Illinois, she received a B.A. Magers took her M.A. from Pennsylvania State University (1927) and in March 1944, the University of Michigan granted her a Ph.D. She was the first female faculty member at Northern to receive a doctorate.

While at Northern, she was a professor in the Language and Literature Department. She was also faculty adviser to the Canterbury Club, editor of the Alumni Newsletter and sponsor of the foreign student group on campus. Over the years she traveled extensively throughout the world. She died as a result of a heart attack suffered as she entered the Peter White Hall of Science to give a final examination.

The Magers-Meyland Residence Halls were dedicated on October 16, 1966. Magers Hall was converted into a faculty office building in 1988.

Magers Hall: *See*: *Quad II*

Magers, Samuel Denis: (1860–January 16, 1919) Magers held degrees from the University of Michigan and the University of Chicago. In the fall of 1911, he came to Northern from Michigan State Normal College (Eastern Michigan University), where he headed the Natural Sciences, Biology and Agriculture Department. From 1911 to 1919, he served as professor of Natural Sciences. He inspired many students to achieve successful careers as scientists and educators.

Professor Magers also found time to analyze water samples for the city health department, engaged in a soil-testing program and tested milk for local and Peninsula dairies. He served as chair of the research committee, which prepared the way for the commission form of government in Marquette.

During the Spanish influenza pandemic (1918–1919), while recovering he fell victim to the disease.

Magers Memorial, Samuel D.: In 1954, the Cambium Club of Northern established an annual award in the form of the "Samuel D. Magers Memorial Trophy," for the purpose of encouraging new techniques in the effective presentation of technical knowledge to the general public. The trophy was provided by his daughter Mildred Magers, who funded a Magers award. The "Samuel D. Magers Tree" honoring him is mentioned in 1966. A plaque honoring Professor Magers is located in West Science. (NCN 03/17/1954)

Magna Carta: As part of the Michigan Sesquicentennial of Statehood in 1987, American Express had a copy of the original Magna Carta visit campus. The exhibition, in April of 1987, attracted over 2,000 visitors.

"Man in Appraisal": Man in Appraisal was a series of lectures and discussions on the human relationship with philosophy, education, science, and the arts. The series was held in Kaye Hall Auditorium in 1957. The following speakers presented: January 3—T.V. Smith's "Man and His Frontiers"; January 22—Ernest O. Melby's "Responsibilities of Higher Education in the Last Half of the 20th Century"; April 11—Karl K. Darrow's "Science in the Modern World": April 25—John Mason White's "Seeing Things." (Program, UA)

Management, Marketing and Computer Information Systems: This unit is part of the Walker L. Cisler College of Business. In the Management Program, students are provided with the theoretical bases as well as the working applications of management, the ability to critically evaluate managerial actions and to apply managerial decision-making skills to future situations.

In the Marketing Program, students are provided with theoretical as well as working applications of marketing. Students are trained to critically evaluate situations and to develop decision-making skills. Students develop the ability to work with others as participating and contributing members of groups or teams.

The main objectives of Computer Information Systems are to apply computer theory to business applications and provide strong dual knowledge foundation in technical and problem-solving skills.

In all three of these areas of study, the global nature of business is stressed. Furthermore, students learn the role of business ethics and have their written, oral and communication skills developed. (*The 1996–97 University Profile*, 1:222–236)

Manic Monday: Manic Monday was a day (03/20/95) hosted by ASNMU Governing Board which provided an opportunity for the campus community to meet area leaders and to celebrate the grand opening of the Wildcat Den in the University Center. Participants in the town meeting included: President William Vandament, ASNMU President Gregg Goetz, Marquette Mayor John Leadbetter and Dean of Students Sandra Michaels, who answered student questions and concerns about the community and the University. (NW 03/23/1995)

Manual Training and Commercial Department: See: Technology and Applied Sciences, College of

Marquette Branch Prison: Since the early days of its existence, Northern has been involved in bringing educational programs to the Marquette Branch Prison. In 1908, Warden James Russell spoke at a Normal assembly explaining the connection between illiteracy and criminality. He invited students and faculty to give concerts and plays at the prison. After a particularly outstanding performance, an inmate, Charles Meyers, composed a melody which he named "The Normal Girl's Dream" and dedicated it to music instructor, Eulie Rushmore. The music was published and the profits went to the Student Girls' League. In 1916, President Kaye and Warden Russell announced that male students from the Normal, supervised by Stephen Stockwell, would teach English classes at the prison three nights a week.

Classes under the Marquette Branch Prison Academic Program were first delivered to the prison in 1972. This program was operated by the Continuing Education office with courses offered on demand. Classes were offered inside the walls and out in the trustee area. By 1983, some 600 students had gone through the program. Mark Stevens was the first to obtain a bachelor's degree through the Program.

In 1981, Northern and Prison officials discussed the development of a more organized and directed program called "The Associate of Arts Program at the Marquette Branch Prison." Grants for the Program were received from the State of Michigan and the Federal government. The program, which began in 1982, operated through Northern's community college function. The full-time coordinator of the Program was Dr. Raymond Ventre. At first, there were eleven courses, which eventually grew to 35 courses. During this time 20 percent of the inmate population was taking some course work.

Then in 1988, Dean Lowell Kafer moved the Program from Continuing Education to the College of Technology and Applied Sciences. At this time vocational education courses were offered. Grants were not received and Prison officials were more interested in vocational training for the inmates. As a result, the Program was disbanded. (MJ 11/24/1916; NW 02/19/1976, 09/01/1983)

Marquette Choral Society: This organization was founded under the auspices of the Music Department in 1971 and continues to perform. Under the Bylaws, the Music Department head appoints the director. It is a course offering (one credit) in the music curriculum. Currently, membership is in excess of one hundred. Highlights through the years include participation in the performance of Beethoven's Ninth Symphony at Avery Fisher Hall in New York City with the Manhattan Symphony Orchestra, their 20th anniversary concert at Hedgcock Fieldhouse featuring Dave Brubeck and the premiere performance of his "Earth Is Our Mother," two appearances in Marquette with Jackson Burkey performing premiere parts of his Mass, and two appearances with the John Anthony Singers from New York City. The Marquette Choral Society also participated in FinnFest in the summer of 1996 with the premiere performance of "Mine Paras Vife."

Directors: Dr. William Dehning, Dr. Douglas Amman, Dr. Steven Edwards, and Dr. Floyd Slotterback.

Marquette City Commission: Over the years, various faculty and staff have been elected to the Commission and related committees. In 1922, President James Kaye (*See separate entry*) was a member of the Board of Trustees of the Peter White Public Library. At the expiration of his term in 1924, John N. Lowe (Biology) became a trustee and remained in that position through at least February 1, 1931. Gunther Meyland of English chaired the Board. In the 1990s James Hendricks (Education) served on the Board. Lynn Halverson (*See separate entry*) (Geography) served in the late 1940s and early 1950s and Howard Swaine (Economics) was mayor and commissioner. Other faculty members have served on the Board of Light and Power, Library Board, and the County Board of Supervisors.

Marquette County Historical Society: Since 1918, Northern and the Society have interacted. Lew Allen Chase (History) was the first secretary and developed the Society's basic collections. Members of the staff and faculty (Richard O'Dell, Richard Sonderegger, Jim Carter, Russell Magnaghi, Ruth Roebke-Berens) have served on the Board of Directors and as Acting Director (Magnaghi, 1980). Director Frances Porter served on the Centennial Committee and the Society has allowed portions of its collections to be displayed on campus. Faculty and students find the resources of the John M. Longyear Research Library invaluable to their studies.

Marquette Development Corporation: In 1968, Northern had the Doxiades Plan (*See separate entry*) to expand the campus into the area bound by the campus, Presque Isle, Wright and Tracy. The University was purchasing homes and moving residents out. To ease their moving problems, the Marquette Development Corporation, formed by the First National and the Union National Banks, had purchased land to the north of Wright Street, generally considered uninhabitable because it was so low. Arrangements were made with Northern to have the soil, which had been removed to make way for the new Learning Resources Building, trucked to the site and used for fill.

The Corporation was dissolved in 1970 after a series of problems. There was a legal struggle with residents and a faculty member, Dr. Robert McClellan (*See: McClellan controversy*) and at that time the Doxiades Plan (*See separate entry*) for campus expansion was pulled back. (MJ 10/06/1970)

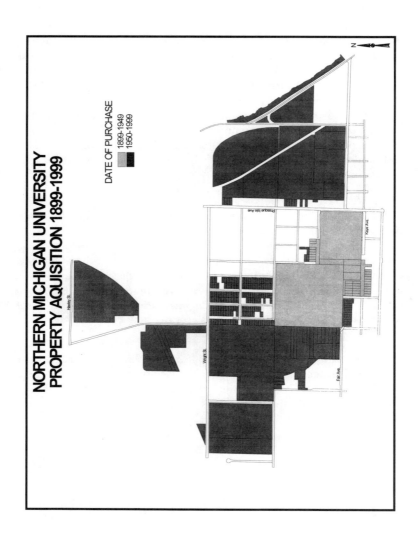

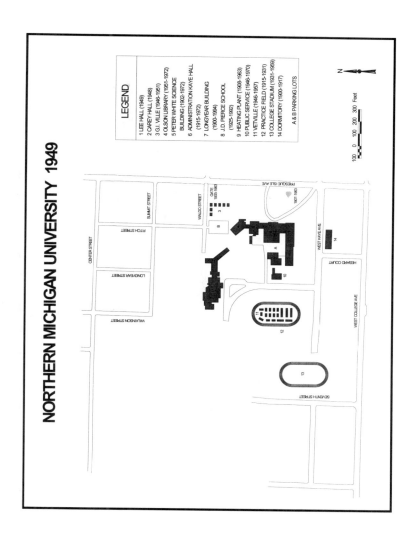

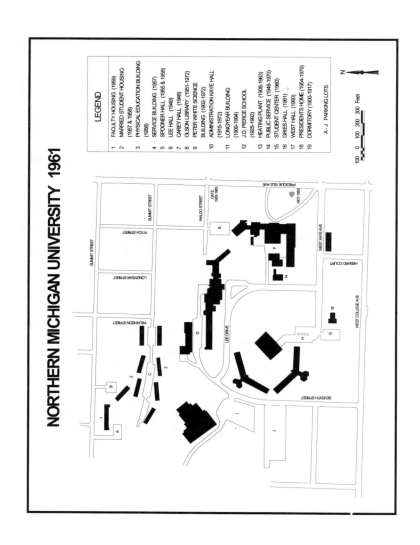

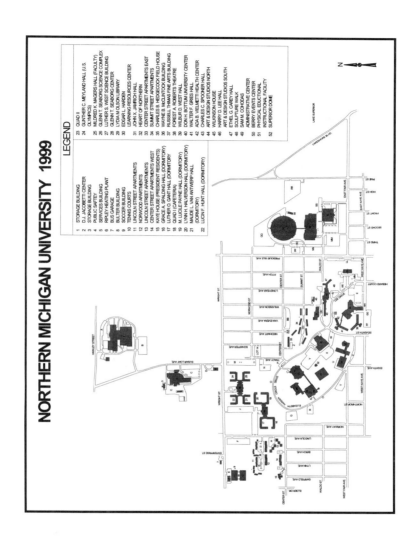

Martin Luther King, Jr.-César Chávez-Rosa Parks Initiative: This was created by the state legislature in 1986 to stem the decline in the number of minority students entering and graduating from college. At the same time, the legislature created the Office of Minority Equity ("OME") located in the Michigan Department of Education, to oversee the implementation of the initiative at the universities. As a result of this initiative, Northern established the King-Chávez-Parks lecture series which brought numerous minority speakers to campus and developed special programs for minority students such as the Gateway Academic Program.

Mascot: Although a popular concept, the story of Northern's mascots is hazy in oral tradition. At the time of the first football game against Hancock High School on October 15, 1904, Northern was known as the "Teachers." At other times they were known as the "Upstaters," "Northerners," "Normalites," and "Northernites."

In the late fall of 1935, after the football season had ended and basketball season was just starting, Coach C.B. Hedgcock announced to everybody that those men who were to be part of the man-to-man defensive unit on the basketball team would be known as the Cubs and those who would play the zone defense would be known as the Cats.

When one of the players asked him why some were Cubs and some were Cats, he said, "well in man-to-man you have to be quicker and because the cubs are the natural offspring of wildcats, bobcats, any kind of cat when they're younger, the man-to-man unit will be known as a Cub, while members of the older, more methodical zone defense group will be know as the Cats . . . the Wildcats."

According to a note in the *Peninsulan* of 1964, Wildcat Willy who was present at football and basketball games, was the protégée of the Chi Sigma Nu Fraternity. The character of Wildcat Willy continued to be used in the 1970s. In the following decade the character took on a formal aspect. A Northern student, Jay McQuillan developed and played the role of Wildcat Willy between 1984 and 1989 Hockey coach Rick Comley saw the use of Wildcat Willy as a means to bring spirit to hockey teams and games.

Since 1995, Wildcat Willy has qualified to compete in a national mascot championship in Orlando, Florida To qualify, mascots have to be in the top 17 nationally. Unfortunately, Willy has not been able to attend because of a lack of funding.

In October 1970, a 38-pound female bobcat named Bobby was purchased with funds donated by Student Activities and the Area Training Center in Marquette. The animal was purchased from a Toronto resident for $500. The bobcat lived in a special cage which was attached to the power plant behind Spooner Hall. Dick Whitman, head of University food services provided the animal with 1 pound of raw meat per day. The animal took its first road trip to a football game with Central Michigan University in late September 1971. During the summer months, the animal was returned to Toronto for living and breeding purposes. Later the animal escaped from its cage and was eventually found in the vicinity of the lower harbor. After this, the animal was returned to its owners, and since then Northern has not had a live wildcat. (Letter from Roy Brigman, '37, UA; MJ 10/16/1904; NN 10/01/1971; NW 09/24/1998)

Mathematics and Computer Science, Department of: The Department of Mathematics was created by the State Board of Education on July 14, 1899. The first instructor who organized the department was Edward G. Maul, who was hired at $900 annually. One of the longest serving math professors was Charles Spooner, for whom a residence hall is named.

Computer Science was not incorporated into Mathematics until 1986. However, Computer courses were offered as early as 1968 and a computer major was introduced in 1978. The Mathematics and Computer Science Department offers majors in mathematics, computer science, computational mathematics, computer programming, mathematics secondary education, and mathematics elementary education. The departmental mission is to offer courses in the above majors and in service to the broader university community. In addition, the department assumes major responsibility for continuing mathematics education of school teachers in the region.

Department chairs and heads: Edward G. Maul, 1899–1900; John B. Fraught,1900–1910; Charles C. Spooner, 1910–1943; Holmes Boynton, 1961–1963; Thomas Knauss, (acting) 1963–1964; Jerome Manheim, (acting 1965–1966; Joseph Harkin, 1966–1967; Donald Heikkinen, 1968–1973; Clarence Stortz, 1973–1976; William Mutch, 1976–1980; Terrance Seethoff, 1981–present. (*Bulletins*; Francis Copper manuscript, UA) Michelle Kangas and Alisa Koski

McCarthyism: A mid-twentieth century political attitude named after Senator Joseph R. McCarthy (R-Wisconsin). It was characterized chiefly by opposition to elements held to be subversive and by the use of tactics involving personal attacks on individuals by means of widely-publicized indiscriminate allegations, especially on the basis of unsubstantiated charges.

The concepts of McCarthyism reached into the life of Michigan's colleges and universities. On March 21, 1952 the Council of Presidents of the compass campuses passed a resolution which was subsequently adopted by the State Board of Education. It stated, ". . . the aims and functions [of the colleges] are in harmony with the American form of government, and are constructive in furthering the American way of life. No organization or its officers, local or national, shall be associated with any subversive groups or so-called fronts." This is an obvious reference to Communist organizations that might try to form on campuses. (*See*: *Oath Card* and *Un-American Activities*)

McClellan Controversy: Dr. Robert McClellan joined the History Department in the mid-1960s as a specialist in Far Eastern and American history. He was known as a social activist and became embroiled in a struggle over private property and academic freedom.

The origins of the controversy go back to the development of the Doxiades Plan (*See separate entry*) in 1966 which called for Northern to purchase land so that the campus would stretch from Lincoln Street on the west to Lake Superior on the east and from Wright Street on the north to Fair-Kaye Avenues on the south. At that time there were plans for a greatly expanded campus and student body. The Marquette Development Corporation (*See separate entry*) was formed to purchase property north of Wright Street and move homes from the south side of the street to the new location. The whole process was highly controversial within the Marquette community.

As part of a class project, Dr. McClellan had his students get involved in the home condemnation project. The people were told that they could fight the process and remain in their homes. President Edgar Harden felt that Dr. McClellan was usurping the President's power and authority and told the Board of Control not to reappoint Dr. McClellan. This was seen as an intrusion on academic freedom and basic University termination policies and regulations which had not been used in the process.

Before Dr. Harden left office in 1967, the Faculty Senate had tried get him to reconsider his recommendation to terminate Dr. McClellan. He refused, and in September 1967 the new Academic Vice President, David Dickson at the request of the Senate, asked Interim-President Ogden Johnson to reopen the case. He, too, refused. As a result, there was general chaos and upheaval during the fall and spring semesters. The Senate resigned. There were class boycotts, resolutions, marches and pickets. The *Mining Journal*, owned by the Panax Corporation, which had two members on the Board of Control, came out against the faculty and students. Despite these actions, the Board reaffirmed its decision to dismiss McClellan on October 27, 1967.

The trouble continued. On May 22, 1968, a suit for violation of the civil liberties of McClellan was filed against President Johnson and on behalf of 137 members of the faculty and the student government Senate. On June 25, an out-of-court settlement was announced and McClellan remained on Northern's staff until his retirement in the early 1990s.

McClintock, Wayne Burr: (April 21, 1889–November 21, 1970) Born on a farm in Bradley, Michigan, McClintock was a graduate of Western Michigan University and Iowa State. He came to Marquette in 1912 from Benton Harbor, where he had been a high school coach. He was a teacher and football coach at Marquette High School and served as principal (1914–1915).

In 1915 he moved to Northern Michigan University, where he became athletic coach and Industrial Arts Director. He was head of the Industrial Arts Department until 1946, retiring in 1949. During these years he developed and expanded Northern's industrial education program.

For many years he was active in athletics, first as player and later as coach. McClintock was widely known for his refereeing throughout the state. He organized the first Upper Peninsula high school basketball tournament held at Northern, and conducted these tournaments for many years.

He was active for a time in the Boy Scout movement and was a life member of Marquette Lodge No. 101, Free and Accepted Masons.

McClintock was a devoted outdoorsman, hunting and fishing in this area for more than 55 years. He was the subject of the "Old Hermit" stories written for the *Mining Journal* by Ernest Rankin. The Industrial Arts Building was dedicated in his honor on April 25, 1965. (MJ 11/23/1970)

Wayne B. McClintock Building: The Fine and Practical Arts Complex was opened for classes in the fall of 1963. This complex was composed of three units: Forest Roberts Theatre, the Thomas Fine Arts Building which houses art, communications and performance arts, and music, and the Wayne B. McClintock Industrial Arts Wing.

The structure is bridged to the central unit by a glassed-in foyer which provides an excellent view of the campus and adjoining terrace. The building was designed by Warren Holmes Company, Architects, Lansing, and the general contractor for the building was Herman Gundlach, Inc., Houghton.

The wing for Industrial Education contains more than 30,889 square feet of laboratory and classroom space, designed for the theoretical and applied aspects of industrial technology. The area contained classrooms with separate areas for drawing and design, electricity and electronics, graphic arts, power mechanics including a drive-in spray booth, general metals laboratory, machine shop including foundry and welding areas, a comprehensive general shop, woodworking shop, and finishing room. Auxiliary rooms included staff offices, conference room, storage room, tool rooms, lumber room, and photography dark room.

As early as 1946, the Department of Industrial Arts had been working on building plans and specifications. The original plans called for a separate facility for the area involved in the applied sciences.

The growing pressure of enrollments led several departments to believe in the construction of a complex. They felt it would be a serious educational error to erect separate buildings for the practical and fine arts. Arbitrary separation of areas of study, failure to integrate skills and ideas, the inability to see relationships between common phenomena and larger concepts being barriers to sound program planning, led to the integration of a facility that provided classes a close proximity of areas while permitting a variety of functions.

Early in 1962, with capital outlay funds of $2,650,000 appropriated by the State Legislature, ground was broken for the Fine and Practical Complex.

This structure was completed in 1964. It was dedicated on April 25, 1965. It was the home of the Department of Industry and Technology until it was relocated in the Jacobetti Center. In 1997 the building was used for nursing classes and the Military Science Department used a portion of two of the bays for storage and classroom space. Plans call for the renovation of the building in the summer of 1999. (MJ 04/26/1965)

McGoff, John P.: (1925–January 21, 1998) The president of the Mid-States Broadcasting Corporation and the owner of the Panax newspaper chain, he became a member of Northern's first Board of Control in 1964 and resigned from the board in 1972. McGoff was a controversial figure whose involvement with publishing in South Africa in the 1970s created a campus controversy. This became heated when in 1979 he gave $300,000 for the McGoff Distinguished Lecture series. (*See separate entry*) Students and some faculty kept up a running struggle with McGoff over the years. In 1988, McGoff took the money back and the series ended. He and his wife donated the Carillons (*See separate entry*) which were dedicated on August 8, 1980. (Hilton, pp. 154, 157, 261; MJ 01/22/1998)

McGoff Distinguished Lecture Series: The Lecture Series was established by the Board of Control on July 6, 1978 to enhance the quality of life of Northern and to contribute to the development of the University as an educational and social institution of greater stature and leadership. This was based on a donation of $300,000 by John and Marge McGoff. Speakers were distinguished in the field of business, industry, public service, the arts, politics, education, religion, professions, the sciences and the humanities. It was further stipulated that the speaker was to give four lectures in a two-week period and remain on campus and participate in academic life and related activities for a minimum of four days.

From the onset there were questions raised by students, faculty and community activists as to the source of the funding which some individuals said was allegedly connected to South Africa's apartheid government at the time. The faculty association (AAUP) disassociated itself with the series in 1979 along with ASNMU. In March 1988, Elie Wiesel (Holocaust survivor and Nobel laureate) withdrew his acceptance of an invitation. On March 23, 1988, McGoff withdrew the funding and the series was terminated.

Speakers brought to campus: Gerald R. Ford, former president (11/15/1978); John Hannah, presidential counselor (11/07/1979); Alexander Ginzburg, Russian dissident(04/17/1980);Herman Kahn, futurist (11/20/1980); Ansel Adams, photographer (03/1981); Alvin Toffler, author (10/05/1981); Edward Albee, playwright (02/16/1982); Howard K. Smith, journalist/author(10/20/1982); Alexander Haig, former Secretary of State/general(04/09/1984);Richard Leakey, paleontologist (03/20/1985). (NW 10/06/1983, 10/13/1983)

Medallion, President's: Also known as "the chain office," the medallion is a silver-plated bronze circular disk, about three inches in diameter. The inner part on the circle contains an engraving of the university seal. Two laurel branches joined at the bottom encircle the medallion. A heavy silver chain connects eleven engraved silver-plated bars. They list each president and their years in office. The Medallic Art Company of Sioux Falls, South Dakota (then in New York City) was commissioned to produce the medallion. It was first used for President John X. Jamrich's inauguration on October 14, 1969. It is worn at commencements and at other university functions on campus by the President. (UA, Jamrich Papers; MJ 10/01/1997))

Men's Get-together: Prior to 1949, men of the faculty hosted the traditional dinner in the fall. It was held on the second Tuesday of the first and second semesters. Featured were pasties, pickles, doughnuts, apples, and coffee. Many men brought their own ketchup bottles. In the winter, the Men's Union (*See separate entry*), a student organization, hosted the gathering. As Northern expanded this tradition declined.

Men's Union: During November–December 1919 meetings were held toward the creation of a Union of faculty men and students. The Men's Union was formed in February 1920. The Council of the Men's Union was officially organized and held its first meeting on January 28, 1924. The goals of the Union were "to express their loyalty to this institution through their efforts to encourage a spirit of cooperation between the various organizations, to promote student interest in the activities of the school, and to further a healthier school spirit." In July 1926 the Union began operating under its new constitution.

By May 1930, the Union was serving as a student council. Two year later it was a leading organization on campus, with every male student a member. In that year, work was carried out, by executive council. The executive council was composed of the two highest-ranking male officers in each class. The organization promoted student interest in activities (Homecoming, Men's Get-Together, Men's Banquet and the Class Rush), fostered healthy school spirit, offered an arena of representation for men at Northern, and encouraged cooperation between the various other organizations. It also sponsored the annual women's banquet. After World War II, the Men's Union was influential in creating the new student government, Northern Student Council (called the Student Senate by the mid-1960s) which later evolved as Associated Students of Northern Michigan University. The Union last appeared in the *Bulletin* in 1956–1957. (NNN 02/04/1924, 07/15/1926; NN 05/20/1930; *Bulletins*) Michelle Kangas

Memorial Field: See: *Athletic Fields*

Meyland, Gunther: (September 15, 1896–August 27, 1966). Born in Milwaukee, Wisconsin, Meyland received his bachelor's degree from the University of Wisconsin and his master's degree from the University of Chicago. He took additional work at Chicago and the University of Michigan.

During World War I, Mr. Meyland served in the U.S. Army. He was the division boxing champion for his weight class. He was civil defense director for Marquette during and after World War II (1942–1954).

Meyland began his teaching career in West Allis, Wisconsin, and was a teaching fellow at the University of Wisconsin before joining NMU faculty in 1924. He was a member of the English Department. Mr. Meyland was adviser of Northern's student newspaper, the *Northern News* for 25 years. Many of his former students became successful authors. He eventually rose to the rank of full professor and became the senior member of the faculty in point of service. For many years, he served as grand marshall of all academic processions.

In addition to his teaching duties, he was a member of the faculty athletic council, coached baseball one year and was debate coach for four years. He was the first faculty adviser to the Tri Mu Fraternity, predecessor of the Tau Kappa Epsilon Fraternity.

Mr. Meyland was chairman of the Marquette County Library Board. His professional affiliations included membership in the Michigan Education Association, Michigan Council of Teachers of English, and the American Association of University Professors. Meyland Residence Hall in Quad II (*See separate entry*) was dedicated on October 16, 1966. (MJ 08/27/1966)

Meyland Hall: *See*: *Quad II*

Michael's Bookstore: This was an attempt to provide the students with an alternative to the Northern Bookstore. The store which was located at 1020 N. Third Street opened on October 11, 1971 and sold general reading material. Later, it tried to compete with the University Bookstore. It lasted for a number of years.

Michigan Association of Governing Boards Awards: Established in 1987, this award is given to two faculty and two students annually. Abbreviations: F–faculty and S–student.

Recipients: Timothy Austin (2-96, S); Jon Bedick (2-94, S); Amanda Brannon (2-96, S); Shirley Brozzo (2-92, S); James W. Camerius (4-95, F); Sarah Caverly (4-95, S); Timothy Clancy (4-88, S); Sara L. Doubledee (4-90, F); Nicole Fende (2-94, S); Robert Glenn (2-97, F); James L. Godell (4-83, F); Brent M. Graves (2-97, F); Gail Griffith (4-90, F); Robert N. Hanson (4-89, F); Anthony Hermann (4-95, S); Lois A. Hirst (2-96, F); Sandra J. Imdieke (4-99, F); Carol Johnson (2-97, F); Rowena Jones (2-92, F); Stewart Kingsbury (5-91, F); Keith Kistler-Glendon (2-98, S); Gregory Kleinheinz (2-93, S); Philip Legler (4-84, F); Russell M. Magnaghi (2-96, F); Ray Mannila (4-89, S); Justin Marlowe (4-99, S); (Stefanie Miklovic (2-98, S); Katherine Payant (2-93, F); Cheryl Peterson (4-89, S); Cheryl Reynolds (2-94, F); Linda Riipi (2-93, F); Karyn Rybacki (5-91, F); Julie A. Schorr (4-95, F); Bruce C. Sherony (4-90 F); Bonnie Southworth (2-93, S); Kelly Ann Srnka (4-88, S); Linda A. Stephen (4-90, S); Thomas J. Sullivan (5-87, F); Jeffrey Szmanski (5-91, S); Zacharias P. Thundy (2-92, F); Karen Toney (5-91, S); Daniel P. Truckey (4-90, S); John Vandezande (4-89, F); Holger Wagner (2-97, S); Jackie Lynn Wainio (4-99, S); Phillip B. Watts (4-99, F); James Wickstrom (2-92, S); Jennifer Zanotti (2-97, S). (University Relations Office)

Michigan Sesquicentennial: In 1987, Michigan celebrated 150 years of statehood. Dr. Russell Magnaghi (History) was the on-campus coordinator. Of particular note was the Sesquicentennial Ball, held in the University Center on January 27, 1987, the visit of the Magna Carta (*See separate entry*) and a theatrical, musical, art and lecture series held during the winter 1987 semester.

Micronesians: In the early 1970s, Micronesians began to attend Northern. By the summer of 1975, about twenty-four Micronesians were attending Northern and a year later there were 30. Many of these Micronesians transferred from Suomi College's two-year program. They were attracted to the Upper Peninsula by an administrator who had worked with the trustee government and started recruiting them. The Micronesians continued to go to Suomi and Northern because they had an established community. Their education was financed by their government, Basic Grants and Work Study programs. In the years that followed, they graduated and their ranks were not refilled. Some of these students remain in the Marquette area. (NW 07/24/1975, 10/14/1976)

Midget Quill: The first John D. Pierce school newspaper initially published in 1916. Earle Parker was the principal at the time.

Military Science, Department of: In 1948, the State Board of Education authorized the four teachers' colleges to request and install Reserve Officer Training Corps (ROTC) on campus. Northern did not begin a program at this time because its application was not accepted. After 1952, the Department of the Army was instructed not to add any more ROTC units. In 1965, President Edgar Harden expressed Northern's continued interest in being considered if the ROTC program was to be expanded. However it was not until 1967 that Northern was invited to file a formal application for a senior ROTC unit.

During the summer of 1967, various meetings were held with ROTC officers and University administrators. Due to the Vietnam War, there were controversial debates over the establishment of this unit. However by the late summer, the ROTC program was approved only if it would be voluntary in nature. In November 1968, Northern was notified that its application had been accepted and meetings were held to discuss the implementation of the program. The ROTC program became known as the Department of Military Science.

The Department of the Army began assigning officers for establishment of the detachment in February 1969. On April 17, 1969, the Defense Department established NMU's Department of Military Science.

Housed initially in the local National Guard Armory, the first classes met in September with an enrollment of 53 students. In the spring of 1971, the Department commissioned its first two lieutenants. In 1973, ROTC was officially opened to women. That year, 13 female students enrolled in the program.

As the Vietnam War caused further protests, anti-war marches were held in front of the Armory. At the same time the ROTC unit maintained a strong community relations program.

Overall the Northern Military Science Department has been a success. During the 1970s, it had a growing enrollment. Provost Robert Glenn played an important part in promoting the unit. Because of its successful Jonathan Livingston Leadership Day program in 1973 and 1974, the Public Relations Society of America awarded the prestigious "Silver Anvil" award to the Northern Military Science Department in the fall of 1974. In 1974–1975 the department moved into the University Center which was an ideal and highly visible location on campus. Into the decade of the 1990s the Department continues to play an important role on campus and is now housed in Gries Hall.

From 1976 to 1982, the NMU Department also hosted Lake Superior State's ROTC program. The Department has received numerous awards from the Department of the Army for management and training excellence. As of December 1998, 305 students have earned their commission through the ROTC program. Twenty percent of them have been women. The unit is also known as the Wildcat Battalion.

Department Heads: LTC James R. Sesslar, 1969–1972; LTC Allen D. Raymond III, 1972–1977; LTC Frank C. Allen, 1977–1981; LTC Donald R. Taylor 1981–1984; LTC Howard R. Schweppe, 1984–1988; LTC Charles P. McCarthy, 1988–1990; LTC Larry W. Davis, 1990–1991; LTC Franklin L. Fiala, 1992–1995; LTC John R. Moschetti, 1995–present. (Lawrence R. Shaw. "Northern's ROTC in the Early Years, 1969–1975." (1995) and Eugene Whitehouse, "Origins of the Military Science Department," (1998), UA)

Miller, Robert: Robert Miller attended Northern in 1933–1934 and was the first mortal casualty during World War II.

Minstrel Shows: The Theta Omicron Rho fraternity was known for its annual "authentic" minstrel show. One of the last ones, called "Are You from Dixie?," was presented on May 21–22, 1958 by the fraternity. (NCN 04/26/1950)

Miss Black Pride: The first Miss Black Pride contest was held on November 22, 1969. The first-place winner was Linda Bolded of Mt. Vernon, NY while the runners-up were Vivian Johnson and Beverly Adams. (NN 12/05/1969).

Money, C. (Cloyd) V. (Vern) "Red": (February 21, 1901–March 19, 1977) Red Money was born in Jay County, Indiana, where he obtained his earliest education. He received a B.S. from Ohio Northern University, Ada (1923), a M.S. (1933) and Dir. P.E. (1956) from Indiana University.

He married Esther McGuffey on December 28, 1927 and they had one son, Robert, of Sault Ste. Marie, a professor at Lake Superior State University (1999).

After graduating from Ohio Northern, he taught physical education classes and coached varsity sports at the secondary level for four years. In 1927, he began a collegiate teaching and coaching career that lasted 41 years. For 28 months during World War II, he was director of a Physical Fitness Program for a Navy V-12 Unit at Valley City State College in North Dakota.

He arrived at Northern Michigan University in 1947. For nine years he carried the entire burden of Northern's intercollegiate athletic and physical education programs. At times he handled as many as five sports during the college year. He initiated the first "grant-in-aid" program for Northern with the Barracks Program after World War II. In 1948, he organized and established the first golf and ski teams. Over the years he organized and conducted the U.P. High School Basketball Tournament and U.P. High School Track meets at Northern. Over 36 coaching clinics were directed by him. His active coaching career, which spanned more than thirty years, ended in 1956 when he assumed more administrative duties as acting head and coordinator of the Department of Health and Physical Education as well as Director of Athletics.

Even with this busy schedule, when Spooner Residence Hall was opened in 1957, he and his wife served as resident advisers. He also found time to assist with the development of plans for Hedgcock Fieldhouse, which was completed in 1958. At one point he wrote all of the news releases for all sports.

In October 1957, he was freed of his athletic directorship duties, became head of the Department of Health, Physical Education and Recreation, and focused his energy on the expansion of the undergraduate program. Money expanded the program and established a master's degree in HPER in 1960. On September 1, 1962 he was promoted to professor and continued as department head. Dr. Rico Zenti succeeded Money as Director of Athletics and Head of Health, Physical Education and Recreation on June 1, 1966. Money retired on September 30, 1968.

After retirement "Red" Money continued to be actively involved in sports recognition. He helped to establish the Alumni "N" Club at Northern. In September 1975, he was one of the originators and organizers of the NMU Sports Hall of Fame. In 1971, he was involved with the establishment of the U.P. Sports Hall of Fame and served as its executive director for a period.

Money was a member of the Ada (Ohio) Masonic Lodge, Rotary, Michigan Sports Sages (president, 1973–1974), Alpha Sigma Phi, and the First Presbyterian Church.

Over the years, "Red" Money was honored for his long career devoted to teaching, coaching and administrative work. On August 16, 1966 he was congratulated for conducting his 20th Annual Coaching School at NMU. He was inducted into the Ohio Northern University (1969), Northern Michigan University (1976), and Upper Peninsula (1976) sports halls of fame. The Board of Control authorized the new name, the C.V. "Red" Money Memorial Field in the Superior Dome on May 2, 1997. The stadium was dedicated with a plaque on September 12, 1998. (MJ 03/03/1973; 03/21/1977)

Moses Coit Tyler Collection. Moses Coit Tyler (1835–1900) was a pioneer and foremost scholar on the historical development of American literature in the eighteenth and early nineteenth centuries. In 1881, Cornell University offered Tyler the first chair in American history in the country. Tyler's working library must be rated by any standard as an important collection of the colonial and early national periods of American history and literature. Northern acquired the Moses Coit Tyler Library through the public spirit of Albert E. Miller, Peter White, N.M. Kaufman and E.N. Breitung in June 1904. The original collection consisted of 2,000 titles comprising 3,000 volumes on American history, theology and literature. The collection brought the total number of books at Northern to 10,000 volumes. The Collection survived the destruction of South/Longyear Hall in 1905 and is the basis of the Special Collections of the Lydia Olson Library. Since late summer 1997, the collection has been housed in the University Archives. (MJ 06/22/1904; *Moses Coit Tyler Collection of the Lydia M. Olson Library*, pamphlet)

Motion Pictures and Videos: The first motion pictures showing scenes of Northern Michigan University were produced by the Delft Theatre in Marquette in the 1920s. The silent film shows Rush Day and the Spring Pageant. The film was "rescued" by alumnus Jack Deo of Superior View Studio in Marquette and is available for purchase.

During the early 1930s, Leslie Bourgeois, owner of The Wicker Shoppe, a popular student ice cream parlor in Marquette, created films of Northern. On June 17, 1998, several canisters of film were located by Alison Crockett among the Bourgeois family. The silent film shows Rush Day in 1930 and 1931. The Bourgeois family graciously donated this and other footage to the University. Rollin Thoren, Northern biology teacher, was the unofficial campus photographer during the 1930s and 1940s. He has preserved some motion pictures of campus.

It was not until the 1960s, with the opening of the WNMU-FM and the Learning Resources Center, that motion pictures were taken on a regular basis. Many film and videos have been preserved by WNMU-TV and some of it is in the University Archives. The Admissions Office has produced a number of films and videos over the years.

Dr. Michael M. Loukinen, a sociology professor, has produced, researched, written and directed four major documentary films. These films include: *Finnish American Lives* (1982), *Tradition Bearers* (1983), *Good Man in the Woods* (1987), and *Medicine Fiddle* (1992). All of these films deal with ethnic life and tradition in the Lake Superior Basin. His documentaries have won top awards at national and international festivals, at the American Film Festival, Council of International Non-Theatrical Events, Chicago International Film Festival, Sinking Creek Film Festival and the National Educational Film festival.

Over the years, faculty and students have developed small documentaries with limited distribution. WMNU-TV has developed a number of commercial videos which have been shown on local television. In December 1998, *Northern at 100: A Century of Memories*, a video produced by Sonya L. Chrisman, was premiered. For this video, on February 23, 1999, WNMU-TV received the award of Best of Category in Documentaries by the Michigan Association of Broadcasting.

Mud Festival: The first Mud Festival was held in May 1967, celebrating the advent of spring and the end of the school year. The week-long event, sponsored by the Residence Hall Association, included such events as an egg throw, root beer chug, sled races, tug-of-wars, wheelbarrow races, a rather primitive obstacle course through the mud, fieldball and softball. All events took place in the "mud area" between Payne and Spalding residence halls. A queen of the Mud Festival was selected and competition at the event was fierce, attracting hundreds of students. It continued to be held into the early 1970s. These events harkened back to Rush Day. (NN 05/16,31/1969)

Muhammad Ali: Muhammad Ali was brought to Marquette by sports promoter, Bill Spagnolo to raise money for the Muhammad Ali Scholarship Fund for needy NMU students. While here, Ali met with University officials, and gave a talk on "Friendship" to an audience of 250 in the Hedgcock Fieldhouse on the afternoon of Saturday, July 9, 1977. In the evening, Ali held a four-round boxing match with Jimmy Ellis, viewed by 1,700. House Speaker Bobby Crim served as the guest referee in the first round. The event was not the success that officials thought it would be, and it actually lost money. While in Marquette, Muhammad Ali looked over Granot Loma as a possible training camp, but nothing came of this interest. (MJ 07/11/1977)

Multi-Cultural Student Services: *See*: *Diversity Student Services*

Munson, John M.: (February 19, 1878–June 22, 1950) The son of Swedish immigrants, Mr. Munson was born in Kane County, Pennsylvania. As a youth he worked as a lumberjack in the Menominee County woods. Seeking an education, Munson attended Ferris Institution (now Ferris State University) where he graduated in 1901 with a bachelor's degree. He received a master's degree from Michigan State Normal College (now Eastern Michigan University) in 1903, and a Ph.B. from the University of Chicago (1911). He taught school in Ingalls, Michigan and between 1903 and 1913, and was superintendent of schools at Clarkston and Harbor Springs. Munson went on to become deputy superintendent of public instruction (1913–1919), and member of the Michigan State Board of Library Commissioners (1913–1917). Between 1917 and 1923, he was director of the training school at Central Michigan State Normal School (now Central Michigan University) and editor of *Moderate Topics*.

In 1923, Munson was appointed president of Northern by the State Board of Education. There are strong indications that he was brought to campus to "clean up" the lax situation and standards which had developed on campus and were protested by Lew Allen Chase. During his tenure, he initiated the first bookstore, promoted academic standards and baseball, invited Ethel Carey to join the staff as dean of women, and operated the institution as a strong executive. In 1927, he introduced a new style of diplomas and certificates that the Board of Education felt should "be brought to the attention of the registrars of other state teachers colleges." He was president of the Michigan Education Association (1926–27). Munson became president of Eastern Michigan University in 1933. A rather complete set of his papers for his years at NMU are located in the Archives.

Munson's Memberships include Phi Delta Kappa, Pi Kappa Delta and Stoics. His honors include 1913 Ed.M. Eastern Michigan University; 1939 LL.D. Ashland College, Ashland, Ohio; and 1942 Doctor of Arts, Wayne State University.

Munson was the only bachelor president of NMU. Upon his death, he was interred in Kane, Pennsylvania. In his will, he left money for the John M. Munson Michigan History Fund (*See separate entry*).

Munson, John M., Michigan History Fund: By the terms of his will, Munson left $100,000 to the Michigan Historical Commission to have a history of the state written. The fund has been used to develop booklets on state history. (*Michigan History* vol. 34 Dec. 1950, 346–351.)

Munuscong Conservation Laboratory: *See: Field Stations*

Museum Collection: In April of 1994, as University Historian, Russell Magnaghi made a preliminary inventory of university-related artifacts which remained on campus. In the summer of 1994, President Vandament unofficially designated Magnaghi a field historian whose job was to collect artifacts. This began the collecting process. The president had personally assisted in the process earlier in the summer of 1993, heading up the collection of the John D. Voelker artifacts.

The Collection consists of University-related items, artifacts from John D. Voelker, Glenn T. Seaborg, Dominic Jacobetti and folk culture items connected with the Center for Upper Peninsula Studies. The items are presently stored for future use in revolving exhibits. The Archives is officially in charge of the museum items. The main processing areas are in the Superior Dome and Jamrich Hall. (NW 02/20/1997)

Music, Department of: In the opening days of Northern, music was not included in the curriculum. Mrs. Longyear donated money so that a music faculty member could be hired. The first instructor was Sophie Linton. She directed a number of quartets, double quartets, and the Normal Semi-Chorus which performed at churches, assemblies and occasionally at the Branch Prison. Linton was so determined that all students learn to sing that until 1915, Chorus was a required course.

In early days, the department was small and devoted itself to music teacher preparation. In 1910, the State Board of Education approved a curriculum leading to a life certificate in the teaching of music and the department began to expand. In 1923, when Linton retired, Conway C. Peters took over. He wrote the music for the song, "Hail Men of Northern" and organized the first all-college orchestra which was 35 strong. The department was helped through the financial aid of the Marquette Music Club. By this time, glee clubs had developed along with the college band. In 1929, President Munson arranged the purchase of green uniforms with yellow accents for the band. Peters was credited with developing the first course in conducting in the state of Michigan. Clubs and organizations developed among the students included the St. Cecilia Society (women's chorus), a string quintet, the glee clubs, the band, and the symphony orchestra. During World War II, Northern had a Women's Symphony Orchestra.

After the war, the department began to grow even stronger when Duane Haskell became head. T. Raymond "T. Ray" Uhlinger was added to the faculty and added to the curriculum so that students could specialize in vocal or instrumental performance or conducting. "T. Ray" organized the Wildcat Golden Jubilee Band in 1949. Meanwhile, Haskell organized a Northern Sinfonietta and recruited members for a Tri-City orchestra. The orchestra gave its first performance in 1949, directed by Allan L. Niemi, his successor. Harold E. Wright arrived in 1948 and led the newly-formed Brass Ensemble. In 1952, Northern offered its first Bachelor of Music degree, which permitted students to take both a major and minor in music. Students could join the Band, Orchestra, String Quartet, Choir or Collegiate Chorale, all of which made tours of Upper Peninsula high schools. Senior recitals were regularly held in Lee Hall Ballroom. Students organized the Klef Klub, which raised money for music scholarships. When President Harden came to campus in 1956, he saw that the marching band needed improvement, and this was done.

When Hal Wright became department head in 1961, he added artists to the department who were skillful performers as well as fine teachers. Lorin Richtmeyer, who took over the Marching Band in 1957, trained the band members to perform at faster cadence, outfitted them in new uniforms with bright gold accents, and prepared a different half-time show for every home football game. He also directed the Concert Band, which presented programs with Raymond Uhlinger's College Choir. In 1961, Jean Hedlund (oboe) and George Papich (violin) formed the center of a new Fine Arts Quartet. From then on, faculty members, as well as senior students in the department, graced regular recitals. In 1963 George Whitfield (pianist) and Eric Shaar (cellist) brought new talent to the Symphony Orchestra and String Quartet. Many of the faculty wrote articles and others composed and heard their work performed locally. Shaar's students built a harpsichord. Financial aid to music students was contributed by the Saturday Music Club. Beginning in 1962, members of the departments of Music, Speech and Physical Education combined to produce a series of Broadway musicals.

In 1965, James McKelvy took over the direction of the Madrigal Singers and turned the group into the Arts Chorale, which demanded long hours of practice and rehearsal. Summer programs in 1965 included Music Camp and Adult Choral Clinic, a Piano Clinic for teachers and a Festival of Music. All of these outreach activities were very successful.

The National Association of Schools of Music first certified NMU's Music Department in November 1969. The department's goal of creating community-wide appreciation for music, supported tours across the Upper Peninsula and the Lower Peninsula, Wisconsin, Ohio, and Canada, as well as special performances in the Bahamas (via an invitation from the USO), and Europe.

In 1971, the Marquette Choral Society (*See separate entry*) was formed with a close link to the Music Department. The head of the department selected the director of the Choral. The department was reaching out to the community at large. In 1967, the marching band was invited to play at the Detroit Lions game. At this time, Eleanor Pool, a faculty member, was selected for the lead part in an opera, "Sister Angelica." The 1962 university production of "South Pacific" was seen as a success. All of the musical groups connected with the department flourished and expanded.

December 7, 1972, was a hallmark day in the history of the department as the National Association of Schools of Music approved Northern's Music Department as a member. In the early 1960s, the band acquired its nickname, "Pride of the North." The band made its television debut during a Green Bay Packer game on November 19, 1961. Over the years, the marching band has played at Chicago Bears, Lions and Packers games. The Music Department has excelled in many areas of endeavors.

Currently, the department supports the Marching Band, Pep Band, Symphonic Band, Jazz Lab Band, Jazz Combos, Percussion Ensemble, University Choir, Madrigal Singers, Lake Effect Show choir, the Marquette Choral Society and a University Orchestra comprised of student and community performers. The department's other special programs include the Computer Aided Music Instruction Laboratory (CAMIL); the Jazz Practice Lab, affectionately dubbed "The Woodshed," houses computerized resources specifically for jazz improvisation and composition; and the Vivace Practice Lab which is equipped with the Vivace musical accompaniment system from Coda Technologies.

Department chairs and heads: Sophie Linton, 1900–1923; Conway C. Peters, 1923–1934; Roy A. Williams, 1934–1946; Duane Haskell, 1946–1949; Allen L. Niemi, 1949–1961; Harold Wright, 1961–1981; Elda Tate, 1981–1995; Donald R. Grant, 1995–present. (MJ 04/28/1947; NCN 02/26/1947; *The 1996–97 University Profile*, 1:131–137)

Musical Chairs: The world record as recorded in the *Guinness Book of World Records* stood at 1,082. For Homecoming 1977, on October 6, the Guinness World Record for the largest game of musical chairs was broken at Memorial Field. 1,674 people participated. Mary Lynn Webster from Halverson Hall was the winner of the game.

Unfortunately, a little later the record was broken, and Northern never made it into the record book. (NW 09/22/1977, 10/13/1977)

Musicals and Plays, (prior to 1924): *See: Expression and Physical Training, Department of*

NASA Educator Resource Center: The room is one of three such teacher resource centers in Michigan sponsored by NASA. The Resource Center, located in the Glenn T. Seaborg Center (*See separate entry*), serves regional educators from elementary grades through the university level. It contains NASA films, slides, and printed information of the nation's aerospace achievements. The NASA Resource Center was originally located in the Lydia Olson Learning Resource Center and dedicated on April 14, 1986.

National Collegiate Athletic Association Champions: Northern teams and individuals have been NCAA champions over the years. They include Football, 1975, NCAA II; Skiing, 1987 and 1988, Men's Nordic Combined National Champions; Skiing, 1991, Women's Nordic Combined National Champions; Hockey, 1991, NCAA I Champions; Women's Volleyball, 1993 and 1994, NCAA II Champions. Individual national champions can be found at the Superior Dome Championship showcase.

National History Day: In the fall of 1982, the Historical Society of Michigan organized a state National History Day. The History Department of Northern became involved in the project under the direction of Dr. Gene DeLon Jones on November 10, 1982. Faculty members judged a variety of projects and the best in various categories were sent to the state contest. The department continued to support National History Day through 1992 until Dr. Jones' retirement. The contest was reactivated by Dr. Russell Magnaghi, director of the Center of Upper Peninsula Studies, and assisted by the history faculty. The reactivated contest was held on April 8, 1998. Dr. Jean Choate became the director in the fall of 1998.

The teachers and students of National Mine School won numerous state contests for their elaborate media-focused exhibits. In 1997, they won the national award for their category. In October, they were honored by the Board of Control. (UA, Univ. Series 47, Minutes of the History Department, 11/10/1982)

Native Americans: In the past a few Native Americans attended Northern and were met with prejudice from students. At various times, Native American speakers came to campus and talked to the weekly assembly or at public lectures. In January 1936, Charles Eagle Plume came to Northern to present a program called "Making Medicine," in which he interpreted Native life through song and dance. Unfortunately, there is little information available about the early days.

Jim Carter, who was in the Office of Research and Development, was interested in developing a special Indian culture and education program. Carter wrote to Senator Robert P. Griffith in 1970 concerning the development of an Indian educational program geared to the Indian cultural heritage, interests and abilities, "rather than force them into our educational mold." The concept was discussed with a number of faculty members who were interested in the project and the idea of a Center for Chippewa Education or a Chippewa Studies Center emerged. The three basic courses would be: native language, folklore, history and anthropology. A possible fourth concentration would be in arts and crafts. On June 29, 1970, there was an important meeting with the NMU Chippewa Education and Culture Program Committee and the Michigan Inter-Tribal Councils (MIC). The latter group represented all the tribes. Many Native Americans from all over the state attended.

By the fall of 1971, there were twenty-three Native students on campus. By 1977, there were forty-six students enrolled in the Native American Program. Northern received a grant of $50,000 for training fifty Native Americans in office occupations in what was called the American Indian Management Training Project. During the decade ending in 1990, the average number of Native students on campus was 136.

As time passed, there were a number of developments in this area. At first, Carter was director as part of his R&D duties until Robert Bailey arrived. The Office of American Indian Programs was created, and Bailey became director (1972–1979). This position was gradually incorporated into the Diversity Programs and the directorship changed. Rosemary Gemill Suardini, 1979–1981; Nancie Hatch, 1981–1995; Rose Allard, 1995–1997; and Michael Teesdale-Sherman, 1997–1998 served in various leadership roles.

Special courses in anthropology were developed by Marla Buckmaster and in history by Russell Magnaghi. Soon after, a Native American Studies Program was developed on paper, but was not approved.

Between 1971 and 1983, Carter and the Native students developed the very successful *Nishnawbe News* (*See separate entry*). There were a variety of cultural programs and lectures presented on campus. "Indian Awareness Week" which began in 1971 was held annually and speakers and programs were featured. Later, there were lectures by Native American speakers funded through the Martin Luther King, Jr.-César Chávez-Rosa Parks lecture series. Seminars, workshops and courses were also presented on reservations in the Upper Peninsula. On a number of occasions, several Native Americans were awarded honorary degrees from Northern: Beatrice Medicine (Humane Letters, 8/79), Vine Deloria, Jr. (Humanities, 5/1991) and LaDonna Harris (Humanities, 4/1994). The last two individuals were commencement speakers.

It was not until 1991 that Melissa Hearn began to discuss the possibility of having a Center for Native American Studies. The Center was developed on paper and was housed in the English Department where Hearn, and later Lillian Heldreth, were faculty. They taught in the program and directed two advisory boards. An interdisciplinary Native American Studies minor was established. In 1993, the Center received a $100,000 grant from the Phillip Morris Foundation for three years. The Center for Native American Studies, which had informally existed in the past, was officially approved by the Board of Control on December 13, 1996.

Although Native Americans had directed the Office of American Indian Programs on campus, they had never been hired as tenure-earning faculty. The first full-time Native American faculty member was Dr. James Spresser (English, 1994–1996). He was followed by Dr. Dennis Tibbetts, named as the first Director of the Center for Native American Studies(Education, 1996–present). Native American instructors have included Don Chosa and Don Abel and Shirley Brozzo who teaches UN 204 Native American Experience. (NCN 01/06/1936)

Newspapers: Since 1919, the students of Northern have published a series of newspapers. The first paper was the *Northern Normal News*, which ran from January 15, 1919 through July 26, 1927. With the title of the institution changing, so did the name of the paper. Between September 20, 1927 and July 20, 1955 it was known as the *Northern College News*. The *Northern News* was published between September 30, 1955 and June 30, 1972. At this time, there were a number of problems between the newspaper and the administration. As a result, the students created an independent publication. However, during the summer of 1972 when the administration wanted to get out news of the summer graduation and other information, there was one issue of the *Northern Michigan University Press* (August 4, 1972).

Since September 14, 1972 the *North Wind* has been published on a weekly basis during the school year. On a few occasions, these newspapers were published during the summer months as well. Between 1919-1929 the editors were faculty members: Doris King (1919), Earle Parker (1921), Parker and A.Bess Clark (1922), Parker (1925), and Blanche de Page (1929). After that, students were editors with a faculty advisor: Bertrand J. Henne (1930), Henry C. Steehler (1931), Edward G.Ferris (1932), Bob Anderson (1933), Bruce K. Nelson (1934), Robert Laurie (in July 1934), George Brotherton and Clyde Kohn (1935), Briaeson Wills and Howard Anderson (1936), Anderson (1937), Edurn McGuire (1938), George H. Nelson (1939), Erich H. Werner (1940), James Hatch (1941, 1942), Helen Ward (1943), Helvi Walkonen (1944, 1945), Robert Alexander (1946), Betty Rose Holliday (1947), Charlotte Meyland (1948), Joe Sullivan (1949), Nola Case and Barbara Lakso (1950), Eugene Maki and Jean Judnich (1951), Elaine Saari (1952), Craig Olson (1953), Dolores Prestay (1954), Ray Saari (1955), Jim Fuller (1956), Doug Moreau and Dee Meyers (1957), Tom Schwalbach and Orton Melchoir (1958, Melchoir (1959), Kathleen Hogan (1960), Sandra Neimeyer (1961), Katherine Anderson (1962), Jane Piirto and Donna Gustafson (1963), Gustafson (1964), James E. Almy (1965, 1966), Almy, Ruth LaVoy, and Jeffery Jurmu 1967), Jurmu (1968), Jurmu and Lowell Easley (1969), Easley and Charles Brunell (1970), Brunell and Ric Wanetik (1971), David S. Haynes ("acted as") and Greg Bell (1972), Don McLennan (1973), Darlene Alonzo (1974), Pan Jansson (1975), J. J. Jackman (1976), Becky Beauchamp (1977), Robin O'Grady (1978), Robin Pettyjohn Stevens (1979), Suzanne Edwards (1980), Kenneth Altine (1981), Mary Body (1982), Todd Dickard (1983), Paul Meyer (interim) and Patti Samar (1984), Samar (1985), Ron Fonger (1986), Dave Gill (1978), James Lyons and Cheryl Peterson (1988), Peterson and Rebecca Ennis (1989), Ann Gonyea (1990), Shana Hubbs (1991), Hubbs and Paul Stieber (1992), Joe Hall (1993), Bob Hendrickson (1994), Andy Goodrich (1995), Michael Murray (1996, 1997), Kristy Basolo (1998). Since its inception some of the advisers have been: Earle Parker, Gunther Meyland, Katheryn Marriott, Paul Ripley, Gerald Waite, Michael Fitzgibbon-Rhea, and Michael McQuade. (NCN 06/14/1939) Michelle Kangas

Nicknames for Northern Students: Teachers: 1904; Normalites: 1923; Northerners: 1923, 1932; Northernites: 1931.

Nishnawbe News: This was a Native American newspaper developed by Native students and first issued in June 1971. Jim Carter was its advisor over the years. It was one of three major Indian publications in the country and was highly respected in both the United States and Canada.

By October 1983, during sharp cutbacks in higher education funding and despite donations the revenues were not enough to continue the paper and it was eliminated. At the time, there was some hope of developing a quarterly, but this never happened. (NW 10/06/1983)

Normal Building: *See*: *Longyear Hall*

Normal Chorus: In 1910, the organization consisted of 100 voices. The purpose of the organization was to give its members an opportunity to study the best known hymns, glees, anthems and operatic selections to become more proficient in sight-singing and to develop the voice.

Normal Council: This Council was also known as the Normal Principals' Council and the Normal Executive Council. It was composed of the principals or presidents of the four normal, or teachers' colleges. They met periodically to discuss policies which affected their institutions. In 1928 the Council became the Council of State Teachers College Presidents (*See*).

Normal Extension Lectures: As early as 1913–1914, Northern, desiring "to be of service in developing and improving the educational work of the various communities," allowed "its faculty members to give single lectures or courses of lectures at educational or social meetings." The faculty presented these lectures as part of their teaching load and were available on Friday evenings and Saturdays. At this time, the available faculty included Gilbert Lee Brown, Flora E. Hill, James H. Kaye (president), John E. Lautner, Samuel D. Magers, Earle M. Parker, Mary A. Proudfoot, Grace A. Spalding, Charles C. Spooner, Steven S. Stockwell, and DeForest Stull. The topics ranged from personal to professional interest. Over the years the faculty have followed similar programs. This was a forerunner of the Speakers' Bureau. (*See separate entry*) (*Year Book of the Northern State Normal School for 1913 and 1914*. Marquette: Mining Journal Company, 1914, pp. 24–29).

The Normal Girl's Dream: *See*: *Expression. . . Department of*

Normal School: A translation of the French term *école normale* (from the Latin, *norma*, a rule or model), the term is applied to a school for the instruction and training of teachers. The first French school so named was intended to serve as a model and was founded in 1834. The term usually refers to a two-year school for training chiefly elementary teachers. The term normal school was an unfortunate misnomer, and its general application led to confusion of ideas. Between 1899 and 1927, Northern was known as the Northern State Normal School.

North End Tavern: The tavern, located on the corner of Center and Presque Isle, was first opened in 1935 by William Winkka. The name and owners changed over the years. In 1948, it was renamed by Olga Winkka, William's wife. From that time, until December 1978, it was a popular student hangout. Then it was purchased by Stevenski's Inc. and reopened on January 13, 1979 as Whiskers Spirits and Eatery. In August 1983, an addition and renovation were completed. During the summer of 1994, a sports bar was added. (MJ 01/19/1997)

The North Gate: Located at the corner of Waldo and Presque Isle, the North Gate was a gift from the Class of 1932. Students donated both money and time to have it constructed during the summer of 1933. Four brownstone pillars, arranged in a semi-circle, formed the nucleus of the entrance and supported the green steel picket fencing which enclosed the corner of the campus. A flagstone walk bisected the area and the space was landscaped. The pillars were actually constructed of an artificial sandstone shipped by truck from Oshkosh, Wisconsin. The Class of 1936 provided the walkway, which passed through the gate. The Gate was removed for parking lot expansion in 1963. (NCN 07/25/1933, 09/19/1933; 10/23/1935 photo).

North Marquette Addition: The addition refers to the area bound by Waldo, Presque Isle, Wright and Tracy Streets. It was originally a wetlands area covered with tamarack trees and wild cranberries and was a haven to mosquitoes. In 1899, when a North Marquette site for Northern was discussed, Peter White sent the Board of Education a letter pointing out the summer breezes out of the north which would make the present Northern site unhealthy because of these swamps. In 1908, a developer began to fill the land and develop a walkway to facilitate the construction of residences from Fair Street to the entrance of the Cliffs-Dow property in the vicinity of Presque Isle Avenue and Wright Street.

In the 1920s, Northern planned on using portions of the land for an athletic field which was never developed. Faculty and married student housing was constructed in the northwest corner of the property in the late 1950s. Plans for an expanded campus took shape in the 1960s, and the Marquette Development Corporation (*See separate entry*) composed of Northern and local banks was created. The idea was to purchase all of the homes and move them to the area north of Wright Street. Some homes on the west side of the area were purchased and either demolished or moved. In 1968–1969, due to the McClellan controversy (*See separate entry*) and the fact that the campus was not going to grow as dramatically as forecasted, the plan to purchase and move the homes in this area was terminated.

Over the years, Northern has purchased homes in the area abutting the campus for office space and open space. A small portion of the land bound by Wilkinson, Schafer, Norwood, and Center Streets remains in its original condition as a low-lying wetland. (MJ 06/19/1908)

North Wind: Created in September 1972 as an independent campus newspaper, it published its first issue on September 14, 1972. *See*: *Newspapers*

Northern College News: The newspaper existed from 1927 to 1955. The purpose of the paper to serve the school to the best of its ability. The *Northern College News* presented news of the institution and announced events. It also served to advertise the college, since it had a large extramural circulation. It was also an outlet for student opinion. The students were responsible for its publication. In 1932, it was published bi-weekly except during August and September. It is available on microfilm in the NMU Archives. *See*: *Newspapers*

Northern Economic Initiatives Center or Corp: *See*: *Northern Initiatives*

Northern Grove: The Grove is an unspecified grove of trees on campus where in 1915 the seniors had their luncheon. Possibly this grove is located on the northeast area of campus by the corner of Waldo and Presque Isle. More likely, it was the orchard property of Jack Anderson on the west side of Hebard Court at Kaye Avenue.

Northern Initiatives: In 1984, when the unemployment rate in the Upper Peninsula was between 18 and 21 percent, President James Appleberry made a decision to increase job growth in the region. At this time, he formed the NMU Business and Economic Assistance Center. The name was changed to the Northern Economic Initiatives Center on December 13, 1985. The purpose of the Center was to support small enterprises in the Upper Peninsula. By 1991, funding for the NEIC came from the state through the Research Excellence Fund. This fund was set aside for each university to assist in research, applied research or applied technical assistance that would lead to economic improvement in the state of Michigan. Other funding comes from national organizations such as the Ford Foundation in New York City, the Joyce Foundation, the Kellogg Foundation and others. The Corporation was created in 1992 and moved off campus. On April 15, 1992 the title "Northern Initiatives" was legally authorized.

By 1998, Northern Initiatives was a non-profit community-oriented business development institution. Its offices are located in downtown Marquette at 228 W. Washington Street. Northern Initiatives offers business counseling and loan programs, in part through an affiliation with the nationally recognized Shorebank Corp. of Chicago. Northern Initiatives focuses on work-force education, business start-up, and expansion loans. The money comes from North Coast Business Industrial Development Corp. (BIDCO), Inc. a for-profit subsidiary of Shorebank.

Presidents: Richard Anderson 1984–1997; Dennis J. West, 1997–present. (NW 10/03/1991)

Northern Center for Lifelong Learning (NCLL): New educational opportunities were made available to retirement-age residents with the creation of this Center in the spring of 1995. NMU provides the group with a workroom in the Superior Dome, where all classes are held. Instructors include retirees and NMU faculty. The annual membership fee is $15. (*Campus* 05/22–26/1995)

Northern Michigan College of Education: The name of the institution between 1941 and 1955.

Northern Michigan College: The name of the institution between 1955 and 1963.

Northern Michigan College Foundation: The Foundation was established in 1962. Monies pledged or donated to Northern were transferred and delivered to the Foundation after its incorporation. The Foundation was administered by a Board of Trustees.

Northern Michigan School of Banking: The School of Banking was conceived in 1964 and begun a year later to meet the ever present need for continuing education in the field of banking. Planned by bankers to serve the specific needs of personnel of "small" banks, the school was staffed by professional banking and business people and University personnel who were interested in further developing banking skills and disseminating a knowledge of new techniques, approaches and concepts in commercial banking. Each student completing the two-year program was presented with a certificate of achievement. The School ended in 1995.

Northern Michigan University: In 1963, the State Legislature created Northern as a self-governing state institution with its own Board of Control through a bill introduced by Representative Dominic Jacobetti. On the morning of March 13, 1963, Governor George Romney signed the bill into law. Individuals at the signing included: President Edgar Harden, Representative Clayton T. Morrison (R-Pickford), Senator Philip Rahoi (D-Iron Mountain), and Representative Dominic J. Jacobetti (D-Negaunee). This was the last name change for the institution. (MJ 03/13/1963, 03/14/1963)

Northern Michigan University Press: The NMU Press was a newspaper which had one issue published on August 04, 1972. (*See*: *Newspapers*)

Northern Michigan University Press: The press was established in 1962 as a function of the Research & Development office. In 1975 it was moved to the Communications office where it became dormant in the late 1980s due to finances, growing demands on the Communications office and staff cutbacks. The Press was reactivated in 1993, under the coordination of the dean of the College of Arts and Sciences, Michael Marsden. Although its publications cover a variety of topics, it has issued more titles in regional studies than in any other field. By 1999, the revived press is a financial success.

University Press Directors: Roy E. Heath, 1962–1966; John Pat Farrell, 1966–1968; Earl A. McIntyre, 1968–1972; James L. Carter, 1972–1993; Michael T. Marsden, 1993–present.

University Press Publications: *Academic Heraldry in America*, Kevin Sheard (1962); *The Free-Living Protozoa of the Upper Peninsula of Michigan*, Francis C. Lundin and Luther S. West (1963); *Current Research in British Studies*, Anthony H. Forbes (1964); *America's Shame and Redemption*, Dwight Lowell Dumond (1965); *Wendell Willkie: Fighter for Freedom*, Ellsworth Barnard (1966); *American Voyageur: The Journal of David Bates Douglass*, Ed. Sydney W. Jackman et al. (1969); *Browning's Analysis of a Murder: Case for The Inn Album*, John Hitner (1969); *ALD: A New Test for Aphasia*, Lon Emerick (1971); *Ojibwa Indian Legends, Wah-Be-Gwo-Nese*, Cheryl Mills King Schauffler (1971); *An Annotated Bibliography of Musca Domestica Linnaeus*, Luther S. West and Oneita Beth Peters (co-published 1973); *Language and Culture: A Book of Readings*, Ed. Robert B. Glenn et al. (1974); *Northern Michigan University: The First 75 Years*, Miriam Hilton (1975); *Reflections*, Praeceptor Humilis, Luther S. West (1975); *Listen to Me: An Anthology of Upper Peninsula High School Writing*, Ed. Christine Johnson et al. (1976); *Cohodas: The Story of a Family*, Wilbert H. Treloar (1977); *Flaming Brands: Fifty Years of Iron Making in the Upper Peninsula of Michigan, 1848–1898*, Kenneth D. LaFayette (1977); *Tuning the Historical Temperaments by Ear*, Owen Jorgensen (1977); *Organization, Training, Search and Recovery Procedures for the Underwater Unit*, Thomas R. Lewis (1979); *Sentinels of the Rocks: From 'Graveyard Coast' to National Lakeshore*, Dennis R. Noble and T. Michael O'Brien (1979); *Words & Images: 31 Lesson Plans for Reading, Art, and English Teachers, Grades K–12*, Thomas Cappuccio et al. (1980); *From the Mississippi to the Pacific: Essays in Honor of John Francis Bannon, S.J.*, Ed. Russell Magnaghi (1982); *Utopia in Upper Michigan*, Olive Anderson (1982); *Lake Superior Journal: Bela Hubbard's Account of the 1840 Houghton Expedition*, Ed. Bernard C. Peters (1983); *Mining in Michigan: A Catalog of Company Publications, 1845–1980*, Le Roy Barnett (1983); *Railroads in Michigan: A Catalog of Company Publications, 1836–1980*, Le Roy Barnett (1986); *Hard Maple, Hard Work*, John Gagnon (1996); *Lake Superior Place Names: From Bawating to the Montreal*, Bernard C. Peters (1996); *A Sense of Place—Michigan's Upper Peninsula: Essays in Honor of William and Margery Vandament*, Eds. Russell M. Magnaghi and Michael T. Marsden (1997); *A Sense of Time: The Encyclopedia of Northern Michigan University*, Russell Magnaghi (1999). Michael Fitzgibbon-Rhea

Northern Michigan University Retirees Association: The association is an organization of faculty and staff retirees established in 1985. (MJ 10/08/1995)

Northern News: The name of a Northern Newspaper published between 1955 and 1972. *See*: *Newspapers*

Northern News-Review: A monthly newspaper, which carried general campus news between 1972 and 1987; originally it was called, *Campus Review*.

Northern Normal News: The name of the first newspaper on campus which ran from 1919 until 1927. *See*: *Newspapers*

Northern Shuffle: A student complaint, nicknamed the "Northern shuffle," goes back to the 1970s. Students say they are shuffled around the campus without any direction or solution to their problems when they seek to take care of enrollment or other business. Attempts continue to be made to make the campus more user-friendly. It is sometimes called the "Cohodas Shuffle." (NW 09/09/1976; 09/03/1998)

Northern State Normal School: This was the name of the University from 1899 until 1927. It was called a normal or teacher's training school. *See*: *Normal School*

Northern State Normal Chapter of the Disabled American Veterans of the World War: *See*: *Federal Men*

Northern State Teacher's College: Northern State Teacher's College was the name of the University from 1927 to 1941. This was done to emphasize the changed status that had come about due to the degree programs.

N.S.N. Daily: A little known newspaper, called the *Northern State Normal Daily* was established in 1910. By June 4th, four issues had been published. The only partial issue of this publication can be found in *Olive and Gold* and no other information exists about this campus publication.

Northerner: An annual or yearbook published in 1947.

Nursing and Allied Health Sciences, College: The School of Nursing and Allied Health was created by the Board of Control in 1968. In 1974, the name was changed to the School of Nursing and Allied Health Sciences. The name was changed to College by Board action on July 1, 1992.

The primary mission of the College is the education of quailed technical and professional health care personnel, from the certificate level through graduate study, who provide direct care and therapy to clients and their families. The College serves the region by providing leadership and sharing knowledge and skills in the provision of professional and technical education in health and health care services.

The College prepares practical nurses, registered nurses at the bachelor degree level, master level nurses in administration and advanced practice, clinical assistants, surgical technologists, clinical laboratory technicians, clinical laboratory scientists, cytotechnologists and speech pathologists.

The College is responsible for the safe practice of its graduates in all health care fields represented in the College by achieving successful pass rates of graduates in licensure or certification exams.

In 1994 the total number of majors was 700. In 1992 of the 178 students who graduated, 90 percent+ were working within four months of graduation. 95–100 percent of all graduates pass licensure/certification exams on the first writing. Within the College are the departments of Clinical Laboratory Sciences, Communication Disorders, Practical Nursing and Nursing (*See separate entries*).

Deans: Margaret Rettig, 1968–1982; Betty Hill, 1982–present. (*The 1996–97 University Profile*, 1:237–245)

Nursing, Department of: As early as 1939, Nursing courses were offered at Northern as pre-professional courses designed to prepare future nurses for additional schooling. Between 1963 and 1968, a baccalaureate nursing program was developed. In 1969, a baccalaureate nursing curriculum was offered to students. Margaret Rettig and Lulu Ervast were instrumental in establishing the four-year nursing program at Northern.

The Department of Nursing offers programs leading to the Bachelor in Science (B.S.N.) and a Masters in Nursing (M.S.N.) The B.S. in Nursing prepares students to function as professional nurses in a variety of hospital and community settings. The B.S. and M.S.N. programs are accredited by the National League of Nursing.

Department Heads: Margaret Rettig, 1969–1980; Phoebe Crouch, 1980–1984;MaryEllen Powers,1984–1989;Elmer Moisio, 1989–present. (*The 1996–97 University Profile*, 1:260–266); *Bulletins*; Karen Hicks, "The Nursing Department," UA). Michelle Kangas

NYA: National Youth Administration was a New Deal program in the 1930s which provided jobs for students attending college. It was actively used at Northern. *See*: *Depression*

Oath Card: Provisions of Act 23 of the Public Acts of 1935 as amended require as a condition of employment in Michigan educational institutions supported by public funds that all employees who are citizens of the U.S. take and subscribe to the following oath or affirmation:

I so solemnly swear (or affirm) that I will support the Constitution of the United States of America and the Constitution of the State of Michigan, and that I shall faithfully discharge the duties of my position according to the best of my ability.

This oath, as required by the law, must be signed and notarized. The law further provides that the requirements of the oath shall not be construed as prohibiting public educational institutions from employing citizens of foreign countries.

Occupational Studies Department: Before the Occupational Studies Department was formed in 1989, courses were offered in Industrial Education at the Skills Center. This department merged vocational programs with associated programs and added a bachelor program. The department includes the widest variety of offerings in the College of Technology and Applied Sciences. Diplomas are offered in Collision Repair Technology and Cosmetology. Certificates in Automotive Service, Carpentry, Heating, Ventilation, Air Conditioning and Refrigeration and Wastewater Treatment Plant Operations. Associate Degrees in Automotive Service Technology, Building Technology, Climate Control Technology, and Wastewater Technology. A baccalaureate degree is offered in Construction Technology.

Department Heads: Elaine Alden, 1989–1991; Walter Anderson, 1991–present. (*Bulletins*; *The 1996–97 University Profile*, 2:316–322)

O'Dell's Party Store: See: *The Wright Place*

Office Information Systems: The unit is part of the Walker L. Cisler College of Business. Two baccalaureate programs are offered: one in office systems and another in business teacher education. The office systems program provides a basic foundation for graduates to progress in office systems career paths to middle management and beyond. The business teacher education program prepares students as certified teachers of business at the secondary level.

Serving the community college role, the department offers one certificate and four associate degrees. The office services certificate provides graduates with introductory skills for employment in an office environment while the office information associate degree graduates with advances skills. In addition, students choosing office information services, legal or medical programs are provided with specialized skills necessary for employment in those fields. The general business associate degree program provides graduates with an understanding of the concepts of business, preparing them for a variety of positions in the business world.

Oldest Remains on Campus: These earliest connections with the past on Northern's campus consist of partial remains located around the campus and in Marquette County. Longyear Hall dated from 1900 and its reconstruction after a fire in 1905. It was demolished in 1993, but its facade has been numbered. Along with the rest of the structure, the remains have been preserved for future use.

Possibly the oldest intact remains is the lower third of the "Heart of Northern" in the southeast side of the Presque Isle parking lot, dating back to pre-1907. The reproductions of paintings and etchings in the Peter White Lounge date to 1906, having been donated by Peter White for the Art Department. Pieces of Kaye Hall (1915) adorn the carillons on campus. The statute of Abraham Lincoln located in the University Center dates from 1916. The next-oldest structure is a brick gate post which once formed the formal entrance to College Stadium which opened in October 1932. Due to a property sale, the structure was placed on property owned by Marquette General Hospital. It is located directly opposite the south entrance of the University Center. The temporary dormitory structures constructed for increased enrollment caused by returning veterans, and called Vetville date back to 1946–1947 and have been relocated at Hotel Place in Harvey and are still in use as rental units. The oldest complete structures on campus are Carey and Lee Halls, which opened in 1948 as a women's dormitory and student union respectively.

Olive and Gold: This was the name of the first class yearbook, published in 1910. It stressed school spirit and "a true reflection of school life." Copies are available in the University Archives.

Olson, Lydia: (January 3, 1880–November 13, 1962) A native of Ishpeming, Lydia Olson was a graduate of Marquette High School and Northern Michigan University. She began her studies at Normal State Normal School in the fall of 1899, the year the university was founded. She went on to be valedictorian of the first two-year class at the University.

Olson returned to Marquette in the spring of 1908 and was employed as a librarian at the Peter White Library, a position she held for six months before becoming librarian at Northern. She continued in this position until her retirement in 1941. This made her the longest serving librarian in the history of Northern, with a tenure of 33 years. During free time she collected and preserved newspaper clippings related to the history of the University and began an embryonic archives.

When the library building was completed in 1951, it was dedicated to her. The name moved when new quarters were opened in 1969 in the Edgar L. Harden Learning Resources Center.

Memberships: Michigan Library Association and the Business and Professional Women's Club. (NN 12/05/1962; *NSNS Yearbook, 1901–1902*) See: Library

Olson Library: See: Library

Olympics: See: United States Olympic Education Center

Open House: Over the last century, numerous open houses have been held on campus especially with the completion of new buildings or renovations. Prior to the dedication of Longyear Hall in July 1900 and the Peter White Hall of Science in October 1902, the buildings were opened to the public. This tradition has continued.

The Academic Mall was dedicated on October 16, 1971, accompanied by an open house of the structures. The biggest open house held on Northern's campus took place on October 5, 1996 when all of the renovations since 1990 were highlighted for the public. Unfortunately, it was poorly attended. (NN 10/15/1971)

Operation Rip Off: This was a campaign to cut down on auto thefts in 1973. (NW 09/12/1973).

Organizations, Student: There have been some 933 organizations associated with Northern students since 1899. The clubs and organizations have ranged from early literary societies, to Greek fraternities and sororities, to religious clubs, to contemporary organizations focused on the environment or sexual preference. A study of these organizations is a study of student interest over the last century. Some records exist and others are sketchy. Check the University Archives, Student Activities records, and the university newspaper for additional information. (Russell M. Magnaghi. *Student Organizations at NMU, 1907–1999*) (1999)

Orientation: All newly admitted freshman, undergraduate transfer and guest students who are planning to enroll for nine or more credit hours on the Marquette campus are required to participate in NMU's New-Student Orientation Program. Orientation programs were offered prior to the beginning of each session. It was not until the 1977–78 *Bulletin* that "new students entering the University for the Fall Semester [were] required to participate in one of the summer orientation sessions offered in June and July." At summer orientation students tour the campus, become acquainted with members of the faculty and staff, take standardized tests, discuss their plans with an adviser and learn the graduation requirements. The Orientation Office oversees the completion of orientation by all new students. Michelle Kangas

Original Plays: Northern students and faculty have written and produced original plays. In 1912, Gertrude Mossler, a replacement for Professor Rushmore, wrote and directed Northern's first musical comedy, "In College Days."

Margaret Rarick, music supervisor in the Pierce School, encouraged original productions. Grade school pupils wrote a Christmas operetta in 1942 based on foreign nations. The next year the upperclassmen wrote an original play, "The S. S. Wolverine." Manthei Howe described the production as having an air of "effortlessness and informality," characteristic, she said, of a "big family party." In the fall of 1994, Dr. Shelley Russell-Parks wrote and produced, "Haywire." (*See separate entry*) (MJ 12/13/1943)

Osiris: Osiris was a literary society founded on October 15, 1907. The name "Osiris" or "Light" was selected because of its symbolic relation to the aim and purpose of this society. The Society disbanded in 1925.

Outstanding Young Alumni Award: The ward was first presented in 1984. Recipients: Rick E. Amidon (2-92); Brenda Bellanger (10-87); Beverly Beauchamp (10-85); Philip G. Blake (10-88); William W. Bowerman (9-92); Kevin Boyle (10-93); Gary Brunswick (10-94); Michele Butler ((10-85); Robert G. Caudill, Jr. (10-88); Jack M. Chiapuzio (10-84); Amy L. Chown (10-96); John C. Cote (10-89); Thomas J. Dahlin (10-86); David C. Forsberg (10-89); Patti P. Holliday (10-84); Thomas F. Huffman (10-88); Gary R. Hughes (10-86); Christ R. Jensen (10-85); David Kanigan (10-95); Patricia Knisley Stepkow (10-88); Donald Kukla (10-93); Stephen G. Lakotish (10-91); Teri List (10-93); Kimberly Maki (10-94); Gerard J. Molitor (10-84); Robert K. Mueller (10-90); Nicolette Nanos (10-87); Carla B. Narrett (10-85); Claudia L. Orr (10-88); Bruce C. Petersen (1-84); Mark F. Pontti (10-97); David L. Prychitko (10-89); Carl Rivord (10-93); Mark Roggenbuck (10-87); Mark H. Ruge (10-86); James Skibo (10-96); Pamela G. Slatter (9-92); Sandra L. Spoelstra (10-90); Robert P. Stefanski (10-91); Bill Streib (10-85); Scott Taube (10-93); Donald Tucker (10-87); Cathy Turner (11-94); Danny L. Wiedbrauk (10-96); Carey Yeager (10-86); Gregory S. Zyburt (10-90).

Pageants: *See*: *Spring Pageants*

Painted Rocks: In an area bound by Tracy and Center Streets and Elizabeth Harden Drive, in front of the Harden Learning Resources Center are located five huge rocks. Following collegiate folklore and tradition, these rocks are painted by various Greek organizations. During the warmer months, the names of Greek organizations on the rocks sometimes change on a daily basis. Infrequently intruders paint and mark the rocks, as happened in the late summer of 1998 when the Lake Superior State swim team put their initials and message on the rocks. This campus tradition has been carried on for over a decade.

Palestra: This was a large, privately-owned, barn-like structure located on the north side of Fair Avenue opposite North Third Street. It was originally built in the Copper Country in 1904. The money was raised and the deal closed by the summer of 1921 to move the structure to Marquette. It took 55 days to take the building apart, ship it by rail, and reconstruct it. The first college hockey game was played there during the first season the Palestra operated. The teams were the University of Michigan and Michigan Tech. It consisted of an ice arena and a second-story dance hall. During the 1920s, it was used extensively by Northern students who would skate and then dance to well-known orchestras. Some time later, the front part containing the dance hall burned.

After World War II, the Marquette Sentinels were formed. They got their name from a brand of antifreeze that one of its sponsors, Cliffs Dow Chemical Company, produced. They played in the Palestra until the early 1960s when they ran out of money and disbanded. The Marquette Iron Rangers, members of the United States Hockey League played there, winning the league title sporadically during the mid-1960s and early 1970s. They also ran into financial problems and disbanded about the time NMU hockey was growing. The Palestra was demolished in 1974. The Lake View Ice Arena, located several blocks to the east on Fair Avenue, replaced this facility. (NW 10/13/1983)

Pan Hellenic Tea: The Tea was held on February 19, 1959 in Lee Hall Ballroom so that female students could become better acquainted with the sororities. Part of the Tea included a Style show of appropriate and inappropriate clothes to be worn at rushing parties. (Source: NN 02/25/1959)

Parking and Speeding on Campus: When South or Longyear Hall was opened for classes in 1900, students arrived either on foot or by the streetcar that passed in front of the campus. By the 1930s, students were commuting from Ishpeming and Negaunee by automobile. Parking places were found on the surrounding city streets.

The situation radically changed in the late 1940s with the construction of GIville and Vetville. Parking places were set for the residents who were veterans, older and owners of autos. With the completion of Carey dorm in 1948, parking was still not a problem because most female students did not have automobiles.

In December 1950 information about parking appears in the Northern College News. At that time student parking was centered near the Union Building (Lee Hall) and along Kaye Avenue. After a heavy snowfall on December 20, notice was given of winter parking rules.

The situation drastically changed with the expansion of the first men's dorm, Spooner Hall, in 1957. The story begins in a July 1957 issue of the *Northern News*. The problems centered around speeders who approached Spooner Hall, illegal parking in a yellow zone in front of Lee Hall, and illegal parking in reserved parking spots for the residents of Vetville.

In October 1957, the Student Council got involved with the parking problems in Vetville and speeding. By November the news journalist covering the story could write, "It appears that the campus parking problem is finally solved." In the days when there was no Campus Security (January 1958) Spooner Hall officials were authorized to issue parking tickets.

In 1959 Public Safety and Police Services (*See separate entry*) was created and became involved in regulating parking. By February 1960, a revised motor vehicle code went into effect. At the same time 106 parking meters were obtained from Park-O-Meter Company of Jackson.

The Presque Isle parking lot was created for the expanding student body in the summer of 1963. During the following years parking facilities were constantly expanded, but never to the satisfaction of the student body or faculty. By 1986, there were 3,373 parking spaces located around the campus. However, many people felt that they were not close enough to main instructional buildings.

In the first half of the 1990s, President Vandament took steps to expand parking on campus. One plan was to create a multi-story lot next to Forest Roberts Theatre, but it was found the cost was too great and few people would want to pay for this type of parking. Between May and August 1996, Lee Drive was realigned between Seventh Street and Kaye Avenue, costing $182,000 which came from the Michigan Department of Transportation. At the same time, a new parking lot was constructed for Carey and Lee Halls, Parking Lot 62 was expanded, and the other lots were regraded and graveled. By 1998, there were 3,762 parking spaces or an increase of 389 spots from the 1986 count. In conclusion, it can be stated that parking has remained an ongoing and major issue over the years on Northern's campus, which despite the greatest of efforts and expenditures of money, does not seem to be resolved in the minds of students. Frequent articles and letters to the editor attest to the problem. (NCN 12-20-1950; NN 07/11/1957; 10/30/1957; 11/27/1958; 01/15/1958; 01/22/1958; NW 10/19/1994).

Passages North: *Passages North* is a literary journal established in Escanaba in 1979 and first edited by Elinor Benedict of Rapid River. It was developed to showcase the work of the Bay Arts Writers' Guild. Until December 1995, Kalamazoo College was its home for five years. Since that time it has been on campus and edited by the English Department. (*Marquette Monthly*, April 1997).

Pasty: On Friday evening, October 20, 1978, as part of Homecoming festivities, the three-man Pasty Planning Commission unveiled what was considered the "world's largest pasty." The monster pasty which was baked in a special oven consisted of: 250 pounds of beef, 400 pounds of potatoes, 75 pounds of carrots, and 25 pounds of onions wrapped in 250 pounds of dough. The Upper Peninsula favorite was consumed by the hundreds who dropped by to see the marvel. (MJ 10/21/1978)

Paul Bunyan: The theme of the legendary woodsman reoccurs connected with dances held on campus. In November 1931, at the Alpha Delta dance, the men were dressed in "woodland garb" and a Paul Bunyan appeared on the scene for the festivities.

In the 1950s and 1960s, the Beta Omega Tu and later the Delta Zeta sororities held an annual Bunyan Ball in the Lee Hall Ballroom and after 1960 in the University Center. Participants dressed "lumberjack" and tried to look like Paul Bunyan. Friday prior to the dance was declared "Plaid Day" and everyone was encouraged to wear mixed and matched plaids. There were a variety of activities: log sawing, the Beta pancake breakfast, and prizes for the beards that were the funniest, scratchiest, nicest-looking, softest, most colorful and the longest. The man with the nicest-looking beard was crown King Paul. A queen with a court were selected for the originality of their costumes.

On the academic side, English professor James Bowman wrote *The Adventures of Paul Bunyan* (New York: Century, 1927), a children's book of romantic folklore. (NCN 12/01/1931; NN 11/14/1957, 10/30/1964)

Payne Residence Hall: Located near Lincoln and Wright streets, Payne Hall was built in 1965 as part of a 25 year expansion project on campus due to the growing number of students. It cost $2,058,000 to complete the project. Architects were Swanson Associates of Bloomfield Hills, Michigan, and the builders were from the Caspian Construction Company of Caspian, Michigan. Dedicated on October 3, 1965, the hall occupies 55,935 square feet. The building was named for Lucille Payne. (*See separate entry*) Michelle Kangas

Payne, M. Lucille: (November 27, 1897–September 1, 1991). Lucille Payne was born in West Lafayette, Indiana. She received her BA from Indiana State College (Terre Haute) and her master's degree from the Teacher's College at Columbia University. She continued graduate work at Northwestern University, the University of Wisconsin and the University of Colorado. Before coming to Northern, she taught in public schools at Parke County and Newport, Indiana; the junior high schools of Bedford and Mishawaka, Indiana; and Pelham, (New York) High School.

Payne came to Northern in September 1930 as a critic teacher in English at the John D. Pierce School where she had special responsibilities for dramatics and forensics. She brought culture to the classroom and applied culture to activities outside the classroom. Senior plays were directed by her and she had charge of most forensic activities. She taught several summer sessions at Northern, and after 1961 devoted all of her time to university classes. For many years, she was the advisor to Gamma Phi Alpha Sorority. Payne was an avid reader and a poet. One of her poems, "Contrasts," was published in the National Poetry Anthology of 1957.

While in Marquette, she participated in many community clubs. She was a member of the Delta Kappa Gamma Sorority, the National Council of Teachers in English, the Michigan Council of Teacher's of English and the Michigan Education Association. She retired in 1963 as assistant professor of English and moved to West Lafayette, Indiana. Payne Residence Hall (*See separate entry*) was dedicated to her on October 3, 1965.

Pearce, Ada Juliette Wellington: (August 22, 1876–July 17, 1958) Ada Pearce was the daughter of George and Ella Wellington of Springport, Michigan. In 1897 when Webster Pearce was employed as superintendent of schools in Springport, he courted and married Ada on

June 23, 1899. They were the parents of four daughters: Dariel, Ella, Gertrude, and Jean and one son, John. She was never comfortable acting as the wife of a college president. On the death of her husband, she moved from Marquette and eventually passed away in Mt. Pleasant, Michigan. (*Daily Times-News* (Mt. Pleasant) 07/19/1958; *Springport Signal* 07/24/1958)

Pearce, Webster Houston: (May 12, 1876–October 10, 1940) Pearce was the fourth president of Northern Michigan University who spent 44 years of his life actively engaged in educational work in Michigan. His long career of teaching paralleled the development of education in the state.

President Pearce was born at Whitmore Lake, Washtenaw County, Michigan, on May 12, 1876. He was the second of three children of Reverend and Mrs. Francis E. Pearce. His father was a Methodist pastor. The family had moved to Michigan from Indiana two years before his birth. After that time, Reverend Pearce served the church in the Lower Peninsula.

President Pearce received a bachelor of pedagogy degree in education from Michigan State Normal College (now Eastern Michigan University) (1901) and a B.A. from Albion College (1904). Then he went on and received his master's degree from the University of Michigan.

Between 1897 and 1902, Pearce was superintendent of schools in Springport, Michigan. It was here that he met and wed (June 23, 1899) Ada Juliette Wellington, daughter of George and Ella Wellington of Springport.

His next assignment took him back to Albion, where he served as high school principal (1902-1905). Then Pearce went to Adrian, for three years and served as high school principal.

This ended his high school career, as he moved up to college teaching. He became associate professor of mathematics at Eastern Michigan University (1909-1916). After five years of service, he became professor of mathematics at Central State Teachers College (now Central Michigan University), where he served from 1917 to 1927. For seven of the ten years that he lived in Mt. Pleasant, he also served as the city's mayor.

His leadership ability as an educator and executive became known throughout the state. In 1927 he was elected to the office of state superintendent of public instruction. He served in this position for six years until he became president of Northern Michigan University in 1933. During his tenure he was faced with the bleak days of the Great Depression, but he brought the institution through it.

President Pearce was known for three qualities: his tremendous capacity for work, his sincerity, and his interest in young people. In his leadership position, President Pearce drove himself until the task was complete. He spent hours at his desk to clear it of work or to prepare the college budget for presentation to the legislature. In order to maintain a close association with the college community, he had an open door policy. Anyone at any time could gain an audience with him. This resulted in a closer association than ordinary between the President and the faculty and the student body. It also crammed his hours to overflowing and necessitated him working into evening hours. Since he lived across Presque Isle (at #1312), he had easy access to his office. As president he was always interested in the students. He had a sympathetic understanding of them and a tolerance for their problems. Although he was caught up by administrative work, he said that he was primarily a teacher and was happiest when he was in a classroom.

Naturally, college policies and events caused friction between the President and the students. However President Pearce was different as evidenced by a student reporter, Manthei Howe, "I have never heard a student (as students do sometimes in relationships with the faculty) accuse Mr. Pearce of insincerity or dishonesty. They, even in disagreement, paid him the tribute of believing him completely sincere."

Pearce's active career came to a halt on July 23, 1940 when he suffered a heart attack at his home. As a result of this, he was confined to his home and was unable to resume his duties with the start of classes in September. He died in the early morning of October 10, 1940.

President Pearce was a member of the First Methodist church in Marquette. He was also a member of the Masonic order and the Marquette Rotary Club. During his seven year's residence in the city, he was an active supporter of civic endeavors. Because of his interest in the community and its problems, he was chosen as principal speaker on many public occasions.

Pearce is not commemorated on Northern's campus. However on the campus of Central Michigan University, an instructional facility built in 1966, was named after this former Central mathematics professor. (*Mount Pleasant Times* 06/23/1927; *Central State Life* 10/16/1940; *Springport Signal* 10/17/1940; *Isabella County Times-News* 10/17/1940)

PEIF Building: The full name is the Physical Education Instructional Facility. Ground-breaking was held on October 19, 1974. The sprawling structure cost $9.9 million, over a million dollars above the original cost.

The building houses a number of specialized features and equipment that physical education instructors felt were sorely needed at Northern. Among these is the Instructional Ice Arena, the first completed section of the building, which was opened at a public ceremony on September 10, 1976. Although the hockey team only used the ice sheet for practice, it had a series of carpeted locker rooms and a warming room for skaters. In order to promote skating among the students, the Health, Physical Education and Recreation Department ordered 250 pair of skates.

Other features of the building included a gymnasium with fixed equipment, a half-court basketball area, an artificial turf area for the football team, a combative area, an exercise room, a dance studio, eight handball courts, eight outdoor tennis courts, a number of classrooms, 34 faculty offices, two saunas and an aquatics area, with a built-in electronic timing system that cost $20,000.

The building was complete in mid-October 1976, and opened for intramural and recreational use. The first major renovation to the building took place with the development of the Vandament Volleyball Arena, which was dedicated in November 1997. This had formerly been the artificial turf room. Over the years, areas have been expanded and uses for areas changed. A climbing wall was added and then expanded. This was also true for the exercise room, which has been expanded. With the construction of the Berry Events Center, the tennis courts were moved to the west end of campus.

For nearly twenty years, the building was not named. In 1997, the Board of Control named the Instructional Wing of the structure after Dr. Rico Zenti. The dedication ceremony took place on September 26, 1998. (NW 09/09/1976) Portions by J. J. Jackman

Pendulum: On April 12, 1995, members of the Physics Club with their adviser, Dr. David Lucas, created the world's largest pendulum. They reserved the Superior Dome, lowered a pendulum from the center of the Dome and conducted experiments. A demonstration is planned for the future.

Peninsulan: See: Annual

Penmanship: Good handwriting was an important skill for teachers, and was a required course. Casey C. Wiggins who came to Northern in 1914 and organized the Commercial Department was the dean of the handwriting teachers. He taught the course until his retirement in 1951, when it was taught by others. Through the decade of the 1950s, students going into teaching had to take a penmanship test. If they were found to be deficient in penmanship, they had to take Business 91 or Education 91: Improvement of Handwriting, which was a two-hour non-credit course. The course ended by the 1960 academic year.

Permanent Museum Collection: See: Art Museum

Persian Gulf War: The war was caused by the Iraqi invasion of Kuwait in August 1990. On January 17, 1991, the allies led by the United States, launched a devastating attack on Iraq from the air. The ground war started on February 24 and lasted 100 hours until President George Bush ordered a cease-fire. During this war, a number of students were called and had to leave their classes. Some took incompletes, and all were allowed refunds. The entire campus community followed the war with interest and concern and were provided constant updates via Cable News Network (CNN).

Personnel Department, Office of the: The Office processes all personnel transactions, provides and processes payroll deductions, administers Federal and State mandates, and negotiates, administers, and produces union contracts. To achieve common purposes, the Office has developed common guidelines for Personnel and Payroll decisions to ensure that all employees enjoy a degree of certainty as to their treatment under varying circumstances, whether prescribed by contract negotiation, statute, or administrative policy. Such an office is critical when in 1999 there are some 1,100 employees (excluding students but not graduate assistants and adjuncts) on the payroll. On July 1, 1997, the Personnel Office merged with Payroll and Employment to form the Office of Human Resources (*See separate entry*).

Peter White: See: White, Peter

Peter White Annex: Constructed in 1906, it consisted of a basement and first floor extending southward from the Peter White Science Hall. It included some classrooms and Northern's first gymnasium which cost $15,000. It was demolished with the rest of the Kaye complex in 1972–1973.

Peter White Fund: The University was authorized to spend money from this fund for research, especially focused on Lake Superior. In 1981, there was $20,000 available for faculty research. Over the years, the fund has developed and increased and is used for faculty research without being limited to the Lake Superior Basin. There are two parts to this Fund: Peter White Scholars Program and the Peter White Equipment Program. Since 1993 the Peter White Fellowship, worth $10,000, is given to a quailed faculty researcher.

Recipients: 1987–Jacqueline Bauman-Waengler(Communication Disorders) "Speech Sound Acquisition and Phonological Process" ($5,000); 1988–John Berens (Library), equipment($2,550); 1990–Ramanchandran Bharath (Management, Marketing), "Use of Information Theory in Knowledge Based Systems" ($5,000); 1993–Louise Bourgault (CAPS), "Mass Media in Black Africa" ($10,000); 1986–Maynard Bowers (Biology) "The Effects of Conjunct Herbicides and Growth Stimulators" ($5,000); 1989–Marla Buckmaster (Sociology), "Paleo-Indian Research in the Upper Peninsula of Michigan" ($5,000); 1986–Michael Cinelli (Art & Design), equipment ($2,330); 1991–Tim Compton (Languages), "Rodolfo Usigli, Giant of Mexican Theater" ($5,000); 1997–Neil Cumberlidge (Biology), "A Cladistic Analysis of the Freshwater Crabs of Africa and South America" ($10,000); 1987–John Farrell (Geography), equipment ($4,850); 1995–John Frey (Chemistry) "Charge-Transfer Complexes of TCNE with Benzene Derivatives" ($9,407); 1987–Thomas Froiland (Biology), equipment ($4,930); 1990–Gail Griffith and David Kingston (Chemistry), equipment ($2,625); 1995–George Gross (Sociology) "Occupational Stress among Corrections Officers ($7,188); 1992–Harry Gunther (Walker L. Cisler College of Business), "An Alternative Approach to Increasing the Availability of Capital to Small Firms" ($10,000); 1988–Michael Loukinen (Sociology) "Chippewa Talk'n Tunes, A Documentary Film Project" ($5,000); 1987–David Lucas (Physics) "Nitromethane Cluster Electronic Structure" ($5,000); 1989–Russell M. Magnaghi (History), "Comparative Colonial History" ($5,000);

Clifford Maier (History-Archivist) equipment ($2,150); 1989–Steve Platt (Psychology) "Breeding For Learning in the Fruit Fly" ($5,000); 1991–Sandra Poindexter (Management, Marketing), equipment ($4,925); 1988–Wanda Jean Rainbolt (HPER), equipment ($1,935); 1988–John Rebers (Biology) "Isolation of Moth Hormone-Responsive Genes" ($5,000); 1990–John Rebers (Biology), equipment ($2,770); 1991–William L. Robinson (Biology), "Preparation of Manuscripts of Publication Results of Woodcock Studies ($5,000); 1986–Jarl Roine (Geography), equipment ($,295); 1990–Shelley Russell-Parks (CAPS), equipment ($4,605); 1998–Shelley Russell-Parks (CAPS), "Historical Play and Production: A Musical Play Based on the History of Immigration in Michigan's Upper Peninsula ($10,000); 1990–Peter Slavcheff (History), "The Temperate Republic: Liquor Control in Antebellum Michigan" ($5,000); 1986–Zacharias Thundy (English) "Buddha and Christ; A Comparative Study of Their Lives and Teachings ($5,000); 1995–Cheryl Reynolds Turton (Nursing), "Health Promotion Beliefs and Behaviors among Ojibwe People" ($10,000); 1988–Frank Verley (Biology), equipment ($4,238); 1991–Frank Verley (Biology), equipment ($5,000); 1986–Phil Watts (HPER), equipment ($1,375); 1988–Phil Watts (HPER), equipment ($5,000).

Peter White Hall of Science: Plans for the "new North wing" were reviewed by the State Board of Education on August 13, 1901, and approved five days later. The contract was awarded to Lipsett & Sinclair of Marquette for $26,790.20. The structure was occupied in June 1902 and accepted by the Board of Education a month later. During the summer the Board voted to name it after Peter White and it was dedicated on October 31, 1902. The Science Hall housed all of the science departments. The physical laboratory was located in the basement. The chemistry lab was on the first floor, and recitation and two other rooms were located on the second floor. In November 1909 a small frame building (12 x 16 feet) was erected in back of the heating plant and was used to house animals used in biological work.

Over the years, repairs and renovations kept the building in good shape. The building was spruced up in October 1925. The dull, dark red walls were covered with white paint. New fans were installed to ventilate the chemistry labs. In the summer of 1941, a contract was let to Beyers Brothers, Marquette, for a new plaster ceiling, wall-washing and crack repair. Using its own funds, the college constructed a greenhouse, 70 by 21 feet, for the Natural Science and Conservation and Agriculture

Departments. It was attached to the west end of the building. Renovation was discussed in July 1950, but the actual renovation took place in 1953. The Science Hall was officially re-opened on September 14, 1953.

At the time, the chemistry department was located on the first floor. The advanced chemistry laboratory was equipped with facilities for analytical and organic chemistry. A darkroom for photography was part of the balance room. As a safety precaution, each one of the laboratories had an emergency shower that could throw 30 gallons of water per minute on burning clothes. Each classroom had tiered seats for better viewing of demonstrations. Dr. Lucian Hunt, head of the department, had his office and private lab on this floor.

Despite the renovations, the quarters became congested with growing enrollments. In 1966 West Science was opened and all science classes were moved across campus. The Peter White structure was demolished in 1972–1973. In late 1998, it was discovered that some of the original scientific equipment and lab tables had been transferred to West Science and were saved for future displays. (Minutes 08/13/1901; NNN 10/21/1925; MJ 07/04/1941; NN 03/05/1956)

Peter White Lounge: When the University Center was renovated in 1993–1994, President William Vandament created the Lounge for student use with money from the Frazier family, descendants of Peter White. The Board of Control approved the name of the lounge on February 8, 1994. In the summer of 1995, it was decorated with a picture of Peter White, and many artifacts and pictures from old Kaye Hall were placed in the lounge. Since that time it has been the scene of memorial services, receptions and symposia. On the north wall, a large series of display cases trace the history of the University along with a series of pictures bought with money Peter White donated to the Art Department between 1905 and 1907.

Philosophy Department: The first Philosophy of Education classes were taught in 1923 and years following by President Emeritus James Kaye. Later, Hubert Bonner taught Philosophy and Ethics from 1931 to 1934. A small number of Philosophy courses were available through the History Department until 1966 when a Philosophy major was offered. During the 1950s and early 1960s, a member of what was then the Department of History and Social Sciences taught an occasional course in Philosophy. The situation was formalized in 1966, when Alastair

Craig was appointed as the first full-time member of the Department of Philosophy. David Dickson, the Dean of the School was his immediate supervisor because of his Humanities background. When Dr. Dickson left, his Associate Dean, chemist Thomas Griffith, became Dean, and Eugene Whitehouse from the Department of History was appointed as Associate Dean. Dr. Whitehouse then became Dr. Craig's supervisor.

A second member, Francis Lee, was added to the Department in 1968. After one year, Professor Lee left for another university, and Dr. Craig died shortly after. They were replaced by Donald Dreisbach in 1969 and James Greene in January 1971. David Cooper was added in the Fall of 1971, bringing the Department up to its current permanent membership of three faculty. All three of the faculty in the Department have doctorates, and all three have been promoted to the rank of full Professor. There have been no changes in permanent, full-time staff since then.

Dr. Whitehouse's title gradually evolved from unofficial supervisor to Acting Head of the Department. Eventually, it was decided to name him "permanent" Head of the Department in 1981. None of these de jure changes brought any significant de facto ones except, perhaps, that the Head is somewhat more likely to get his mail in that capacity directly, without undue delay. This situation continued until July 1, 1994, when Dr. Whitehouse resigned as Associate Dean and returned to the Department of History. At that time, Dr. Barry L. Knight, head of the Department of History was queried as to whether or not he wanted to become the head of the Department of Philosophy. As a result, beginning in July 1995, the Department had a new head when it was reattached to the History Department. At this time, the department moved from offices in Carey Hall to Magers Hall within the confines of the Department of History.

Currently the Philosophy department has two major mission functions. First, the department offers a major and minor to those who wish to specialize in Philosophy. Second, courses are offered for students wishing to elect Philosophy courses to fulfill liberal studies requirements. The Philosophy department also sponsors an interdisciplinary program in Religious Studies.

Department Heads: Eugene Whitehouse, 1977–1995; Barry Knight, 1995–present. (*Bulletins; The 1996–97 University Profile*, 1:144–150)
Michelle Kangas

Physical Education Instructional Facility: See: PEIF Building

Physical Sciences, Department of: From 1899 to 1911, this department consisted of biology, chemistry and physics and was known as the Department of Physical Sciences. In 1911, biology split into its own department called the Department of Natural Sciences (*See*: Biology).

Classes were taught in the Peter White Science Hall, which had been constructed in 1902. From the beginning, the department offered labs in the physical, botanical, zoological, and chemical sciences. In the early days "General Geology" was also offered in this department. By 1910, the *Bulletin* could boast that the labs were "second to none among western normal schools." At this time, the lab fees were: chemistry, $1.00, and 50¢ each for botany, physics and zoology.

Although Northern offered a vast selection of science courses, the Bachelor of Science degree was not offered until 1926. This was eight years after the Bachelor of Arts was first offered in 1918. As the years passed, the selection expanded into classes such as the History of Chemistry, Twentieth Century Physics, Radio Communication, Heat, Hygiene and Bacteriology, as reported in the 1935–1936 *Bulletin*.

As Northern expanded in the 1960s, changes were made in this department. In 1962, the two departments separated and became independent. (*See*: *Chemistry* and *Physics*).

Department chairs: William McCracken, 1899–1907; Thomas C. Hebb, 1907–1916; Walter Ferguson Lewis, 1917–1931; Dell S. Garby, 1931–1947; Lucian F. Hunt, 1947–1962.

Physics, Department of: Between 1899 and 1962, physics was taught under the label "Physical Sciences." Classes were taught in the Peter White Hall of Science, which was remodeled in the fifties. By the early sixties, it was obvious that a new facility was badly needed, and the West Science Building was constructed and opened in 1966.

The Physics faculty has remained around five members since the 1960s. The introduction of computer courses (*See*: *Computers*), which occurred during the mid-1970s, was a big change in the department. In 1972, the Sprinkle (*See separate entry*) telescope was donated to the University and an observatory was placed in operation three years later. The addition of an astronomy class had drawn non-majors to lectures of 50–80 students. One of the big recent changes to the department has been courses for majors and minors are now primarily lab courses instead of lectures. The Physics Department has never had a graduate program. In 1997, the Physics Department offered courses for majors and minors and background work in other curricula: engineering, allied health sciences, biology, chemistry and education. Finally, the department offers courses for the natural sciences/mathematics requirement in Liberal Studies.

Department chairs and heads: Francis Cooke, 1962; Donald H. Baker 1962–1968; Robert R. Wagner, 1968–1976; William W. Ralph, 1976–1979; Duane K. Fowler, 1979–1987; Ralph, (interim) 1987–1988; Fowler, 1988–present. (Source: *The 1996–97 University Profile*, 1:151–157) Jay Brennan

Pierce, John D.: (1797–1882) A New England clergyman who came to Michigan as a frontier missionary. He was named the first superintendent of public instruction (1836–1841) and he was the first independent administrator of education under a state constitution in the United States.

During his tenure in office, Pierce drew up plans for the organization and support of a system of primary schools, provided for the establishment of the University of Michigan, and set up procedures for the sale of lands granted to the territory for the support of public education. Pierce organized the state into school districts and helped formulate state school laws that required appointment of school inspectors, provided for a library in each district, governed the length of schooling and established qualifications for teachers. Ground plans for a model schoolhouse that were used throughout Michigan were drawn up by him. His plan for the state university provided for a board of regents, establishment of the first three academic departments and the initiation of a building program. Pierce started and edited *The Journal of Education* (1838–1840) which was the first common school journal in the Midwest. Once out office, he supported legislation that established the state's first normal school, which later became Eastern Michigan University (1849). In 1927 the training school on campus was named in honor of him. *See*: *John D. Pierce School*. (Kim Sebaly. "John David Pierce" in John F. Ohles, ed. *Biographical Dictionary of American Educators*. vol. 2 (Westport, CT: Greenwood Press, 1978), 1034–1035)

Pin, Official: In the spring of 1907, a committee composed of faculty and students met to review designs for a school pin, "to be recognized for all time as the official pin worn only by members of the senior class, alumni, and members of the faculty."

The pin was small and consisted of the central figures of the Michigan state seal, in gold, surrounded by a narrow band of olive upon which were the words, "Northern Michigan State Normal" in gold letters. The outer edge was gold, irregular in form, as in the case of a seal stamped on wax.

From the evidence available, Northern was the first Michigan institution to adopt an official emblem for such a purpose. The design was adopted, samples were procured and a supply was ordered. (MJ 04/13/1907)

Pine Tree Logo: *See: Signature*

Pingree, Hazen Stuart: (1840–1901) Pingree was the Republican governor of Michigan (1897–1900) who signed the bill which created Northern State Normal School on April 28, 1899. He was known for his progressive attitude and programs which pre-dated the Progressive Era.

Placement Office: *See: JOBSearch*

Planning and Analytical Studies, Office of: The origins of this office go back to the Harden years when the Office of Institutional Research was created in 1964 and Kalmer Stordahl was its founding director. The North Central Accreditation report for 1984 noted that Northern's lack of a management information system and informational infrastructure hindered its ability to plan. As a result, in the following year the Division of Institutional Research and Planning was created. The office was also known as the Office of Institutional Research and Management Information Systems, and Planning and Analytical Studies.

The mission of the office is to develop and oversee the University's long-range planning processes and to ensure the integration of budget and planning. This office provides primary administrative support to the faculty and staff, who are directly responsible for student learning and development. The office is also concerned with the development of databases, analytical tools and policy studies in support of the planning process and decision making.

The office was moved from Human Resources to Finance and Administration in October 1992. Paul Duby became associate vice president and he is assisted by R. Gavin Leach, the Budget Director.

Directors: Kalmer Stordahl, 1964–1984; Paul B. Duby, 1984–1992; vice president 1992–present. (*The 1996–97 University Profile*, 2:82–87) Alisa Koski

Plant Operations, Department of: The Department is in charge of the operation of the Central Heating Plant and bringing heat and air conditioning to all of the buildings on campus. In a larger arena, it is in charge of architectural, electrical, custodial and grounds maintenance on campus. Over the last century, this department has developed from a custodian hired to tend classes at Old City Hall to a staff of nearly ninety. (*The 1996–97 University Profile*, 2:70–75)

Playboy Magazine: In Northern folklore, there is a story that says Northern was highlighted in an issue of *Playboy* in the late 1960s as a major party school in the nation. A search of these issues did not uncover such a story.

Polaris: *See: Annual*

Police Academy: The U.P. Law Enforcement Development Center, a consortium of police agencies and the NMU Criminal Justice Department, announced an agreement with the Sawyer Base Conversion Authority to establish a police academy on the former base in early March 1995. The authority agreed to lease the Sawyer pistol and rifle firing range plus several adjacent buildings. The 17-week course prepares students for police work in any of the 50 states and started on July 1, 1995. Today the program is headed by Ken Chant, director of the Department of Public Safety and Police Services and the Center. (MJ 03/04/1995)

Political Science, Department of: Before 1962, Political Science courses were offered through the History and Social Science Departments. On July 14, 1899, the State Board of Education created a position in History and Civics which was filled by Principal Dwight Waldo. This was the forerunner of the Department.

Today, the Political Science department involves four major areas of responsibility: 1. Undergraduate programs in fields of Political Science, Pre-Law, Public Administration, and Education are designed to develop talented and ethical leaders and educators; 2. Liberal arts courses are offered to create awareness and understanding of political processes; 3. Graduate programs in Public Administration prepare individuals for government and non-profit agency employment; 4. The department assists in the study and resolution of political and administrative problems on local, state and regional levels.

Department heads: Miodrag Georgevich, 1962–1975; Robert Kulisheck, 1976–1998; Steven Nelson, (Acting) 1998–present. *(Bulletins;* Larry Harness, The Political Science Department," (1995), UA; *(The 1996–97 University Profile,* 1:158–164) Michelle Kangas

Posthumously Awarded and other Degrees: Over the years the University has presented the relatives of deceased students who did not receive their degrees with a posthumous degree. Some individuals who were awarded degrees: Nancy Devlin Kennedy (1992, M.A.); Colby B. Trinka (1995, B.S. with Honors); Donna Kuster (1998, B.S.).

On July 2, 1998, the University awarded 102-year-old, Cecelia Loch Parrott of Stephenson, Michigan an honorary baccalaureate degree. The ceremony was attended by university officials and staff: President Bailey; board members Sam Benedict, Robert Berube and Ellwood Mattson; Russell M. Magnaghi and Connie Williams. It was also witnessed by dozens of relatives and friends.

Powwow: The first Native American powwows were held on campus in the 1970s. Since 1991, the "Learning to Walk Together" powwow, sponsored by the Anishinabe Club, has been held. Singing, dancing, visiting and observing are all part of the celebration. Crafts are also sold.

Practical Nursing, Department of: Practical Nursing at Northern began in 1958. It was a one-year training course designed to provide school and clinical training that would result in the mastery of knowledge and skills needed to perform the duties of a practical nurse. In 1990, the Practical Nursing program went from giving a nonacademic diploma to an academic certificate program. In 1992, the director's title was changed to a department head.

Today, the program prepares practical nurses to provide care to patients in hospitals, nursing homes, physician's offices, home health care agencies and health clinics. A surgical technology program is also offered and prepares graduates to assist surgeons and other members of the operating team. One-year certificates are offered. In 1984, the department moved into the D.J. Jacobetti center.

Heads, Directors, Coordinators: Elizabeth Vickers, (director) 1957–1961; Marion Judish, (assistant director) 1961–1962, (director) 1962–1964; Marion Ferzacca, (supervisor) 1964–1966; Therese Johnson, (supervisor) 1966–1971; 1971–1984 Mary Sundberg, (coordinator) 1971–1984); 1984–1986 Marjorie Vidlund, (head) 1984–1986); Marjorie Vidlund, (cluster manager) 1986–1989, (director) 1989–1991 Marjorie Vidlund; Gloria Clocklin, (director) 1991–1992, (head) 1992–1995; Cheryl Karvonen, (director) 1995–present. (*Bulletins*; *The 1996–97 University Profile*, 1:267–273) Michelle Kangas

Pre-Professional Programs at NMU: As early as 1939, two and four year programs were offered as preparatory courses for professional study based on the requirements of the University of Michigan. Pre-professional programs in 1939 included Dentistry, Engineering, Forestry, Law, Medicine, Nursing and Pharmacy. In 1973, the pre-medical program was established. Today, pre-professional programs offered at NMU include Architecture, Dental, Engineering, Law, Medical, Optometry, Pharmacy and Veterinary. The Art and Design, Chemistry, Physics, Biology and Political Science departments assist in preparing students for professional study. Michelle Kangas

Presidential Homes: Until 1954, the president of Northern Michigan University lived in a variety of locations and circumstances. The first principal, Dwight B. Waldo (1899–1904) with his wife and two children rented the Richard Parker home at 422 East Ohio Street. With the completion of the Longyear Dormitory in 1900, they moved into the dorm. He was followed by James Kaye (1904–1923) who lived in a home at 629 High Street.

By 1922, the State Board of Education gave serious consideration to provide presidents of the normal schools with a residence. On March 11, 1922, after considerable discussion, the Board unanimously adopted the resolution that residences for the four presidents be provided. Unfortunately, the State Administration Board of Michigan did not act on the matter and nothing came of this resolution.

As a result, bachelor President Munson (1923–1933) rented rooms at 322 E. Ridge Street. Both Webster Pearce (1933–1940) and Henry Tape (1940–1951) lived with their families at 1312 Presque Isle, across the street from the college. This home had been constructed by mathematics professor John Faught around 1903. Seven years later it remained the only house on Presque Isle and over the years it was occupied by Northern faculty members. Between 1948 and 1954, the Tapes lived in an apartment at 416 E. Hewitt.

The State Board of Education decided to construct the first state-owned presidential residence in the early 1950s. In June 1952, authorization was given to appraise a site for the new home. Officials at Northern consulted about an architect beginning in June 1953, and in August the decision was made. In late 1954, the new home at 537 W. Kaye (across the street from the south entrance of the University Center) was completed and ready for occupancy. The architect was Harry W. Gjelsteen and the contractor was Arthur Mercure. It consisted of three bedrooms, kitchen, dining room, study, living room, and partial basement (4,065 square feet). It was occupied by the Tapes, Hardens, Johnsons and Jamriches.

Over the years, the residence went through a number of changes. In January 1969, approval was given by the Board to construct an addition on the home, which was undertaken by contractors LaBonte and Adams. With the proposed expansion of Marquette General Hospital onto the site, in October 1978, the Board authorized a new residence on Center Street.

In July 1979, the Board moved to accept the bid of Dickinson Homes and Quality Concrete for the construction of the new residence. The structure, constructed by Dickinson Homes in Iron Mountain, was modular in form and trucked to the site. It is located at 1440 Center Street and was first occupied by the Jamriches. On November 15, 1979, the Board of Control named the new residence after President James H.B. Kaye and officially called it "Kaye House."

First occupied in 1980, it consists of 7,183 square feet on two floors. It is surrounded by gardens and a two-acre rustic garden to the north of the residence. It is frequently used by the president for official dinners and receptions. Since 1980, it has been occupied by the Jamriches,

Appleberrys, Vandaments and Baileys. In the fall of 1997, important renovations were belatedly made to the residence. (Source: Marquette City Directories; Minutes SBE, 1922; NCN 11/08/1954; News release 11/15/1979)

Presidential Longevity:

19 years (1904–1923) James B.H. Kaye—retired and taught for an additional 9 years at NMU

16 years (1940–1956) Henry A. Tape—retired

15 years (1968–1983) John X. Jamrich—retired

11 years (1956–1967) Edgar L. Harden—became president of Story Auto and Michigan State University President

10 years (1923–1933) John M. Munson—became president of Eastern Michigan University

8 years (1983–1991) James L. Appleberry—became president of the American Collegiate Association

7 years (1933–1940) Webster H. Pearce—died in office

6 years (1991–1997) William E. Vandament—retired

5 years (1899–1904) Dwight B. Waldo—became president of Western Michigan University

10 months (Sept. 1, 1967–June 30, 1968) Ogden E. Johnson—retired

Presidential Receptions: Over the century, Northern presidents have held receptions. In June 1908, President James Kaye had a reception for the faculty and students at his home at Hewitt and High Streets. After 1915, receptions were held in the foyer of Kaye Hall. The location moved to the Lee Hall ballroom after 1949, and to the University Center in the 1960s. Mrs. Harden invited all new freshman women to a reception in her home. The most elaborate receptions held in recent years were those orchestrated by Patricia Appleberry between 1983 and 1990. Some of them had themes and others were grand picnics held in front of Carey Hall. Today, the President has an official reception for all university personnel in late August at the University Center.

President's Award for Distinguished Citizenship: See: Distinguished Citizenship

President's Ball: First presented in 1991, the ball honors the President of the University. The semi-formal dinner and dance was originally held in February and is now held in March. It is attended by students, faculty and staff. In 1997, some students became so involved with the affair that dance lessons were sold out in preparation for the dance.

President's Division: The Division was established during the Appleberry Administration (1983–1991). Under it, the mission of the President of the University is to serve, at the pleasure of the Board of Control, as the Chief Executive Officer of the institution. As such, the President is charged with the development of administrative policies, programs and procedures to guide the operations of the University. The President also implements and directs such policies as the Board of Control may adopt. The President provides leadership in areas of the educational growth and development of the institution, seeking and maintaining those accreditations which are deemed to be in the best interest of the University. The President serves as the chief spokesperson for the University in relations with various external constituencies, especially the State Legislature and the Office of the Governor, as well as alumni, individual and group donors, and other support groups.

The Division is composed of Vice Presidents for Academic Affairs, Student Affairs, Finance & Administration, University Relations; Director of Public Safety, Athletic Director, Affirmative Action Officer and Internal Auditor. (*The 1996–97 University Profile*, 2:8–14)

President's Lifetime Achievement Award (LAA): As Northern marked its Centennial observance this award was created and approved by the Board of Control on October 16, 1998. The LAA recognizes an individual whose lifetime is truly outstanding, marked by a rich and enduring body of work in any of a number of endeavors. The recipient should have some connection with Northern or with the Upper Peninsula but does not have to be a resident of the area. The first award will be presented at spring commencement 1999.

Presidents: Dwight B. Waldo (1899-1904); James H. B. Kaye (1904–1923); John M. Munson (1923-1933); Webster H. Pearce (1933–1940); Henry A. Tape (1940-1956); Edgar L. Harden (1956–1967); Ogden E. Johnson (1967–1968); John X. Jamrich (1968–1983); James B. Appleberry (1983–1991); William E. Vandament (1991–1997); Judith I. Bailey (1997–present).

Presidents, Acting: Over the years, for a variety of reasons, individuals have been made acting president for a temporary period of time. Professor J. E. Lautner was officially appointed on July 13, 1921 by the State Board of Education in the absence of President Kaye. During the latter part of President Tape's tenure when he was ill, Walter Gries a member of the Board of Education, filled the position. Jack Rombouts served as acting president for Dr. Jamrich, and in the fall of 1974 when President Jamrich was on a trip of South Africa, the then provost, Robert Glenn served as acting president.

Press, Northern Michigan University: *See*: *Northern Michigan University Press*

Preston, Bessie Madeline: (September 1, 1883–June 19, 1904) Marquette native and daughter of a Jamaican barber, Ms. Preston was the first graduate of color from Northern in 1903. She taught mathematics at Booker T. Washington's Tuskegee Institute, but died thirteen months after graduation.

Preston, Charlotte "Lottie": (August 10, 1881–May 19, 1901) Marquette native and daughter of a Jamaican barber. She would have been the first graduate of color from Northern if death by consumption had not intervened.

Principals: When Northern Normal was established, the head of the institution was known as the "principal." At this early period, the State Board, acting under the provision of the law, made the heads of the Marquette and Mt. Pleasant Normals principals under the jurisdiction of the "president" of the Ypsilanti Normal. When the Marquette citizens learned of this, they were disgruntled at having a school (as they thought) be merely a feeder for the Ypsilanti Normal. They felt that they had been deceived and had won only an empty victory.

It was not until 1908 that the heads of the Normal schools were called "presidents." Northern's principals: Dwight B. Waldo, 1899–1904; James H. B. Kaye, 1904–1908.

Printing: At first, any printing that was needed on campus was contracted out to local print shops. The faculty used mimeograph machines, which produced copies with purple print. The use of these machines continued until the early 1970s when they were gradually replaced by xerox machines.

As Northern developed in the late 1950s, there was a change in approach. The college was moving toward becoming an independent institution with its own facilities. As a result, in November 1957, the college purchased the printing equipment, paper stock and other supplies from the Iron Ore Printing Company in Ishpeming which had published the *Iron Ore* newspaper. Since that time, Northern has had a self-printing capacity.

Printing is presently under Administrative Information Technology, which is a part of the Finance and Administration Division. After 1975, the printing shop was located on the first floor and basement of Cohodas Administration Building. In the early 1990s, a satellite station was located in Magers Hall. Today the print shop produces a wide variety of brochures, posters, programs and just about anything that an individual would need. (*The 1996–97 University Profile*, 2:46–51)

Prison: See: Marquette Branch Prison

Production and Audio-Visual Services Department: Under Learning Resources, the Department has a two-fold mission. Production/Operations provides WNMU-FM and WNMU-TV public broadcasting operations and University administration with television, and audio and graphics services. The Department produces television programs for WNMU-TV including major documentaries which have been distributed regionally and nationally, weekly series, and four major fund raising events annually. These have included: NMU commencement, High School Bowl, Media Meet, "Ask The Doctors," "What's Up?" and Public Eye News. It has also produced documentaries highlighting topics of community and regional interest, such as *Superior Destiny*, *Superior Celebration* and *Northern at 100: A Century of Memories*.

The Department also produced selected videos in support of University internal communications, marketing, student and faculty recruitment and alumni development. Some of these productions have included "Northern Notebook," the annual alumni videos, the faculty recruitment program and videos for the U.S. Olympic Education Center. This also includes Northern video promo for airing on Public TV 13 and regional television stations. All productions must conform to RS-170A broadcast standards. The graphics unit produces visual materials for print, video and live presentations. In 1996 this unit produced the first official Northern flag from a vague description in the minutes of the State Board of Education. Two years, later Melinda Stamp designed the Centennial banners which have been placed around campus and have become popular icons of the Centennial celebration.

Audio-Visual Services is responsible for planning, developing and executing a wide range of technological activities which support Northern's administrative and public service missions. This unit draws heavily on support from all other areas of the Learning Resources Division. (*The 1996–97 University Profile*, 2:234–239)

Prophecy, Peter White: When South or Longyear Hall was dedicated on July 3, 1900, Peter White gave a speech, "The Northern Normal School and the Struggle to Get It." Towards the end of it, he made an interesting prophecy about Northern's future: "As our efforts here for establishing this school took twenty-five years another generation will be here then, trained to desire liberal education and to achieve it by graduates and teachers of this school. These buildings then will be here and there will be more of them. This will be as a result of slow and careful selection and addition, a comfortably housed library, distinct from the one in Town, of 20,000 volumes. There will be five hundred of our graduates at work in our schools, and one thousand students in the school itself. There will be a gymnasium and careful training in reasonable physical culture and practical hygiene. There will be laboratories for botany, chemistry and physics, and a small but well-equipped observatory. The U.S. Weather observatory will be at this school. There will be an Assembly Hall with a fine pipe organ, and notable examples of the arts will adorn the walls, corridors and pedestals. The school will have been kept free from harmful political influences, and have taught the school boards how to choose teachers without reference to favoritism and partisan influence.

"A true progressive conservatism will have been maintained and manly men and womanly women, all of ripe culture will have been always found in charge of every department of the school. The courses will have been lengthened to four years of advanced study beyond the High School curriculum, and the degree of the school be known and respected at least throughout the State. If you think I am too sanguine, look at the past year and multiply it by 25 and you will see I am modesty itself, as a prophet." Most of what Peter White said came true within a few years. (UA; Peter White Papers, Detroit Public Library, microfilm Reel 3 [1969] Part 83, Peter White Public Library).

Propylon Nonprofit Housing Corporation: In July 1978, members of this nonprofit legal entity approached the Board of Control to develop a residence facility for up to twelve severely physically handicapped. Specifically they were seeking a parcel of land located to the northwest of the West Science Building and between Elizabeth Harden Circle Drive and Norway Street. By 1985, the land was exchanged and construction was soon begun. The facility allows residents to attend classes at Northern if they desire.

Provost: This position was created in May 1974 by the Board of Control. The provost was considered the ranking officer of the institution directly below the president. He was responsible for all educational and academic activity within and outside the University. He acted in the president's name and his authority when the president might be absent from campus. Robert Glenn, the former dean of the College of Arts and Sciences, who began his duties on July 1, 1974 was to date the only individual to hold this position. In 1984, when Alan Donovan replaced Glenn, the position of provost was abolished and returned to that of Vice President for Academic Affairs.

Psychology, Department of: When Northern opened, Psychology, as part of Education, was offered to prepare future teachers for "everyday human contact." Courses and faculty were limited. In 1957, Dr. Jean Rutherford came to Northern and the department began to grow. The first psychology major was offered in 1964 and old courses were eliminated and new ones added. By 1968 the department had become independent of the Education Department.

In 1972, Dr. Pryse Duerfeldt became head of the department. During his 25-year tenure, he led the department in creating a student-oriented program which produced students who were well prepared for the next stage of their careers. Three program tracks were developed and implemented: a General Program for students with a general liberal arts focus, a Program for graduate school-bound students and a Behavior

Technology emphasis. A fourth track, Community psychology was developed, but never implemented due to a lack of funding. All programs were founded on hard data and scientific methodology.

Faculty teaching, research and community work became augmented by student apprentices and these apprenticeships became an integral part of the teaching-learning process. In some years, nearly 60 percent of the graduates went on to graduate schools around the country. The department developed and regularly used evaluation methods for all aspects of the program so that advising, teaching, service, alumni placement and other functions were quantified and could be used by the department and by each faculty member both as a tool for improvement and a statement of performance. As a result, the department set an evaluation and outcome model that others could emulate. By using this program feedback and maintaining regular contact with and receiving feedback from its alumni, the department was able to continually reconsider and improve its programs, learning opportunities and the way in which they were offered.

Today, the department promotes the discovery, transmission, and application of the scientific principles of psychology within the University and the community. In the context of programs and courses that are nurtured by the data of current knowledge, direct student involvement in the process of research, teaching and service, and quality of advisement, that mission is interpreted to include: 1) educate students to think critically and creatively about both the practical and theoretical aspects of the science of psychology; 2) advancing the frontiers of psychological science and communicating this science to the University and the community; and 3) preparing students for success in the next stage of their careers.

Also, the Psychology Department started the university's longest-running public colloquium. First opened on a weekly basis over 19 years ago, the Psychology Colloquia today continue on monthly and bi-weekly schedules.

Department Heads: Joel West, (acting) 1969–1970; John W. P. Ost, 1970–1972; Wilbert Berg, (acting) 1972; Pryse Duerfeldt, 1972–1997; Harry Whitaker, 1997–present. (*The 1996–97 University Profile*, 1:207–213; Jay Brennan, "Department of Psychology," (1995) UA; *Bulletins*) Michelle Kangas

Public Safety and Police Services, Department of: In the early days of Northern, the small complex did not need a special police force. In October of 1903, John Peters began work as the night watchman and assistant janitor at $45 per month. The head custodian oversaw the buildings and their safety.

On October 22, 1956, an agreement was entered into between Northern and the city of Marquette to deputize the college groundsmen and firemen in the heating plant. In March 1959, the *Northern News* noted that traffic violations would be referred to the on-campus traffic council. Then two months, later students conducted a spring raid consisting of a water fight and panty raid on Carey Hall. The city police were called and arrested six bystanders. This caused people to question the fact that only one night watchman protected a physical plant worth $13 million and there could be a dangerous demonstration by students. In the coming months, the Office of Plant Security, was created and C. Duane Stambaugh became the chief.

In February 1960, the first motor vehicle code developed by a student-faculty traffic committee, Stambaugh, and the state Board of Education was published (*See*: *Parking and Speeding on Campus*). Vehicle registration had come to Northern. Soon after the first parking meters appeared on campus as did ever expanding parking lots which had to be monitored. There was also general agreement that there was not enough parking on campus. As the number of students increased so did the need for better public security. New regulations went into effect by an expanding department.

Over the years, the department has undergone a series of name changes reflecting its direction. Called Campus Safety, the Board of Control changed its name to the Department of Public Safety and Police Services on July 11, 1979.

By 1997, the Department had under its jurisdiction: police services, escort services, crime prevention, fire prevention, Right to Know Training, lost and found, building security, vehicle registration, parking, and TTY-Hearing Impaired services.

Directors: C. Duane Stambaugh, 1959–1969; William Lyons, 1969–1979; Kenneth Chant, 1979–present. (*The 1996–97 University Profile* 2:33–38; NN 05/20/1959, 06/03/1959, 02/24/1960, 03/30/1960, 05/11/1960)

Public Services Division: In 1956, this division was created and continued Northern's traditional services to off-campus students and teachers through extension and correspondences courses which went back into the 1920s. It also expanded Northern's offerings in the field of vocational education by taking over the administration of the practical nursing training program from the Marquette Public Schools and combining the program with psychiatric aide training formerly offered by Newberry State Hospital.

The Division's Consultant in Management Development (first Kenneth Weller and later Bob Vanderburg) organized management training classes for employees of industrial, commercial, and service firms throughout the Upper Peninsula and at K. I. Sawyer Air Force Base. The employees of the city of Marquette were one of the first groups to complete the classes for supervisors. Courses in collective bargaining, mine safety, steward training, labor history and law were organized by Martin Duffy, the Labor Education coordinator. Edward Sell, the Administrative Teacher Trainer, provided assistance to forty-two school districts interested in improving their counseling and vocational education programs. The consultant in Community Development helped the communities of Manistique, Gladstone, and Baraga Counties to analyze their strengths and weaknesses and make plans for future development. At the end of the Division's first five years, the Annual Report, 1961–1962 showed that nearly 50,000 people had been helped by the Public Services Division that year as compared to about 14,000 in 1957. Nearly 22,000 people had attended conferences on campus. Several thousand high school students attended the science fair, forensic tournaments, basketball workshops, Senior Day, music festivals and Band Camp.

By 1961–1962, the Division had initiated certification programs for training and retraining unemployed and under-employed workers. These programs were made possible by funds from the Vocational Division of the Michigan Department of Public Instruction, and a grant of $126,000 from the Area Redevelopment Act for instruction, facilities and equipment, plus a loan of machine equipment by the National Industrial Equipment Reserve through the office of the Secretary of Defense.

By the mid-1960s, the office of the vice president for Public Services included: Business and Industrial Programs; Area Training Center (later this would become the Jacobetti Center); Experimental and Demonstration Project; Practical Nursing Center; Conferences; Field Courses and Correspondence; Community Services.

During President Harden's administration (1956-1967) the Public Services Division was involved in evaluating educational training programs along with Georgia Institute of Technology. Northern was involved because of its wide experience gained in the field of vocational and technical education, through the federally-supported Area Training Center and other manpower programs conducted on campus. These programs had been established by the Tumpane Company of Marietta, Georgia, a firm engaged in international operations. In 1968 and 1969 Claude Bosworth, vice president of the Public Services Division and Russell Adams went to Saudi Arabia and for the third time since 1965 to Thailand.

During the administrative reorganization under Dr. Jamrich, the Public Services Division became the Division of Continuing Education and Extension (*See separate entry*).

Director: Claude A. Bosworth, 1957–1970 (NN 07/28/1959; MJ 07/16/1969; Hilton, pp. 149–150) Miriam Hilton

Purchasing Department: The old State Board of Education Minutes show that the Board had to give its approval for even the smallest items that were purchased. Items were purchased in small amounts and stored around the campus. During the Harden administration (1956–1967) as the institution gained its University status, this Department emerged. Two of the original people connected with the development of the Department are Kathy Poisson and Robert Sibilsky.

The mission of the Purchasing Department and related areas, including Central Stores and Receiving, Equipment Inventory, Mail Services, Printing Services, Risk and Insurance, and the Transportation Office, is to provide the maximum service and administrative supports levels to faculty and staff who are directly responsible for student learning and development. (*The 1996–97 University Profile*, 2:88–93)

Quad I: Quad I consists of Spalding and Gant and Payne and Halverson Residence Halls. In 1956, Northern experienced an increased enrollment. In preparation for future housing, the University purchased land between Wright Street and Lincoln Avenue around the National Guard Armory. Swanson and Associates of Birmingham, Michigan were the architects while the Caspian Construction Company in Caspian, Michigan were the builders. Spalding and Gant halls make up the "Quad I" area and cost $2,860,000.00 combined. In 1964 the first half of Quad I was completed with Gant and Spalding Halls equally sharing 112,080 square feet. Both halls were dedicated on November 22, 1964. In the summer of 1972, the University opened both halls to visitors to rent as an option instead of staying at a hotel. This was met with strong opposition from local innkeepers and was halted.

During the following year, 1965, Payne and Halverson Residence Halls were completed, totaling 111,870 square feet. They were dedicated on October 3, 1965. (NMU Building Survey; NN 01/22/1958, 06/30/1972) Alisa Koski

Quad II: Quad II consists of Magers and Meyland, Hunt and Van Antwerp Halls. The first two halls totaling 117,410 square feet were completed in 1966 and dedicated on October 16. Hunt and Van Antwerp Halls were completed in 1967 and dedicated on June 9, 1968. The latter halls totaled 117,410 square feet and cost $6 million.

With the decline in enrollments, part of the Magers-Meyland complex was closed in 1980s and put into mothball status with a few rooms used for office space. Phase I renovations were begun on Magers and the first floor was occupied by: Economics, History, Academic Senate, AAUP, and Education in the fall of 1988. In 1989 construction was renewed and an essential elevator installed. The Phase II renovation project was completed in 1991 and the entire building opened to the A&S Dean's office, Business, Language, Political Science and Nursing. This renovation project cost $2,100,000.

The Meyland portion houses the U.S. Olympic Education Center. The offices are located here as is the lobby and rooms for the visiting athletes.

The Quill: This was a magazine that was first published on November 25, 1914 with Earle M. Parker as the editor. It was a general information and literary magazine. It was hoped that *The Quill* would "stick and serve an end quite beyond its comprehension." The last issue was published in July 1918 and was followed by the newspaper, *Northern Normal News*. (*The Quill* 11/25/1914) *See*: *Newspapers*

Quonset Hut: At the end of World War II with an anticipated influx of students, President Henry Tape negotiated with the U.S. Army in San Francisco to purchase two Quonset huts as war surplus material. They were used as warehouses in connection with planned veterans' housing which was underway by late November 1946. They were located midway between Cohodas and the University Center.

These structures were used for a variety of purposes, but were allowed to deteriorate. One was attached to the old cafeteria and another was attached to Kaye Hall and in 1965 was used by the chemistry department. The hut attached to the old cafeteria in its latter years was used for its toilet facilities and for storage. By the late 1960s, they remained a link with World War II and similar structures were found on campuses across the country. The final remains of the Quonset huts were removed with the demolition of the Kaye Hall complex and the construction of the west parking lot in 1972. (NCN 11/27/1946)

Radio Station: The first radio station on campus was WBI. It was a short-wave radio station which started operations in early January 1922. The station was initiated by President Kaye on January 25. It was operated by Harry Bottrell of Ishpeming, a former United States Navy wireless operator. Besides receiving broadcasts from Pittsburgh and Chicago, it broadcast basketball tournament scores. (NNN 02/15/1922; NMU Archives) *See*: *WNMU-FM*

The Raven: Female student disk jockey who in 1994–1995 had a popular radio program on WUPX. Characterized by her jet black hair and black painted nails, she was the delight of the air waves and received mail from inmates at the Marquette Branch Prison. Her identity remains a mystery.

Recreational Facilities and Services: This service was formed in the spring of 1993. An administrative department, its purpose is to provide Northern students and the community with facilities and services used for recreation. The department is responsible for the daily operation of Hedgcock Fieldhouse, the Physical Education Instructional Facility (PEIF) and the Superior Dome. The department provides student employment opportunities. Services provided to the public include membership programs to the facilities, intramural and informal athletic opportunities and non-credit instructional programs. Other services include banquet and conference space. The staff includes a director, four assistant directors and a support staff of secretarial and student employees. Within the facilities there are opportunities which include ice skating, tennis, wall climbing, swimming, aerobics, gymnastics, basketball, volleyball, football, and other sports.

Director: Kenneth Godfrey, 1993–present. (Source: Paper by Steve Sickle, "Recreational Facilities," UA; *The 1996–97 University Profile*, 1:35–40). Michelle Kangas

Registrar's Office: The registrar is responsible for registering students, keeping academic records and corresponding with applicants and evaluating their credentials. The first Registrar at Northern was Doris I. Bowron, who also served as secretary. In 1915 she had the title "Secretary and Registrar." By 1924, Bowron's title was simply "Registrar," and she performed the duties of this position only.

The Registrar is responsible for keeping accurate student records by verifying that students meet degree requirements, and by monitoring the records to make them available for the student's use. The Registrar is also responsible for registration, scheduling, transfer credit evaluations, publishing bulletins and course schedules, releasing Grade Point Averages for the Dean's List, transcripts, grades, attendance records, degree audits, advance placement exams, and sending records which verify financial and athletic eligibility. The newsletter of the Registrar's office is *Update*.

Registrars: Doris I. Bowron, 1915–1924; Alma Olson 1924–1926; Luther O. Gant, 1926–1960; Clarence Bjork, 1960–1968; James Hoffman, 1968–1971; Harry Rajala, 1971–1989; Gerald Williams, 1989–1994; Marilyn Robbert, 1994-present. (David Buchanan, "Registrar's Office," (1995) UA; *Bulletins*; *The 1996–97 University Profile*, 1:41–46) Michelle Kangas

Reserve Officer Training Corps also ROTC: See: *Military Science, Department of*

Residence Centers: Over the years as part of Northern's commitment to Public Service, residence centers have been created at various locations around the Upper Peninsula. On January 21, 1952 the State Board of Education considered approving Sault Ste. Marie as a center for

Curriculum Problems 408. In the 1960s, centers were established at K. I. Sawyer and Kincheloe Air Force Bases, Iron Mountain-Kingsford. By the late 1980s, many of these centers were closed. It was not until the presidency of Dr. Bailey that plans were developed to open or re-open Centers in Escanaba, Iron Mountain, Ironwood and Sault Ste. Marie.

Residence Hall Governments, and University Apartment Advisory Boards: These governments are formed all over campus. They are designed to build a strong community and a comfortable living environment by planning activities for their community members. Through the government, students can socialize in individual living areas as well.

Resolutions and Citations of Appreciation, Tribute, Welcome from the Board of Control: Under special circumstances the Board of Control passes special resolutions and citations for individuals and organizations.

Recipients: James B. Appleberry (5-91); Aspen Ridge School (National History Day; 10/98); Wilbert A. Berg (12-80); Governor James J. Blanchard (5-85); Claude A. Bosworth (condolences to wife, 1-70); Henry J. Bothwell (7-77); Jeanette S. Bowden (9-88); Sandra Bruce (5-97); Rev. Louis C. Cappo (9-71); Richard Celello (5-97); Cleveland Cliffs Iron Company (2-74, 8-75, 3-77); Sam M. Cohodas (8-70;2-74;7-75;9-78;7-80;8-85); Willard Cohodas (10-94); James M. Collins (5-91); Rick Comley and NMU Hockey Team (5-91); Walter C. Drevdahl (12-74); Leo F. Egan (4-95); Arnell A. Engstrom (10-68); Carl A. Erickson (6-72); Escanaba High School Football Team (12-81); John L. Farley (2-76); Republic of Finland (12-81); Thelma H. Flodin (3-73); Charles L. Follo (9-71); William R. Ford (9-71); Lincoln B. Frazier (3-76); Edwin O. George (5-70); Robert B. Glenn (4-84); Gogebic Community College (8-82); Thomas Griffith (7-71); John A. Hannah (2-69); Robert N. Hanson (4-84); Edgar L. Harden (8-67); Edward F. Havlik (4-95); Ralph E. Huhtala (3-77); Ishpeming High School Boys Basketball Team (4-95); Dominic J. Jacobetti (6-72, 2-80, 5-86); John X. Jamrich (9-72, 4-83); Hugh Jarvis (5-93); William K. Jensen (9-78); Richard Jones (2-96); The Kresge Foundation (9-78); Lake Superior and Ishpeming Railroad (8-66, 8-67); Lake Superior State College (10-71); Adrian N. Langius (10-73); Samuel Logan (5-93); James Malsack (7-89); Marquette General Hospital (7-81); Marquette High School Boys' Hockey Team (3-77; and 4-95); Marquette High School Debate Team (3-77); Marquette High School Girls' Basketball Team (2-77); John P. McGoff (1-72); Mr. and Mrs. John P. McGoff (1-78, 11-78);

Michigan Technological University (8-85); Microptics, Inc. (owner R. L. Kampe) (3-76); James W. Miller (12-73); Glenn G. Moreau (3-73); Mott Community College (6-73); Munising Board of Education (12-80); National Mine School for National History Day (10-97); Jacquelyn R. Nickerson (4-83) Allan L. Niemi (12-80); Susan D. Nine (5-91); Bishop Thomas L. Noa (3-77); Norway High School Football Team (12-80); School of Nursing (4-79); Byron W. Reeve (9-73); Margaret A. Rettig (4-82); William C. Roege, Jr. (9-72); Jack R. Rombouts (11-78); George W. Rusch (2-76); Bishop Charles A. Salatka (11-77); Sawyer Air Force Base (11-79, 5-81); Ellen Schreuder (5-97); Larry J. Sell (4-83); Lyle F. Shaw (5-91); Shiras Institute (4-77); Kenneth J. Shouldice (5-82); Leonard H. Snyder (9-80); Jacob A. Solin (5-71); Theodore B. Southerland (4-73); Stephenson High School (5-81); Roland S. Strolle (7-74); Suomi College (3-72, 5-82); Union National Bank and Trust Company (8-67); United Steelworkers of America Local 4950 (10-70); Leo Van Tassel (7-77); Willis F. Ward (1-66); Wayne State University (7-81); Bert J. Whalen (12-71); Wildcat Football Team (12-75, 12-81); WNMU-FM (12-88); Women's Swimming and Diving Team (4-82); Women's Volleyball Team (12-93); Katherine G. Wright (7-89)

Retirees and Service Awards Luncheons: The first luncheon was held on April 9, 1979. At the luncheons individuals are given a pin with the University logo and the number of years of service (10, 15, 20, 25, 30). If 35 or more, the individual received a pin with a diamond without a number. Beginning in 1998, watches are given in place of the latter.

Rhino Run: During the 1970s, sometimes in the middle of homecoming or other spirited times of the school year, "bar-hopping" or "pub-crawling" was made into a sport called the rhino run. The rhino run boasted candidates from various organizations who were renowned for being able to hold their liquor. They were pitted against each other in a bar-to-bar marathon. (NW 09/04/1975)

"The Right to Try": An early form of such a program was initiated by President Munson, who allowed World War I veterans to enter Northern even though they had not completed high school. A more progressive concept was developed and promoted by President Harden (1956–1967) after he had been influenced by the desperate conditions of the Great Depression in Iowa and after he read Thomas Minehan's *Boy and Girl Tramps of America* (New York 1934) which discussed the desperate social conditions of the Depression. He felt that everyone

needed a chance to improve their lives with a college education. It was a controversial concept on Northern's campus, and after Harden left it was gradually modified. However, the concept remains part of Northern's mission.

Ring: In the spring of 1957, the administration and the Student Council discussed plans for the creation of a Northern ring which would be purchased by students and alumni. On March 27, 1957 a contract was signed by Bob Tupper, president of the Student Council and Mrs. Christian, manager of the bookstore and representatives of L.G. Balfour Company. The first rings were available in the fall of 1957. (NCN 04/17/1957)

Ripley, Harvey G.: (December 24, 1878–August 23, 1959) Born in Sault Ste, Marie, he came to Northern as the first engineer after the central heating plant was constructed in 1908. Ripley was with the Maintenance Department (1909–1925) and then President Munson made him Superintendent of Buildings and Grounds and Stationary Engineer (1925–1945). He retired, and in 1951 he returned to work and stayed until 1957. The new heating plant at the corner of Wright Street and County Road 550 was dedicated in his honor on June 27, 1975. (MJ 07/25/1945; 08/24/1959)

Risk and Insurance Management Department: The Department has one Administrative/Professional employee with clerical support shared with the Purchasing staff. The manager is responsible for systematically identifying loss exposures, analyzing them and applying sound risk management techniques to them for the minimization of financial loss to the University. Additional risk management duties include the preparation of insurance specifications, negotiating and analyzing insurance coverages, contract review and claim adjusting. *See*: *Purchasing*

Roberts, Forest: (October 15, 1901–March 28, 1997). Roberts was born in Tabor, Iowa. He received his education at Graceland Junior College (1919–1921) and State University of Iowa (1921–1923) where he received his B.A. and master's degree. He also took graduate courses at the University of Wisconsin (1930) and the University of Southern California (1940–1941). He married Esther Ruth Salter of DePere, Wisconsin in June 1925.

Prior to coming to Northern, he taught at Graceland Junior College (1923–1927) and J. Sterling Morton High School in Cicero-Berwyn, Illinois (1928).

In the summer of 1928, he and his wife Esther moved to Marquette where Roberts began his tenure in the English Department at Northern. Through his efforts, the University established the Department of Speech (now Communication and Performance Studies) in 1955. Mr. Roberts was selected as department head. Affectionately known throughout the Upper Peninsula as "Mr. Speech," Professor Roberts was Northern's Director of Forensics (1928–1963), Director of the Upper Peninsula Forensic and Debate Leagues (1932–1964), manager of the U.P. Debate League (1933–1938) and served as an official Certification Officer for the Michigan State Department of Speech Pathology (1943–1964). He also established NMU's first courses in drama and directed many productions which toured the Upper Peninsula (1928–1943); he even acted several roles. His last Marquette performance was in "The Snow Goose" in 1988.

While at NMU, Mr. Roberts was also faculty chair of the Alumni Relations committee and a lifelong member of the Michigan Education Association which culminated in a term (1962–1965) on the MEA Board of Directors.

Active in community affairs, Mr. Roberts was co-founder and president (1936–1939) of the Marquette Community Concert Association and accepted many other community responsibilities.

In his retirement, the family maintained a home on Middle Island Point where he and his wife, Esther, spent the summer. She died in 1993. In the summer of 1994, Mr. Roberts conducted an oral interview detailing his life in the Upper Peninsula.

Northern Michigan University honored him on several occasions. In 1969 the Little Theatre was renamed in his honor (*See: Forest Roberts Theatre*). Then in 1987, he was awarded an honorary doctorate of Humane Letters. Finally the Forest A. Roberts Scholarship was established in his honor. (MJ 04/01/1997)

Roosevelt, Eleanor: (1884–1962) The wife of President Franklin Roosevelt visited the campus and presented a lecture which opened the assembly series on October 4, 1956. The title of her talk was, "Changes in the United States in the Past 50 Years," in which she stressed the role of United States leadership in the world. She talked to an audience that filled Kaye Hall Auditorium. Northern had negotiated for five years to get her to come to campus (MJ 10/04/1956; NN 10/10/1956)

Rose Ceremony: The Rose Ceremony was held each spring to honor senior girls graduating from Northern. Its origins went back to 1935. At that time, the daffodils from the centerpieces of the Student Girls' League Banquet were distributed to seniors at the end of the evening. The 1936 dinner program included the "Senior Flower Ceremony," and in 1937, each senior girl received a yellow rose. Though the banquet itself was discontinued in later years, the Rose Ceremony was continued until 1973. (NCN 04/10/53 pg.5; 05/15/1958; *Peninsulan* 1955; Hilton, p. 93) Michelle Kangas

Roundtable: As the administrative staff grew larger during the Harden administration, Dr. Harden regularly consulted with staff members who were invited to breakfast at his "Roundtable."

The RoundTable: This publication was produced by the History Department, under the editorship of Dr. Peter Slavcheff, between October 1991 and February 1993. It was funded from a variety of on-campus sources. The authors were students, faculty and staff. A complete set of back-issues is available in the University Archives.

Rugby Club: Known as the Moosemen, the non-varsity male rugby team was established in 1977 and continues to be popular. It is self-financed.

Rush: The Freshman-Senior Rush was a tradition at Northern going back to 1909. At that time, the students amused each other with rousing serenades, parades and even with capturing the refreshments of the other class parties. The rush usually took place in December, and they also had "Rally Day," at which time they all gathered in the auditorium and yelled for their home towns. Each tried to make their yell the loudest. The two classes carried this spirit of group competition even into sports. Until 1921, they had female basketball teams which joined the inter-class competition with the males.

The Freshman-Sophomore Rush became institutionalized in the 1920s and lasted until World War II. The Men's Union, the Student Girls' League and the Druids organized Rush Day to replace the traditional junior (first-year) hazing. On the appointed day (usually in June) the faculty and students went to Presque Isle Park for a lunch and then a series of games and contests. One event, called the bag tussle, included pushing the large medicine ball filled with hay from one territory to another with opponents seized and tied. The Rush was physically violent and involved kidnaping class officers, but was encouraged by the editors of the *Northern Normal News* as an important campus tradition. The Rush Day ended with a parade and dance in the evening.

In 1930, activities were severely curtailed because all of the students had just been vaccinated against smallpox. Dr. Lloyd Howe, campus physician, did not want to risk infection and that year the activities took on a more athletic approach. During the early 1930s, these events were recorded on film by Leslie Bourgeois and are housed in the University Archives.

This quaint event of the early 20th century ended in 1946. Actually Rush Day was temporarily halted by World War II. Then when students tried to revive it in 1946, it was found that most of the juniors were battle-hardened veterans who would destroy the regular seniors. In early May, the Men's Union and the Faculty Rush Committee met several times and decided to terminate this tradition. Furthermore, the whole concept of Rush had outlived its usefulness. (NCN 10/23/1935; NNN 05/19/1925, 06/17/1925, 05/18/1926; NCN 05/15/1946; Hilton, pp. 72–73).

Russell Thomas Fine Arts Building: The structure is the central unit of a three-unit complex which includes the Forest Roberts Theatre and the Wayne McClintock Building. Designed by the architectural firm of Warren Holmes Company of Lansing, the building was constructed by Herman Gundlach of Houghton at the cost of $2,650,000. Work began in September 1962 and was completed a year later. Originally known as the Fine and Practical Arts Building, it was dedicated to Russell Thomas on October 10, 1965. For two and one-half decades he had shared his love and knowledge of the arts with the students and faculty at Northern Michigan University. From the beginning, the music department has been located on the first floor. Until 1994 the former Home Economics Department was housed on the second floor, while the Art and Design Department continues to have classrooms on the third floor. The office of UP North Films was also located in the building. In 1995–1996, a $1.1 million project saw the second floor renovated to provide offices for the Department of Communication and Performance Studies (CAPS) faculty and construction of a forensics laboratory and an upgrade of classrooms and HVAC systems on the first and second floors. In the fall of 1996, the offices of CAPS were relocated in the building while Art & Design continued to use their facilities there. (MJ 04/15/1963; Dedication folder, 10/10/1965, UA)

St. Johns, Harold L.: Mr. St. Johns was the first male student to graduate from Northern in 1901.

Sauna: During FinnFest on August 10, 1996, the World's Largest Sauna was created on the north end of Memorial Field. Dave Savolainen of Negaunee planned the event. The blue and white tent was heated to 121 degrees by two 400,000 British thermal unit diesel-powered heaters, donated by American Eagle of Marquette. 658 people packed into the tent and records were sent to the *Guinness Book of World Records*. The old record of 304 participants had been set in Finland by sea scouts. (MJ 08/11/1996)

Sawyer, K. I. Air Force Base: The original airport and later the air base was named after Kenneth I. Sawyer, Marquette County road commissioner. Located some 16 miles southeast of Marquette the air base was originally the airport for Marquette County and was opened in early 1949 for commercial service. The Cold War soon changed the status of the airport. The Defense Department sought to expand the northern perimeter of its Air Force bases for national security. Some 14,000 acres were available. On January 24, 1955, the airport was leased to the Air Force for 99 years. The first commander of the base, Lt. Col. Robert Brocklehurst assumed his duties on April 8, 1956. Until the Strategic Air Command entered the scene in 1958, the county shared airport space with the Air Force.

Sawyer was the home of the 56th Fighter Wing, and there were two tenant units, the 4042 Strategic Wing and the Sault Ste. Marie Air Defense Sector. The Sault unit's SAGE Operation at Sawyer, manned by U.S. and Canadian airmen, was the Upper Peninsula's "nerve center" for NORAD's vast radar coverage of North America. On January 1, 1964, control of the base passed to SAC's 410th Bombardment Wing, and other units were either absorbed or deactivated.

The air base was a city of some 10,000 residents and the second largest community in the Upper Peninsula. From the earliest days, Northern played an active role maintaining cordial relations with the Air Force and offering numerous undergraduate and graduate academic programs at the Base for the airmen and their families. For many years, Northern held "K. I. Sawyer Appreciation Day" each fall in conjunction with a football game.

When the Base officially began its closing process in 1993, Northern began to notice the loss of several hundred students which had a negative impact on University enrollments. The Base was finally closed in 1995.

The Base Conversion Authority began at that time to start a reconversion of the site. Presidents Vandament and Bailey have served on committees to help the reconversion process. (Jim Carter, "Many Airports Served Marquette County during Nearly 90 Years of Aviation." *Marquette Monthly* No. 127 (May 1998):14–19)

Scholarships: Two categories of scholarships are available to Northern students. They consist of 15 University Scholarships, established by the Board of Control beginning in 1964. There are over 115 endowed scholarships. The first endowed scholarship honoring Margaret Wallace was created in 1934. In 1955 and 1959 scholarships were created honoring Gilbert L. Brown (Education) and James C. Bowman (English) and the others followed. For a complete list check the latest university *Bulletin*.

Sculpture Walk: The Walk is located to the southeast of Lee Hall. The concept was developed by Michael Cinelli and Wayne Francis of the Art and Design Department in 1994. They sent out invitations to artists throughout the United States to donate pieces to a Sculpture Walk. By the summer of 1995, seven sculptures were in place and others followed. Sculptors and their works include: Mara Admitz Scrupe (Washington, D.C.) "Garden IV: Desire" (steel, wood, mixed media, 14'h x 20'w x 25'l, 1995); Rico Eastman (Santa Fe, NM) "Geocon Spire" (steel form, 1997); Lorrie Goulet (New York) "Aurora" (limestone female form, 17" x 37" x 10", 1995); Suzanne Johnson (Detroit area; bronze female form, 3' x 2' x 2', not placed); Bill Leete (Marquette, MI; wood form, 1998); Sol LeWitt (New York) "Complex Form MH8, 1990" (painted aluminum, 5' x 4' x 4', 1995); Peter Maqua (Ontario) "Iron Spirit Lodge: The Western Door" (cast iron bowl and structure, 6' x 6'd, 1995); John Mishler (Chicago area) "Dream Walk" (welded steel form, 10' x 6' x 6', 1995); Mike Todd (Los Angeles) "Snake Charmer" (steel, 13' x 3' x 3', 1995); David Warner (Boston area), "Kinesthesia II" (welded steel, 8' x 3' x 3', 1995); Dale Wedig (Gwinn, MI) "Shape and Color" (painted steel, 10' x 3' x 3', 1997); Marvin Zehnder (Marquette, MI; ceramic form at main entrance of Lee Hall, 1997).

Seaborg, Glenn T.: (April 19, 1912–February 25, 1999) American chemist. An Ishpeming, Michigan native, Dr. Seaborg was a professor and later chancellor at the University of California, Berkeley. During World War II, he worked at the University of Chicago on the development of the atomic bomb. Later, he was chair (1961–1971) of the U.S. Atomic Energy Commission. He shared with Edwin M. McMillan the 1951 Nobel Prize in chemistry for work in transuranium elements. Seaborg is co-discoverer of the elements plutonium, americium, curium, berkelium, californium, einsteinium, fermium, mendelevium and nobelium. The Seaborg Center and Science Complex (*See separate entries*) are named after him. (MJ 02/26/1999)

Seaborg, Glenn T., Center for Teaching and Learning Science and Mathematics: Announcement of the creation of the Center was made in August 1985, and named after Dr. Glenn T. Seaborg, a native of Ishpeming, nuclear chemist and Nobel laureate. Its objectives are to provide: programs that support the teaching and learning of science and mathematics at all levels, but particularly in the elementary and secondary schools of the Upper Peninsula; mathematics and science teacher training; professional development opportunities for teachers; and enrichment experiences for students. It is connected with the College of Arts and Sciences and is housed in West Science.

The Center offers graduate programs in mathematics and science education and provides in-service, undergraduate and pre-college offerings in science, mathematics and computer education. As one of Michigan's state-supported centers for science and mathematics, the Seaborg Center offers leadership, student services, professional development, curriculum support, community outreach and resource clearinghouse services.

Directors: John O. Kiltinen, (interim) 1985–1986; Duane K. Fowler, (interim) 1986–1987; Phillip T. Larsen, 1987–1992; Fowler, (interim) 1992–1993; Peggy A. House, 1992–present.

Seaborg, Glenn T., Science Complex: The Complex will consist of a new science building on the northwest edge of the Academic Mall (*See separate entry*), together with a renovated and expanded Luther S. West Science building (*See separate entry*). This is the largest capital outlay for a structure on campus, and it will be the largest facility when completed.

The project design for the Complex was announced in December 1997, conducted by TMP Architects. On April 23, 1998 schematic designs were approved by the State of Michigan Legislative Joint Capital Outlay Subcommittee (JCOS). Dr. Glenn Seaborg, students and departments heads led a groundbreaking ceremony and the preliminary design was approved by JCOS on June 11, 1998. In September, the fast-track construction process began and Phase IA contract was awarded. A month, later Phase IA construction began. The project is scheduled to be completed in August 2001 when Northern moves into renovated West Science.

The new structure will consist of 128,000 gross square feet on three levels with a footprint 160 by 245 feet or 39,000 square feet with a height of 60 feet. The exterior finish material will be face brick with precast concrete accent. The renovated West Science Building will consist of 142,370 gross square feet on three levels with a footprint 207 by 234 feet plus a new Seaborg Center entrance measuring 51 x 103 feet and a height of 48 feet. The new greenhouse will be 32 x 41 feet.

The facilities will have academic occupancy of 2,825 persons and will house 171 faculty and academic department offices, 14 conference rooms, 6 computer labs, 124 laboratories, 30 classrooms and 84 support rooms. There will be an additional 100 to 150 parking spaces provided.

The cost of the structure and renovation is $46.9 million—$35.2 million from the State of Michigan; $11.7 million from NMU. Northern's share is to be secured through existing revenues, bond sales and fundraising from individuals, corporations and foundations. (*Seaborg Science Complex Fact Sheet,* 1998).

Seal of the University: In the years prior to 1961, the official Northern seal consisted of the state of Michigan seal surrounded by the name of the institution at any particular time. In 1960–1961 as Northern Michigan College was working towards university status, President Edgar Harden wanted an new and identifiable seal. He asked Clair Hekhuis, director of Information Services, to create the new seal that was distinctive of the developing university. As Hekhuis recounted in 1997, "I put a lot of thought into it and what I thought would be representative of what the University was doing and what we thought it should be doing." Gene Sinervo, an artist in the graphic design unit of the television station, provided the artistic talent.

Hekhuis was concerned that every symbol on the Seal would have meaning. He had discussed the matter with President Harden and got some of his general ideas before he actually began the project in earnest. The outline of the Upper Peninsula is prominent as it identifies the major service area of the University. In the center is the torch of learning. Below that is the block "N" which Hekhuis kept despite opposition that such lettering is never part of a seal. He thought it was important because Northern was seeking badly needed recognition. The stars stand for Northern's four-dimensional program of instruction: undergraduate and graduate studies, public service and research. The two circles symbolize continuity.

The design was developed by Hekhuis and Sinervo, and the finished product was presented to President Harden who approved of the design. It seems that as of May 3, 1961 the use of the official seal was in place. On March 28, 1962, the design was presented to the State Board of Education for its approval which was done on April 11. Thus there were two seals using the above-described design: one used by Northern Michigan College from May 3, 1961 to March 12, 1963 and the other from that date forward when Northern received university status.

At this time, there was no discussion of how the Seal would be colored. In 1986 this matter was dealt with by a Committee. For specific information on coloration and use of the seal contact the Learning Resources Division and the Communications and Marketing Office. (Clair Hekhuis interview, 07/07/1997, UA; NN 05/03/1961).

Senior Picnic: The picnic was an annual event held by the senior class, usually in late May. Families and guests were invited for the day. At this time graduation was in mid-June so the weather was pleasant for a picnic. In 1950, the event was held at Champion Beach on May 27. This tradition gradually declined and is no longer held. (NCN 04/26/1950).

Services Building: Originally this complex consisted of merely the Birdseye Building (*See separate entry*). In the mid-1990s, the new building was constructed and opened in the fall of 1996. It houses: Public Safety, Facilities Operations, Business Services, Engineering and Planning, Plant Operations and Central Receiving. It covers 88,439 square feet and cost $9.9 million.

75th Anniversary Celebration: President Jamrich appointed an executive committee to plan the commemoration of this anniversary which lasted from September 1974 to May 1975. Throughout the period, a series of lectures, exhibitions and events were held by various departments. A special Mid-Year Commencement Luncheon was held on December 21, 1974, which also concluded Finnish Culture Week. Leo O. Tuominen, Finnish ambassador to the United States gave the commencement address. It was during this time that the motto, "Working to Put Tomorrow in Good Hands" came into use on campus.

The elaborate 75th Anniversary Dinner was held on May 10, 1975 in the University Center (social hour) and C. B. Hedgcock Fieldhouse (banquet) attended by 1,846 guests and dignitaries. Included in the festivities were a five-foot high birthday cake with 75 candles, choral groups and an address, "The Biology of the 20th Century" by Leonore Romney. It was on this occasion that the President's Award for Distinguished Citizenship was presented to six Upper Peninsula residents: Guido Bonetti (Ishpeming), Albert Gazvoda (Calumet), Malcolm McNeil (Crystal Falls), Geraldine Noyes (Ironwood), President Raymond L. Smith of Michigan Technological University and Jean Worth (Escanaba).

Two publications were unveiled. They included, Miriam Hilton's *Northern Michigan University: The First 75 Years* and Luther West's volume of original poetry, "Reflections" which was presented to President Jamrich. (MJ 12/23/1974, 05/10/1975, 05/12/1975)

Severance Incentive Plan (SIP): The plan went into effect in 1996 and nearly 10 percent of Northern's employees retired under SIP in 1996–97. The plan was set up to provide the University with $2.6 million in salaries and benefits, but also created many open faculty positions to be filled. Of the 72 faculty and staff that participated in the SIP, 46 retired as of July 1, 1997. From 1992 to 2000, the College of

Arts and Science will replace 50 percent of its faculty. It was noted that overall, every tenure track position is approximately a million dollar investment. (NW 10/02/1997)

Sheard, Kevin: (1916–) Sheard was an associate professor of Business Administration from 1959 through 1963. He was a scholar on vexillology and academic heraldry and the author of *Academic Heraldry*, the only book of its kind on the topic and the first book published by the NMU Press (*See separate entry*). In 1962, he designed the masters degree academic hood along with the University flag. In 1996 he provided critical details on the University flag, and in May of the following year he presented the first official flag to the Board of Control and was honored for his services to the University.

Signature: The University has had two logos, or signatures, in recent years. A logo, as opposed to an official seal (*See separate entry*) must have a simple design, be readily recognizable and often convey the impressions of the institution it represents. The Board of Control adopted the logo as the official logo of the University at its meeting on July 17, 1975. The logo was designed by the Reverend Raymond Johnson, who at the time was pastor of St. Peter's Lutheran Church in New York Mills, Minnesota. Johnson was a Munising native who graduated from Northern in 1964, majoring in art and social services. His design was selected from over 30 entries in a logo contest which the then Board of Publications and Communications sponsored.

The logo bore the letters "NMU," and with the pine tree, identified the north where such trees of beauty predominate. It communicated a sense of serenity, simplicity, and majesty which are characteristic of the Upper Peninsula environment. The logo presented a growing pine, and the clear presentation of the uncharted future as represented by the open space surrounding the pine. The University is preparing the students for this future. The logo manifested the unity and cohesiveness of the University as it pursues its mission of instruction, research and public service. It also shows the dynamism of Northern—it is bound on all sides, but only temporarily, like the growing pine which is forging through the top as it seeks to realize its full growth potential. This logo was used on stationery, pins, pennants, etc. until December 31, 1988.

Over the years a variety of unofficial logos were used, and by September 1987, Howard Yeoman, coordinator of Marketing Services noted that there was confusion over Northern's logo. President James Appleberry established the Graphic Identity Standards Task Force whose mission it was to create a new logo. Members of the Task Force included Yeoman, chair, Russ Ault, Cameron Hadley, Sheila Johnson, John Kuhn, Paul Mattson, Laura Raab, Eric Smith and Roger Wissler. Through a series of meetings and market research, the Task Force worked with the University community to create a new logo. The new graphic identity sought to: enhance recognition of the University; bind together diverse activities throughout the institution; and signal change.

The new logo was presented to the Board of Control on December 16, 1988. Yeoman said "free-flowing lines and rounded corners, impressions of nature such as a tree or water, and the University's colors, were incorporated into the logo." The use of the new logo went into effect on January 1, 1989 and there was a year phase-in period. At this time the term "logo" was replaced with that of "signature."

In July 1994, a temporary addition was adopted to the signature with the addition of "1899–1999" located at the bottom of the icon. Use of the signature began in 1994, but had to be used on printed materials circulating off-campus from April 28, 1998 through December 31, 1999, after which time it will be suppressed. At no time could business cards be made using the "1899–1999" signature.

The signature is regulated through the university editor in the Communications and Marketing Office and through guideline publications. For information regarding the use of the signature see: *Northern Michigan University Graphic Identity: Standards for Use of the Official NMU Signature* (1990) and *Rules for Using the Official University Centennial Signature* (1994). (NW 11/10/1988; Board of Control Minutes 07/17/1975, 12/16/1988).

SIP: See: *Severance Incentive Plan*

Sit-In: See: *Demonstrations, Student*

Skiing: Northern's first ski team appeared in the *1961 Peninsulan* as an all-woman five member team. There was a ski club formed in 1955, which consisted of 30 men and women. Known as the Tempo Ski Club, it "originated one evening when a nucleus of ski enthusiasts called a meeting of all persons interested in skiing." The club had its own ski shop on campus to store and repair their skis. Men's and women's teams were competing by 1962. The competition was limited to downhill skiing, but cross country competition was introduced in 1973. Training opportunities are ideal with the long winters and numerous skiing facilities.

Coaches: Miodrag Georgevich; Roland Schwitzgoebel; George Ozburn; Lowell Meier; Russ Luttinen; Don Hurst; Karen Kunkel; Dominic Longhini; Barb Kipley; Guy Thibodeau. (*Peninsulans*) Michelle Kangas

Skiing, Women's: The first official women's ski team began in 1971 with alpine and nordic competitions. Before the team formed, women could join the Tempo Ski Club, a student skiing organization formed in 1955. In 1980, the women's skiing program was dropped, but seven years later nordic skiing was reintroduced. In 1996, alpine skiing was added. (*See Skiing* for coach listing.) (*Peninsulans*; Sports Information Office) Michelle Kangas

Smoking on Campus: In 1930, it was noted that there was an "unwritten law" that did not allow smoking on campus. Dean Ethel Carey was known to enforce the law. Students had to go to the sidewalk of Presque Isle Avenue and step off in order not to violate this rule. Actually these regulations were developed by the State Board of Education for all teachers' college and implemented by Dean Carey, who is blamed for them.

Until 1946, Northern had a tradition against smoking anywhere on campus. With the return of veterans, President Tape was forced to allow smoking on campus but outside of buildings at the recommendation of the State Fire Marshall. At the time, there were fire concerns in the Kaye Hall complex.

With the construction of new buildings, smoking was allowed in the halls. However in some instances, faculty smoked either cigarettes or pipes in classrooms. It was common to find students and university personnel smoking in the cafeterias, offices, and dorms. On January 1, 1987 smoking was again outlawed by the Board of Control and state law. In January 1992, the University issued its "Smoking and Tobacco Use Policy" which was promulgated across the campus. By it, smoking is allowed only in specially designated areas around the campus. For a period in the early 1990s, it was common to have students chew tobacco in class and spit in soda cans. By the latter part of the decade, this had terminated as well. (NCN 11/04/1930; NCN 02/10/1947; NW 01/16/1992).

Snow Queen Contest: *See: Union Board*

Snow Days: In the early days of Northern's development, when faculty and students lived within walking distance, or (until the early 1930s) could take a streetcar to campus, there was little concern for snow days. However, once commuting began in the 1930s from outlying communities, a larger problem developed. In the 1950s, the faculty called for a system to alert the university community of impeding blizzards and tornadoes.

A policy evolved over the years. At first, and as late as Provost Robert Glenn's tenure (1974–1984), it applied only to faculty and students. All staff were expected to report to work. Later this policy was changed to essential staff only, after the union threatened a grievance after one particularly bad day when the police closed the roads to all traffic.

In an October 1983 *North Wind* article, Provost Glenn outlined the policy. Presently, a snow day is called by the office of the Academic Vice President. The University tries to remain open, but when the weather conditions become treacherous, the Vice President in consultation with the director of Public Safety and the local weather service, makes a decision to close the University. On an average, the university closes 2–3 times a year. In 1998, due to mild conditions, there was only one afternoon cancellation. The closure can be for a whole day or a portion of it. In January 1997, Public Safety announced a new number 227-BRRR (2777) people can call to find out about the status of the University. Besides this number, the University notifies radio and television stations throughout the Upper Peninsula. (NW 10/01/1983; *Campus* 01/26–30/1998)

Soccer, Women's: The women's soccer team at Northern began in 1996. That year the schedule of competition included opponents from Wisconsin, lower Michigan, Pennsylvania, Ohio and Minnesota. The coach for the 1996 season was John Peppler. In its first year, the team posted a record of two wins and nine losses. In 1997, the team was coached by Milton Braga and played 13 games, losing all. Braga continues into the 1998 season. (Sports Information Office) Michelle Kangas

Sociology and Social Work, Department of: The first Sociology classes at Northern were taught by John E. Lautner. In 1958, Dr. Richard F. O'Dell became Head of a department called History and Social Studies, under which Sociology was taught. Sociology was then separated from that department in 1962 to form the Department of Economics and Sociology with Dr. Jean R. Pearman as the chair of the Sociology division.

Between 1965 and 1968, the Economics and Sociology Departments separated, forming their own departments. During that time the Sociology Department divided further into a Sociology, a Social Work (or Social Services) and an Anthropology component.

By 1974, the Department of Sociology and Social Work consisted of 12 people, seven persons in Sociology, three persons in Social Work, and two persons in Anthropology. In 1987 there were 14 faculty members in the Department, namely eight Sociologists, five Professors of Social Work and one Anthropologist.

By 1994–1995, the Department could report that it had as the major component of its mission the responsibility of preparing undergraduate students for work in the disciplines of Sociology and Social Work. Sociology students receive preparation in theory and research methods along with other sub-specialties leading to degrees in Sociology and Applied Sociology. These majors are qualified for employment in entry-level research positions and in some positions involving human services. Social Work students, earning the bachelors in Social Work in the Social Work program accredited by the Council on Social Work Education, receive an education oriented toward generalist practice. They are prepared for entry-level social work positions and for graduate work in social work programs where they can receive advanced placement.

Department chairs and heads: Emil H. Vajda, 1967-1975; Cornell R. DeJong, 1975-1979; Kenneth W. Kelley, 1979-1982; Richard D. Wright, 1982-present.

(Gloria Slade "The Sociology Department" (1995), UA; *The 1996–97 University Profile*, 1:214–220) Michael Fitzgibbon-Rhea

SOLAR: The acronym for "Student Online Access Registration" which allows a student to register via phone or computer went live in March 1998 and was used for Summer and Fall registration. A personal identification number (PIN) is necessary to enter the system. Available on the web version of SOLAR are: academic information (majors, minors, adviser, GPA), course schedule, grades, unofficial transcript, biographical data, holds, information restrictions and student account information. In the future, Financial Aid information will be available as well. (*Campus*, 10/5–9/1998)

Sons of Thor: A local fraternity which was started in 1914, Sons of Thor eventually became Theta Omicron Rho. (NCN 05/23/1962)

South Wing: *See*: *Longyear Hall*

Spalding Residence Hall: *See*: *Quad I*

Spalding, Grace Allen: (1870–December 25, 1957) Born in Evanston, Illinois, Spalding attended high school there. She completed undergraduate work at Columbia Teachers' College and Pratt Institute and Columbia University, both in New York. Before coming to Northern in 1904, she taught for a few years at Evanston. Spalding was head of the Art Department at Northern from 1903 until 1938. She also taught art in the summer at Chautauqua, New York and also at Museé de Louvre, Paris in 1912.

She continued her study of art in the United States and Europe. In 1907, she studied in Florence and in 1918 at the University of California. During the period 1921–22 she studied in Paris, attending the Academie Colorossi, the Academie Delacleuse and the studio of Richard Miller. In 1926, she took another leave of absence and spent 30 weeks studying in France and Italy. Her last leave was in 1931, when she studied at the Fogg Museum, Harvard University and at the Metropolitan Museum, New York before going to Europe for travel and study in Greece and Italy.

After her retirement, she made her residence in Marquette and spent the winters in Oklahoma and California. Her paintings, exhibited in New York and Chicago as well as in Marquette, sold well, particularly those of her favorite subject, the fall woods near Lake Superior (especially at Middle Island Point), carpeted with scarlet huckleberry bushes. In 1956 she was honored at an exhibit of her paintings in Lee Hall. Some of her pieces of art are part of the Permanent Art Collection. Spalding Residence Hall was dedicated in her honor on November 22, 1964. (NCN 09/20/1938; 01/25/1958; MJ 12/27/1957)

Speakers' Bureau: The forerunner of the Bureau was the Normal Extension Lectures (*See separate entry*) created in 1913. In the early 1960s, Natural Science, the first of what became three speakers bureaus, was established, followed by Social Science (1974) and Humanities not long after. The Bureau filled the University's Public Service mission and the faculty were willing and available to speak to schools and groups throughout the Upper Peninsula. These were originally under Continuing Education.

Each of the three bureaus was handled by a committee of faculty from the respective departments, one of them serving as coordinator. Brochures listing the speakers and their topics were made available to the public.

The Bureaus successfully cooperated until the late 1970s, when the faculty lost interest. In 1981, responsibility was transferred from the Dean of Arts and Sciences to the Office of the Provost. The program became "orphaned" and passed from the scene. In the late 1980s, there was a study of "reviving" the bureau but nothing came of it. The concept was revived in the fall of 1997, and Professor Emeritus Elisha Greifer developed a report which was presented to the College of Arts and Sciences. A year later, Dr. Ray Ventre was the director of this new service to the community.

Remnants of the bureau remain. The Arts and Sciences faculty are listed in the Media Resource Directory, "a listing of faculty and administrative staff expertise." The Seaborg Center and some area schools have funds for visiting faculty activities. Some of the science departments and others have personal contacts for similar activities. In addition the Conference Department sometimes recommends faculty (on an ad hoc basis) as resource people on panels at conferences held at Northern. (UA, Elisha Greifer. "Speakers Bureau—Initial Report," 11/20/1997)

Special Studies Program: This two-year program leading to an Associate of Applied Science degree was developed in 1976. Students interested in this associate degree program develop a program of study, following either the minor track or planned program option with a faculty advisor. This was created as an extension of the Individually Created Program. (*See separate entry*) There is also a year program leading to a certificate.

Speech and Hearing Clinic: In 1962, a Speech and Hearing Clinic was available at Northern. The clinic offered "free diagnostic and remedial facilities for students with speech problems, e.g. articulation, voice, stuttering, etc. In addition, hearing appraisals are performed." Today, the same services are offered free of charge to students. The clinic is operated by the Communication Disorders Department. The speech clinic is located in the basement of Carey Hall and the audio lab is in the basement of Lee Hall. (*Bulletins*) Michelle Kangas

Speech Department: See: Communications and Performance Studies

Speed Bumps: In the late summer of 1974, Provost Robert Glenn had speed bumps placed along Elizabeth Harden Circle Drive. People bitterly complained in the *North Wind* and coupled with them being an obstacle to snow removal, they were removed by January 1975. (NW 10/17/1974)

Sponberg, Harold E.: (September 26, 1918–April 26, 1975) Dr. Sponberg was the first Vice President of NMU. He received his education at: Gustavus Adolphus College, St. Peter, MN (B.A. 1940); University of Minnesota (M.A. 1942); Michigan State University (Ph.D. 1952).

Prior to coming to Northern, he was the director of extension at Michigan State University. On July 1, 1956 he began his term as the first Vice President of Northern, joining newly appointed President Harden. He remained in the position until September 1961, when he became President of Washburn University (1961–1965) in Topeka, KS. Sponberg was also president of Eastern Michigan University (1965–1974). He was active in the local and state communities and authored a book on parliamentary law. (MJ 04/28/1975)

Spooner, Charles Cutler: (August 20, 1872–October 7, 1950) Born in Ware, Massachusetts he attended Amherst College and was a classmate of Calvin Coolidge. He received a M.S. from Amherst in 1902 where he was a member of Phi Beta Kappa. Later he did additional work at the University of Chicago in mathematics and physics. Spooner married Ella Brown Jackson in Salida, Colorado on June 26, 1902.

His first-year teaching position was in a country school in New Hampshire where he remained half a year. Then he moved to Salida, Colorado and for three years taught in an academy followed by two years in a high school. He taught in Salt Lake City for seven years.

During the summer, Mr. Spooner attended the University of Chicago.

In the fall of 1910, Mr. Spooner joined the Northern, faculty. Throughout his career at Northern he occupied the same two classrooms. Spooner was the head of the Mathematics Department between 1923 and 1943. In the early days, he coached the basketball team at a time when Michigan Tech was the only college available to play, and thus the team had to resort to playing high school teams. Throughout his tenure at Northern, Spooner was active in state and faculty activities. He retired in June 1943, and on July 10, 1946 the State Board of Education awarded him emeritus status. Spooner Residence Hall was dedicated on June 16, 1965.

The Spooners were avid travelers, and fishing was his favorite sport. He was a member of: Lions International, Free Masonry, Mathematical Society of America, Amherst Alumni Club and the Marquette County Historical Society. In 1938, Spooner was elected as a Fellow of the American Association for Advancement of Science.

Ella Spooner was a poet. In 1949, she published her first book of verse entitled, *This Broad Land*. Two years later she published a volume of poetry, *From Mountain to Shore*. (NCN 07/23/1943, 04/01/1942; NN 09/30/1955)

Spooner Hall: The earliest discussion for a men's dorm went back to the late 1940s. In April of 1954, approval was given for the construct of a new dorm. The architectural firm was the Warren Holmes Company. The funding was provided by the Ann Arbor Trust Company.

The eastern end of Spooner Hall, the first all-male residence hall at Northern, was completed for 1955 fall occupancy. The building housed 108 men on three floors. Two men lived in each room. The rooms contained double deck beds, a six-drawer chest, two closets, a double study desk and a book shelf. There was a bathroom between each two rooms to be used by four residents. There was also a dining room, three conference rooms, lounge, recreation room, trunk storage room and a laundry. At that time, the charge for room and board was $279.50 per semester. The western or second addition was completed in the fall of 1958. Spooner Hall formerly had a dining room attached to it but since the 1970s, this room has been used as a classroom for the Department of Art and Design. It consists of 61,349 square feet. Although the hall was named after Charles C. Spooner by the State Board of Education on June 23, 1955, it was not formally dedicated until June 6, 1965.

In 1962, Spooner Hall became coed. It was an "Honor Hall" and the women lived on the third floor. It continues to be used as a residence hall. (NCN 09/29/1954, 09/30/1955, 05/29/1957; NN 09/28/1962)

Sports Hall of Fame, NMU: The purpose of the NMU Sports Hall of Fame is to recognize Northern Michigan University alumni who have distinguished themselves in the field of athletics, either by virtue of their performance on athletic teams representing the University or by meritorious efforts in behalf of athletics either as an undergraduate or in years after leaving the University. Consideration is also given to those who have made other significant contributions to the athletic program at Northern. The program is operated through Alumni Relations.

Past Inductees-

1976: Bob Armstead '65, F.L. "Frosty" Ferzacca, Morgan "Muggs" Gingrass '51, Burt Gustafson '52, C.B. Hedgcock, George McCormick '52, Mike Mileski '62, C.V. "Red" Money, Len St. Jean '64, Albert Treado '31, Rico Zenti '32.

1977: Stan Albeck, Curt Harper '62, G. Vance Hiney '26, R. Victor Hurst, Curt Marker '67, Tom Schwalbach '60, Gus Sonnenberg '18, Gene Summers '66.

1978: George Blommel '61, Joe DeCook '30, Rollie Dotch, Wayne Monson '61, C.J. "Mink" St. Germain '42, Gary Silc '63.

1979: Harry Anderle '27, Dr. Henry S. Heimonen '35, Henry E. Lindeman '48, Thomas Neumann '63, Edwin B. Olds '42, C. James Soli '39, Patrick Stump '66.

1980: Richard Bonifas '48, Michael Boyd '70, William R. Hart '51, Allan Ronberg '30, Duane O. Soine '65, Eugene Valesano '62, Olaf Vickland '31, Oscar Wassberg '30.

1981: Harold "Babe" Anderson '43, Eber C. Carlson '28, Rod Coe '58, Gil Krueger, Bill Rademacher '64, Al Sandona '62, Norm Slough '42.

1982: Tim Kearney '73, Jack Mauro '65, Jack Nelmark '31, Frank Novak '62, Jerry Pangrazzi '54, Ray Ranguette '35.

1983: Art Allen '53, Gil Canale '56, Alvin "Dutch" Cummings '37, Francis "Curly" Hetherington '48, Benedict Montcalm '48, Con Yagodzinski '67.

1984: Gil Damiani '73, Gerry Goerlitz '62, Bill Koski '67, Norman "Boots" Kukuk '41, Barbara Patrick, R. Thomas Peters, Jr. '55, Ted Rose '70.

1985: Axel Anderson '54, Allen Ische '67, Milton "Mickey" Johnson '28, Karen Kunkel, Robert Pecotte '64, Jack Refling '48.

1986: Glen C. Brown, W. David Cade '64, Donald R. Elzinga, M.D., David Fleet '66, Pertti Reijula '76, Jack Schils '52, Wayne Sickler '62, Louis Taccolini '52.

1987: Gil Heard '70, Dick Koski '64, Ed Kukuk '48, Jim Meyer '69, Barbara Perry '71, Fritz Wilson '58.

1988: C. Richard Bye '50, Thomas J. Fagan '35, Byron J. Johnson '68, Stephen R. Mariucci '77, Lowell E. Meier, Reginald D. Peters '68, Daniel J. Stencil '76.

1989: Richard R. Ambrosino '70, Jerry Glanville '64, Lonnie R. Holton '70, Kenneth F. Hruska '66, Arthur E. Koski '43, Walfred "Mike" Mickelson '52, Kathy Talus '52.

1990: David Freeman '53, Carol Hammerle '70, Tom Izzo '77, Tom Laidlaw '80, Marshall Treado '31, Steve Weeks '80.

1991: Steve Bozek, Steven Contardi '67, Edward "Matt" Gleason '37, Clifford Puckett '50, Donald Trost, Robert A. Villemure '38.

1992: Phillip J. Kessel '81, Terry B. Nyquist '65, Rexford M. Terwilliger '57, Stanley W. Whitman '50, Earl Wilkins '31, Warren E. Wilson '57.

1993: Gordy DeLuc '62, Francine Malindzak '83, Irving Soderlund '49, John Spuhler '69, Francis Vetort '41, Donald Waddell '80.

1994: John H. Beaumier M.D. '53, William D. Brodeur '60, Julie Campbell '83, John A. Chrisant '70, Robert W. Pearce '61, Michael C. Strebel '62.

1995: Leslie F. Coduti '68, Edward J. Egan '80, David B. Ghiardi '61, Joel D. Hanner '76, Michael E. Matter '72.

1996: George R. Barber '73, Roy E. Brigman '37, Lloyd H. Carr '68, Guy T. Falkenhagen '73, Dale A. Kaiser '61.

1997: 1975 Football Team, Lori Burke '85, Carl Nystrom, Steve Spangenberg '80, Denise Zanoni '87.

1998: The 1991 Hockey Team, Randy Awrey '78, Rick Comely '73, Bill Joyce '80, Bob Jurasin '85, Tom Kirby '51, John Mehki '76, Joe Stemo '80.

Sports Information Office: The Office was created in 1965 because Northern's sports program had expanded and the sports area could not be adequately handled by the News Bureau alone. At that time, Gil Heard was hired as the first Sports Information Director. In 1997, the Office was transferred from Communications and Marketing to Athletics and the facility was moved from Cohodas to Zenti Instructional Wing (PEIF). Directors: Gil Heard, 1965–1988; Tony Tollefson, (acting) 1989; Jim Pinar, 1989–present.

Sports Training Centers: This area was developed under the direction of Karen Kunkel in the mid-1980s with the coming to campus of the U.S. Olympic Education Training Center. Located under the Finance and Administration Division, its overall mission is to provide training and educational opportunities for athletes and to prepare and train them to become Olympic champions. The Centers are concerned with assisting student athletes (whether current or retired) through the academic program at Northern. It also coordinates a variety of regional, national and international training camps, competitions and coaches' educational programs. The Center represents Northern on: Governor's Council on Physical Fitness, Health and Sports, Food Service Advisory, CCHUB, Recreational Services Advisory, and Superior Nordic Training and Recreation Complex Committee. It also works with the HPER Department on-campus and Marquette General Hospital off-campus. In 1999 director Jeff Kleinshcmidt oversees a staff from Center headquarters in Meyland Hall. (*The 1996–97 University Profile*, 2:94–99).

Sprinkle Observatory: In the Fall of 1972, Nell Sprinkle donated a 12-inch reflecting telescope (12-inch, F:6 Newtonian telescope with a precision equatorial drive), the mirror on it hand-crafted by her husband Lloyd, to Northern. In 1974, Northern purchased the dome which encompasses the entire telescope from Ash Dome Company. The mount on which the telescope sits was purchased from Beyers, Inc. By 1975, the Sprinkle Observatory was ready to be used. Located on the roof of the West Science Building, the observatory is used by students in astronomy classes, visited by middle and high school students, and is occasionally used by the public. The roof of the dome has a narrow, mechanical opening. The entire dome roof rotates 360 degrees to allow observers to see beyond what is possible with the naked eye—distant galaxies, planets, comets. A photographic lens can also be attached to the telescope. Michelle Kangas and Alisa Koski

Spring Break: In the past, when classes ended in mid-June, Spring Break coincided with the Easter week. Since 1973, it takes place in mid-semester. Many students seek refuge from the cold and snow in sunny climes to the south. Ads for travel to these locations are placed as inserts in the *North Wind*.

Spring Pageant: This was an event developed by the Physical Education Department. Active in the 1920s it was held in June. All of the women in gym class were involved in the pageant. In 1924, the different seasons were represented by flowers and there were group and individual dances. The May queen arrived with ladies in waiting, heralds and pages. In 1924, The Pageant was held "on the heart of the campus." This tradition declined in popularity by the 1930s. (NCN 06/02/1924)

Spruce Hill: This was a 50-foot twin engine diesel yacht donated to the University by John McGoff in April 1977. The plan was to use the boat for Lake Superior research by University biologists and chemists.

In early 1978, $10,000 in repairs were made to the vessel. In August, a major underwater research project was conducted involving a shipwreck study off Isle Royale. It was soon found that the vessel was impractical and costly, and on April 27, 1979 the Board of Control authorized its sale at the price of $105,000. There was also another vessel called the *Merlin* which was owned for a short time by the University and sold for $9,000. Proceeds from the sale of these ships were transferred to the Endowment Fund and interest used for research related to Lake Superior.

Stadia/Stadium: *See*: *Athletic Fields*

State Board of Education: The Board was established by Act 138 of the session laws of 1849. The Constitution of 1850 made the membership elective and the Superintendent of Public Instruction *ex officio* a member. The Constitution of 1909 designated the Superintendent of Public Instruction as a member and secretary of the Board. Section 6 of Article XI of the constitution further stated: "The State Board of Education shall consist of four members . . . It shall have general supervision of the state normal college and the state normal schools, and the duties of said Board shall be prescribed by law." The law prescribed that "the Board is hereby authorized and required to prescribe the course of study for students, to grant such diplomas and degrees and issue such licenses and certificates to the graduates of the several normal schools of the state as said Board of Education shall determine." Northern became independent of the Board on March 13, 1963.

Straits Bridge Festival: Anticipating the completion of the Mackinac Bridge in 1958, Dr. Richard O'Dell (History) chaired a committee which planned to use the occasion as a symbol of social integration. In the prospectus (developed as early as 1954) it was stated, "The Festival [referred to by some as a mini-world's fair] not only will provide a vehicle for rejoicing over the completion of a monumental physical task. In its own right it will help to draw together many cultural threads in modern life in the hope that through a new synthesis the prospect of total peace can replace that of total catastrophe." The events were planned to be held on Northern's campus in 1959. Unfortunately given the complicated nature of the event, it was never held.

Streaking and Streakers: Streaking and streakers were phenomena which hit college campuses in the mid-1970s. Individuals would abruptly run through a crowd stark naked. The first two Northern students to streak in Marquette ran down Washington Street on March 17, 1974 and were arrested by the city police for indecent exposure. On March 20th a *North Wind* editorial challenged students to streak, and this resulted in massive streaking during the following week. On December 7, 1993 an unidentified male student streaked through the Academic Mall in honor of Northern women's volleyball champions in 20 degree weather. (MJ 03/18/1974,03/20/1974; NW 03/20/1974, 03/27/1974, 12/09/1993). Michelle Kangas

Student Activities and Leadership Programs Office: Created in 1962, the Student Activities and Leadership Programs Office has responsibilities in several major areas of extracurricular and co-curricular student life at NMU. The office coordinates services for over 170 student organizations that register annually, advises student programming organizations (concerts, films, lectures, Homecoming, Winfester, Family and Human Relations), coordinates the NMU Volunteer Center (which provides volunteer opportunities for students), coordinates a leadership initiative including programs and workshops, and provides the Service Learning Initiative which provides support to faculty members interested in bringing service-learning opportunities into their classrooms. The office began as a committee, was later called the Student Activities Office, and received its current name in the Fall of 1994.

Directors: Beulah West Zettle, 1965–1968; Terry Nyquist, 1968–1969; Carol Huntoon, 1969–1976; Ron Stump, 1976–1978; David Bonsall, 1978–present. (*Bulletins*; SALP Office) Michelle Kangas

Student Affairs Division: Previous to 1969, the Office of Student Affairs was known as the Office of Student Personnel Services. Between 1923 and 1956, a Dean of Men and a Dean of Women were in charge of Student Affairs. In 1956, the offices of Dean of Men and Dean of Women were combined and became known as the Office of the Dean of Students. In 1961, a new office was created with wider prerogatives than the Office of the Dean of Students, namely the Office of Student Personnel Services. At this time, the Office of the Dean of Students became a subdivision of the Office of the Vice President for Student Personnel Services. Over the years, the Vice President for Student Personnel Services became responsible for several other subdivisions as well. In 1969, the Office of the Vice President for Student Personnel Services was renamed the Office of the Vice President for Student Affairs.

The mission of the Division is to assist students and faculty to achieve their educational goals. In 1997, the Division included: 1. Admissions; 2. The Hub Student Resource Center: Counseling Center, Academic and Career Advisement Center; 3. Dean of Students: Disability Services, Student Support Services, Upward Bound, Vocational Support Services; 4. Financial Aid; 5. Food Services; 6. Health Center; 7. Housing and Residence Life; 8. JOBSearch; 8. University Center and Campus Activities: Bookstore.

Through these units, the Division develops and implements the University's enrollment management plan, ensures a campus living-learning environment that contributes effectively to the growth and development of students, administers student services and support programs which promote student development and enhance student life. Finally it provides the recognized communication linkage between students and the administrative structure of the University. (*The 1996–97 University Profile*, 2:101–106.

Student Army Training Corp (S.A.T.C.): In 1918, President Kaye was notified by the U.S. Army that Northern could establish a S.A.T.C. if one hundred men of draft age could be registered. Through faculty visits throughout the Upper Peninsula, 104 men were registered. The old dormitory was reopened and the men were housed and fed there. The men received $30 per month as regular army privates, and Northern received reimbursements for housing and food. Due to the Spanish flu pandemic which closed Northern in the fall of 1918, the men were quarantined in the old dormitory and were never able to date the female students as they hoped to do. This program was terminated in January 1919.

Student Code of Conduct: Assistant Dean of Students Norman Hefke (1968–79) was instrumental in developing the Student Code of Conduct which was published in 1969. For the first time in print, the booklet outlined regulations and rules that students had to follow. It also outlined the procedures of due process, whereby students are tried by their peers. These matters are handled by the Dean of Students.

This eventually became the *Northern Michigan University Student Handbook: Student Rights and Responsibilities, Student Code, University Policies and Related Documents*. The Board of Control approved its revision on December 16, 1994 and its was issued to the University community in January 1995. It is periodically updated. (Amy Henderson. "History of the Office of the Dean of Students (1995), UA).

Student Commencement Speaker: Started in 1988, the selection of a speaker is administered through the Dean of Students Office. *Past speakers*: Laura J. Ballweg (12/98); Fred Bratumil (12-88); Christopher Charboneau (5-93); Laura Engler (12-93); Sharon Fousek (5-92); Richard T. Haverkate (4-89); Jeannie Jafolla (5-91); Tammie Johnson (12-90); Carie Kaniszewski (4-95); William R. Kroeger (4-88); Nancy Krusic (12-89); Chante M. Lasco (12-96); Virginia Liedel (12-97); Matthew Lorenz (4-94); Meghan Marsden (5-98); Diane Nelson (12-92); Emily Peterson (12-94); Melanie Ryan (4-96); Rebecca Slough (4-90); Robin Soine (12-91); Cem Tanova (5-91). (University Relations Office)

Student Council: Origins of the Student Council go back to 1941, when members of the Men's Union and the Student Girls' League worked on a new constitution for a Student Council. Their work lapsed with the coming of World War II. They were active again in the late 1940s and saw their dream realized on January 23, 1947, when the articles of a newly-organized student council were approved by President Tape.

In May 1948, a group of students circulated a petition to organize a student council. It was strongly backed by the faculty who were approached. The Constitution written by June 1948, was presented to the administration, faculty and students for revision, and suggestions were evaluated. The document was revised by the end of the term. The main purpose of the Council was the promotion of better relationships between the faculty and students of Northern.

On December 15, 1948, the student body, by a vote of 554 to 25 votes, passed the new constitution on which student government would be based. Along with a faculty adviser chosen by the Council, each class was represented by three students nominated and elected by the whole student body.

On January 25, 1949 the first election for the Student Council was held. Its first officers consisted of Bud Vecellio, president; John Bittner, vice president; Joseph Sullivan, treasurer; and Jean Jackson, secretary. The newly elected Student Council met for the first time on Monday, February 21. At the time the agenda was set to reread the Constitution and write bylaws.

This form of student government was not adequate, and there were problems with representation. On May 25, 1965, by a vote of 1282 to 89, the Northern students ratified a new constitution of the student body and student government association. The new constitution replaced the former "Council" system and provided for increased representatives (from 17 members to 35) who were called senators. Furthermore, the Student Government Association (now called the Student Senate) was divided into executive, legislative and judicial branches. The Judicial Review Board (consisting of one justice and four associate justices) was responsible for the interpretation of the Student Government constitution and any constitution referred to it by any student organization.

The Student Senate voted on March 25, 1969 to accept a constitution proposed for Northern's student by the Senate Self-Evaluation Committee. On April 22 the student body by 44 percent voted in the new constitution which created ASNMU.

The Student Senate met for the last time on April 29, 1969 and in the fall was replaced by Associated Students of NMU (*See separate entry*).

Presidents: Oswald Vecellio, 1949; Dick MacNealy, 1950; John Pantalone, 1951; Bob Kline, 1952; Craig Olson, 1953; Paul Gingrass, 1954; Bill Pearson, 1955; Bob Tupper, 1956; Robert Bordeau, 1957; George Aune, 1958; Dennis George, 1959; Roger LaBonte, 1960; Dave Blomquist, 1961; Jim Surrell, 1962; Edward Havlik, 1963; Dick Landi, 1964–1965; Don Keskey, 1966–1967. (MJ 01/27/1949; NCN 02/10/1947, 12/10/1948, 01/06/1949, 03/03/1949, 10/12/1949; NN 05/21/1965, 05/28/1965; Hilton, p. 132)

Student Discretionary Activity Fee: All graduate and undergraduate students carrying six or more credit hours taught on the Marquette campus must pay a $19.95 fee for each fall and winter semester. The fee is appropriated to student organizations to provide funding for their activities. The Office of the Dean of Students is responsible for administering the Student Activity Fee and for providing an adviser to the Student Finance Committee. The Student Finance Committee (*See separate entry*) is an all-student group appointed by student government. The SFC is responsible for making decisions regarding budget requests from registered student organizations. Currently, the student newspaper (*North Wind*), the student radio station (WUPX) and the Student Art Gallery receive pre-established amounts of money. Northern Arts and Entertainment, along with Platform Personalities receive regular amounts of funding from the fee. The adviser of the SFC and the Student Activities and Leadership Programs Office assist student organizations in requesting funds. The first Student Activity Fee of $5.00 was charged in the 1973–74 Academic Year. Michelle Kangas

Student Finance Committee (SFC): A standing committee of ASNMU (*See separate entry*), it is entrusted with the allocation of funds from the Student Discretionary Activity Fee (*See separate entry*). Any registered student organization wishing to sponsor a program or activity that will benefit the student body may apply for funding. Examples of past expenditures include: concerts, dances, films, lectures and special events.

Student Girls' League: Organized in the fall of 1911, the League did much for the social and moral welfare of the students. Committees from the League met all incoming freshmen, took care of the new students, showed them Northern, showed them to their rooming and boarding places and helped "the new students to get into the best life of the school and to avoid anything that might be harmful to them." The League held social parties, published a calendar for a number of years, established a School Honor Standard, and published a *Handbook of Northern* for graduating high school seniors.

By 1932, it was a leading organization with every female student a member. The executive council of the League consisted of the two highest ranking women officers of each of the classes. The purpose of the organization was to help every woman enjoy her life at Northern. The organization promoted student interest in activities and encouraged cooperation between the various other organizations. It cooperated with the Men's Union in sponsoring student activities. Some of its activities during 1932 included: the annual Men's banquet, Get-Together Party, the annual pasty supper, a Leap Year Matinee Dance and the Women's Banquet. The League held a series of open-house teas on Saturday afternoons in the recreation rooms. Interesting programs which utilized latent talent such as ping pong, dancing, singing, card playing and dramatic ability were popular. In the 1940s the League was instrumental in creating student government in the form of the Student Council (*See separate entry*).

By February 1957, there was common feeling that the name Student Girls' League should be changed to Associated Women Students, a national organization that they had joined in 1956. On February 28, 1957 the women voted for the name change which passed.

The Associated Women Students remained a viable organization affiliated with the Intercollegiate Association of Women Students, the only national women's student government group in the United States. Every undergraduate woman became a member of this organization upon registration. With the creation of Association Students of NMU (ASMMU) in 1969 this organization ended. (NCN 02/27, 03/13/1957; *Bulletin*, 1913–1914, pp. 14–15) Michelle Kangas

Student Government: Since the founding of the institution, students have had a variety of organizations which dealt with their concerns and affairs. Two of the earliest organizations were the Men's Union and the Student Girls' League (*See separate entries*). In 1949 the Northern Student Council (*See separate entry*) was created and in 1965 became the Student Senate. ASNMU (*See separate entry*) was created in the spring of 1969.

Today, student government organizations give students a great opportunity to hold leadership positions and have an impact on Northern. The role of students in government positions ranges from student government representatives to serving on the All-Student Judiciary. *See*: *All Student Judiciary* (ASIO), *Associated Students of NMU*, *Resident Hall Governments*, etc., *Student Finance Committee* (SFC).

Student Government Association: *See*: *Student Council*

Student Handbook: *See*: *Student Code of Conduct*

Student Resource Center: *See*: *The Hub*

Student Senate: *See*: *Student Council*

Student Support and Disability Services: Under the Student Affairs Division, this Department seeks to help low income, first-generation students with disabilities develop skills and motivations necessary to persist in college, graduate and pursue a suitable career. The Department (primarily funded by the U.S. Department of Education) serves 210 eligible students per grant year.

The Department is responsible for identifying and selecting eligible students for participation in the program, conducting an individual needs assessment and providing services to facilitate academic excellence, personal growth, and adjustment to the university environment. Specifically, the department provides the following services: academic support and disability-related services; specialized tutoring, basic/study skills development, personal growth workshops and academic and career advisement; interpersonal counseling; social and cultural enrichment and student advocacy. A parallel responsibility is to serve as a liaison between Northern students with disabilities and Northern personnel concerning the rights and responsibilities of all parties involved in accordance with the law and common practice. Directors: Masud Mufti; Pamela Motoike, 1997–1998; Linda Anderson, 1998–present. (*The 1996–97 University Profile*, 2:137–142)

Study Skins: A collection in the Biology Department in the form of stuffed animals, bottled items, skeletons and skins or pelts which was started in 1902 with the opening of the Peter White Hall of Science. The informal collection has been augmented over the years by faculty and student researchers, road kill, and donors. The collection is primarily an instructional tool.

It consists primarily of Upper Peninsula specimens. Professor John Lowe (1919–1938) developed a fish collection. Dr. William Robinson (1964–1998) collected specimens from the McCormick Tract (1970s), the Huron Islands, and the Huron Mountain Club. There are a number of special parts to the collection: African sub-Saharan mammals, line ground squirrels from Marquette County, California specimens, and wolves. One rather spectacular item is a timber wolf in an exhibition case in the hallway by the Biology Department. (Interview with William Robinson, 12/15/1998, UA)

Suffrage: See: *Women's Suffrage*

Summer College: See: *Summer School*.

Summer Institute: In the spring of 1983, Northern was selected as a site for the State Board of Education's Summer Institute for 125 gifted children in 10th and 11th grades in mathematics and art and design. This was supported by a state grant to five colleges. The Institute was successfully conducted for several years before Michigan Tech was awarded the grant. Later the Institute operated under the Seaborg Center.

Summer School: The first summer session at Northern was held in 1900. It was primarily for teachers and it cost $3.00 for the entire six-week term. Housing in the dormitory was $3.75 a week.

Since that first season, summer school has been offered every summer since then. Usually the summer program was advertised months in advance. During the course of the summer, the visiting students were provided with social programs, tours, special speakers in the field of education (in 1907 Booker T. Washington was an invited speaker who had to decline the invitation because of other commitments) and the publication of the campus newspaper. At first it was geared to teachers who were upgrading their certification. Later, the course work expanded into other fields than education.

In preparation for Summer 1996, the Summer College was created to emphasize that this session was a critical component of the year-round curricular effort. The "Summer College Advisory Committee" was established to provide leadership in the development of an integrated Summer College curriculum.

The Superior Dome: Building a large all-events center at Northern was first proposed in the spring of 1971. However, it remained an unrealized dream until the mid-1980s when Northern was promoted as the site of a U.S. Olympic training/education center. With strong support from Governor James Blanchard—who also pledged state funding for a facility which could be used for Olympic training—NMU's bid won approval of the U.S. Olympic Committee in February 1985. While the Center took up residence in an existing University building, and commenced operations on July 1, 1985, it was not until the following January that NMU submitted a formal program statement that called for the construction of a Sports Training Complex.

Constructed with special State of Michigan funds ($21,800,000) the structure was completed and named The Superior Dome in September 1991. The first event, a football game with the University of Indianapolis on September 14, attracted 7,942 fans; the Homecoming football game with Ferris State saw 8,432 in attendance with the addition of portable bleachers.

It is the world's largest wooden dome structure, constructed of 781 Douglas fir beams and 108.5 miles of fir decking. The structure covers 5.1 acres under one roof and it rises to the height of a 14-story building. Permanent seating capacity: 8,000; the building capacity: 16,000.

One of its unique characteristics is the artificial synthetic playing turf which is the largest piece of retractable turf in the world. The turf is floated out on an air cushion and controlled by twelve computerized winches. It takes approximately two hours to set it up, and it retracts in thirty minutes. The turf is suitable for football, soccer, softball and field hockey. The synthetic playing surfaces are suitable for a variety of sports including, tennis, badminton, volleyball, basketball, 200-meter track and more.

Unfortunately, the original plans had to be downsized and the structure remained in an incomplete state. In 1995, Phase II was completed.

Costing $2.1 million it consisted of construction of five locker rooms, five carpeted classrooms/meeting rooms, one state-of-the-art classroom with theatre seating (accommodates 75), concession stands (northwest and southwest entrances), "Superior Souvenirs" retail store, and administrative offices located at the southwest entrance. An "EZ Tickets" outlet is located in the administrative offices.

Concerned about the limited use of the structure, President Vandament, working with the University Historian, began to expand its focus to include museum spaces to promote the heritage and natural environment of the Upper Peninsula. In 1994, the President obtained mining equipment which was located on the south side of the structure a year later. All of the historical exhibitions have been developed by Dr. Diane Kordich (Art & Design) with student assistants. Artifacts from the Cohodas Room in the Cohodas Administrative Center were relocated in the Cohodas Room during the summer of 1995. The President's Room is located on the north side of the structure. In early 1995, four large exhibition cases were completed and by the fall, one was filled with "NMU National Championships." During the summer of 1996, under the on-going direction of Dr. Kordich, the natural environment case was completed along with much of the work on the "Legends of the Upper Peninsula" case. During the summer of 1998, the last of the Phase I exhibit cases dealing with the ethnic groups of the Upper Peninsula was completed. In late 1996, work was completed on the Labor Hall of Fame Exhibition.

The building is also the home of the NMU Sports Hall of Fame. Under the capable supervision of Ken Godfrey, the use of the structure has been greatly expanded. The Dome was the scene of an NBC Today program with Willard Scott in April 1995.

The major events held in the Dome include NMU commencement (first held May 1, 1993); high school football games (regular season and playoffs); NMU football games; car, boat, builder, and food shows; high school track meets; softball tournaments; and conventions.

The Dome is used by the general public for walking and jogging, informal recreation and intramural sports, NMU classes and athletic practices. The Superior Dome is also a rental facility available as: the entire facility, classrooms/meeting rooms, or playing courts.

Swimming (Men): Men's swimming became a varsity sport during the 1959–1960 season. Burt Gustafson was the first coach, followed by Mike Milaski, who coached the team from 1961 through 1966. Don Trost became the head coach in 1966 and remained through 1980, when the sport was dropped because of budgetary constraints.

During Trost's tenure, there were nearly 100 All-American NCAA Division II swimmers. There were also two national champions. Mike Mehki won the 1-meter diving board in 1975, and Dwight Hoffman won the 1-meter and 3-meter diving in 1979 and again in 1980.

Northern hosted the NCAA Division II national men's swimming and diving championships in the spring of 1979. *Coaches*: Don Trost, 1966–1980; John Bransfield (Diving), 1978–1979. Gildo Canale.

Swimming (Women): Introduced as a sport in 1977, the women's swim team has had continued success. The program can boast 21 All-Time National Champions in swimming and diving events. In 1992, Northern won their first GLIAC conference championship and placed 2nd in the NCAA championships. Coach Anne Goodman James was honored in 1992 as GLIAC coach of the year. Swimmers from Northern have received many regional and national recognitions.

Coaches and Career Records: Joan Peto-Hopkins, 1978–1986, 51 wins, 34 losses; Anne Goodman James, 1987–1996, 63 wins, 26 losses; Karl Zueger, 1997–1998, 4 wins, 1 loss; Chris Coraggio. 1998–present. (*1997 Media Guide*, Sports Information Office) Michelle Kangas

Tape, Flora S.: (March 25, 1891–May 21, 1981). The daughter of William and Bertha (Knopf) Simmons, Tape was born in East Jordan, Michigan. She married Henry Tape, future president of Northern Michigan University in East Jordan on September 2, 1913. Their only child is Gerald F., who was a member of the Atomic Energy Commission in the 1960s. She was a member of the Congregational Church. (*Ypsilanti Press* 05/22/1981).

Tape, Henry A.: (May 10, 1889–August 2, 1962) Dr. Tape was born in Caledonia, Michigan. He was a student at Michigan State Normal College (now Eastern Michigan University, 1911–1912) and received a B. A., (1917) and an M. A. (1920) from the University of Michigan. In 1939 he received his Ph.D. from Teachers College at Columbia University (1939). He was the first president to hold this degree.

He married Flora Simmons on September 2, 1913 and had one son Gerald F., who was a member of the Atomic Energy Commission.

Prior to coming to Northern, Dr. Tape had a long history as an educational leader. From 1906 to 1908 he was a rural school teacher in Kent County, and for the next two years (1908-1910) he was superintendent in Hudsonville, Michigan schools. After completing advanced college work, he became superintendent in Milan, Michigan where he remained from 1913 to 1923. After receiving his master's degree, he joined the faculty at Michigan State Normal College in 1924. He was principal of the Lincoln Laboratory School, six miles south of Ypsilanti. Later he became an associate director of training and professor of education at MSNC.

The State Board of Education appointed him president of Northern Michigan University on October 29, 1940. During his presidency, he had to guide Northern through a difficult period. There were the last years of the Depression, the difficult years of World War II and the turbulent post-war years.

When Tape arrived on campus, the University had only four buildings. He oversaw the development of GIville and Vetville and the surplus cafeteria as stop-gap measures. It was during his administration that veterans returned to campus by the hundreds and swelled the student ranks.

He oversaw the construction of the first women's residence, Carey Hall and the first student center, Lee Hall (1948). This was followed by the construction of the Lydia Olson Library and its audio visual center (1951), the remodeling of the Peter White Hall of Science (1953), additions to the connector wings on Kaye Hall, and the construction of Charles Spooner Residence Hall for men (1955). During his administration, the name of the institution was changed by the State Board of Education to Northern Michigan College of Education, and then in 1955 it was changed again to Northern Michigan College.

President Tape retired in 1956. He spent his summers with his son on Long Island, New York and his winters at Daytona Beach, Florida.

Memberships included: National Educational Association, Michigan Educational Association, Kappa Delta Pi, Phi Delta Kappa. He belonged to Michigan Schoolmasters and Rotary and was a Congregationalist and

Free Mason. Tape was the co-author of *The Community School*. (NCN 11/06/1940; *Milwaukee Journal* 08/04/1962; *Who's Who in the Midwest*, 1954, p. 802).

Technology and Applied Sciences, College of: The College of Technology and Applied Sciences is home to five departments: Aviation, Consumer and Family Studies, Electronics, Industrial Technologies and Occupational Studies. Diplomas are offered in Collision Repair Technology and Cosmetology. Certificates are offered in Automotive Service, Carpentry, Culinary Arts, Heating and Air Conditioning/Refrigeration and Wastewater Treatment Plant Operator. Associate degrees are offered in Science, Applied Science and Technology. Bachelor degrees are offered in Arts or Science. The college's mission is to serve both traditional and non-traditional students, while providing opportunity for those already employed in their occupational specialties.

The early history of what is now the college dates back to 1908 when Lottie Turner taught a course in Manual Training, though her specialty was drawing. By the 1980s, many were training for positions in industry. The College was established on July 1, 1986 and it has always been located in the D.J. Jacobetti Center. The industry majors were integrated to form the School of Technology and Applied Sciences, which in 1992 was renamed the College of Technology and Applied Sciences.

Deans: James Suksi, 1986–1990; Elaine F. Alden-Pontillo, 1991–1993; Virginia Slimmer, 1993–1998; Phillip Beukema (acting), 1998–present. (*Bulletins*; Showcase Display at the Jacobetti Center; Telephone interview with William Rigby; Kauko Wahtera interview, UA; *The 1996–97 University Profile*, 2:275–282) Michelle Kangas and Alisa Koski

Telestar: Telestar was a satellite system for telephone communication. On October 4, 1962 President Harden made what was believed to be the first Telestar call from any college campus. He talked to Dr. Carl Sieveking, a Hamburg, Germany attorney whom he had met the previous summer.

Television Station: *See: WNMU-TV*

Tennis (Men's): Throughout its history Northern, has had tennis courts located at various locations on campus (*See: Athletic Fields*). Men's varsity tennis began in the late 1940s, and continued through 1985, when the sport was dropped because of budgetary constraints. Most of the players over the years were Upper Peninsula products and produced many fine seasons.

Coaches: Victor Hurst, 1920s; Dominic Longhini, 1976; Leisuke Ito, 1977–1978; Charles Drury, 1979–1981; Kirk Schmidt, 1982–1983; Jim Jackson, 1984–1985. Gildo Canale

Tennis (Women's)*:* Before becoming an official women's sport at Northern, tennis was played for recreation and through intramural competition. Tennis became a sport in 1978 and remained until 1980. The sport was added again in 1992.

Ten O'Clock Charlie's: The former Tip Top (*See separate entry*), this student watering hole was popular in the mid-1980s and became crowded every night especially around 10:00 p.m., when for ten minutes, a shot of a liquor of the night was sold for 50¢. Unable to keep its lease, Chad Norton, the owner, moved to the old Marquette Bakery to the north which was destroyed by an arsonist. Norton then built a new facility which later became the Sweet Water Café.

The Thaw: A journal of student literature, known in years past as *The Dark Tower* has became *The Thaw*. Students are limited to two poems and one piece of prose each. In 1997 Jacqueline Flicker, was in charge of the publication. In 1998, the name was changed to *A Rumor of a Thaw*. (NW 01/23/1997; Teresa Kynell "Department of English" 03/09/1999)

Thomas Fine Arts Building: See: Russell Thomas Fine Arts Building

Thomas, Russell: (June 12, 1896–March 1, 1988). Dr. Thomas was born in Glen Lyon, Pennsylvania. During World War I (September 1917 through June 1919) he served in the U.S. Army. In 1924 he graduated with a B.A. from the University of Michigan where he was a member of Phi Beta Kappa. He taught in the public schools of Howell for three years. In 1927, he entered the graduate program in English at Michigan and received his doctorate in 1931.

On June 22, 1928, he was married to Helen Matson of Hancock, Michigan. They had two children: Norman and Charlotte.

Between 1931–1934, he taught at Sioux Falls (SD) College. He served as supervisor of instruction at the Hanover Township (PA) Public Schools (1934–36), and taught at Slippery Rock (PA) State College from 1936 to 1939.

In September 1939, he became professor of English at Northern Michigan University and head of the Department. While a faculty member, Dr. Thomas chaired the Assembly Program Committee for several years. Also, he was instrumental in the initiation of the Marquette Community Concerts in the late 1940s. His research specialized in English usage, an area in which he published several scholarly articles. In 1964, as part of the University's Arts Recognition Year, he was given a special award for his contributions to the arts in general and to language and literature specifically.

He retired on June 30, 1964. The Russell Thomas Fine Arts Building (*See separate entry*), which was first known as the Fine and Practical Arts Building, was dedicated to him on October 10, 1965 because of his interest in the arts.

Memberships: National Council of Teachers of English; Phi Beta Kappa; Marquette Masonic Lodge 101; and the First Presbyterian Church of Marquette. (MJ 03/07/1988)

Ties: President Jamrich was characterized by the bow tie which he always wore. He started wearing one after his military service, and the practice evolved from clip-ons to tying his own. In July 1994 he donated a bow tie which he wore to all 45 commencements during his administration to the Museum Collection. President Vandament, who wore a regular tie, pointed out that the way to keep it clean at meals is to turn it around.

Time Capsule: Records of time capsules in campus buildings are obscure. However there is evidence of two of them on campus. One is in the cornerstone of the Thomas Fine Arts Building put there by President Harden in 1962. Another one is in the West Science Building cornerstone placed there in 1966, uncovered in 1996 and returned unopened. ASNMU has plans for a time capsule to be opened in 2099.

Tip Top Café: Located at 503 North Third Street, this was a popular bar and restaurant that was owned and operated by Rose and Nick Arger from the late 1940s through the early 1980s. Friendly Gert Johnson, the cook, knew most of the students who frequented the Tip

Top. It was best known for its hamburgers and milk shakes and Friday fish fries. *See: Ten O'Clock Charlie's*

Tobacco Use: *See: Smoking on Campus*

Track & Field (Men's): Northern students were able to engage in track and field when classes ended in mid-June. Men's organized track and field took place in 1926 and remained a varsity sport until 1971 when the sport was dropped because of budgetary constraints. In 1938, Northern ran in the Michigan Intercollegiate track meet.

The highlights of the program included Al Washington tying the world indoor record. On January 14, 1961, at Central Michigan University, Washington ran the indoor 60 yard dash in 6.0 seconds, which was at that time the world record. Curt Harper won the State NAIA championship in the discus in the same year.

Coaches: C. B. Hedgcock; C. V. Red Money; Burt Gustafson; Mike Mileski; Don Trost; Pat Arsenault; and Al Claremont. (NCN 05/25/1938; MJ 01/16/1961)

Track & Field (Women's): The first track and field meet at Northern was held in June of 1926. Men and women competed. At the meet, Mary Stanek broke the world record for the 50 yard dash, but the time was not officially recorded by the women's athletic association. The first official track team was formed in 1927 and was coached by Victor Hurst and C. B. Hedgcock. (NNN 06-15-26, 04-04-27)

Traditions: The history of life on campus has been influenced by evolving traditions over the century. Many of them are desirable and their educational importance cannot be underestimated, while others have proven to be disruptive. Both have existed on campus.

In the first fifty years of campus life, there were a number of positive traditions. Evergreen or Ivy Day (*See separate entry*), a transplant from eastern colleges, saw students say and sing farewell to Northern and then plant a tree or ivy as a memorial. The giving of a class gift (*See separate entry*) saw the statues of Lincoln (*See separate entry*) and St. George come to campus, where they are on display in the Peter White Lounge. Other more elaborate gifts like the North Gate (*See separate entry*) donated in 1932 have been lost to time. Weekly assembly or chapel (*See separate entry*) was a tradition that most students and faculty were happy to see go in the 1960s. The Christmas celebration in the foyer of Kaye Hall was one tradition that old-timers remember fondly. Others that are also gone include beanies or pots, the Rose Ceremony, Paul Bunyan Ball, the Rose Ceremony and the old Heart of Northern (*See separate entries*).

School spirit drives many traditions. Between 1900 and 1949 each class has its own unique colors and class song. In the 1920s and 1930s, the snake dance, done by faculty and students at the end of a football game on the field was popular. The most infamous tradition was Rush Day (*See separate entry*) which lasted from around 1909 to the start of World War II. School spirit and physical violence was the order of the day.

Homecoming (*See separate entry*) is the oldest tradition on campus dating from 1935 and flourishes. Winfester dating from 1958, with its activities and snow statues, continues to be popular. Beginning in 1969, there was the Mud Festival (*See separate entry*) celebrated for several years. On an academic note the Honors Banquet (*See separate entry*) which began as a convocation in 1956, continues to be a traditional spring-time event. Summer Orientation is another old tradition dating from the 1950s.

Some modern traditions have been developed by First Impressions (*See separate entry*). This student group was created to foster new traditions on campus. They created the Holiday Dinner tradition and the President's Ball which was first held in 1991.

The Leadership Recognition Banquet is an important spring function, which many students do not miss. In the fall of 1998 the Free University (*See separate entry*) was revived with Discovery Daze. Fall Fest has become a first-day-of-class tradition, during which student organizations advertize themselves with information tables and local businesses welcome the university community. A new tradition was the change of radio station WBKX from cable to WUPX, an on-air station. As a result, this station has become popular with students around town.

Some traditions have died or are declining. The infamous Rhino Run (*See separate entry*) of the 1970s is gone as is the Lawn Picnic last held in front of the University Center in the summer of 1995. Although Greek organizations (*See separate entry*) are alive and well, their golden age was between 1965 and 1975. Activities like the popular Sunday Night Movie which started around 1985 is waning due to videos, cable television and satellite dishes. The Arctic Plunge (*See separate entry*), which sees students jump into a frigid Lake Superior, is a tradition for the heartier students on campus.

There are some traditions among the faculty. When Northern's enrollment was small, there was closer contact between students and faculty. Home parties and dinners were common. The student-faculty dinners on campus, served by the Home Economics Department, were popular and united the community. A dream of many faculty has been the creation of a successful faculty club, either on or off campus. Lunch and a Friday afternoon social in the Charcoal Room (*See separate entry*) was about as close as we came to this type of club. The carrying of the university mace at commencement started in 1970, became dormant and was revived in December 1998.

Northern's traditions continue to develop and evolve on campus. They are based on the times and the tastes and interests of the community.

Training School*: See: Laboratory School*

Tree Day*: See: Evergreen Day*

Tri Mu Fraternity: Tri Mu Fraternity was organized on December 19, 1922. One of its founders was John Voelker who was responsible for the writing of the Tri Mu song (lyrics only, melody is the Purdue fight song) and initiation ceremony. The three "Ms" stand for mind, morals, and muscle. The Tri Mu house, which was at 425 W. College Avenue, was in a building corporation controlled by Tri Mu alumni. In 1961, the members of the fraternity decided to become a chapter of Tau Kappa Epsilon, a national fraternity. The building corporation refused to turn over the house to the chapter of the national fraternity. The house was sold and the proceeds from the sale were given to the University to establish an endowed scholarship fund to provide scholarships to descendants of Tri Mu.

Tubby's Playhouse: Beginning in the mid-1970s, the grounds at 908 Center Street, (corner of Center and Tracy Streets) were decorated with old Marquette street lights, jerry-built cannons, a pump, bird feeders and houses, park benches, a swing and a Santa's sleigh on the roof. The yard had a red, white, and blue color scheme for the Bicentennial. This was the former home and then "playhouse" of Edward "Tubby" Bernard, who had lived there for 38 years. For many, this was an eccentric campus landmark. Several years ago, the remaining artifacts were removed. (NW 10/14/1976)

Tuition: Over the years, tuition for Michigan residents has dramatically changed along with the cost of living. Back in 1900–1901, the price for room, board, books and registration cost $58 for a 12-week session. By 1917 the amount rose to $102, and by 1930 it was between $125 and $154. A decade later, the estimated total expense per semester was between $151 and $203, climbing to $316 to $375 by 1950–1951. Twenty years later, just to take 13–18 credits came to $220 and still there was room and board and related fees for physical education ($6–$10) and application ($10). By 1980, it was more difficult to calculate tuition, but for a Michigan undergraduate it cost $32.50 per credit. In January of 1995 the University looked into tuition alternatives. The result was the flat-rate tuition which in 1998 was $1,527 for 12–18 credits. (*Bulletins*; NW 01/12/95)

Un-American Activities: With the coming of the Cold War and the start of the Korean War in June 1950, there was a concern that Communists had infiltrated some American institutions such as colleges. The Smith Act made it a crime to advocate the overthrow the government by force or violence. These fears are found in *Mining Journal* editorials in late 1950.

In this atmosphere, a vigilante committee was formed in late 1950 in Marquette by representatives of various civic organizations. The purpose of the group was to uncover un-American activities in the Marquette area, and they identified a Northern faculty member. In response to these actions the Faculty Council, chaired by Holmes Boynton, met in special session to review the charges against this unidentified faculty member or others if they were accused. The Council supported the faculty member feeling that he was "a good American citizen." Additional information on this incident is lacking, but the incident shows that even Northern's faculty came under suspicion. An editorial in the *Northern College News* in an oblique way wrote of scapegoats and a witch hunt, possibly in reference to this development. (NCN 01/17/1950; MJ 12/12,20,27/1950)

Underground Publications: During the era of protest in the late 1960s and 1970s, a number of underground publications were published and distributed on campus as alternatives to the regular media sources. Unfortunately, there is not a complete run of any of these publications in the University Archives.

Cogito, an anti-Vietnam War publication came out in May of 1967 and was one of the earliest underground publications. In February 1969 the organization Zaca was established on campus. Its plan was to publish *Peace Weekly* "the people's paper put out by the people for the people." Several issues of *Peace* were published before the administration sought to terminate its distribution on campus. President Jamrich rapped the paper for "character impugnment and the irrelevant use of obscenity." *Student Action*, a national publication, was distributed in the spring of 1969. A similar publication which came out at this time was *Campus Mirror*.

In the spring of 1969 the admissions office, alumni relations and many administrators were dissatisfied with the *Northern News*, which did not "help them disseminate their positive image" so wrote the editors. They called for an "administrative underground" announcement sheet of "all the good things" that happened at Northern similar to one published at Central Michigan University.

In the 1970s, this trend continued. *University Free Press* was published in March 1971. On October 31, 1972, *Black and White Bi-Monthly* was printed as an "alternative to the printed media." It was concerned with political and social issues. *The Broadsheet* was published in 1977 and its associated *Tuesday Committee* came out in 1978. There were probably other underground publications distributed on campus, but they have been lost to time. (NN 03/28/1969, 05/16/1969)

Union Board, Lee Hall: The Union Board was a board whose task it was to program social, recreational and cultural activities for the college Union Building. During orientation week they got new freshmen acquainted with college life. Their goal was to provide the students with something to do over the weekend. Activities ranged from free record sock hops, to dancing lessons on Thursday, ballroom dancing, jazz concerts during Homecoming Week, bowling, billiards and ping pong tournaments. In 1958, the Board met with their counterparts at Michigan Tech to exchange ideas. A year later, the Board held an all-event weekend, snow queen contest (the first in Michigan) and a jazz concert. It was also in charge of the Lake Superior Creative Arts Association exhibit in April and the Art Show in May. At the end of the month, the Board held a formal faculty and student tea. The Board was dissolved with the opening of the Don H. Bottum University Center in 1960. (NN 02/18/1959; 02/25/1959).

Union Building: See: Lee Hall

Unions, Labor: There are five labor unions on campus. The first, American Federation of State, County, and Municipal Employees (AFSME) was organized on May 12, 1966 with a vote of 109 to 5 favoring adoption of bargaining rights. This was the first AFSME on a college campus in Michigan. AFSME included all non-academic employees with the exception of secretarial, supervisory and security personnel. The first contract was approved in October 1966.

It continues to operate to the present and includes custodians, line workers, and those in food, kitchen and grounds. The number of members has declined over the years due to the consolidation of a number of kitchen facilities.

The American Association of University Professors (AAUP) was organized on May 6, 1975 when out of 280 eligible faculty, 151 to 90 voted in favor of organizing. Because of past problems, the faculty sought more self-determination and control over policy or "shared authority." The first contract was approved on July 1, 1975. The membership of the AAUP consists of all non-supervisory staffers at the University holding academic rank except those teaching in the Jacobetti Center.

The United Automobile, Aerospace and Agricultural Implement Workers of America-Technical, Office and Professional, Local 1950 (CT) was organized on October 15, 1975. This union includes all of the clerical technical people—secretaries, bookstore sales people, audio-visual people, mailroom workers, lab technicians in biology and chemistry, printing services folks, cashiers—on campus. The other, United Automobile, Aerospace and Agricultural Implement Workers of America—Technical, Office and Professional, Local 2178 was created on June 23, 1981 and their first contract was approved on May 13, 1983 with wages retroactive to July 1, 1981. Its membership includes all of the administrative professional people on campus.

The first employee strike in Northern's history began on August 18, 1981 and involved United Auto Local 1950. It resulted following unsuccessful mediation efforts between the university and its 176 clerical and technical workers. It ended three days later with an acceptable contract.

The Northern Michigan University Faculty Association, which includes the faculty in the Jacobetti Center, was organized in 1981. Their contract was approved in May 1982, though made retroactive through July 1, 1981. At the time they were represented by Michigan Educational Association (MEA). (MJ 05/14/1966, 05/07/1975, 07/25/1981, 08/08, 11, 13, 15, 18, 19, 20, 21/1981)

United States Olympic Education Center: The year 1965, begins the history of the USOEC. At that time, Northern Vice President of Research and Development, Dr. Roy Health proposed that Northern be designated as an Olympic Training Center. At that time there were no Olympic Training Centers in the United States. Soon after, Upper Peninsula businesses and citizens formed the Great Lakes Training Site Association, under the direction of Burton Boyum of the Cleveland Cliffs Iron Company, to obtain a training center at NMU. Next, Northern made a request to the U.S. Department of Commerce/Economic Development Administration for technical assistance to develop an NMU Winter Sports Facility for training athletes and coaches for international competition.

In the spring of 1966, the Federal government and the U.S. Olympic Committee expressed interest in a proposal for a winter sports area at Northern. Little came of that at the time. A decade later, Northern and local residents presented a proposal to designate NMU as an Olympic Training Center to the U.S. Olympic Site Selection Committee. In 1980, former President Gerald Ford urged the OTC to consider Northern as an Olympic Training Center. In the spring of 1982, NMU created the Great Lakes Sports Academy to develop and support top U.S. athletes without the Olympic designation.

With strong support from Governor James Blanchard—who also pledged state funding for a facility which could be used for Olympic training—NMU's bid won approval of the U.S. Olympic Committee in February 1985. While the Center took up residence in an existing University building, and commenced operations on July 1, 1985, it was not until January 1987 that NMU submitted a formal program statement calling for the construction of a Sports Training Complex.

In February 1988, three Northern Olympic Training Center's athletes competed in short track speed skating at the first Olympics after being designated an Olympic facility during the Winter Olympic Games in Calgary, Canada.

The U.S. Olympic Training Center unfortunately did not attract enough participants and a change was made. In 1989, it was designated the first and only U.S. Olympic Education Center. The Center, with its offices and dormitory space, is headquartered in Meyland Hall. It has its own newsletter, *Inside View*.

At the Winter Olympics in February 1992, at Albertville, France, Cathy Turner earned a Gold Medal and the Relay Team a Silver Medal in short track speedskating. A month, later USOEC boxer Vernon Forest became the first American to win the 139-pound world title. He was also a member of the U.S. Olympic team for the Summer Games in Barcelona, Spain. In August, USOEC Chris Jongis, became the first American to win an Olympic contest in Badminton. In February 1994, USOEC athletes accounted for four of America's record 13 medals during the Winter Olympics at Lillehammer, Norway. In short track speed skating, Cathy Turner won the 500-meter event (gold), Amy Peterson won the 500-meter event (bronze), the women's relay team won the 3000-meter event (bronze), and the men's relay team won the 5000-meter event (silver).

In April 1995, USOEC Boxing Coach, Al Mitchell, was selected Head Olympic Boxing coach and the USOEC Team Physician Dr. John Lehtinen, Head Physician for the Centennial Olympic Games (1996) in Atlanta, Georgia. During the Olympics in July, three USOEC boxers, Zahir Raheem (Bantamweight/119-pounds), David Reid (Light Middleweight/156 pounds) and Lawrence Cley-Bey (Super Heavyweight/201+ pounds) represented the United States on the U.S.. Olympic boxing team at the Atlanta games. USOEC boxer, David Reid recorded the only U.S. boxing medal, when he captured a Gold Medal with a third-round knockout.

In June 1995, the state of Michigan began selling special motor vehicle license plates, featuring the Olympic rings, with the proceeds benefitting the USOEC.

University Advancement Division: In 1994, this Division had as its mission to serve the University's priorities for available external sources of funding and to maintain an ongoing relationship between the alumni and Northern.

During the period of 1988–1994, fundraising expense was improved to 16.8 cents per dollar raised (excluded deferred gifts and 6.3 cents per dollar raised and identified). Between mid-1989 and December 1994 the Division raised $27.1 million in planned gifts for the future use of the University. It actively solicited for the Walker L. Cisler College of Business endowment and the gifts and pledges exceeded $650,000. Some of its other accomplishments include: a) improved undesignated monies as a percentage of total cash from $38,966 (3.2%) in 1987 to $483,587 (23.4%) in 1994; b) wrote and presented two white papers on "The Capital Campaign," and "The Case Statement," which led to the first iteration of a case statement for Northern in 1994; c) moved the Development Fund from 87.2% general fund support in 1987 to 16.3% seven years later; d) improved total assets of the Development Fund from $2,303,498 in 1987 to $4,393,979 in 1994—an increase of $2,091,481 or 90.8%. In 1994 a fee schedule was designated and installed which generated more than $184,000, but due to its unpopularity it was subsequently abolished.

Despite the success of this Division, it was eliminated in mid-1995 and transferred into the University Relations and Development Division (*See separate entry*). The Director of Development-Athletics was included in Intercollegiate Athletics. See: *Development Fund*

University Apartment Advisory Boards: See: *Residence Hall Governments, etc*

University Art Museum: See: *Art Museum, University*

University Center: Named after Don H. Bottum, it was constructed in sections, beginning in the summer of 1959. The original wing and first addition of the building was constructed by Miller, Davis and MacDonald, Inc., Kalamazoo and completed in 1960. The original wing covers 55,400 square feet. In the beginning, the original two-story wing contained a public cafeteria, dining and game rooms, student and faculty lounges, a television lounge, a barber shop, offices and an information desk. Michigan State University Cooperative Extension Service also occupied offices in this wing, which facilitated cooperation between the two institutions. The Northern Michigan College Student Center was formally dedicated on October 22, 1960.

The second addition to the Center was begun in late April 1963 and opened in the fall of 1964. It was also designed by Miller, Davis and MacDonald and constructed by Proksch Construction Co., Iron River, Michigan. The new complex which added 45,000 square feet to the complex, enabled Northern to further develop various student activities and programs in public service, conferences and alumni relations. This addition also included the store, student council offices, the West Hall dining room, and other facilities. On May 22, 1964 the Center was named after Don H. Bottum by the Board of Control. It was formally dedicated to Don Bottum on September 10, 1966.

The south wing of the University Center was designed by Ralph Calder and Associates of Detroit and was completed in 1966. The new addition, covering 50,000 square feet, accommodated the expanding conference program and included student recreation rooms, meeting rooms, a bowling alley and offices.

This was also the location of the President's office and associated meeting rooms until the opening of the Cohodas Administrative Building in 1975. In February 1993, the John Voelker Collection was exhibited in the "apartment" room in the south wing. It was popular and attracted many visitors until it was closed in December 1995 and was relocated in the Superior Dome. Excess pieces of the collection were relocated in the rooms as part of an alumni exhibition.

Talk of a major renovation of the UC began in the spring of 1991. By December, the project was in the hands of Giffels, Hoyen, Basso of Troy, Michigan. The Center had remained in its original condition until 1993–1994, when it was totally renovated and made more user friendly through a $7,000,000 project. One of the major innovations was to create one air conditioning and heating system in the building which had been constructed in sections over the years.

When the building was rededicated on September 24, 1994, Don H. Bottum joined in the celebration via telephone. A heritage theme has been used throughout the structure. The Peter White Lounge (*See separate entry*) is the location of statues of St. George and Abraham Lincoln and numerous reproduction art works from Kaye Hall. In 1995, a link (*See: Connector Link*) connected the second floor to Gries Hall (*See separate entry*) which had become a faculty office building. With this renovation the Don H. Bottum University Center has become more of a focal point on campus. In August 1996 Alumni Relations office was relocated to the Center.

In 1994–95 the Center implemented some 4,280 room reservations in the UC and billed more than $288,000 in food/beverage charges. At this time, the total attendance was 158,861. Also operated on site is Willy's Snak Shak which provides film services, novelty, convenience items, tickets and UPS services. Annual special events held in the building include: UC Main Event (some ten events), and the annual Halloween and Holiday parties. (*The 1996–97 University Profile*, 2:185–190); (NN 06/03/1959; MJ 04/19/1963, 09/06/1966; NW 03/14/1991, 09/26/1991, 12/05/1991)

University Center and Campus Activities Department: This Department is under the Student Affairs Division. Its mission: is to maintain the University Center facility; provide services and promote programs that are responsive to commuter and nontraditional students' developmental needs; provide extracurricular social and educational programs for students; and to support the conference and continuing education needs of the campus community. The Department Director also oversees the Bookstore and Conference Department. The mission also includes initiating programs which foster a sense of community among the University community, alumni, retirees and guests, and which meet the special needs of students' parents. (*The 1996–97 University Profile*, 2:185–190)

University Courses: These courses were so designated because they are not specifically attached to a department but serve the entire academic community.

University Harbour Park: *See*: *Lake Front Property*

University Relations and Development Division: As early as 1937, there were faculty committees which handled areas concerning relations: College News, Correspondence and Extension and Enrollment. The origins of this Division go back to the late 1950s during the administration of President Harden. An Information Office was formally established, and after 1964 with the creation of the Board of Control, the office of Secretary to the Board was made operational. Clair Hekhuis served briefly as Secretary, and then was followed by Jack Rombouts, who came to Northern in the early 1960s and soon after was offered the position of Assistant to the President and Secretary of the Board.

By the late 1960s, there were Communications, Campus Development and Capital Outlay, Publications, and Research and Development offices under the university relations division. By 1977, Matthew Surrell was Vice President for University Affairs. Surrell has held this position through a number of name changes. In 1984, the office was called

University Relations and is now called University Relations and Development. The Division was created during the Appleberry administration. By 1998, the areas under this Division included: Communications and Marketing, Development Fund, Learning Resources (which includes WNMU-FM and WNMU-TV) and Alumni Relations (*See separate entries*).

The mission of the University Relations Division, under the direction of a Vice President, is to provide technical and professional support and services needed to provide marketing strategies and plans which communicate the University Mission to its various constituencies and also has the mechanisms to obtain feedback from them. University Relations is dedicated to: a) supporting major initiatives enunciated by the President; b) fostering positive image enhancement; c) serving as the marketing arm of the University; and d) serving as an in-house consulting agency for University offices seeking to carry out their missions, providing communications and marketing support.

The second part of the Division's mission is that of the Office of the Secretary of the Board of Control. The secretary oversees the needs of the members of the Board and the President of the University in his capacity as an ex officio member without vote. The Secretary of the Board reports to and is accountable to the President.

Past directors, secretary to the Board of Control or vice presidents of this Division: Clair Hekhuis (1964-1966), Jack Rombouts (1966-1978), and Matthew Surrell (1978-present). (*The 1996–97 University Profile*, 2:197–209) Alisa Koski

University Women: The organizational meeting of the wives of the faculty members was held on March 18, 1926 at the home of Ethel Carey. The objectives of the organization were social and educational: to preserve and strengthen friendship among its members to assist any Northern committee whose objectives were similar to those of the organization and to foster a spirit of community service. Over the years the name of the organization has changed. In 1926 they were known as Faculty Wives, then University Wives (1968) and finally in 1970 they called themselves NMU Women and included wives, faculty and/or women on the professional staff. Later they were named University Women.

In the early years, they met monthly in different homes and had a speaker or social hour. Their Bicentennial Project in 1975–1976 was to plant a grove of trees to the southwest of the Learning Resources Center which remains a tribute to their foresight. Over the years, the University Women have continued as an active organization on campus.

UP North Films: *See: Motion Pictures and Videos*

U. P. Wildcats: On February 7, 1942 a group of Northern students left Marquette to begin their training at the U.S. Naval Air Base in Glenview, Illinois. Because nearly all of them had attended Northern, they were named the "U.P. Wildcats." They included: Walter Bietila (Ishpeming), Patrick Brennan (L'Anse), Blake Foard (Marquette), Clint Gondreau (Marquette), Ralph Gunville (Munising), Ralph Hannula (Ishpeming), Robert Hupy (Gladstone), Bob Johnson (Marquette), Albert Jokela (Negaunee), Norman "Boots" Kukuk (Marquette), Tom Lagan (Marquette), Toivo Lauri (Rock), Howard Mott (Marquette), Al Nurkala (Marquette), Albert "Curly" Nyquist (Marquette), John Lellow (Negaunee), Melvin Pritchard (Onaway), Orlando "Spig" Spigarelli (Iron Mt.) (NCN 03/12/1942)

Upper Peninsula Center for Educational Development: This Center was established in 1985 and operates out of the Department of Education. It is located in Magers Hall.

Upper Peninsula Hall of Fame: On January 22, 1958, Northern offered its facilities for a U.P. Hall of Fame honoring outstanding athletes. Later, the Hall of Fame was moved to the Lakeview Arena. In the early 1990s, a group of citizens approached President Vandament to relocate the Hall in the Superior Dome. Eventually they decided to remove the Hall of Fame to Iron Mountain, where it is located today.

Upward Bound Office: The United States Department of Education and Northern Michigan University sponsor the Upward Bound Program, a year-round educational opportunity program for high school students to develop skills for success in post-secondary education. Northern Michigan University students serve as tutors in all academic areas to area high school students who meet program qualifications. Students in the program are from families which meet federal income guidelines and/or where neither parent has completed a four-year college degree. There is no cost to program participants. Upward Bound holds two sessions: one during the high school academic year, and one six-week summer program held on NMU's campus. Along with workshops, Upward Bound provides experiences, as well as social, cultural, educational, personal, and occupational development. An office staff consisting of two Learning Skills Specialists and one Secretary are employed in the Upward Bound office which moved from Wilkinson Street (where it was located since its inception in 1980) to the Cohodas Building in the Winter of 1998. (*Upward Bound* pamphlet, Upward Bound Office; *The 1996–97 University Profile*, 2:143–148) Michelle Kangas

USOEC: See: *United States Olympic Education Center*

Van Antwerp, Maude: (August 17, 1887–September 29, 1970). Maude Van Antwerp was born in Vermont, Illinois and received her B.S. from Western Illinois University (1921) and her M.A. from Columbia University (1926). Before coming to Northern, she had been a high school principal in Illinois and an instructor at Kent State University. Van Antwerp began teaching in the NMU English Department in September 1928. Her specialty was reading techniques and remedial reading. She also served as advisor to the NMU chapter of Kappa Delta Pi, the National Education Society. She retired in 1953 and had a residence hall dedicated to her on June 9, 1968. (MJ 10/06/1970)

Van Antwerp Hall: See: *Quad II*

Vandament, Margery R. Lampe: (February 16, 1931–) Mrs. Vandament was born in Quincy, Illinois. She married William Vandament on February 2, 1952. Throughout the years, the two Vandaments worked as a team, moving some eighteen times in their careers. In the various communities she has lived, Mrs. Vandament was committed to public service and worked with the Girls Scouts, League of Women Voters, Planned Parenthood (Binghamton, NY), Veterans' Administration Hospital and Meals on Wheels (Long Beach, CA). In Marquette, she volunteered her time at Marquette General Hospital's Hospitality House and involved herself with a study group, University Women, served on the advisory boards of the University Art Museum and the First Nighters Club and on the city's board of Child and Family Services.

Throughout her years at Northern, Mrs. Vandament worked with her husband. She accompanied him to alumni meetings around the country and on a student trip to South Africa. She received an honorary degree, Doctor of Public Service, in May 1997. The Vandaments retired to Long Beach, California. (*A Sense of Place*, pp. 257–260).

Vandament, William E.: (September 16, 1931–) Dr. Vandament was born in Hannibal, Missouri. He received his B.A. from Quincy College (1952) and an M.S. from Southern Illinois University (1953). He received an M.S. and Ph.D in Psychology from the University of Massachusetts (1963, 1964). While in graduate school, he was a NDEA fellow (1961–1964). Between 1954 and 1961, he was a psychologist at the Bancon Clinic in Racine, Wisconsin.

Dr. Vandament married Margery R. Lampe on February 2, 1952. They have two daughters: Jane Louise and Lisa Ann.

At the State University of New York, Binghamton Dr. Vandament was an assistant professor (1964–1969), university examiner and director of institutional research (1969–1973), and assistant vice president for planning and institutional research (1972–1976). In 1976, he moved to Ohio State University (Columbus). Here he served in a number of capacities: executive assistant to the president and director of budget and resources (1976–1979), and vice president of finance and planning (1979–1981). At New York University in New York City he was senior vice president of administration (1981–1983). Between 1983 and 1987 he was provost and vice chancellor for academic affairs for the California State University System at Long Beach. He was a trustee professor at California State University, Fullerton (1987–1992).

Dr. Vandament came to Northern in June 1991, as interim president; everyone was so pleased with him that he was asked to become full-time president in the spring of 1992. He provided a new direction and spirit to the university community.

In September 1991, Dr. Vandament was faced with a $1.3 million cut in the state appropriations which included $600,000 for operation of the U.S. Olympic Education Center and $480,00 in state contributions to the Michigan Employees Retirement System. He immediately invited the university community to suggest ways to reduce expenditures or increase revenues. In October he convened a group to develop strategy and tactics for "rescuing" the USOEC which was the beginning of an ongoing effort. In June of 1992, having been named full-time president two months earlier, he had to face 1992–1993 budget cuts of $2.8 million and elimination of 49 positions. In August, he established the University Priorities Committee composed of faculty, staff and students to advise him on institutional goals and resource allocations. He also encouraged the campus community to use the UPC to make themselves heard on vital issues.

He testified in February–March 1993 on the university's appropriation level for the first time since the ousting of Rep. Dominic Jacobetti as chair of the Michigan House Appropriations Committee. In response to his work, the Board of Control extended his contract for a year in April, citing his outstanding work. In July, he commended the NMU Chapter of the American Association of University Professors for voluntarily foregoing a portion of their negotiated pay raise to assist in addressing the University's pending budget deficit.

During the year 1994, the Board extended his contract for an additional two years. Soon after, he told the University community of the need to focus on core educational programs and enrollment marketing. It was his position that although the budget was being cut, the University should try to move forward. He declined a personal pay raise at the end of the year.

In 1995, he had to face the third consecutive round of budget cuts, and he proposed consolidations and cutbacks to cover $1.28 million shortfall in the general operating budget. For the third time, the Board of Control extended his contract to terminate on August 31, 1997.

Tinkering was an avocation for Dr. Vandament. Thus, he was personally involved with many of the expansion projects on campus. A grand open house was held in October 1996. The public was invited to see the results of five years of intensive construction, expansion and renovation. This included the renovated Don H. Bottum University Center ($5.9 million, 1993), Gries Hall/Health Center ($4.2 million, 1992–1993), Phases I ($21.8 million, 1992–1993 budget) and Phase II ($3.3 million) in the Superior Dome, Heating Plant/Service Building/Infrastructure ($19.5 million, financed in 1992–1993 and completed in 1996), Learning Resources Center ($1.8 million, 1993–1994), and Thomas Fine Arts ($1.1 million, 1994–1995). Other notable but less costly projects included: remodeling of the Turf Room in the PEIF into a women's varsity volleyball court, two recreational basketball courts, and locker rooms for women's varsity swimming and volleyball (1994);

renovation of the PEIF ice rink into an Olympic-size ice sheet (1995); remodeling of the former Service Building into an Art and Design Studios North (1995); realignment of Lee Drive and expansion of adjoining parking lots (1996); and laying of computer cables connecting student computers in residence hall to the University's main frame (1996). The Vandament administration in 1996 won approval of state funding for the $46.9 million Glenn T. Seaborg Science Complex which includes renovation of the Luther S. West Science Building, construction of the Seaborg wing to house the science and mathematics center named in his honor, and construction of a massive unnamed building. By the time he left in July 1997, the Heart of Northern was re-established on campus.

Throughout his tenure at Northern, Dr. Vandament was concerned about the economy of the Upper Peninsula. In August, 1993, he established a temporary office at NMU to assist community leaders to jump-start the process of converting K. I. Sawyer Air Force Base to civilian use. Two years later, he told the Michigan Jobs Commission Regional Forum in Escanaba that the Upper Peninsula must take control of its economy. He also played an active role in the Lake Superior Jobs Coalition's work to revive K. I. Sawyer.

Dr. Vandament had a strong sense of history. For a number of years during his presidency, he had to face the problem of demolishing J. D. Pierce School and Longyear Hall. Although the latter was demolished in 1993, he made provisions for dismantling and storing the building's facade for possible future use. On April 20, 1994, Dr. Vandament convened the Centennial Committee composed of area residents and alumni as well as faculty, staff and students to begin preparing for Northern's Centennial in 1999. At the same time, he announced the appointment of Russell Magnaghi as University Historian. Between 1995 and 1997, he served with Secretary of State Candice Miller as co-chair of Michigan Week. He also directed the development of the Peter White Lounge with its historic orientation and displays, and the creation of the Cohodas Room and the Heritage Center in the Superior Dome. In the development of these sites, he used faculty and students. For his efforts, he was awarded the History Department's Dwight B. Waldo Ward in June 1996 for promoting the study of history and creating campus displays. A year later, he was similarly honored by the Historical Society of Michigan with the Charles Follo Award.

Over the years, Dr. Vandament could be heard playing his coronet at hockey games and other functions. He and Mrs. Vandament attended as many activities on and off campus as they were able. At times, they covered for each other, depending on the event. He was a frequent speaker on campus and throughout the Upper Peninsula, talking about psychology and the local economy.

Dr. Vandament gave the Northern commencement address in December 1996. At the May 1997 commencement, he received an honorary Doctor of Letters.

For his retirement, there were a series of parties which culminated on July 11, 1997 in a dinner and grand tribute by the community. At this time, besides the numerous accolades and gifts he and Mrs. Vandament were presented with a festschrift, *A Sense of Place, Michigan's Upper Peninsula: Essays in Honor of William and Margery Vandament* (1997) which was written and published by the faculty. In an editorial a few days later, the *Mining Journal* called his "interim" term exemplary.

He retired from Northern on July 15, 1997 and he and Mrs. Vandament returned to Long Beach. On November 9, 1997, the couple returned to Marquette for the dedication of the Vandament Volleyball Arena. (*A Sense of Place*; MJ 11/04/1997, 07/17/1997, 06/19/1997; NW 08/28/1997; Jim Carter, Chronology (05/06/1997) in the NMU Archives).

Veteran Student Services: Services have been offered to veteran students, active duty personnel and dependents of disabled or deceased veterans attending Northern since 1973. The office was called Veterans Affairs until 1989. Special services offered include: processing VA paperwork, academic counseling and tutoring, tuition assistance and loan programs, referrals and a bi-semester Newsletter and an educational benefits handbook. Recipients are determined by the Veterans Administration and are expected to attend classes and maintain a 2.0 GPA. (*Bulletins*) Michelle Kangas

Veterans Memorial: The Vietnam War (1964–1975) was only two years old when the 1966 pledge class of Chi Sigma Nu fraternity was instrumental in getting a large boulder placed on the north side of the Don H. Bottum University Center. On this boulder they placed a metal plaque inscribed: "In Memory of Northern Michigan University War Veterans, Chi Sigma Nu Fraternity Pledge Class, 1966." On May 25,

1966 fraternity president, Thomas McLoughlin of New London, Connecticut presented the memorial to President Harden representing the University community. The invocation was given by Rev. Glenn G. Weber, Newman Club chaplain for NMU and Marquette Diocesan district superintendent of schools.

As the Vietnam War progressed, the boulder lost its memorial status and became the focal point of antiwar and general protests and demonstrations on campus. In the process, the metal plaque was torn from the rock. The years passed, the antiwar protests ended, and the history and purpose of the rock were lost.

In 1997, as part of the University's Centennial project to properly identify buildings and sites and provide the public with their historical significance, plans were made to recreate the plaque. On September 25, 1998 a new bronze plaque replacing the lost plaque was rededicated.

There are two plaques honoring Northern veterans in the west corridor of the University Center. The Military Science office in Gries Hall has a memorial exhibit honoring World War I Upper Peninsula servicemen. (MJ 05/25/1966)

Veterans Housing: After World War II, the student population at Northern soared due to the G.I. Bill, which provided educational benefits to veterans. As a result, there was an immediate need for housing for both single and married students. President Tape negotiated with the federal government to obtain war-time housing units for two locations on campus. The first of these was known as GIville and was located in the corner bound by Waldo and Presque Isle. Seven compact housing units, home to fourteen families were located in the area. The women did their laundry in special facilities in the basement of the Peter White Hall of Science. In August 1951, the Board of Education authorized removal of these facilities with the completion of the Lydia Olson Library.

The better-known veteran housing was, Vetville. It was located in the area south of present Lee Hall and west of Cohodas at the east entrance of the Bottum University Center. The housing units were originally constructed for use during World War II and were purchased by Northern for instant housing at the end of the war. Construction on the housing units began in the fall of 1946. There were two types of units suitable for family use. The first type was complete with two bedrooms, a kitchenette and a living room. This type of unit rented for $30 a month. The second type was similar in construction to the Waldo Street units, but was larger (16 x 20 feet). Each unit had separate bedrooms and was furnished with a kitchenette and a living room that could be adjusted into sleeping quarters. This unit rented for $22 a month.

Each family dwelling was furnished with oil heater, ice box, electric water heater and electric range. There was closet and drawer space as well as a bath.

By mid-October of 1946, all but four of the fifty-five family units had been contracted for. Students were encouraged to check with L. O. Gant if they desired accommodations.

The administration erected four temporary men's dormitories. These buildings, 150 x 20 feet were divided into three sections, each 50 feet long. These three sections were identically constructed and furnished.

The three sections were subdivided to form six apartments approximately 25 feet long. Each apartment had two bedrooms accommodating two men apiece, and one study room for four men. The apartments were furnished with double-decked cots, lights and a bath. These accommodations were spartan and small. One of these structures was known as "The Barracks," and was used to house the athletic teams. The rent for each apartment was $13 a month. In March 1947, unmarried male students started to move into the four large dormitories, while married students moved into seventeen family units.

With plans for the construction of Spooner Hall and married student housing on the north side of campus, the State Board of Education approved their removal on February 7, 1957. They were sold to a local developer, removed in the late 1950s and relocated at Hotel Place in Harvey. The site was cleared of foundations and prepared for construction of the Don H. Bottum University Center in May–June 1959. The structures still stand in Harvey and Northern students continue to reside in them. (NCN 10/16/1946, 03/12/1947)

Vielmetti, Ada Burt: (April 16, 1902–April 23, 1986). Ada Vielmetti was born in Ishpeming and graduated from Ishpeming High School in 1918. She attended Lawrence University in Appleton, Wisconsin and received her degree from Wesley Memorial Hospital School of Nursing in Chicago. She also attended the School of Public Health at the University of Michigan.

Before coming to Northern in 1947, she served with Lawrence University and the Chicago Children's Memorial Hospital, and was a community nurse at Norway-Vulcan in Dickinson County. She was also a nurse for the Negaunee Public Schools.

At Northern, she lectured in the Effective Living classes and was given Instructor rank. She served as Head Nurse and Administrator of the Health Service for 19 years and then served as Head Nurse for four more years during the time that Dr. Osmo Niemi, Dr. Darrell Thorpe and Dr. Barbara Lyons were Health Service Directors.

Until Northern had a full-time medical doctor, Vielmetti ran the Health Center. She scheduled several local medical doctors to come in for an hour or two a day, as their time permitted. Some of the physicians included Doctors Bennett, Casler, Cooperstock, Howe, Matthews and Swinton. She worked with the architects and can be given credit for having helped to design the University Health Service facility. She was a motivational spirit who helped to establish the outstanding Health Service which eventually developed on campus. She retired in 1968.

Vielmetti was president of the Michigan Nurses Association and the Michigan College Health Service Association, and was active with the Michigan Heart Association. She was also a member of the P. E. O. Sisterhood, a member of the Faculty Emeriti of NMU, and was very active in the First United Methodist Church, having served on the church's World Service Guild. In recognition of her years of service and guidance, the Health Center (*See separate entry*) was dedicated to her on October 16, 1976. (MJ 04/26/1986)

Vietnam, Local Effect: The Vietnam War (1964–1975) was closely examined across college campuses and caused numerous protests and debates. At Northern, however, there were factors which decreased the number of anti-war protests. Many of Northern's students at the time were children of immigrants. To these children, supporting the government was like saying "thank you" for letting them become citizens. Many young men wanted to serve in the war because their fathers did. Also, church was influential in the Upper Peninsula. God, country and honor were strong values.

There were some antiwar protests on campus and in 1969, some fasted for one meal and donated money to charity. There was an antiwar publication called *Peace* which was, at first, rejected by President Jamrich but still survived. In 1969, 28 students and three faculty protested the

ROTC unit on campus, but there was a larger pro-ROTC protest. Throughout the war years marches, lectures and protests were held on campus. Fortunately violence was not part of the protest. (Kevin Esposito, "The Local Effect of Vietnam," UA) Michelle Kangas

Vital Issues I: The first series was a three-day conference on Vital Issues held at Northern on May 22–24, 1952. It was developed under the direction of Dr. Richard O'Dell of the Department of History. The purpose of the conference was to promote unity and effective leadership in several fields of our national life by presenting outstanding leaders and authorities in these fields: Dr. Ruth Alexander, economist; Stuart Chase, economics writer; Norman Cousins, editor of the Saturday Review of Literature; Albert Deutsch, authority on health and welfare; Frank Fernback, CIO Associate Director of Research; John B. Martin, Jr., Auditor General of Michigan, Republican; Dr. Arthur Mauch, Professor of Agricultural Economics, Michigan State University; Dr. Paul McCracken, professor of Business Conditions, University of Michigan; Robert E. Novy, Vice President in Charge of Operations of the Inland Steel Container Company; Dr. J. Marvin Peterson. Director of Research, Federal Reserve Bank of Minneapolis; Reverend Basil R. Reuss, Department of History, St. Norbert College; Dr. Frederick K. Stamm, minister and author; Lawrence P. Walsh, Democratic Party chair for Ontonagon County. The conference was sponsored by Northern, the University of Michigan, Michigan State University, and by business, industrial, labor and education groups and by both major political parties in Marquette County. It proved to be a success, attracting a cross-section of the local community. (MJ 05/21/1952; NCN 05/14/1952)

Vital Issues II: Professor Emeritus Richard O'Dell revived the concept of this series as a Centennial program in 1996. The Centennial Committee promoted the idea which was co-chaired by Vice President Phillip Beukema and Dr. David Prior. When Prior left the University in July 1998, Michael Marsden became the new co-chair. The Committee members included: John Andrews, James Camerius, Erin Fleck, Stephenie Hugo, Lewis Peters, Marcus Robyns, Paul Suomi, and Nick Vivian. The topics of the series included: "Investing in Diversity" (September 25, 1998); "Geopolitical Forces" (January 28–29, 1999); "Sustainable Environments" (March 25–26, 1999); and "Sports and Society" (July 8–10, 1999).

Vocational Skill Centers: *See: Jacobetti Center*

Vocational Support Services: The VSS office is under the Division of Student Affairs. It provides academic and personal support to special populations students in the University's one-and two-year programs. Among its specific duties: to administer and meet the requirements of the Carl Perkins Grant for Special Populations; provide the College Transition Program as an integral component of the University's overall effort in retention; administer and meet the requirements of the Single Parent/Displaced Homemaker and Sex Equity Grants; and act in a liaison capacity between the Office and University committees and offices. (*The 1996–97 University Profile*, 2:149–155)

Volleyball (Women): Women's volleyball was introduced as a sport at Northern in 1974. In recent years, the volleyball program at Northern has become outstanding in NCAA competition. In 1991, the team made it to the NCAA Quarterfinals. In 1993 and 1994, the Wildcats claimed NCAA Championship titles. In 1992 and 1995, Northern received runner-up honors in the tournament. 1996 brought a third place finish in the NCAA to Northern. Many players from Northern's volleyball program have received national, regional and GLIAC honors.

Coaches and Records (wins-losses-ties): 1974–75 Kathy Wainio 10-17-0; 1976 Luanne Larrison 11-13-0; 1977 Jane Scheper 6-20-0; 1978–80 Mark Hunt 85-44-7; 1981–88; Terrie Robbie 194-135-0; 1989–1993 Jim Moore 123-55-0; 1994–1997 Mark Rosen 99-12-0; 1998 Toby Rens. (*1997 Volleyball Media Guide*; *North Wind* 1997–98; Sports Information Office) Michelle Kangas

Volunteer Center: In 1992, Northern began to operate a Volunteer Center located in the University Center. The center is designed "to promote and recognize the volunteer efforts of the students, student organizations, faculty and staff of Northern Michigan University." The center helps provide potential volunteers with an interesting and exciting opportunity. Up-to-date lists of volunteer opportunities available in Marquette County are kept. Some local opportunities include Habitat for Humanity, Special Olympics, Big Brothers/Big Sisters, U.P. 200 Sled Dog Race volunteers, and tutoring of area students.

Director: David Bonsall 1992–present. (NMU Volunteer Center brochure) Michelle Kangas and Alisa Koski

Waldo, Dwight Bryant: (June 13, 1864–October 29, 1939). Waldo was born in Arcade, Wyoming County, New York and in 1873 the family moved to Plainwell, north of Kalamazoo. He attended the Michigan Agricultural College (now Michigan State University; 1881–1883) and then entered Albion College where he received an M.A. (1890). While at Albion he concentrated on history and civics under Professor F.M. Taylor. While an undergraduate, Waldo served as an alderman in town. After graduation, he taught history and German in the preparatory department of the college. In January 1890, he entered graduate school at Harvard University, studying American history under Albert Bushnell Hart and economics under Dr. F.W. Taussig.

In the Fall of 1890 he went to Beloit College (WI) as an instructor in history and economics. Later he became chair of political science and economics at Albion (1892–1899). Waldo proved to be very popular with the students and won their respect with his interest in them (both in and out of the classroom) and his superior ability as a teacher. He had been prominent on the athletic field and continued to support Albion sports, especially baseball.

In early 1898 when the newspapers wrote of a future normal school at Marquette, Waldo discussed the idea of a professorship with his colleague in modern languages, Richard C. Ford. The latter told Waldo that he would discuss the matter with the state superintendent of education, Jason E. Hammond, in Lansing. Ford was cordially received and during the discussion with Hammond, Ford formally presented Waldo's name as a candidate for principal at Northern. This was followed by a tremendous number of letters of recommendation from a variety of educators, businessmen, ministers, and politicians. The Board of Education was impressed with Waldo, and on June 23, 1899 he was appointed the first principal.

Between June and August, Waldo made several trips of Marquette in order to develop a teaching staff and curriculum. In mid-July, the Board working with Waldo decided on the north Marquette location for the new school. In the midst of these arrangements, Waldo announced that the start of classes would be on September 19, 1899. Although contractors staked out the future Longyear Hall by late August, the structure would not be ready for Fall occupancy. As a result Waldo and Superintendent Hammond were out negotiating for temporary quarters. The city of Marquette provided accommodations for classes in the second floor of the Old City Hall on Washington Street.

In mid-August, out of a list of some 125 candidates, William McCracken was the first teacher appointed and would be in charge of the science department. Waldo's staff was rapidly created.

Besides having to deal with space and staff, Waldo also had to have students. On September 7, Waldo and County School Commissioner F.D. Davis took a train to Champion, Michigamme and Republic to promote the new school. The numerous articles in the *Mining Journal* about the school also acted as an advertisement.

When classes began, all was prepared and it was noted that the students would get to work without any experimentation. Waldo worked hard to be ready for the fall semester.

During the summer months, Waldo commuted to Marquette to oversee the development of the school, while his family remained in lower Michigan. On August 30, Waldo and his family arrived in the late afternoon. Prior to this time, he stayed at the Clifton Hotel but now he would need permanent housing. In early September, they rented the Richard Parker house at 422 East Ohio Street.

With the basic plans for the new school being implemented, Waldo could oversee the construction of South (later Longyear) Hall. F. D. Charleton had a complete plan for the entire future complex completed and in Waldo's hands by October. The contractors, Lippsett & Gregg of Sault Ste. Marie were working on the structure and eventually provided everything but the heating for $22,000.

During the years from 1899 to 1904, Waldo was kept busy with the construction of South Hall and the Peter White Hall of Science, promoting the school to prospective students, and increasing his faculty. He also found time to teach and was the first history professor at Northern teaching history and civics.

In the midst of this work, Waldo's wife passed away on January 30, 1903, which added to his concerns. The Board of Education was impressed with his work, and in the spring of 1904, Waldo was appointed principal of Western State Normal School (now Western Michigan University). He proved to be an active and dynamic leader and builder and went on to become a nationally known educator. He retired as professor emeritus on September 1, 1936. Waldo was a Republican in his politics and a Presbyterian.

The memory of Waldo continues in Marquette. The city named a street in his honor on the north edge of campus, and within the Longyear Forest (*See separate entry*) there is Waldo Pond. The History Department has the Waldo Award (*See separate entry*).

Waldo, Dwight B., Award. Since 1986 the History Department has awarded the "Dwight B. Waldo Award" to an individual or institution that improves the teaching ability and quality of the History Department. This award honors the first professor in the department (1899–1904). Since 1986 it has been awarded to: Clifford Maier for his archival work (1986); Martin L. Dolan for establishing the Phi Alpha Theta chapter on campus (1987); Msgr. David Spelgatti for an Italian-American oral history collection (1990); Willard Cohodas for donating Holocaust materials (1994); President William E. Vandament for promoting history on campus (1996).

Waldo, Lillian Trudgeon: (June 28, 1883–February 26, 1976) She was Principal Waldo's second wife. A native of Vulcan, Michigan, Ms. Trudgeon attended Northern and was an honor graduate of the class of 1904. Originally she was scheduled to be the third-grade critic teacher in the training school. However the situation rapidly changed. Waldo was appointed principal of Western in April 1904. She and Waldo were married on September 14, 1904. After her husband's death in 1939, she continued to live in Kalamazoo. (MJ 03/11/1976)

Waldo, Minnie Strong: (June 27, 1865–January 30, 1903). A native of Vicksburg, Michigan where her father was a farmer, she attended the Michigan Female Seminary at Kalamazoo and Kalamazoo College (a year each) and two years at Albion College. While visiting friends in Lansing, she met D.B. Waldo, then a student at the Michigan Agricultural College (MSU). The acquaintance continued at Albion, while both were students and after Waldo became a member of the college faculty. The marriage took place at the home of her father, Ezekiel December 31, 1890. They had three children: Rollin (1891–1892), Herbert (b. June 1893) and Ruth (b. September 1895).

In September 1899, the family moved to Marquette when Waldo assumed his duties as principal of Northern State Normal School. From July 1, 1900 until her death, Mrs. Waldo was librarian of the Normal school.

In Marquette, besides her duties as librarian, she took care of her family in quarters in the dormitory. In 1902 she became ill with "a terrible disease." The best medical advice was sought, but to no avail. She died on January 30, 1903 at St. Luke's Hospital. Funeral services were conducted on Sunday afternoon, February 1 at the Normal dormitory by Reverends J.M. Rogers and E.A. Elliott. She was buried in Vicksburg, Michigan (MJ 07/24/1899; 02/02/1903; *Vicksburg Semi-Weekly Commercial* 02/03/1903)

Walker L. Cisler College of Business: See: Business, Walker L. Cisler College of

Washington, Al: See: Track and Field

Washington, Booker T.: (1856–1915). The famous African American educator was scheduled to deliver a lecture on Northern's campus in the summer of 1907, but had to cancel due to a busy schedule at Tuskegee Institute in Alabama. (MJ 07/13/1907)

WBXX: See: WUPX

Weapons on Campus: The question of firearms on campus goes back to the decade of the 1960s. There was one unauthenticated report that in 1967 students and faculty called for the removal of firearms from campus. There is no evidence that anything came from this concern.

In the spring of 1970, the issue was reopened. It was centered around a series of national and local developments. At that time, the shooting of students at Kent State University during the Vietnam War caused a reaction on campus. During this time, there was a rumor heard by many that Black students had been fired on by white students. On May 4, 1970, Dean Lowell Kafer issued a memo that possessing firearms on campus was in violation of a regulation. This was followed by a regulation issued by President Jamrich on May 13, stating that all firearms must be stored with Public Safety.

On February 27, 1987 a revision of Administrative Policies entitled, "Weapons Registration: Weapons and Ordinance on Campus" was issued. The Ordinance states that "No person...shall use, carry or possess (whether on his person or subject to his control) any weapon or any explosive device at any place on the campus..." The ordinance defines a weapon as "any rifle, shotgun, handgun or other lethal or dangerous device which is capable of casting a projectile" whether it is loaded or not. This is the basis of the present regulation.

From 1970 until 1997, these arms were stored in Public Safety's gun lock-up in Lee Hall and then in the Services Building. In the fall of 1997, College of Arts and Sciences Representative Phil Webb called for a clarification of this policy. This caused debate on campus. After several weeks, University attorneys wrote that there was no conflict between university and state policy. Today regulation remains in force. (NN 05/15/1970, 05/20/1970, 05/22/1970, MJ 05/20/1970, *Detroit Free Press* 05/14/1970; NW 01/23/1997; MJ 09/21/1997)

West, Luther: (September 6, 1899–December 14, 1985) Dr. West was active in teaching, research, writing and administration. West began his teaching career at Cornell University where he received the B. S. degree in 1921. He was an instructor in parasitology and medical entomology until 1925, when Cornell awarded him the Ph.D.

West became professor of biology and eugenics at Battle Creek College in Battle Creek, Michigan in 1925. He was appointed dean of arts and sciences at Battle Creek in 1933 and held that position until 1938, when he joined the Northern faculty as professor and head of the Biology Department.

During World War II, (1943 to 1945), West was chief of the medical entomology section, division of parasitology at the Army Medical Research and Graduate School, Army Medical School, in Washington, D.C. It was during this period that he began his study of malarial control in the Caribbean and South Atlantic Commands. He returned to Northern in December 1945.

Later, as a scientist-consultant to the World Health Organization of the United Nations (1952–1953), he conducted extensive research into fly control in eastern Mediterranean countries and elsewhere, a project which took him to England, Switzerland, Egypt, Jordan, Syria, Lebanon, Greece and Italy. His report on this subject was published in 1953.

Concerning the role of research and teaching, Dr. West explained, "One complements the other. I wouldn't give up teaching for research or vice versa. Both are too important to me. I think a teacher should be concerned with new developments in his field, with the hope that he might add his own contribution. Through personal example, the teacher also encourages creative scholarship in his students."

As Northern grew and expended, the School (later College) of Arts and Sciences was created and on July 1, 1962, West became the first dean. At the time he felt that "the whole realm of science, arts and letters must assume the responsibility of providing the cultural and general aspects of higher education." He resigned as dean and retired from the University in 1965.

His most highly regarded publication was the *Manual of Tropical Medicine* which was only one of his many publications. The others include a college text: *Eugenic Aspects of Race Betterment, The House Fly-Its Natural History, Medical Importance and Control.* There was also a joint authorship of *Practical Malariology.* He also published *Free Living Protozoa of the Upper Peninsula of Michigan.*

His interest in music and the academic life produced another work less academic, perhaps, but equally close to Dr. West's heart: "Hail Northern," a ceremonial hymn he wrote for Northern's Golden Jubilee in 1949. Today it is Northern's official Alma Mater (*See separate entry*). The West Science Building (*See separate entry*) was dedicated to him on August 20, 1966. (NN 04/04/1962, 07/02/1962; MJ 12/16/1985).

West, Luther, Science Building: See: *West Science*

West, Wilbur D.: (December 21, 1902–January 29, 1960) Dr. West was born in Boston, Massachusetts and received his bachelor's and master's degrees from Springfield (MA) College and his doctorate in psychology from the University of Michigan. He was coach of gymnastics at Michigan from 1930 to 1933. While working for his doctorate, he was a graduate assistant in the Psychology Department at Michigan (1933–1936). He was married to Beulah Neir and was the father to Rebecca Ann, Priscilla Ann and Charles Henry.

Upon receiving his degree, West became head of the Psychology Department at Wittenberg College (Springfield, OH; 1933–1943). At one time, he was associated with the YMCA as assistant physical director in Toledo and associate physical director in Boston.

He came to Northern in 1948 from Western Michigan University, where he directed an experimental school camping program and served on the student personnel services staff. At Northern he served as director of counseling and guidance (1948–1959). On July 1, 1959 he became Dean of Students. Unfortunately he took ill and died in early 1960.

West was a member of the American Psychological Association, American Personnel and Guidance Association, Michigan College Personnel Association, Michigan Education Association, and the Michigan Psychological Association. He was a member of the First Methodist Church in Marquette. West Residence Hall (*See separate entry*) was dedicated on October 2, 1960. (MJ 01/29/1960)

West Residence Hall: The hall was needed because enrollment in the fall of 1958 had reached 1,743, having doubled since 1956. Construction on the three-story dorm was begun in the summer of 1959 on the site of the former outdoor track and football field. The architects were Ralph R. Calder of Detroit and Harry W. Gjelsteen of Marquette. Bonds for construction of West Hall were repaid through room rentals, fees and earnings of the building. The structure is 59,282 square feet in size. It was dedicated to Dr. Wilbur West (*See separate entry*) on October 2, 1960. (NN 06/03/1959)

West Science: As enrollments increased in the late 1950s, there was a growing demand for modern science facilities. The Peter White Science Hall, dated from 1902, and although it had been renovated several times, it had out-lived its usefulness. The fact that Dr. Emerson Garver was forced to conduct his experiments in a makeshift hut attached to Kaye Hall during 1961 proved the point. Plans were developed to construct a new science facility in a newer quarter of the campus.

West Science was designed by Waller Halmeslo. The plans were carried out by J. Cullen, Inc. of Janesville, Wisconsin. The building was dedicated on August 20, 1966 and named in honor of Luther West (*See separate entry*), former biology department chair and dean of the College of Arts and Sciences. The structure covers 130,787 square feet and includes laboratories, classrooms, lecture halls and offices. It is currently home to the departments of: Biology (second floor); Chemistry (first floor); Geography (second floor); Mathematics (first floor); and Physics (ground floor). The building also includes a plexiglass greenhouse, the Sprinkle observatory (second floor; *See separate entry*), and the Glenn T. Seaborg Center (first floor; *See separate entry*).

The ground floor is made up of three elevated lecture halls and laboratories. The first floor has classrooms for mathematics, a reading room, laboratories, herbarium and a computer lab. The second floor contains a cartography lab, classrooms, seminar rooms and laboratories.

Thirty years of use have taken their toll on West Science. Plans are currently underway to completely renovate, modernize, and expand the structure. The completion date for this massive renovation is August, 2001. (MJ 08/12/1966) *See: Glenn T. Seaborg Science Complex*

Whiskers Spirits and Eatery*: See: North End Tavern*

White, Peter*:* (October 31, 1830–June 6, 1908). A pioneer and founder of the city of Marquette, White became a successful businessman, state legislator and philanthropist. As early as 1875, he saw the need for a college in the Upper Peninsula. It was through his efforts in 1899 that Northern was established.

After Northern was located in Marquette, White led a group to donate land on the south side (Adams and Division Streets) of the city to the State Board of Education as a site for the new school. Although it was rejected because of discrepancies in the title, White continued to work for the betterment of Northern. For a number of years he anonymously donated $1,000 annually for the development of an art collection.

At the time of his funeral in 1908, afternoon classes were canceled at Northern. The honorary pall bearers included President Kaye, Dr. Lewis Anderson, and John Lautner.

The Peter White Science Hall (*See separate entry*) was named after him, as is the Peter White Lounge (*See separate entry*) in the Don H. Bottum University Center, and the Peter White Fund (*See separate entry*) which is used to fund faculty research. Descendants of his family maintain close ties with Northern. His famed prophecy (*See: Peter White Prophecy*) for Northern was made in a speech given by him on July 3, 1900. (MJ 06/22/1908)

Wild Cat Den: *See: Food Service*

Wildcat Battalion: *See: Military Science, Department of*

Wildcat "Bobby": *See: Mascot*

Wildcat Den*: See: Food Service*

Wildcat Room: *See: Izzo-Mariucci Academic Center*

Wildcat Willy*: See: Mascot*

Wild Cat Squadron*: See: U. P. Wildcats*

Wilkinson Street Building*:* This is a modern ranch-style home next to University property, that was purchased by the University and used by a number offices and programs. It was home to the Northern Economic Initiative Center in the 1980s. Later, the Upward Bound Office was located there until 1998.

Winfester: Formerly known as "All Events Week," this activities week occurs annually at Northern. The first All Events Week was from February 28 to March 1 in 1958. Snow Statues were built, contests were organized on campus, a campus sweetheart was crowned and a dance was held. Today, the snow statue and contests (like tug-of-war and broomball) are still a tradition. The annual Winfester dance is still held on Saturday night. All Events Week was known as Winter Funfest in 1970, then as Winfester from 1973 to present. (NN 02/26/1958, 03/06/1958, 02/27/1970; NW 02/21/1973) Michelle Kangas

Women's Athletic History*:* Varsity athletics for women at the intercollegiate level for Northern Michigan University students began in the fall of 1968 when the University sported its first all-female team in field hockey.

The program for women was initiated through the efforts of Karen Kunkel, Del Parshall and Barb Patrick, staff members in the Department of Health, Physical Education and Recreation, who prepared a rationale that was approved by the University's Board of Control. A game against Central Michigan University that autumn marked the start of the modern era in women's athletics at NMU. The coach of that initial team was Patrick, and her squad consisted of 12 "first team" players and nine "second team" players. The first team played three games that fall and recorded a 2-1 record.

Field hockey remained the only NMU sport exclusively for women until the 1970–71 season when basketball was officially added to the program. It was discontinued after the 1983 season, compiling a 122-69 record in 16 seasons, all coached by Patrick.

The first basketball coach was Parshall, who also coached a first and second team. The first team played two games in 1971 and won both. The so-called "B" team program was discontinued after the 1976 season.

Although Northern coeds had competed on the men's ski teams earlier, and had even been awarded their varsity "N," the first women's team took the slopes in 1971–1972 in both alpine and nordic competition. Kunkel, who served as the first women's athletic coordinator at Northern, was also the coach of the first women's ski team.

Volleyball was added to the program in the fall of 1974 with a 12-player roster and a six-match schedule. The team had a 4-2 record under the guidance of Kathy Waino, a Marquette resident who coached the team on a part-time basis.

Gymnastics and swimming became intercollegiate sports for women in the 1977–78 academic year and tennis became the seventh women's sport in the fall of 1978. Lowell Meier, the longtime men's gymnastics coach, inaugurated the women's program with seven gymnasts and eight meets. The team was 4-4 and finished sixth in the state championship meet. That squad was actually Meier's second women's team at NMU. He put together a team in 1968 that competed in a brief schedule, but the squad disbanded after the one season. Joan Peto Hopkins began the women's swimming program with a predominantly freshman squad of 12. The team had a 1-6 record in dual competition and took part in two invitational meets.

Debbie Kazmir, a graduate assistant, coached the first tennis team. The nine-member squad competed in eight matches and had a 5-3 record. Tennis and skiing, however, were casualties after the 1979–80 academic year. A budget crunch in the state of Michigan forced cutbacks in higher education, and these two sports, as well as two in the men's program, were discontinued.

Patrick served as women's athletic coordinator from 1974 to 1976, was appointed assistant athletic director in 1977, succeeding Lu Darr, who served in the post for one year, and was named associate athletic director in 1983.

The program became affiliated with the Intercollegiate Athletic Association for Women in 1974 and with the National Collegiate Athletic Association in 1982. Patrick served as AIAW Division II national vice-president and Michigan AIAW-II state commissioner prior to NCAA affiliation.

The University hosted two AIAW national championship events, skiing in 1979 and Division II swimming in 1981, and four athletes won individual AIAW championships. Francine Malindzak was the first female All-American and the University's first double national champion, male or female, when she won the slalom and alpine combined skiing titles as a freshman in 1979. Two years later another freshman, Lori Pebbles, won the Division II three-meter diving championship.

In 1982, swimmers and divers were AIAW-II runners-up and set national records while winning five events. NMU's first female NCAA champion, senior diver Jodie Stout, captured the one-meter crown in Division II in 1983, becoming the University's fifth individual national title holder. She was a member of the first NMU female team to qualify for an NCAA national championship event. One year later, at the 1984 NCAA-II gymnastics championships for women, junior Lori Farell became the University's first national champion in that sport when she placed first in the floor exercise competition.

The basketball, field hockey and volleyball teams won Michigan AIAW-II state championships—basketball in 1980 and 1981, field hockey in 1979 and 1980, and volleyball in 1979—and the field hockey team reached the AIWA national championships in 1979 before being eliminated in the consolation quarterfinals.

Anne Goodman James replaced Joan Peto Hopkins in 1987 and continued NMU's national swimming success. She led the Wildcats to NCAA finishes of fifth place or higher in nine out of 10 seasons, including a second-place standing in 1992. Overall, the swimming and diving program has produced 21 individuals who have earned national titles in individual events or relays as well as a pair of NCAA Division II Swimmers of the Year—Kristen Silvester (1990, 1991), and Xia Fujie (1995)—and one Division II Diver of the Year—Debbie Duncan. Goodman James earned Swimming Coach of the Year in 1988 and 1991, while Milton Braga was named Diving Coach of the Year in 1997.

Mike Geary, who took over women's basketball in 1988 and enjoyed immediate success by posting a 24-4 win-loss mark, has guided the Wildcats to 20-win campaigns on eight occasions and is NMU's all-time coaching victory leader. He has led Northern to seven NCAA Tournaments and to the "Elite Eight" in two of the last three seasons to make the Wildcats a perennial national contender. Individually, Northern has had three players receive All-America honors—Julie Heldt (1993), Shana DeCremer (1997) and Kris Manske (1998).

Jim Moore arrived prior to the 1989 volleyball campaign and began the process which elevated the NMU program's status to that of a national power. The Wildcats reached the national finals in 1992, before capturing Northern's first women's national team title in 1993 at Hedgcock Fieldhouse. Mark Rosen took over the reins in 1994 and continued the Wildcats' success with a repeat NCAA title. Northern now has appeared in the last seven NCAA "Elite Eights" and has produced 10 volleyball All-Americans as well and a pair of two-time Division II players of the year in Stacy Metro (1992, 1993), and Liu Jun (1995, 1996). Moore and Rosen each received National Coach of the Year honors following NMU's title campaign.

Sten Fjeldheim (1986–94, 1997–present) returned to coach NMU's cross country and nordic ski teams after serving as the U.S. Ski team's assistant coach/junior development coordinator. He led the Wildcats to their first-ever national title in NCSA competition in 1991. In 1992, Sara Kylander was the first NCAA All-American in nordic skiing as well as a U.S. Junior World Team member, while Susan King, a former champion (1987–88) is a two-time Olympian (1994, 1998). Fjeldheim also guided the women's cross country team to its lone GLIAC title in 1991.

During the decade of the 1990s, NMU has added women's teams in the sports of tennis (1992), coached by Troy Mattson; alpine skiing (1995), coached by Jill Rogers; and soccer (1996), coached by Milton Braga.

In 1984, Patrick was elected to the University's Sports Hall of Fame, becoming the first woman so honored. Other female inductees include Karen Kunkel (1985), Barb Perry (1987), Kathy Talus (1989), Carol Hammerle (1990), Francine Malindzak (1993), Julie Campell (1994), Denise McDowell (1997), and Lori Farrell (1997). Suzan Travis-Robyns

Women's Center: The Women's Center started after a Northern conference on women's roles in society in 1973. "At the end of the conference there was a unanimous call by all the delegates who were there, all the women who were there, to start a women's center," remembered Sally May, who has been involved with the organization since its inception and who served as its director for many years. Gail Griffith was instrumental in presenting these ideas to the Board of Control on July 20, 1973.

The Center opened on December 11, 1973. For its first seven years, the center was affiliated with Northern under Continuing Education. In September 1977, the Center received a grant to fund a halfway house for women with alcohol and drug abuse problems. Then in October 1980, the Center was discontinued at Northern and the organization successfully struck out on its own. It is currently located on South Front Street in Marquette. Director (on campus): Holly Greer, 1973–1980. (NW 09/22/1977; MJ 01/21/1998)

Women's Suffrage: In 1912, Michigan's women's suffrage was defeated by the voters. Determined not to be defeated again, the women of Marquette, led by Mrs. Abby Roberts, formed the Women's Welfare League. League committees, including women from Northern, dealt with civic beautification, smoke abatement, juvenile recreation, and the quality of movies shown in the local theater. Even more important was the selection of delegates to the state Equal Suffrage Conventions of 1914 and 1915. Eight delegates went each time. Among them, both years, were Mrs. James Kaye and Abby Longyear Roberts.

In 1914, Charlotte Perkins Gilman, a national leader in education and the equal suffrage movement, spoke on "Votes for Women" in the city hall at the invitation of the League. At a mass meeting in the Normal Auditorium in the spring of 1915, Northern students contributed $15 to the State Equal Suffrage Association. At this time, Elizabeth Byers, a 1909 alumna of Northern, was appointed legislative secretary of the Michigan Woman Suffrage Association, headquartered in Lansing.

Finally, in 1918, when Michigan women won the right to vote, the first women to register in Calumet were Northern alumnae Marie and Lucille James; and in Adams Township, Cora Dolittle Jeffers. (DMJ 04/06/1914; NNN 02/15/1919; Hilton, pp. 52–53) Miriam Hilton

Women's Welfare League*: See: Women's Suffrage*

WNMU-FM: On August 13, 1963, Northern received a license from the Federal Communications Commission to operate Public Radio 90, WNMR-FM. By February of 1963, the station was established as a non-commercial educational FM station. The station was initially located in Lee Hall and moved to the lower level of the Learning Resources Center in 1969. Original wattage of the station could reach a 15–20 mile range. The antenna was on a 50-foot tower on the 42-foot Lee Hall building. In 1971, WNMR became an affiliate of National Public Radio. Two years later, the station was operating seven days per week and 12 hours per day. Lectures and local concerts were broadcast. In 1974–75, a 15 member NMU Broadcast Advisory Board was formed and a name change was instituted in July of 1974, making the station WNMU-FM. A new 950-foot transmitter antenna was installed six miles east of Republic, Michigan, allowing the station to reach all of the Upper Peninsula and Northeast Wisconsin. Grants allowed more improvements to be made. Fundraising began in 1976, and $490.50 was raised that year. The station nearly closed in 1980, but fundraising allowed the station to remain in operation. In 1995, $53,000 was raised in a two-week period.

Today, the station has expanded more than tenfold since 1963. It provides a 24-hour per day, 365 day per year, broadcast programming service, including Emergency Broadcast Systems announcements. Programming includes news, music of all kinds, commentaries, the arts and local concerts. The mission of the station is to produce programs and to highlight the University as a repository of talent, ideas and information.

Station Managers: Bruce Turner, 1963–1970; Phil Hartzell, 1970–1972; Steve Dupras, 1973–1989; Jim Miskimen, 1990–1992; Susan Sherman, 1993–present. (Todd Jobbitt, "History of WNMU-FM," (1995), UA; *The 1996–97 University Profile*, 2:243–246) Alisa Koski

WNMU-TV: WNMU-TV, Public TV 13, licensed by the Federal Communications Commission as a noncommercial television station, is responsible for the broadcast of public and cultural affairs and informational and instructional programming to the diverse audiences it serves in the Upper Great Lakes region. It functions as a major public service arm of NMU broadcasting and the educational services the institution provides, and enhances the quality of life throughout the region.

The history of the campus television station goes back to 1963 when it was WNMR-TV. A community antenna served approximately 33 communities in the Central Upper Peninsula. An Instructional Communications Division was created in 1962. Originally located in the former ballroom of Lee Hall, the station moved to the bottom floor of the Learning Resources Center in 1970. By 1972, a new transmitter was built in Ely Township. An 1,100-foot tower with a 110-foot antenna produced 316,000 watts of power and allowed Channel 13 to go on the air. Now, viewing was expanded to the entire Central Upper Peninsula and Northeast Wisconsin. Originally, the station was designated Channel 19, but only channels two through 13 were available to viewers in the area, so the frequency was changed.

Before 1975, the station was funded with federal and state government money, with an additional contribution from the University. In 1975, funding was cut and fundraising began. The first fundraiser netted $975.00. Currently, there are three fundraisers a year. In 1975, the station's name was changed to WNMU-TV. A year later, with a grant from the U.S. Department of Health, Education and Welfare, the station began color broadcasting. Presently, additional grants allow new equipment to be purchased. A satellite transmitter was added in 1978, allowing programming to be received directly, instead of on the large two-inch tape system which was previously used. WNMU-TV is the only public television station in the Upper Peninsula.

By the mid-1990s, the station provided a broadcast signal (17 hours a day, 7 days a week) to viewers in 14 of 15 Upper Michigan counties, seven northeast Wisconsin counties, and Sault Ste. Marie, Ontario, which included Emergency Broadcast Service announcements. The station coordinates the acquisition and scheduling of in-school TV programs and college credit telecourses on behalf of participating Upper Peninsula public school organizations and institutions of higher learning (Bay de Noc and Gogebic Community Colleges and NMU). Regularly produced are local news, public affairs and phone-in programs in response to ascertained community needs and issues, and other educationally-related programs. The station has developed local and regional community outreach programs independently or in conjunction with PSB national initiatives such as U.P. PLUS Task Force, U.P. Head Injury Alliance and U.P. Tobacco Health Coalition. Station Manager: Bruce Turner, 1963–present. (*The 1996–97 University Profile* 2:246–251); *Bulletins*; Tim Nelson, "WNMU-TV," (1995), UA) Michelle Kangas

Women's Rugby Club (The North Stars): The non-varsity Club was established in 1994. The North Stars play throughout Michigan and Wisconsin. Five to seven games are played in the fall and three to four games are played in the spring. The North Stars annually play in the Michigan Cup held in April, in which 27 rugby teams from Michigan, Ohio and Ontario compete.

World Records: Since 1961, a number of world records have been equaled or broken on campus. These events have included: Al Washington running the indoor 60 yard dash in 6.0 seconds, Musical Chairs (1977), Pasty (1978), Pendulum (1995) and Sauna (1996). Northern is also home to the world's largest wooden dome with the largest piece of retractable turf in the world. (*See separate entries*)

World War I: When World War I began in the summer of 1914, Northern Normal and Marquette were quietly enjoying the warm weather. During the next four years, the faculty and students followed the war through newspapers and periodicals. In June 1915, Kaye Hall was opened for use and during the war years various performances expressed the spirit of the times. In 1916, over 100 students vied with each other in "The Contest of the Nations" — each group interpreting a different national character in story, song and dance. A year later proceeds from the performance of "Hiawatha" by the children of the training school were donated to Belgian Relief.

The war came home on April 6, 1917, when President Wilson signed the declaration of war. In 1918 and 1919, war rallies and memorial services filled the auditorium, which became a patriotic war center for the Upper Peninsula. Faculty and special lecturers visited the campus and actively promoted the war effort and patriotism. The Training School created a Junior Red Cross organization to help with the war effort. During one drive, Northern contributed over $3,000. The Glee Club Concert in 1919 was called "To Arms for Victory." In the spring of 1918, soldiers from Camp Custer near Kalamazoo presented the play, "A Day in Camp Custer" in Kaye Auditorium and raised $1,200. Some of the female faculty systematically worked in food conservation.

During this time, a unit of the Student Army Training Corps (SATC; *See separate entry*) was established on campus in the fall of 1918. The old dormitory was their base of operation. Unfortunately, the flu epidemic of 1918–1919 kept them quarantined, and with the end of the war they were disbanded.

In the city of Marquette, a home guard of nearly 300 young and older men was formed. The idea was to prepare enlistees so they would be ready when they were called up. Some 45 faculty and male students joined and drilled on campus as a company on Monday and Wednesday afternoons.

A number of students enlisted, and the enrollment for the fall of 1917 dropped a bit. Other young people did not attend Northern because as positions opened with the enlistment of men, they could get good-paying jobs. Among the faculty, a number served in a variety of capacities. Della McCallum of Home Economics went to Camp Jackson, South Carolina and instructed student nurses dietetics at the U.S. Army School of Nursing. O. H. Horrall, an assistant in the Psychology Department, received an early commission as a psychology expert and then went on to do reconstruction work in France. Earle Parker, the Latin teacher, worked for the Red Cross and was scheduled to go to France or Italy before the war ended.

Federal Men (*See separate entry*), was organized in 1921 and consisted of World War I veterans. Later it became Northern's chapter of Disabled American Veterans. (Hilton, p. 44)

World War II: With the coming of the war, Northern went through dramatic changes. In 1940 there were some 500 students enrolled. With the outbreak of the war on December 8, 1941, most of the male students and some females entered the various services. By the fall of 1944 term, there were only 26 male and 201 female students. During the war years, the enrollment stayed below 250. Many social activities such as Rush Day, Homecoming, Men's Get-Together, and the yearbook came to an end for the duration. The last yearbook published was the *1942 Polaris* which students dedicated to former classmates in military service. When Don H. Bottum, Dean of Men, held the last Men's Get-Together in his dining room in 1944, there were only seventeen in attendance.

Students entered all branches of the military. When a group of former students trained at Glenview, Illinois, they formed the U.P. Wildcat Squadron (*See separate entry*). Others, because of their skiing expertise, served in the Tenth Mountain Division. The campus kept in touch with its former students and faculty in the service by sending them the *Northern College News*, and the men and women frequently corresponded with former faculty members. The History Department maintained other information sources such as the "World News of the Week" bulletin board in the Kaye Hall foyer and a new European survey course.

By the summer of 1943, there were 337 Northern men in the service and seven had given their lives. The first to be killed was Ensign Robert Miller, who had been a student back in 1933–1934.

During the war, Northern took the lead in the local war effort both on and off campus. The Northern community was organized into fifteen committees under the direction of the Office of Civilian Defense. The warning crew scheduled all staff members, including President Tape, to keep four-hour watches on the high school roof. George Butler, whose specialty was agriculture, became the chair of Marquette's Victory Garden development program. Students in Home Economics served sugarless cookies and "Bohemian tea" at their parties and provided meals for visiting military and government groups. A series of adult education classes in nutrition were conducted for the Upper Peninsula Nutrition Committee. At other times, the students presented exhibits on economical meal planning and made-over clothes. When local farmers needed help, a special course was offered in Farm Machinery. By 1943, even though women had been admitted to the Bench Work class, there were only six students enrolled in the Industrial Arts Department. At the onset of the war, a variety of new mathematics courses were offered for students, who knew they would enter the service. C.B. Hedgcock (*See separate entry*) taught a first aid course for defense workers and Northern's physical education students. He also built an obstacle course on the playing field to meet the specifications of the Navy V-7 program.

During the war, many faculty left for teaching positions at other institutions, and others enlisted due to the reduced enrollment. Biology's Luther West became a captain in the Army in March 1943 and worked as an entomologist.

Due to the social disruption in Michigan caused by the war, there was a growing need for teachers. In 1942 the State Board of Education temporarily revived the limited teaching certificate, which required only two years of college training. Students were reminded to do their patriotic duty and remain in college. Northern arranged extension, evening and short summer courses to help students rapidly complete certification requirements.

The end of the war brought a flood of veterans back to campus who used the G.I. Bill for their education. By October 1946, the enrollment soared to a record-breaking 929 students. Military surplus housing known as GIville and Vetville and the "new" cafeteria were constructed to provide housing and food services for both married and single veterans. The influx of veterans brought to a close long-standing traditions such as Rush Day and no-smoking on campus. Northern was entering a new era.

Wrestling: The first organized wrestling team at Northern was formed at the end of the Spring term in 1926. Six wrestlers, coached by C.B. Hedgcock, competed for one season only. The wrestling program was reinstated as a varsity sport in 1966 and coached by Ed Brown for two seasons. Ken Koenig coached from 1969 through 1974. His best finish was 10th in the nation in the NCAA College Division.

In 1975, Bob Fehrs became coach and remained through 1978. His team finished sixth in the nation in 1978. Bill Dotson coached from 1979 through 1980, and his team finished fifth in the nation in 1980. Between 1981 and 1985, Mike Duroe coached, and his team's best finish was fifth in the nation in 1984. The last coach was Robin Ersland (1985–1986) who saw the wrestling program dropped because of budgetary constraints.

National champions in wrestling were: Steve Spangenberg at 142 lbs in 1980; Gil Damiani (heavy weight) in 1973; and Mike Howe (heavy weight) in 1981. (*Kawbagam*, 1926, *Peninsulan*, 1966–80) Gildo Canale and Michelle Kangas

The Wright Place: This is a party store and deli located at the corner of County Road 550 and Wright Street. Situated across from campus, it has been used by students living in the residence halls for years. It started out as a ramshackle store called O'Dell's and was rebuilt in the 1970s. For a while in the 1980s it housed a Wendy's as well.

WUPX: Known as WBKX until the 1990s, WUPX is the student radio station at Northern. Also known as "Radio X," the station's programming is handled by students with supervision from a station manager. WBKX began in 1971, broadcasting from Lee Hall and is now located on the first floor of the Don H. Bottum University Center. WUPX sponsors concerts and campus events throughout the year. (*Bulletins*) Michelle Kangas

Ygdrasil: A literary society founded on October 15, 1907. The name is associated with the legend of Ygdrasil taken from Norse mythology, and is symbolic of "The Tree of Life." All students had to belong to this organization or Osiris (*See separate entry*) and attend frequent meetings. The Society disbanded in 1925. (C.R. Murphy. "Yggdrasil, the Cross and the Christmas Tree," *America* 12/14/1996)

Zenti, Rico N.: (June 27, 1910–December 24, 1977). Born in Gwinn, Michigan, Dr. Zenti graduated from the University of Michigan in 1932 where he was class president and lettered in football and basketball. He taught in the Gwinn and Negaunee school districts and was a referee throughout the Upper Peninsula.

At the beginning of World War II, he enlisted in the U.S. Navy, attained the rank of lieutenant commander and served as head of physical rehabilitation at St. Alban's Naval Hospital in Long Island.

Zenti earned his master's degree at Wayne State University and a doctorate at the University of Michigan. In 1947 he joined the Wayne State faculty, serving as coordinator for the development of the university's Fred C. Matthaei Building for physical education and athletics. In recognition of his services, he was selected one of the first recipients of WSU's College of Education Faculty Honor Award.

In 1966 he became director of athletics, physical education and intramurals at Northern. He initiated varsity swimming, wrestling, gymnastics and skiing, and was responsible for introducing women's varsity athletics. He stepped down as athletic director in 1969.

Zenti also prepared the document that resulted in legislative approval of NMU's Physical Education and Instruction Facility, which opened in 1975. He was the first to present the initial concept of an indoor all-sports building to the University's administration. This eventually led to the Superior Dome (*See separate entry*) which opened in 1991. He promoted the selection of the city of Marquette and NMU as the joint sponsors of the Olympic trials in the biathlon event in 1966. Zenti was active in the U.P. Special Olympics program and was responsible for Northern's involvement in the organization of the first Special Olympics Spring Games.

The Metropolitan Detroit Alumni Association of NMU was established with his help, and he served as its president. Recipient of Northern's Distinguished Alumni Award in 1966, he was inducted in the NMU Sports Hall of Fame as a charter member in 1976. When he retired in 1975, he received the designation of professor emeritus from Northern's President and Board of Control.

He was a member of the Marquette Rotary Club, Marquette Golf and Country Club, Golden Wildcat Club, "N" Club, Phi Delta Kappa, and was a charter member of Northern's President's Club.

For his numerous efforts at developing and promoting all aspects of the athletic programs at Northern, the Instructional Wing of the Physical Education Instructional Facility (PEIF) was named in his honor on September 26, 1998.

1899 - 1927

1927 - 1942

1963 -

1942 - 1955

1955 - 1963